ASSER International Sports Law Series

More information about this series at http://www.springer.com/series/8858

Antoine Duval · Ben Van Rompuy
Editors

The Legacy of *Bosman*

Revisiting the Relationship between EU Law and Sport

ASSER PRESS

Springer

Editors
Antoine Duval
ASSER International Sports Law Centre
T.M.C. Asser Instituut
The Hague
The Netherlands

Ben Van Rompuy
ASSER International Sports Law Centre
T.M.C. Asser Instituut
The Hague
The Netherlands

ISSN 1874-6926 ISSN 2215-003X (electronic)
ASSER International Sports Law Series
ISBN 978-94-6265-119-7 ISBN 978-94-6265-120-3 (eBook)
DOI 10.1007/978-94-6265-120-3

Library of Congress Control Number: 2016935566

Published by T.M.C. ASSER PRESS, The Hague, The Netherlands www.asserpress.nl
Produced and distributed for T.M.C. ASSER PRESS by Springer-Verlag Berlin Heidelberg

Printed on acid-free paper

This Springer imprint is published by Springer Nature
The registered company is Springer-Verlag GmbH Berlin Heidelberg

Series Information

Books in the *ASSER International Sports Law Series* comprehensibly chart and analyse legal and policy developments in the emerging field of European and international sports law. Within scholarly publishing, the series is the most cited in its area and uniquely features contributions from the leading sports law scholars. It is a valuable resource for practitioners, academics, sports officials, and anyone interested in or impacted by sports and the law.

The series is developed, edited and published by the ASSER International Sports Law Centre in The Hague. The Centre's mission is to provide a centre of excellence in particular by providing high-quality research, services and products to the sporting world at large (sports ministries, international—intergovernmental—organizations and federations, the professional sports industry, etc.) on both a national and an international basis. As a pioneer in the field of European and international sports law, the Centre has established a worldwide network of academics and practitioners and co-operation agreements with various sports law institutes and centres in Europe and beyond.

Apart from the Series, the Centre edits and publishes *The International Sports Law Journal*

Series editors

Prof. Dr. Ben Van Rompuy, Editor-in-chief
e-mail: b.van.rompuy@asser.nl

Dr. Antoine Duval
e-mail: a.duval@asser.nl

Marco A. van der Harst, LL.M.
e-mail: m.van.der.harst@asser.nl

Editorial Office

ASSER International Sports Law Centre
T.M.C. Asser Instituut
P.O. Box 30461
2500 GL, The Hague
The Netherlands
www.sportslaw.nl

Foreword

The first thing to do for the Court of Justice of the European Union with an incoming case is to choose the judge rapporteur and the Advocate General responsible for the opinion. The date of registration determines the President of the Court, responsible for the nomination of the judge rapporteur, and the First Advocate General, responsible for the nomination of the advocate general competent for the case. In the *Bosman* case the date of registration was 6 October 1993. The next day, a partial replacement of the Court took place. So the outgoing President took no decision on the *Bosman* case. The nomination of the judge rapporteur took place after that date. Ole Due was the Court's President, and Marc Darmon the First Advocate General. Together, they nominated the same persons originally nominated for the first *Bosman* case C-340/90, registered 15 November 1990. The President (already Ole Due) had then nominated as judge rapporteur Federico Mancini, and the then First Advocate General Francis Jacobs had nominated myself as competent Advocate General. In the second *Bosman* case C-269/92, registered on 15 June 1992, these nominations had been maintained. On proposition of the judge rapporteur and the Advocate General the full assembly of the Court decided to keep the case before the full court. Mancini was a football fan and reader of the 'Gazetta dello Sport'. His *référendaire* Vittorio Di Bucci[1] was in charge of the case. I had a *référendaire* named Gerhard Grill,[2] who was also very knowledgeable about football. He was charged with the preparation of the case.

The parties to the case, the European Commission and the French and Italian governments, handed in briefs and participated in the hearing on 20 June 1995. The Italian Prime Minister at that time was Silvio Berlusconi. The French minister for culture and justice, Jaques Toubon, even assisted at the hearing. For their part, the Danish and German governments participated only in the hearing. Originally, the German (Kohl) government had not intended to join the procedure. But at the

[1]Now director and principal legal advisor, legal service of the European Commission.

[2]Now director at the European Ombudsman.

demand of the State government of Baden-Württemberg it acted at the hearing on the side of the football associations, like France and Italy. Indeed, the finance minister of Baden-Württemberg at the time was Gerhard Mayer-Vorfelder, who was also presiding the VfB Stuttgart, a prominent German Bundesliga club. The only government that sided with Bosman was the Danish government. The best pleadings in my mind were made by the agent for the Commission, Ms. Wolfcarius who, different from the earlier written submissions of the Commission, pleaded in favour of Bosman. After the hearing there was a dinner of the Court in honour of the French minister. Returning home that evening I watched the late edition of the German first TV news programme, which gave a rather positive report of the hearing.

My opinion in this case was scheduled immediately after the summer recess of the Court. So it had to be prepared during the summer vacation. But before we could start, the opinion for another case (C-101/94) had to be finished. Its presentation was scheduled for July 13 1995. After that I had planned a trip to the 'Châteaux de la Loire'. Before leaving I discussed the line to be followed in the opinion with Gerhard Grill. He drafted the opinion and faxed chapter after chapter of the draft to the various 'châteaux' of the Loire Valley. I studied them and returned them to Mr. Grill with my comments. There were few comments.

Much attention was given to the question of admissibility of the preliminary questions raised by the national court. Both questions (on the transfer system and especially the nationality clause) were considered to be inadmissible by several governments and by the Commission in its written submissions. We considered the arguments against admissibility on more than 12 pages and refuted them. We saw no reason for the Court not to give the preliminary ruling and the Court followed us.

During the preparation of the opinion I received several phone calls from the German political world offering more information on the subject. I thanked them for the offer, but told them I could only use information that was also in the hand of the judges and that the occasion for sharing such information had been the hearing. So there was no use in giving me now such information. In no other case in my career of almost 14 years at the Court have I been exposed to such efforts to take influence on a case. The political influence and power of football cannot be overestimated. Another example illustrates this fact. After the judgement I was invited to participate in a broadcast of the second German TV channel (ZDF)—'Das aktuelle Sportstudio'—together with a representative of the football associations to talk about the consequences of the judgment. A few days before the event I got a fax from the moderator that the discussion would not take place because the representative of the football associations was unavailable. If you switched on the broadcast that Saturday you could however see the representative of the football associations criticizing the judgment and nobody contradicted him.

As you probably know, the opinion pleaded for the admissibility of the case and for the incompatibility of the football rules with the freedom of movement for workers seen as containing a general prohibition of restrictions on the freedom of movements, a prohibition of discrimination on grounds of nationality, and a prohibition of agreements restricting competition. The echo of the opinion in the media was split in two camps. The general media and especially the UK media were favourable to my views. In fact, it is probably the only case in my career at the Court for which I have been stopped in the streets, clapped on my shoulders and commented: Well done! On the other side, the media close to sport in general and particularly to the national football associations and UEFA were very critical.

Not being satisfied with the opinion, UEFA requested the Court to order a measure of inquiry with a view to obtaining fuller information on the role played by transfer fees in the financing of small or medium-sized football clubs and the consequences of their possible disappearance. After hearing my views on the matter, the Court considered that the application should be dismissed. Indeed, it was made at a time when the oral procedure was closed. The Court held that such an application could be admitted only if it relates to facts which the party concerned could not put forward before the close of the oral procedure. This was not the case here. Moreover, the question was raised whether the aim of maintaining a balance in financial and competitive terms, and in particular that of ensuring the financing of smaller clubs, could be achieved by other means such as a redistribution of a portion of football income from television—in particular by Mr. Bosman in his written observations. Obviously the football associations had been confronted with that issue even before the hearing. The opinion treated this matter under the heading 'Maintenance of the financial and sporting equilibrium'.[3]

So the stage was set for the rendering of the judgement.

The judgement largely followed the opinion. Thanks to it, for the first time, millions of people learned that in 'Europe' they have individual rights and judges who protect them. This book celebrates the importance of the *Bosman* judgement as a fundamental case for the application of EU law to sport and for the dialogue that it fostered between sports governing bodies and the EU institutions. The book, which covers a wide range of subjects, demonstrates the living legacy of the *Bosman* ruling.

Prof. Dr. Carl Otto Lenz
Advocate General at the Court of Justice in *Bosman*

[3](para 218–234).

Contents

Editors and Contributors

About the Editors

Antoine Duval is a Senior Researcher for International and European Sports Law at the T.M.C. Asser Instituut in The Hague. He defended his Ph.D. on the interaction between Lex Sportiva and EU Law at the European University Institute in Florence in 2015, where he was the conveyor of the Transnational Law Working Group. His research focuses mainly on the place of law in a transnational context and he uses lex sportiva as a case study. He is the editor of the ASSER International Sports Law Blog and co-editor of the Yearbook of International Sports Arbitration.

Ben Van Rompuy is a senior researcher at the T.M.C. Asser Instituut, where he heads the ASSER International Sports Law Centre, and he is also a Visiting Professor of Competition Policy at the Free University of Brussels (VUB). His main research interests lie in the field of EU competition law and internal market law, with a specific focus on its application in the media and sports sectors. He has published widely in this area and frequently acts as a legal expert for media companies, sports associations, athletes, and public authorities. He holds a Ph.D. in law from the VUB (on the role of non-economic public policy considerations in EU antitrust law enforcement) and held visiting scholar positions at Georgetown University and New York University.

Contributors

Mattias Derlén LL.M., LL.D. is a Senior Lecturer and Associate Professor at the Department of Law, Umeå University, Sweden. His areas of interest include law and language, constitutional EU law, and empirical legal research. In the area of law and language he is mainly interested in multilingual interpretation of EU law from a practical legal perspective. His recent interests include multilingual interpretation of the case law of the Court of Justice of the European Union as well as issues of legal integration. In the area of empirical legal research he is part of two large, interdisciplinary research projects, where methods from example network analysis are used to analyse the case law of the Court of Justice as well as Swedish courts.

Borja García is a senior lecturer in sport management and policy at Loughborough University (United Kingdom). He is an expert in European Union sports policy, which he has researched with an agenda-setting theoretical framework, and the impact of EU policies and regulations on the governance of professional sport, especially football. He has published extensively in international academic journals, such as Journal of European Public Policy, Public Administration or the Journal of European Integration. He was one of the principal investigators of the groundbreaking FREE (Football Research in an Enlarged Europe) Project, funded by the European Commission's FP7. Moreover, he is one of the founding members of the Association for the Study of Sport and the European Union. His research was a pioneer in applying political sciences concepts to the study of EU sport law and policy, showing new lights on the dynamics of the interplay between professional football stakeholders and the institutions of the European Union.

Simon Gardiner is a Professor of International Sports Law at Leeds Becket University and has worked at a number of universities in the UK and in Australia including Middlesex University and Griffith University in Queensland. He has been an active researcher in the area of sports law for over twenty years and has an international reputation. His particular research interests include sports governance and the regulation of sports-related corruption, racism in sport and the construction of national identity and athlete mobility in sport. He has been involved in funded research projects and consultancy for a range of sports bodies and has worked with the European Union concerning a number of projects. He is widely published including lead author and editor of the UK's principal student-targeted textbook, namely Gardiner et al, Sports Law that is due to be published in its fifth edition in 2016.

Arnout Geeraert is a Post-Doctoral Fellow at Leuven International and European Studies (LINES), University of Leuven, Belgium. He develops the Sports Governance Observer for Play the Game/ Danish Institute for Sports Studies. His current work explores the role of the European Union in international sport through different theoretical lenses and looks into elements of good governance in sport organisations in general.

Johan Lindholm LL.M., LL.D. is a Professor of Law at Umea University, Sweden, where he teaches and does research in the fields of constitutional law, European Union law, sports law, and empirical legal studies. He is an author and editor of several books in these fields, including both research monographs and text books. He continues to publish frequently and wildly, including articles in leading international journals such as Common Market Law Review, European Law Review, Columbia Journal of European Union Law, and the International Sports Law Journal.

Richard Parrish is the Director of the Centre for Sports Law Research at Edge Hill University in the UK. He has provided sports law and policy advice to the European Union and European governments through his membership of the European Commission's

High Level Expert Group on Sports Diplomacy, the Commission's Group of Independent Sports Experts and his participation in the EU's TAIEX programme. He was also Specialist Adviser to the House of Lords Inquiry into Grassroots Sport and the European Union (2010/11). He has authored a number of influential reports for the European Parliament and the European Commission, including the main reports into nationality discrimination in Olympic sports and European football. He is the author of two monographs and three edited collections exploring the interface between sport and EU law. He is the Honorary Chair of the Association for the Study of Sport and the European Union. He is an editorial board member of the International Sports Law Journal, the International Journal of Sports Policy and Politics, Sport and the Law Journal and the European Sports Law and Policy Bulletin.

Katarina Pijetlovic is a Senior Lecturer in EU law and sports law at Liverpool Hope University. She is the author of "EU Sports Law and Breakaway Leagues in Football" (2015), an editorial board member at LawInSport.com, and a peer-reviewer for the International Sports Law Journal. She is the receiver of numerous academic awards and distinctions, and regularly presents at international conferences and seminars on various topics of EU and international sports law. Dr. Pijetlovic occasionally acts as a legal representative of athletes, clubs, and leagues. Previously, she served as a researcher in EU competition and sports law at the University of Helsinki, a lecturer in EU law at Tallinn University of Technology, and a visiting scholar in sports law at St. John's University, in New York.

Oskar van Maren is a Researcher for International and European Sports Law at the T.M.C. Asser Instituut in The Hague. He holds an LL.M in European law from Leiden University (The Netherlands) and wrote a master thesis on EU State aid rules and Spanish football. His academic interest lies mainly in the involvement of EU law in sport. He is the managing editor of the International Sports Law Journal and editor of the ASSER International Sports Law Blog.

Stephen Weatherill is the Jacques Delors Professor of European Law in the University of Oxford. He also serves as the Deputy Director for European Law in the Institute of European and Comparative Law, and is a Fellow of Somerville College. His research interests embrace the field of European Law in its widest sense, although his published work is predominantly concerned with European Union trade law. He has been writing about sports law in Europe for almost thirty years now.

Roger Welch Ph.D., LLM, LLB was, until 2010, a principal lecturer in employment law in the Business School at the University of Portsmouth, where he is now a visiting research fellow. He has written extensively on collective and individual employment rights, and is the lead author of Employment Law (with Caroline Strevens), published by Pearson in its Living Law series. He is an original and ongoing author of Sports Law, edited by Simon Gardener and published by Routlege. With Simon Gardiner, he has written extensively on employment contracts in professional sport with particular emphasis on the ongoing legacy of the *Bosman* ruling in the contexts of player mobility, the regulation of transfer systems and the compatibility of player nationality quotas with European Union law.

Abbreviations

ACP	African, Caribbean and Pacific Group of States
AG	Advocate General
BER	Block Exemption Regulation
CAS	Court of Arbitration for Sport
CJEU	Court of Justice of the European Union
DG	Directorate General
DRC	(FIFA) Dispute Resolution Chamber
ECA	European Club Association
ECB	England and Wales Cricket Board
EEA	European Economic Area
EEC Treaty	Treaty establishing the European Economic Community (Treaty of Rome)
ELPA	Elliniki Leskhi Aftokinitou kai Periigiseon (Greek Automobile and Touring Club)
EP	European Parliament
EPFL	European Professional Football Leagues
EUR	Euros
FFP	Financial Fair Play
FIA	Fédération Internationale de l'Automobile
FIFA	Fédération Internationale de Football Association
FIFPro	Fédération Internationale des Associations de Footballeurs Professionnels
FOA	Formula One Administration Ltd
G14	Group of 14 European football clubs
GBER	General Block Exemption Regulation
INEA	Institute for European Affairs
IOC	International Olympic Committee
ISC	International Sportsworld Communicators
ITC	International Transfer Certificate
MOTOE	Motosykletistiki Omospondia Ellados NPID (Greek Motorcycling Federation)

MRSPC	Minimum Requirements in Standard Player Contracts
NYC	New York Convention
PA	Principal-agent
PFA	Professional Footballers' Association
PFSC	(UEFA) Professional Football Strategy Council
PSC	Players Status Committee
RSTP	(FIFA) Regulations on the Status and Transfer of Players
SGB	Sports Governing Body
SME	Small and Medium-sized Enterprise
TFEU	Treaty on the Functioning of the European Union
UCI	Union Cycliste Internationale
UEFA	Union Européenne de Football Association

Chapter 1
Introduction

Antoine Duval and Ben Van Rompuy

Abstract In this introduction to the edited volume, The Legacy of Bosman. Revisiting the relationship between EU law and sport, we provide some background on the aim and methodology of the book. We start by outlining the reasons for exploring the legal and political transformations triggered by the Bosman judgment over the last 20 years and beyond. Most importantly, we argue for a shift in the way the ruling is commonly interpreted. The Bosman decision of the CJEU is widely perceived in the literature and in public opinion as a deregulatory intervention by the Court. This, in our view, is a misconception that necessitates a re-reading of the ruling. We suggest that the Bosman case is displaying a democratic ethos. The duty of justification it imposes on the transnational private regulations of sports governing bodies is of a genuine 'counter-democratic' nature. The last part of the introduction offers a short overview of the chapters included in the book.

Keywords Bosman · EU law · Lex sportiva · Sports law · Free movement · Competition law

Contents

A. Duval
European and International Sports Law, T.M.C. Asser Institute, The Hague, The Netherlands
e-mail: a.duval@asser.nl

B. Van Rompuy (✉)
T.M.C. Asser Instituut, The Hague, The Netherlands
e-mail: b.van.rompuy@asser.nl

B. Van Rompuy
Vrije Universiteit Brussel, Brussel, Belgium

A. Duval and B. Van Rompuy (eds.), *The Legacy of* Bosman,
ASSER International Sports Law Series, DOI 10.1007/978-94-6265-120-3_1

Is the 20th anniversary of the *Bosman* ruling[1] a sufficient reason to revisit this old case on which so much has already been written? Is there still something interesting to say about *Bosman*?

We believe the answer is a resounding 'yes' and we count on this book to demonstrate it.

Unlike most judgments of the Court of Justice of the European Union (CJEU), which get lost in legal limbo over time, the relevance of the *Bosman* judgment has endured. It is a central case in the systematic structure of EU law, as demonstrated by the latest scholarship studying its position in the complex network of CJEU jurisprudence.[2] It is also a mythical case, one that gives flesh to the idea(l) of a European public sphere. *Bosman* is probably the only case decided by the CJEU that normal European citizens are susceptible to know. A simple google search will show its actuality and the permanence of its shadow in the public discourse on football and sport in general. It is fair to say that many people discovered the existence of the CJEU when it rendered this decision, as Advocate General (AG) Lenz vividly recalls in the preface to this book. This spotlight on the CJEU is the longest-lasting legacy of the *Bosman* ruling and probably its greatest service to the European cause.

Bosman taught generations of EU lawyers that EU free movement rights apply 'horizontally' to transnational private regulations of *inter alia* sports governing bodies (SGBs). In fact, this was already evident from the CJEU judgment in *Walrave and Koch*,[3] delivered twenty years earlier, but the popularity of football (in comparison to motor-paced cycling) helped drive this point home. Since *Bosman*, we also know that a simple non-discriminatory restriction of the free movement right of a worker needs to be justified and proportionate if it is to be compatible with EU law. In addition, we know that sporting regulators can invoke specific legitimate objectives (such as maintaining competitive balance or encouraging the recruitment and training of young players) to justify the restrictions they impose on the freedom to work of professional athletes. This general analytical framework for applying EU law to sport has not changed since 1995. Nonetheless, there are still academic lessons to be learned from *Bosman*. Law is a living object. The seemingly static structure of the legal framework developed in *Bosman* should not overshadow the unforeseen and dynamic nature of the transformative legal changes it has triggered. The hyper-activism of the European Commission after *Bosman*, primarily on the basis of the EU antitrust rules, compared to its passivity in the aftermath of *Walrave and Koch* and *Donà*,[4] illustrates the political and institutional choices at play. *Bosman* opened a Pandora's Box. The world of sport, and

[1]Case C-415/93 *Union Royale Belge des Sociétés de Football Association and others v. Bosman and others*, ECLI:EU:C:1995:463.

[2]See the chapter by Derlén and Lindholm in this volume.

[3]Opinion of Advocate General Warner in Case 36/74 *Walrave and Koch v. Union Cycliste Internationale*, ECLI:EU:C:1974:111.

[4]Case C-13/76 *Gaetano Donà v Mario Mantero*, ECLI:EU:C:1976:115.

its *lex sportiva*, entered in legal communication with EU law, and has been dialectically engaged with it since then.[5] EU law was successfully used by a variety of actors to implicate the EU in the sporting world. This implication takes many different forms, e.g. the initiation of antitrust and State aid investigations,[6] the adoption of a White Paper and a Communication on sport,[7] and the introduction of a European social dialogue committee for professional football.[8]

This edited collection of contributions from leading scholars takes stock of this multifarious afterlife of the *Bosman* case. It explores how a set of legal formula and principles introduced in *Bosman* have on the long run triggered widespread social, legal, political, and institutional transformations that fundamentally affected the sporting world. In a way, this book demonstrates that one can understand the impact of a legal case only retroactively by analysing at a distance the practical changes it has provoked.[9] On that metric, *Bosman* deserves a special mention as a fundamental, symbolical milestone for the involvement of the EU in the sporting field.[10] Through various case studies, on specific aspects of the EU's involvement in sport, the chapters cover many of the domains in which spill-over effects of the *Bosman* ruling have been felt. Some of the authors also envisage the potential way forward, engaging partly in prophesising. By doing so, they demonstrate that *Bosman* has not run out of symbolic fuel yet, its spirit is still around. The case remains a beacon, a fundamental reference to which EU lawyers and administrators turn when they are confronted in one way or another with sporting matters.

20 years after *Bosman*, its legacy is well alive. The trajectory of EU sports law and policy can only be understood with reference to this case as a founding moment. The genealogy of its impacts presented in this book demonstrates both its currency and the depth and variety of its effects. The hundreds of commentaries published in the immediate aftermath of the case were sometimes, as legal commentaries often are, repetitive in their analysis and paraphrasing the decision.[11] For many of them, their added value in academic terms was relatively limited. However, the sheer mass of writings did probably contribute to the mythical status and symbolic force of the *Bosman* case. With the advantage of the temporal distance, this volume adds different (and less chartered) layers of analysis to the discussion.

---

[5] In general on this legal relationship, see Duval 2015b.

[6] See the chapters by Pjetlovic and Van Rompuy and Van Maren in this volume.

[7] Commission White Paper of 11 July 2007, COM (2007) 391 final - White Paper on Sport.

[8] See the chapter by Parrish in this volume.

[9] A point made recently by Antoine Vauchez in a draft paper on file with the author.

[10] It has been duly recognized as a 'classic' of EU law by Azoulai and Maduro 2010.

[11] See for an incomplete overview of the existing commentaries the annotations collected by the CJEU at http://curia.europa.eu/jcms/upload/docs/application/pdf/2009-05/notes_89-04.pdf. Accessed 1 December 2015.

1.1 Re-reading *Bosman*: From Deregulation to Democratization

1.1.1 The Deregulatory Myth

The *Bosman* case has been understood by many as a purely deregulatory ruling.[12] The chief narrative being that the CJEU, driven by an alleged neoliberal bias, engaged in a radical deregulation of football, as it was doing in other economic and social fields.

The ruling clearly fostered negative integration when it provided that nationality quotas are to be abandoned. This led to the Europeanization of the labour market for professional football players and, more broadly, sportspeople. On the one hand, it is fair to argue that the CJEU might have underestimated the destabilizing effects on sporting competitions which are, in football at least, still mainly structured on a national basis. There is some empirical evidence substantiating that the inflow of non-nationals in certain country might have discouraged the local training of young players in some countries.[13] On the other hand, we are not witnessing, as the CJEU predicted, a loss in interest in clubs featuring non-national or local football players. This was a key argument in favour of the nationality quotas in the *Bosman* case. UEFA, URBSFA and the French, German, and Italian Governments argued that *'those clauses serve to maintain the traditional link between each club and its country, a factor of great importance in enabling the public to identify with its favourite team and ensuring that clubs taking part in international competitions effectively represent their countries'*.[14] In fact, supporters' loyalty is a more complex phenomenon that is not chiefly dependent on the nationality (or local character) of the players fielded on the pitch.[15] A recent study has shown that *'without any ambiguity [...] the influx of foreign players following the Bosman ruling has not fundamentally altered supporters' capacity to identify with their club'*.[16] The assumed xenophobic bias of supporters invoked to defend the maintenance of nationality quotas has not materialized in practice. This is good news for the EU, and a powerful rebuttal to those that perceive football fans as intrinsically prone to chauvinist behaviour.

Moreover, the European Commission and the CJEU have been willing - if corroborated by evidence - to acknowledge the collateral damages arising out of

[12]For a caricature of this point of view see Manzella 2002.

[13]CIES Football Observatory Monthly Report Issue no. 9 of November 2015, Record low of club-trained players in Europe. http://www.football-observatory.com/IMG/sites/mr/mr09/en/. Accessed 1 December 2015.

[14]Case C-415/93 *Union Royale Belge des Sociétés de Football Association and others v. Bosman and others*, ECLI:EU:C:1995:463, para 123.

[15]For a detailed analysis of the fan behaviour to the internationalization/europeanization of squads see Ranc 2011.

[16]Ibid., p. 163.

the *Bosman* ruling and to tolerate regulatory mechanisms designed to tackle these externalities. For example, the Commission informally condoned the introduction by UEFA (and national federations) of a lighter version of nationality quotas: the homegrown player rule.[17] Similarly, the Commission indicated its political support for UEFA's Financial Fair Play Regulations.[18] And, most famously, it agreed to the introduction of a reformed FIFA transfer system in 2001.[19] The CJEU, for its part, has also been willing to accommodate the regulatory objectives of the SGBs. It has recognized the need for transfer windows in the *Lehtonen* case,[20] the proportionality of anti-doping rules in its *Meca-Medina* decision,[21] and the legitimacy of a training compensation system in the more recent *Bernard* ruling.[22] If there is a deregulatory ambition in the CJEU's sporting jurisprudence it is very well hidden. In fact, what the EU institutions are keen to preserve is the free movement of sportspeople in Europe. Directly discriminatory nationality quotas remain a no-go. However, the CJEU is well aware of the need for multilevel regulations (private and public) in sport, and very much ready to give the green light if they are properly justified.

This is the heart of the message one should derive from the *Bosman* ruling and its aftermath. The misleading deregulatory narrative of *Bosman* that prevailed until now has been a blessing for some SGBs willing to find a scapegoat to blame for their failure to regulate their own sport. Furthermore, this narrative also eclipsed a fundamental dimension of the *Bosman* ruling: its 'counter-democratic' function in a transnational space.

[17]Commission Press Release of 28 May 2008, IP/08/807 UEFA rule on 'home-grown players': compatibility with the principle of free movement of persons. http://europa.eu/rapid/press-release_IP-08-807_en.htm. Accessed 1 December 2015. Yet, the effectiveness of the measure remains controversial, see: University of Liverpool and Edge Hill University (2013) Study on the Assessment of UEFA's Home-Grown Player Rule. Study for the European Commission EAC/07/2012. http://ec.europa.eu/sport/library/studies/final-rpt-april2013-homegrownplayer.pdf. Accessed 1 December 2015.

[18]Commission Press Release of 21 March 2012, State aid: Vice President Almunia and UEFA President Platini confirm Financial Fair-Play rules in professional football are in line with EU state aid policy. http://europa.eu/rapid/press-release_IP-12-264_en.htm. Accessed 1 December 2015.

[19]Commission Press Release of 6 March 2001, IP/01/320 Commission President Prodi welcomes outcome of football transfers talks. http://europa.eu/rapid/press-release_IP-01-320_en.htm. Accessed 1 December 2015.

[20]Case C-176/96 *Jyri Lehtonen and Castors Canada Dry Namur-Braine ASBL v. Fédération royale belge des sociétés de basket-ball ASBL (FRBSB)*, ECLI:EU:C:2000:201.

[21]Case C-519/04 P *David Meca-Medina and Igor Majcen v. Commission*, ECLI:EU:C:2006:492.

[22]Case C-325/08, *Olympique Lyonnais v Olivier Bernard and Newcastle United FC*, ECLI:EU:C:2010:143.

1.1.2 The 'Counter-Democratic' Function of *Bosman*

Bosman should in our view be interpreted as an instance in which the CJEU tried to impose a democratic check on the exercise of transnational authority by SGBs in football and beyond.[23] The control of the proportionality of the transfer system (and to a lesser extent of the nationality quotas) embodies the 'counter-democratic' function of the *Bosman* ruling.[24] In *Bosman*, the rules of the football federations were not considered per se contrary to the EU free movement rights. Rather, the justifications raised to defend their compatibility were deemed insufficient. In fact, as far as the transfer system is concerned, the less restrictive alternatives (i.e. the centralized redistribution of media rights revenues) proposed by AG Lenz, and indirectly endorsed by the CJEU in its ruling, were extremely restrictive of the economic freedom of clubs.[25] This framework of justification is the main legacy of the *Bosman* ruling.

Over time, it was transposed to the area of EU competition law. Because the CJEU had confined itself to the application of the free movement rules in *Bosman*, despite the guidance from AG Lenz in his opinion, the European Commission initiated the application of the EU competition rules to the sports sector. In the aftermath of *Bosman,* a growing number of notifications and complaints prompted the Commission to examine certain sports-related activities that were not considered contentious in the past. Regarding economic activities generated by sport, the growing commercialization of professional sport, closely related to developments in the European audiovisual sector, was the main catalyst for enforcement action. Regarding organizational sporting rules, however, *Bosman* had significantly cast a shadow on the idea that they, particularly given the commercial context in which they operate, could escape assessment under EU law. When the CJEU for the first time applied the EU antitrust provisions to a sporting rule in *Meca-Medina*,[26] it finally dismissed the notion of a 'purely sporting' exception in the context of EU competition law. It identified the *Wouters* proportionality test as the appropriate method to assess sporting rules under the antitrust provisions: as long as the rule is inherent and proportional to a legitimate objective in the interest of sport, the restrictions caused by that rule are not caught by the prohibition of anti-competitive practices.

---

[23]This claim is elaborated on in Duval 2015b.

[24]'By 'counter-democracy' I mean not the opposite of democracy but rather a form of democracy that reinforces the usual electoral democracy as a kind of buttress, a democracy of indirect powers disseminated throughout society–in other words, a durable democracy of distrust, which complements the episodic democracy of the usual electoral-representative system.' Rosanvallon 2008, p. 8.

[25]Opinion of Advocate General Lenz in Case C-415/93 *Union Royale Belge des Sociétés de Football Association and others v. Bosman and others*, ECLI:EU:C:1995:293, paras 218–234.

[26]Case C-519/04 P *David Meca-Medina and Igor Majcen v. Commission*, ECLI:EU:C:2006:492.

Hence, the most valuable heritage of the *Bosman* case is that the private regulators of sport have to justify and explain the proportionality of their rules. This undeniably endows the judiciary with an important political power, reminiscent of a much-dreaded *Gouvernement des juges*.[27] Yet, in a transnational context in which sport's private rulers are everything but democratically elected and inevitably escape the control of an absent global state, this turn towards a strong counter-democratic check on the SGBs is a (much) needed development.

In that regard *Bosman* has played, and still plays, a crucial function. The CJEU as an institution, and EU law as a legal system in general, are well placed to personify this counter-democratic ethos in the transnational sporting context. Indeed, SGBs, and FIFA in particular, have successfully secured an autonomous regulatory space by blackmailing national states. They are able to impose their conditions upon states willing to host international sporting competitions and use aggressive political tactic and threat to defend their autonomy and their authority.[28] Their power derives from their monopoly on the organization of mega-events, like the FIFA World Cup or the Olympic Games. SGBs are also able to play with one of the characteristic trumps of multinationals in a globalized world: they (ab)use the exit option.[29] In other words, by having the ability to leave a country or to choose one, these organizations can exercise a form of modern blackmail to shape the legal environment in which they operate and attract the favours of national politicians. This power asymmetry between international federations and national states, however, evaporates when the EU gets involved.[30] For example, the EU has no national team and does not compete for the organization of the Olympic Games. Moreover, for FIFA to threaten to ban all EU Member States would mean threatening to ban all the most successful (and wealthiest) national football federations. This explains why *Bosman* is of such importance (beyond the world of sport): it shelters the state from a direct confrontation with the SGBs and empowers national courts to stand up to them on the basis of EU law.

This power of EU law has been utilised in many different instances over the twenty years since *Bosman*. The FIFA regulations concerning the transfers of players, as well as those regulating the profession of agents,[31] were subjected to the critical review of the European Commission under its power to enforce EU competition law.[32] The same is true for the institutional structure and rules of the

[27] As pointed out by one of the legal advisers of UEFA, see Zylberstein 2008.

[28] On FIFA see García and Meier 2015. On the IOC see James and Osborn 2011.

[29] On the strength of the exit option of multinationals see Beck 2005.

[30] This asymmetry-breaking function of the EU has been emphasized by political philosophers and sociologists, see Habermas 2001 and Beck and Grande 2007. But also by EU scholars, see Menon and Weatherill 2008.

[31] Case T-193/02, *Laurent Piau v Commission*, ECLI:EU:T:2005:22.

[32] See the chapter of Duval in this volume.

Federation Internationale de l'Automobile (FIA) at the turn of the century.[33] In both cases, the SGBs were forced to change their rules in order for them to be deemed compatible with EU competition law. Similarly, the EU was instrumental in improving the privacy rights of athletes in the fight against doping. The intervention of the so called *Article 29* Working Party was decisive in driving a reform of the Data Protection framework applying to the World Anti-Doping Code.[34] The mere threat of the use of EU law to challenge the transnational private regulations put in place by the SGBs forces them to think in terms of proportionality of their measures and to better balance the various interests of the affected actors when doing so. In this context, the rise of the Court of Arbitration for Sport (CAS) as a key institution in the regulation of global sport can only be understood with *Bosman* in mind.[35] It is because of the irritation of the *Bosman* ruling that CAS finally became the 'Supreme Court of World Sport'. CAS is far from perfect, its independence has been challenged recently by the Oberlandesgericht München in the *Pechstein* ruling,[36] but it offers a promising embryo of a separate judicial power to solve transnational sporting disputes. In the absence of an international sports court instituted by national states, it is a useful forum to approximate a judicial level playing field for the world's finest athletes and clubs. In short, *Bosman* is a 'reflexive'[37] judgment: it triggered changes to the normative and institutional structure of the so-called *lex sportiva*, but it did not aim at destroying it altogether.

EU law after *Bosman* (and already in *Bosman*) was not blind to the particular demands of the sporting world. On the contrary, as has been tirelessly reminded by lone but powerful voices, EU law was (and still is) extremely generous in its assessment of the compatibility of transnational sporting regulations.[38] Nevertheless, the rhetoric deployed by SGBs, namely that the EU disregards the peculiarities of sport, has been an extremely potent smokescreen.[39] It is a lobbying

[33]See Notice of 13 June 2001 published pursuant to Article 19 (3) of Council Regulation No 17), concerning Cases COMP/35.163—Notification of FIA Regulations, COMP/36.638—Notification by FIA/FOA of agreements relating to the FIA Formula One World Championship, COMP/36.776—GTR/FIA & others [2001] OJ C 169/5.

[34]See the Opinion 3/2008 by Alex Türk of 1 August 2008, on the World Anti-Doping Code Draft International Standard for the Protection of Privacy. http://ec.europa.eu/justice/data-protection/article-29/documentation/opinion-recommendation/files/2008/wp156_en.pdf. Accessed 1 December 2015; See also Second Opinion 4/2009 by Alex Türk of 6 April 2009, on the World Anti-Doping Agency (WADA) International Standard for the Protection of Privacy and Personal Information, on related provisions of the WADA Code and on other privacy issues in the context of the fight against doping in sport by WADA and (national) anti-doping organizations. http://ec.europa.eu/justice/data-protection/article-29/documentation/opinion-recommendation/files/2009/wp162_en.pdf. Accessed 1 December 2015.

[35]Duval 2015a.

[36]On this case see Duval and Van Rompuy 2016.

[37]On the notion of reflexive law, see Teubner 1983.

[38]See in general the work of Stephen Weatherill on EU law and sport.

[39]Garcia and Weatherill 2012.

strategy gone right. So right that the idea of a neoliberal EU in sporting affairs has entirely occulted the fact that FIFA and UEFA themselves were actively driving the commercialization of football and cashing in substantial revenues which, apparently, ended up in the deep pockets of the administrators rather than trickle down to the bottom of the football pyramid. The public, misled by an offensive of charm picturing the traditional values of football under the ruthless attacks of an army of heartless European technocrats, has been wilfully fooled. The truth is very far from this. The EU (and the European Commission in particular) has left a wide scope of autonomy to SGBs. Instead, EU law provides a few (much-needed) legal weapons to weaker stakeholders in sport (mainly the athletes, but also the clubs) to challenge the regulatory status quo. However, like a constitutional review in a national context, this instrument has inherent limitations. SGBs 'only' face a duty to justify their decisions and this duty is tamed through the omnipresent reference to the notion of the specificity of sport. One would be at pain to identify a recent case in which FIFA or UEFA were unable to justify their rules.

Bosman is a Pandora's box that cannot (and should not) be locked ever again. It provides for a permanent right for athletes, clubs, and supporters to have the right to contest, criticize, and challenge the regulations put in place by the SGBs. The European and national courts (and competition authorities) are a new forum to debate the necessity (and *in fine* the legitimacy) of the regulations adopted. *Bosman* offers a legal and political response in a world undergoing an uncertain transnationalization process. It is a check on the emerging transnational powers and authorities, be they SGBs or multinationals, standard setting bodies, or non-governmental organizations. By imposing a proportionality test onto FIFA and UEFA, the CJEU recognized their capacity to pursuit legitimate objectives and to work for a transnational common good, but also the need to bind their power as Ulysses to his mast.[40]

1.2 The Structure of This Book

Each chapter in this book tackles a different aspect of the legacy (and origin) of the *Bosman* ruling. The case is used as a starting point by the authors to reflect from a variety of theoretical perspectives and methodologies on its influence over time on EU law and policy in the field of sport.

The book starts with Borja Garcia's chapter looking back at the social roots of the *Bosman* ruling. The chapter aims at showing that the ruling did not come out of the blue, but was the result of a complex evolution inside and outside the foot ball world. *Bosman* is identified as an accelerator of a process that led to what is known as 'modern football'. From a macro perspective, Garcia reconstructs the broader historical (in particular economic) context surrounding the ruling. He then

[40] The metaphor is borrowed from Teubner 2012.

focuses on the micro context of the *Bosman* case through an in-depth study of the actors of the case and the complex interactions between their interests. Garcia concludes that the *Bosman* ruling is only a piece of a broader transformation of European football and cannot be understood in isolation from this transformation.

The Chap. 3 by Mattias Derlén and Johan Lindholm provides a fascinating study, based on the cutting-edge use of network theory, of the position of the *Bosman* judgment in the network of CJEU judgments. They demonstrate that the *Bosman* ruling is exceptional due to its profound and long-lasting influence on the CJEU's case law. This influence goes way beyond the realm of sports and extends primarily to four areas: the jurisdiction of the CJEU in matters of preliminary rulings, the use of the fundamental freedoms against private entities, non-discriminatory obstacles to the internal market, and the temporal effects of CJEU judgments. They conclude that the case's legacy is due to the fact that the ruling is well written, well reasoned, well known, and well connected. The chapter concludes that the ruling has had a transformative impact on the reasoning used by the CJEU outside of the relatively narrow sporting field. It anchors, in tangible facts, the widespread belief of a remarkable legacy of the *Bosman* ruling.

The Chap. 4 by Simon Gardiner and Roger Welch tackles the narrower question of the fate of nationality quotas and more broadly the transfer system in football following the *Bosman* ruling. They analyse closely both FIFA's proposal for the introduction of a 6 + 5 rule and UEFA's imposition of a homegrown player rule, and argue that both are likely to infringe EU law. To replace it, the authors support a comprehensive social dialogue agreement between FIFA, UEFA, and FIFPro as a reflexive legal strategy to create a reformed international transfer system, which would enhance player mobility and secure a true competitive balance between the clubs.

Chapter 5 by Antoine Duval offers a fresh look at the evolution of the FIFA Regulations on the Status and Transfers of Players (RSTP) after the *Bosman* ruling. The author retraces, through a study of the European Commission's investigation into the FIFA transfer system, the complex multi-level law-making process that led to the adoption of the FIFA RSTP. Thereafter, he assesses the autonomous institutional underpinnings and normative power of the FIFA RSTP, highlighting the emergence of a peculiar form of transnational regulation, enforced with the help of FIFA's internal tribunals and the CAS. This autonomous, highly institutionalized system is revealed as the direct legacy of the *Bosman* case, and of the Commission's attempt at nudging the regulation of the transfer system by FIFA. Hence, the chapter emphasizes the reflexive nature of the intervention of the EU Institutions into the realm of *lex sportiva*.

Chapter 6 by Katarina Pijetlovic addresses the application of EU competition law to organisational rules in the sports sector. Pijetlovic retraces in detail the case law of the CJEU and the decisional practice of the European Commission in their application of the EU antitrust provisions to sport cases. In doing so, she highlights the evolution of the tests applied from *Bosman* onwards to determine the compatibility of organisational rules with EU competition law. Thus, she points out the centrality of the objective justification test and its progressive transplantation from internal market law into EU competition law. In her words, it becomes the 'ultimate test' for the regulations of SGBs after the *Meca-Medina* ruling of the CJEU in 2006.

Chapter 7 by Ben Van Rompuy and Oskar van Maren turns attention to the application of the EU state aid rules to public support measures for professional sport. Until very recently, this pillar of EU competition law remained an anomaly in the story of EU sports law. The authors explain why the financing of sports infrastructure and professional sports clubs only now, 20 years after *Bosman*, are on the radar of State aid control. Considering the general policy dynamics of EU State aid law and policy, they argue that the late appearance of enforcement efforts is not as remarkable as it may appear. The extension of the reach of State aid control to new sectors or new forms of aid has typically been the result of external constraints on the European Commission's independent agenda-setting abilities. In the case of sport, it was primarily the case law of the EU courts that triggered the recent surge in formal investigations and decisional practice.

Chapter 8 by Richard Parrish offers a critical look at the introduction of the European social dialogue committee in professional football. He traces back the emergence of the social dialogue to the liberalizing effects of the *Bosman* ruling on the transfer system. The author reviews the work of the committee since its inception in 2008 and provides a sobering account of its achievements to date. As pointed out by Parrish, the first agreement signed in 2012 has faced important difficulties at the implementation phase and since then the committee has been incapable of agreeing to other arrangements. Yet, the author remains hopeful that on the long term the European social dialogue will prove a necessary mechanism for a better governance of football.

Chapter 9 by Arnout Geeraert looks at the *Bosman* ruling from a political science perspective and builds on insights derived from the classical principal-agent framework. Highlighting the influence of *Bosman*, the chapter explores the limitations and opportunities of the EU's power in relation to SGBs. His fundamental claim is that EU law can offer a powerful shadow to force institutional and governance reforms of the SGBs. This power, however, is not unlimited as SGBs have been able to limit the capacity of the EU to intervene through various strategies. Geeraert concludes his chapter by offering some concrete policy advice for a more ambitious EU sports policy, oriented at improving the governance of the SGBs.

The closing chapter by Stephen Weatherill is an evolutionary study of the transformative effect of the *Bosman* ruling on the academic field. The author shows that EU sports law and policy as an academic discipline was almost non-existent before the *Bosman* ruling, in short it was a 'lonely world'. However, after the decision, a small but active community of scholars interested in the interaction between the EU and sport flourished. Or, as he so eloquently puts it, '*Bosman changed the pace of EU sports law–from backwater to fast flowing current*'.

References

Azoulai L, Maduro MP (2010) The past and future of EU law. The classics of EU law revisited on the 50th anniversary of the Rome Treaty. Hart Publishing, Oxford

Beck U (2005) Power in the global age: a new global political economy. Polity Press, Cambridge

Beck U, Grande E (2007) Cosmopolitan Europe. Polity Press, Cambridge

Duval A (2015a) The Court of Arbitration for Sport and EU law: Chronicle of an encounter. Maastricht J Eur Comp Law 22(2):224–255

Duval A (2015b) La Lex Sportiva face à L'Union européenne: Guerre et Paix dans l'espace juridique transnational. PhD Thesis, European University Institute, Florence

Duval A, Van Rompuy B (2016) Protecting athletes' right to fair trial through EU competition law: the Pechstein case. In: Takács T, Lazić V, Van Rompuy B (eds) Paulussen C., Fundamental rights in international and European Law: public and private law perspectivesT.M.C. Asser Press, The Hague, pp 245–278

García B, Weatherill S (2012) Engaging with the EU in order to minimize its impact: sport and the negotiation of the Treaty of Lisbon. J Eur Public Policy 19:238–256

Habermas J (2001) The postnational constellation. MIT Press, Cambridge, Massachusetts, United States

James M, Osborn G (2011) London 2012 and the impact of the UK's olympic and paralympic legislation: protecting commerce or preserving culture? Mod Law Rev 74:410–429

Manzella A (2002) La dérégulation du football par l'Europe. Pouvoirs 101:39–47

Meier H-E, García B (2015) Protecting private transnational authority against public intervention: FIFA's power over national governments. Public Adm 93:890–906

Menon A, Weatherill S (2008) Transnational legitimacy in a globalising world: how the European Union rescues its states. West Eur Politics 31:397–416

Ranc D (2011) Foreign players and football supporters: the old firm, Arsenal. Manchester University Press, Manchester, Paris Saint-Germain

Rosanvallon P (2008) Counter-democracy. Politics in an age of distrust. Cambridge University Press, Cambridge

Teubner G (1983) Substantive and reflexive elements. Mod Law, Law Soc Rev 17(2):239–285

Teubner G (2012) Constitutional fragments: societal constitutionalism and globalization. Oxford University Press, Oxford

Zylberstein J (2008) The specificity of sport: a concept under threat. In: Blanpain R, Colucci M, Hendrickx F (eds) The future of sports law in the European Union. Beyond the EU reform treaty and the white paper. Kluwer Law International, The Hague, pp 95–106

Chapter 2
He Was not Alone: Bosman in Context

Borja García

Abstract This chapter analyses the social, political, historical and economic context of the Bosman case. The chapter argues that Bosman needs to be understood as yet another stage of a continued process of commercialisation and transformation in European football: players fought to transform their employment conditions since the 1960s; clubs questioned the legitimacy of UEFA to regulate European football and organise club competitions as they wanted a larger share of the commercial profits of the game; finally, political institutions in Brussels started to exert pressure on football governing bodies to modify the international transfer system. The chapter argues that, taking these into account, major transformations in the governance and regulation structures of football were needed, and they would have happened even without the Bosman ruling. Consequently, Bosman cannot be seen, on its own, as the only cause of the transformation of modern football in Europe. Finally, the chapter dedicates some space to Jean Marc Bosman's legal team composed by Luc Misson and Jean-Louis Dupont. It was their legal expertise what made a challenge before the Belgian and European courts also possible.

Keywords Bosman ruling · Football · Globalisation · Nationality quotas · Right to retain

B. García (✉)
Senior Lecturer in Sport Policy and Management; School of Sport, Exercise and Health Sciences, Loughborough University, Leicestershire LE11 3TU, UK
e-mail: b.garcia-garcia@lboro.ac.uk

A. Duval and B. Van Rompuy (eds.), *The Legacy of* Bosman,
ASSER International Sports Law Series, DOI 10.1007/978-94-6265-120-3_2

Contents

2.1 Introduction

The main message of this chapter is to explain that Jean-Marc Bosman was not a lone ranger; his case was the culmination rather than the starting point of a process of change in European football. *Bosman* (on its own) did not destroy European club football either, as claimed by the then president of UEFA Lennart Johansson.[1] Thus, this chapter provides the context to understand the circumstances under which Jean-Marc Bosman decided to take his contractual dispute to court. Only when looking at the case within its wider context, one can understand the consequences of the CJEU's ruling. It is not possible to grasp what has happened after the ruling without taking into account the socio-political and economic reality of European football in the late 1980s and early 1990s.

The chapter argues that *Bosman*[2] should not be considered as the origin of what some have called recently 'modern football',[3] but perhaps just as an accelerator of a process that was already in motion when, for example, the Premier League and the UEFA Champions League kicked-off in 1992 (three years before the ruling). Moreover, it is quite difficult to sustain that these changes would not have happened with a different decision of the Court in *Bosman*. If the Court would have found in favour of UEFA and the Belgian Football Association (FA), this may have slowed down the process of transformation of football; but given the development and globalisation of professional sport since 1995,[4] we would have gotten to the current point one way or another.

The chapter proceeds in four steps. First, it analyses the problems in the regulation of footballers' working conditions that led to conflicts between the players, on one

[1]Johansson, This Ruling Is Nothing Short of a Disaster. The European, 21 December 1995.

[2]Case C-415/93 *Union Royale Belge des Sociétés de Football Association and others v. Bosman and others*, ECLI:EU:C:1995:463.

[3]See Giulianotti 1999, p. 168 et seq.

[4]See for example Niemann et al. 2011.

side, and clubs and governing bodies, on the other. A long term perspective of those conflicts is necessary to understand why and how Jean-Marc Bosman took his case to the Belgian court. Second, the chapter reviews briefly the historical and economic development of football, with a special focus on the transformations from the 1970s. Here, the chapter addresses the economic context of European football, especially the liberalisation of the television market in the 1980s and 1990s. In the fourth section, the chapter enters into the political, legal and personal context of the *Bosman* case, analysing the role played by Luc Misson and Jean-Louis Dupont, the player's legal team. Finally, the chapter concludes with an overall analysis of the different elements that made a case and a ruling such as *Bosman* possible.

2.2 The Transfer System and Nationality Quotas: A Governance Problem

The first section of the chapter analyses the regulation of footballer's working conditions that, at the end of the day, were the rules challenged by Bosman's legal team before the courts. However, here we have taken a non-legal point of view. In doing so, we invite the reader to consider the *Bosman* case well beyond its legal confines, particularly in relation to the balance of power among the stakeholders involved in the game.

Thus, if we adopt a governance perspective to the players market, the first point to note is that the control structures of football traditionally positioned players at the bottom of the football pyramid.[5] This is a result of the way in which player registration works. Clubs must register their players with their respective national federation or league to participate in competitions. In turn, it is the responsibility of these governing bodies to regulate and decide which players can be registered to play in the competitions they organise. Football governing bodies have traditionally adopted two sets of norms to regulate the employment and registration of footballers: transfer systems and nationality quotas.[6]

2.2.1 The Transfer System

The so-called transfer system is a set of rules that regulate the circumstances under which players can move from one club to another. Transfer systems were said to protect small clubs that dedicate their resources to train and educate young players, so that the richest clubs cannot just 'steal' the players once they had finished their grass-roots education.[7]

[5] Tomlinson 1983, p. 173.

[6] Lanfranchi and Taylor 2001, p. 218.

[7] Roderick 2006, p. 116.

The origins of the transfer system can be traced back to the days when English football first turned professional. In the 1880s, the English Football League created a system of player registration that prevented players from changing clubs during the season. Moreover, Football League rules required the player's club permission for any transfer to proceed at the end of the season,[8] hence creating the 'retain and transfer principle'.[9] The retain and transfer system did not change much until the 1960s. If anything, it made things even more difficult for players, as the system went global and was adopted by leagues and governing bodies world-wide.[10] The foundation of FIFA 'led to the formalisation of the transfer system at the international level'.[11] FIFA adopted a comprehensive set of regulations on international transfers in 1953.[12] FIFA normally implemented its transfer regulations world-wide, but between 1979 and 1995 UEFA dealt with international transfers within its territory and operated an arbitration scheme in case of disputes.[13] Following *Bosman* in 1995, FIFA decided to regain control over the implementation of the transfer system in UEFA's territory, thus being the sole authority for international transfers world-wide.

Challenges to the transfer system came, naturally, from the players. It first began at the national level, when footballers' unions protested against the regulations governing transfers between clubs within their own country. Perhaps unsurprisingly, the first challenges came from England. The English Professional Footballers' Association (PFA) stepped up its fight to modify footballers' employment conditions in the early 1950s; the object of the PFA's attack was the retain and transfer system and the regulation of the maximum wage.[14] The occasion came with Newcastle United's refusal to grant a transfer to George Eastham in December 1959, hence, making use of its right to retain the player.[15] Eastham, with the support of the players union, decided to challenge in court the English transfer system, arguing it was in breach of restraint of trade regulations.[16] The result of the proceedings was that the judgment found in favour of the player, as it considered that the retention elements of the transfer system went beyond what was necessary to ensure that clubs were able to protect their legitimate interests.[17]

---

[8]McArdle 2000, p. 19.

[9]Roderick 2006, p. 116.

[10]McArdle 2000, p. 25.

[11]Lanfranchi and Taylor 2001, p. 216.

[12]Opinion of Advocate General Lenz in Case C-415/93 *Union Royale Belge des Sociétés de Football Association and others v. Bosman and others*, ECLI:EU:C:1995:293, para 20.

[13]UEFA, Vision Europe, the direction and development of European football over the next decade, p. 16. http://www.uefa.com/newsfiles/374875.pdf. Accessed 21 July 2015.

[14]Greenfield and Osborn 2001, p. 76.

[15]Ibid., p. 79.

[16]Ibid., p. 80.

[17]*Eastham* v *Newcastle United Football Club Ltd. and Others* [1964] 3 All ER 139; See also Greenfield and Osborn 2001, pp. 80–81; McArdle 2000, pp. 27–28.

Thus, *Eastham* precipitated the introduction of a new transfer system in England which addressed the concerns of the ruling, eventually dismantling the retain principle. It should be no surprise, then, that following *Eastham* the PFA continued its efforts to get better working conditions for the players. In 1961, the maximum wage[18] was abolished.[19] Platts and Smith point out that these developments cannot be understood in isolation, nor can they be disconnected from the wider social and economic development of English football and English society.[20] A similar claim is made in this chapter, albeit for the wider European context, as we argue the need to understand *Bosman* as part of a process.

Therefore, the momentum that started in England with *Eastham* and the abolition of the maximum wage jumped over the channel to 'the continent'. In France, the footballers' trade union negotiated in 1969 with the French league the abolition of the 'life contract which had bound players to a club until the age of 35'.[21] The agreement stipulated that, at the end of a contract, players were free to sign with whichever employer they chose. The negotiations between the players, clubs and the French FA were not smooth and there were even suggestions in 1972 that the agreement needed to be reversed. This prompted French footballers to call for a strike.[22] France was not the only country where players decided to fight for their working rights. In Spain, professional footballers challenged the so-called *derecho de retención* (right to retain)[23] in the late 1970s and early 1980s. The Spanish Footballers' Union (*Asociación de Futbolistas Españoles*, AFE in its Spanish acronym) called three strikes in the period between 1979 and 1982. The first two strikes, in 1979 and 1980, had a considerable impact bringing Spanish professional football to a halt.[24] The third strike in 1982 led to the intervention of the national government to facilitate an agreement between clubs, the Spanish FA and the players.[25]

[18]An agreement by the clubs and the governing body to limit the salary of the players (i.e. what we call nowadays a salary cap, but without the players' agreement).

[19]Platts and Smith 2010, p. 650.

[20]Ibid., p. 645 et seq.

[21]Lanfranchi and Taylor 2001, p. 217.

[22]The French strike: a rough guide. Goal, 7 October 2008. http://www.goal.com/en/news/8/main/2008/10/07/900511/the-french-strike-a-rough-guide. Accessed 21 July 2015.

[23]The right to retain stipulated that clubs could retain the registration of players at the end of their contract by offering a 10 per cent salary rise. Players were unable to move to other clubs without the consent of their employer. See La retención en el fútbol español, práctica 'esclavista' hasta 1979. El País, 29 March 1985. http://elpais.com/diario/1985/03/29/deportes/480898805_850215.html. Accessed 21 July 2015.

[24]González, Histórico: Se consumó la huelga de futbolistas. El País, 4 March 1979. http://elpais.com/diario/1979/03/04/deportes/289350006_850215.html. Accessed 21 July 2015; González, La asociación de futbolistas mantuvo la huelga, pero jugarán casi todos los profesionales. El País, 11 April 1982. http://elpais.com/diario/1982/04/11/deportes/387324003_850215.html. Accessed 21 July 2015.

[25]González, Los futbolistas desconvocaron oficialmente la huelga. El País, 13 April 1982. http://elpais.com/diario/1982/04/13/deportes/387496825_850215.html. Accessed 21 July 2015.

In their struggle with clubs and the national FA, Spanish footballers achieved the abolition of the right to retain and a transformation of the transfer system and other employment conditions.[26] Not only that, but in 1985, as part of these negotiations, the Spanish government adopted a decree (RD 1006/85), whereby professional sportspersons could terminate their contracts upon the payment of a proportionate compensation to their employer.[27] Thus, it was a decade before *Bosman* that in Spain football players were granted similar rights to those that the Court recognised in 1995 to Jean-Marc Bosman. Again, this is a clear indication that the judgment of the CJEU in 1995 was by no means revolutionary.

There is no evidence available to establish a formal link between the different 'liberation' movements of football players in different countries, but there is clearly a pattern whereby footballers in the 1960s and 1970s challenged their situation at the bottom of the football pyramid as they mobilised to improve their conditions.

2.2.2 Nationality Quotas

Nationality quotas are intended to fix the maximum number of non-national players that a club can field in any given game. Nationality quotas are normally justified as a means to ensure the quality of national teams and to maintain the identification of the supporters with their club.[28] Although the concept of nationality quotas is relatively simple, it is difficult to trace the evolution of the implementation of quotas in European football. This is due to the variation among countries.[29] Despite these asymmetries, quotas are based on a common principle; the differentiation between national and foreign players.

Whilst the transfer system was quickly institutionalised at the international level, nationality quotas remained a matter for national FAs for a long time,[30] which contributed to a diversity of regulations in this area.[31] For example, in Italy, the national FA permitted from 1947 the recruitment of five foreign players per club; however, it later banned all foreign players from 1966 to 1980.[32] Similarly,

---

26 La retención en el fútbol español, práctica 'esclavista' hasta 1979. El País, 29 March 1985. http://elpais.com/diario/1985/03/29/deportes/480898805_850215.html. Accessed 21 July 2015; Paradinas, El derecho de retención de futbolistas, a punto de desaparecer. El País, 1 June 1979. http://elpais.com/diario/1979/06/01/deportes/297036015_850215.html. Accessed 21 July 2015.

27 La retención en el fútbol español, práctica 'esclavista' hasta 1979. El País, 29 March 1985. http://elpais.com/diario/1985/03/29/deportes/480898805_850215.html. Accessed 21 July 2015.; See also García et al. 2011.

28 Roderick 2006, p. 116.

29 Lanfranchi and Taylor 2001, pp. 218–219.

30 Ibid., pp. 49–50.

31 Greenfield and Osborn 2001, p. 85.

32 Lanfranchi and Taylor 2001, p. 96.

in Spain foreign players were allowed until 1962, when a total ban was introduced; in 1973 a quota of two per club was adopted.[33] Thus, there was a wide diversity of nationality quotas in Europe with changes in regulation linked most of the time to the performances of the national teams in the World Cup or the European Championship.

Nationality quotas, however, were not attacked by footballers' unions. Logically, national unions of footballers endorsed any regulation that protected their members from competition by foreign players. It is in this area of nationality quotas that *Bosman* arguably made a bigger impact. And perhaps in this respect the judgment was more ground-breaking and slightly more distanced from its wider context. One needs to be cautious with this line of reasoning though. Whereas the implications of *Bosman* for nationality quotas were perhaps stronger than for transfers, it is nevertheless possible to find traces of important contextual developments suggesting that the evolution of professional football was heading towards (at the very least) a relaxation of nationality quotas.

Nationality quotas found opposition, naturally, in those employers (clubs) willing to sign foreign players. Thus, in 1976 the CJEU issued a preliminary ruling in *Donà,*[34] a case that originated in Italian football. In *Donà* the CJEU noted clearly that nationality quotas were contrary to European law. The Court pointed out that the prohibition of discrimination based on nationality does not apply only to the action of public authorities, but also to any rules aimed at regulating employment and services (i.e. rules adopted by football governing bodies and/or clubs).[35]

Donà could have been a severe blow for nationality quotas in club football, but in fact they remained in place for another 20 years. This was possible because the reaction of other EU institutions to the CJEU ruling was relatively conciliatory. This timid reaction helps to explain, perhaps, why *Bosman* was perceived as such a shock by European football stakeholders.[36] In 1978, following negotiations with the European Commission, UEFA agreed that it would authorise clubs to hire as many foreign players as they wanted, but that they would be restricted to just fielding two such players in any game.[37]

The Commission engaged in further negotiations with UEFA again in 1984 when Commissioner Peter Sutherland requested the end of restrictions for EU players, but no progress was really made and nationality restrictions remained in place.[38] This of course was changed abruptly by *Bosman*, which prompted UEFA and national FAs to abolish nationality quotas for EU players almost immediately after the ruling.

---

[33]Ibid., p. 97.

[34]Case C-13/76 *Gaetano Donà v Mario Mantero*, ECLI:EU:C:1976:115.

[35]Ibid., para 17; See also Case 36/74 *Walrave and Koch v. Union Cycliste Internationale*, ECLI:EU:C:1974:140, para 17.

[36]García 2007, p. 205.

[37]European Commission (1996) Note de la DG4 présentée à la Commission: Conséquences de l'arret Bosman; affaire C 415/93 de la Court de Justice. SEC 212/1.; See also Case C-415/93 *Union Royale Belge des Sociétés de Football Association and others v. Bosman and others*, ECLI:EU:C:1995:463.

[38]Parrish 2003, p. 91; Greenfield and Osborn 2001, p. 85.

2.2.3 *Low Political Visibility*

Up to this point, this chapter has explained how the regulation of the players market was heavily debated well before *Bosman*. By December 1995 the employment conditions of football players had been debated throughout Europe for more than twenty years. *Bosman* and its outcome were not a surprise. It was a question of visibility rather than something completely new or unexpected. The reaction of the European Commission to *Donà* illustrates this point perfectly. The Commission's reaction indicates that football was not at that time a priority; otherwise, they would have been more assertive. Moreover, in the mid-1970s, football was not the major commercial industry that it is today. Challenges and protests to the transfer system and nationality quotas increased over time just as the commercialisation of the game developed thanks to the possibilities offered mainly by television. Therefore, it is almost impossible to separate the regulation of players' employment conditions to the historical and economic development of football as an industry in Europe.

2.3 Football, from Entertainment to Industry

This section briefly depicts the evolution of football from a mere leisure activity in British schools, where it was born, to the highly important economic industry that it has become. Specific attention is paid to the development of football after the Second World War and, more concretely, to the importance of television in shaping modern football.

The origins of football as a game are difficult to trace, for 'characters have been depicted kicking a ball in Egyptian relics, religious paintings, Grecian vases' and it even 'existed in ancient China and Japan, in the Americas before the Europeans arrived, and in most European countries long before it became officially recognised'.[39] At the beginning of the nineteenth century, football was played in public schools all around England, although the formats and rules of the game were very different from place to place: Rugby, Harrow, Shrewsbury all had their particular version of a game played between two teams and involving a ball.[40] Football was well established in the English public schools by the middle of the nineteenth century, but none of the schools played against each other, and, as a result, the rules were numerous and inconsistent.[41]

Amidst different efforts to find a common format for the game, Ebenezer Cobb Morley called a meeting of representatives from clubs in the London area with the purpose of 'forming an association with the object of establishing a definite code

[39]Murray 1994, p. 1.

[40]Marples 1954, p. 107.

[41]Murray 1994, p. 13.

of rules for the regulation of the game'.[42] The meeting, held on 26 October 1863 at the Freemasons Tavern in London, was the foundation of the London Football Association. At that time the London FA was just one of many FAs around the country with the Sheffield FA being the main competitor.[43] In 1877 both FAs reached a compromise agreement, with the London FA standing virtually as the sole authority of the game in England and being called simply 'the Football Association' without any location attached to it. By 1905 the Football Association had 10,000 members.[44]

The Football Association had no option but to recognise professional football in July 1885.[45] In 1871 the Football Association introduced the Challenge Cup[46] and in 1888 the first league competition (the Football League) was played.[47] The 1880s witnessed a surge in the popularity of football, closely linked to the social transformation brought about by the Industrial Revolution in England. It can be argued that, from that moment on, football has not ceased to grow as an economic activity, reaching the levels that made *Bosman*, the Premier League, the UEFA Champions League and even the Qatar 2022 World Cup possible. It is exactly for these reasons that one needs to understand this historical and economic evolution of football in order to grasp fully the importance of *Bosman*. The work of Richard Giulianotti is useful to explain football's development, as he provides a socio-cultural account that brings together the economic growth of the game with its impact on other social dimensions. Thus, Giulianotti divides football's development into three stages: 'traditional', 'modern' and 'post-modern'.[48]

The 'traditional' period lasted until after the First World War and it was marked by 'the establishment of the game's rules, their international diffusion and the formation of national associations to administer the sport under the aegis of ruling elites'.[49] The 'modern' era of football is sub-divided into three periods. 'Early modernity', running from the 1920s to the Second World War. During that time the Olympic Games and the World Cup cemented football's global status. During this period football became the major national sport in Europe and Latin America, players started to emerge as national heroes and earn better than average wages, but they lacked long-term security.[50] The 'intermediate modernity' of football lasted from the post war period to the early 1960s. In this period continental confederations (such as UEFA) emerged as another tier of governance for the game and, above all, television became more prevalent in family homes, making the

[42]Ibid., p. 14.

[43]Ibid.

[44]Ibid., p. 15.

[45]Giulianotti 1999, pp. 4–5.

[46]Murray 1994, p. 17.

[47]Giulianotti 1999, p. 5.

[48]Ibid.

[49]Giulianotti 1999, p. 166.

[50]Ibid., p. 167.

skills of top players known world-wide.[51] 'Late modernity' ran from the early 1960s to the late 1980s. Consumer culture and youth culture had a massive impact on the game, with players becoming superstars and icons of modernity (Manchester United's Northern Irish star George Best is one of the best examples); revenues from sponsorship and merchandising gradually started to overcome gate-receipts as the first source of income for clubs.[52]

2.3.1 'Post-modern' Football

This gets us to what Giulianotti in his sociological framework called football's 'post-modern' era which began in the late 1980s and has been evolving ever since. In general, many others (including academics, but especially football activists that proclaim to be 'against modern football'[53]) have adopted the label of 'modern football' to designate this era of European and global football. Regardless of the semantic distinctions, the meaning behind the concepts is very similar. According to Giulianotti, post-modern football has entailed a major commercialisation of the sporting activity and the influence of television companies in controlling clubs and financing the game.[54] Brand new or totally refurbished stadiums became a symbol of this new era of football, where television deals and ticket distribution policies maximise income, but may in turn damage the interests of the most dedicated supporters.[55] In the 'post-modern' era fans represent a new middle class, 'a new kind of football spectator keen to produce and consume a variety of football media'.[56] With television revenues multiplying the benefits of top clubs, tournaments have become a huge business and elite players enjoy higher than ever wages, especially after the *Bosman* ruling.[57]

In his analysis, Giulianotti himself refers to *Bosman*, but it can be seen above that this is clearly embedded in a narrative of commercialisation and change of

[51]Ibid., p. 168.

[52]Ibid.

[53]See for example Cloake, Why Stand Against Modern Football? NewStatesman, 23 August 2013, http://www.newstatesman.com/business/2013/08/why-stand-against-modern-football. Accessed 22 July 2015; The Stand Against Modern Football fanzine. http://www.standamf.com/. Accessed 1 September 2015.

[54]Giulianotti 1999, p. 168. See also Webber (2014) No longer the people's game: Karl Polanyi and the double movement 'Against Modern Football', Football Research in an Enlarged Europe (FREE) Conference, Loughborough University, 24–25 October 2014. http://www.free-project.eu/documents-free/Working%20Papers/Webber%20No%20Longer%20the%20Peoples%20Game%20Karl%20Polanyi%20and%20the%20Double%20Movement%20Against%20Modern%20Football.pdf. Accessed 22 July 2015.

[55]Giulianotti 1999, p. 169.

[56]Ibid.

[57]Ibid.

European football that started well before the Court delivered its verdict in December 1995. What Giulianotti points out, and it is recognised in this chapter as well, is that *Bosman* was undoubtedly an accelerator that had important consequences, not least the increased wage levels for top players in Europe. Another important point in Giulianotti's analysis is that the modernisation and commercialisation of European football has come hand in hand with the increase in revenues from selling the game's broadcasting rights. The reality of modern (or post-modern) European football cannot be understood without mentioning the importance of television. This is another important piece in the *Bosman* jigsaw.

2.3.2 From European Cup to Champions League: The Arrival of 'Sportainment'

The Champions League is UEFA's top flight competition for football clubs. It is the current version of the European Champions Cup that was established in 1955. The European Champions Cup was born as a competition for the league champions of various European countries. FIFA, the world's football governing body, insisted at the time that the competition would be organised by UEFA; thus, the competition 'consolidated UEFA's role in European football as the sovereign organisation with regard to pan-European competitive structures'.[58]

Arguably, the evolution of the European Cup is one of the best examples of the economic transformation of football. The arrival of the Champions League when the *Bosman* case was already in the courts, but three years before the CJEU ruling, is yet another element to explain the consequences of *Bosman*. It is perhaps also possible to consider that both the Champions League and *Bosman* are actually stages of the same process. So they are symptoms, rather than the cause, of European football's transformation. For this reason, any analysis of *Bosman* and its context would be incomplete without taking into account European club competitions.

The European Champions Cup was played in almost the same format from 1955 to 1991. In the late 1980s and early 1990s the concept of a European league (as compared to a knock-out competition) was advanced by AC Milan chairman and, importantly, media mogul Silvio Berlusconi.[59]

UEFA responded to these movements and introduced modifications to the competition format of the Champions Cup. It was in the 1991–1992 season when the quarterfinal and semi-final rounds of the European Champions Cup were replaced with two groups of four teams, the winners of which went directly to the final. The competition was rebranded and renamed as the UEFA Champions League for the

---

[58]Holt 2006, p. 22; See also Dietschy 2013.

[59]Holt 2006, pp. 30–31; See also Holt 2007.

1992–1993 season.[60] Over the next decade the competition would undergo several transformations, the most important of which was arguably the increase in the number of participating teams,[61] allowing for more matches to be played and, in turn, increasing the revenue from broadcasting rights.

The dynamics leading to the transformation of the old European Champions Cup into the Champions League have been researched at length, normally in the context of the wider commercialisation of football. There is a consensus that two main forces were behind the changes: (i) the development of digital and satellite channels willing to broadcast more European football and (ii) the growing awareness by the top football clubs of their economic potential, which in fact led to some clubs threatening to set up a break-away European football league outside UEFA's umbrella.[62]

The breakaway proposals and the formation of the G-14 in the 1990s have a twofold implication. First, in economic terms these movements suggest a clear interest by top professional clubs in the commercialisation of football. In other words, the football market was clearly re-shaping, and with a bigger 'cake' available clubs (and other stakeholders) wanted a bigger slice of the profits generated by the industry. Second, in governance terms those proposals signal a clear un-ease of the clubs with the decisions of the governing bodies. It is necessary to remind that similar breakaway moves were taking place at national level, with, for example, the top 22 clubs in England forming the Premier League in 1992. Thus, clubs were yet another stakeholder that sought to reposition themselves in the governance structures of European football. In this context, the clubs were following similar dynamics to the players. Whereas the latter had to recourse to strikes, protest and legal challenges to be 'heard', the former decided to organise new breakaway national leagues and threatened with similar moves at European level, but at some point they also considered to use the EU as an alternative policy/governance venue with clear interest in certain competition policy investigations.[63]

In conclusion, the historical development of European football has seen increased commercialisation that reached a peak with the so-called post-modern (or modern) football. In this post-modern era, the de-regulation of Europe's

[60]Ibid., p. 31.

[61]In the 1997–1998 season the participation in the Champions League was open for the first time to clubs other than the national league champions. Under the current format, up to the fourth team in Europe's top ranked leagues can qualify for the tournament, albeit for the preliminary round.

[62]In basketball, some clubs and professional leagues broke away in 1991 from the sport's main governing body (FIBA) to form the Union of European Leagues of Basketball (ULEB) and organise their own competition called the Euroleague. For some years, the Euroleague co-existed with FIBA's own European Champions Cup, both trying to attract the top teams in Europe. At present, the Euroleague has finally established itself as the top European club competition in basketball.

[63]For a good summary of these dynamics involving EU institutions, clubs, players and governing bodies re-shaping the governance of European football, see García 2007 or García and Meier 2012; See also Geeraert et al. 2013.

audiovisual market is paramount to understand the blossoming of football as an industry. In turn, these factors are extremely important to understand *Bosman*. Indeed, it has been argued that the creation of the Premier League and the Champions League and, finally, *Bosman* cannot be seen in isolation, but rather as incremental stages of the same process.

Having analysed both the context of the players market and the wider economic development of football, the chapter moves now to discuss the political and legal environment in which Jean Marc Bosman challenged the international transfer system.

2.4 The Political Context and the Ability of Luc Misson

This section tackles a final dimension to round up our analysis of the context in which *Bosman* came about. Here we focus on two main elements. First, the political context at European level, and especially the increasing hostility towards football governing bodies in Brussels. Second, the section dedicates some attention to the importance of Jean Marc Bosman's legal team, led by Luc Misson and assisted by Jean-Louis Dupont. Although FIFPro had been contemplating for some time mounting a legal challenge against the international transfer system, Jean Marc Bosman's decision to frame his case in relation to freedom of movement of workers cannot be understood without reference to both Misson and Dupont. Although the latter has perhaps reaped the 'benefits' of popularity since 1995, it was the former's militant interest in the expansion of freedom of movement rights that most impacted their approach to the case.

2.4.1 Increased Hostility in Brussels

This chapter has already analysed how the European Commission's mild reaction to the CJEU ruling in *Donà* helps to explain the lack of reform in the international transfer system for a long time. And, as such, it was a contributing factor to Jean Marc Bosman's decision to go to court. However, that cautious approach to the governance and regulation of football steadily changed in Brussels during the late 1980s and early 1990s. The rather hostile position of the European Parliament towards UEFA during those years is of particular interest. Whereas it is not possible to find formal links between the hostility of EU institutions towards UEFA and the ruling of the Court in *Bosman*, this again should be seen as yet another contextual element to consider that Jean Marc Bosman was indeed not alone when going to court; and that the judgment was perhaps less a surprise than many wanted to believe.

The European Parliament addressed the issue of footballers' employment conditions in 1989 when it adopted a report on the freedom of movement of professional footballers drafted by the Dutch Christian Democrat James Janssen van Raay.[64] Van Raay was elected to the European Parliament in the first elections in 1979 and he was a Member for 20 years, stepping down in 1999 after completing his fourth term. More importantly, Van Raay was one of FIFPro's founding fathers in 1965. He had a long history of involvement in players' unions as chairman of the Dutch footballers association and FIFPro.[65]

The Van Raay report was extremely hard on football's employment regime. It considered the transfer system 'a latter-day version of the slavery trade'.[66] The EP also criticised strongly nationality quotas as being contrary to the provisions of the EC Treaty.[67] The report requested the Commission to start legal proceedings against UEFA, national FAs and/or individual clubs with the aim of abolishing the transfer fee system and nationality quotas.[68]

Thus, six years before the ruling, but just a few months before Bosman started his legal challenge, the European Parliament adopted a resolution questioning the legality of the international transfer system and nationality quotas under EU law. Given Van Raay's affiliation as FIFPro Chairman, his report does not only indicate the interest of the Parliament in that matter. It also suggests an increase in the political awareness of players' unions to the point of using the supranational level (i.e. the European Parliament).[69]

The Van Raay report had an effect on other EU institutions. The European Commission decided to threaten UEFA with heavy fines should the restrictions to free movement remain in place.[70] It was at that point, after protracted negotiations with Commission Vice-President Martin Bangemann that UEFA came up with the so-called 3+2 formula to progressively lift nationality quotas in European football.[71]

For the Commission this was just a provisionally *bona-fide* scheme to give football authorities some time to put their structures in line with EU law before moving towards the progressive abolition of nationality quotas.[72] The European Parliament,

[64]Resolution of the European Parliament of 11 April 1989, A2-415/188 on the Freedom of Movement of Professional Football Players in the Community, OJ C120.

[65]Lanfranchi and Taylor 2001, p. 221.

[66]Resolution of the European Parliament of 11 April 1989, A2-415/188 on the Freedom of Movement of Professional Football Players in the Community, OJ C120, para 1.

[67]Ibid., para 4 et seq.

[68]Ibid., para 16.

[69]García and Meier 2012.

[70]McArdle 2000, p. 38; Greenfield and Osborn 2001, p. 85.

[71]The 3+2 formula was agreed between the Commission and UEFA on 18 April 1991; See UEFA, Agenda for the 8th UEFA conference for presidents and general secretaries of member associations (Montreux, 20 September 1991) and UEFA (1992) Report of the Secretary General for the years 1990 and 1991). The 3+2 formula was to be applied first in the top-divisions of professional football, being extended to the rest of non-amateur football by the end of the 1996–97 season.

[72]L'UEFA veut-elle la guerre? La Dernière Heure, 19 January 1996; La UE tomará los cuartos de final como prueba en la sentencia Bosman. El País, 19 January 1996.

on the other hand, criticised the agreement, considering it an unacceptable concession by the Commission to football authorities.[73]

It should be clear by now that the closer one gets to December 1995 the easier it is to find clear elements in support of a liberalisation of footballers' employment conditions. The political context analysed here added yet another layer of pressure to football's governance system. The traditional (and rather stable) pyramid of European football, with players' employment conditions at the very bottom, was under threat from many angles: the commercial interest of television operators, the economic desires of clubs, the political questions of EU institutions, and, of course, the demands of the players. In this context *Bosman* was just the straw that broke the camel's back. Considering the multitude of economic, social and structural changes that European football was undergoing in the late 1980s and early 1990s, the icing on the cake to get to *Bosman* was the knowledge and intellectual curiosity of Jean Marc Bosman's legal team.

2.4.2 The Importance of the Legal Team Behind Jean-Marc Bosman

The history of the *Bosman* case is well known. Jean-Marc Bosman saw his transfer from RC Liège to US Dunkerque collapse at the end of his contract with the former. In his situation, Bosman decided to take legal action against RC Liège and the Belgian FA. When looking for legal advice, Bosman decided not to go to his parents' lawyer, but rather to a certain Jean-Louis Dupont, whose girlfriend at that time was a long-term friend of Bosman. Crucially, Dupont was a young graduate in European law employed by Liège-based lawyer Luc Misson, who had already some experience in cases regarding freedom of movement. Luc Misson is a well-respected Belgian lawyer, specialised in European law. In a personal research interview with this author, Luc Misson did not hide his federalist and pro-European views, which he very much identifies with the period of the Delors Commission.[74] In the early 1980s, well before getting to know Jean-Marc Bosman, Luc Misson wrote some academic articles on the employment regulations of football players and the freedom of movement provisions in the Treaty.[75] Dupont himself had studied for some time the regulations of sports governing bodies and their conflicts with EU law, as he had a particular academic and intellectual interest on the topic during his studies. He was convinced that sport should be brought in line with EU law.[76]

---

[73]European Parliament (1994) The European Community and sport. Committee on Culture, Youth and the Media, A3-0326/94.

[74]Interview with Luc Misson (Liège, 6 June 2006).

[75]Ibid.

[76]For more on Jean-Louis Dupont's background and agenda, see Bent et al. 2000, pp. 9–22.

Another element that should not be underestimated is the fact that in the 1980s and 1990s the CJEU was clearly in the mood to widen the interpretation and scope of the Treaty's fundamental freedoms. In this respect, the knowledge and ability of Luc Misson was paramount for the outcome of the *Bosman* case. It was also important for the design of the legal strategy that brought up the demand for a preliminary ruling in the proceedings between Bosman and his club, the Belgian FA and UEFA. As Misson explained to the author of this chapter, he considers himself a specialist in freedom of movement because, before *Bosman*, he was involved in several cases in that area. In those cases the Court found in favour of the 'workers' and decided to extend the definition of 'worker' (and consequently the provisions on freedom of movement) to new social groups.[77]

Thus, Bosman's lawyers were of the opinion, from the start, that the only way to deal with the case was to go the European route. The player himself felt so badly treated by his club and the Belgian FA that he was extremely angry, so he wanted 'to make the transfer system explode if possible'.[78] In that situation, both Misson and Dupont agreed that the only way ahead was to challenge FIFA and UEFA regulations on transfers and nationality quotas before the CJEU. In a way, the *Bosman* case was the result of the personal situation of a football player, combined with the desire of a legal team to explore the boundaries of the right to free movement, and the links between EU law and sport. It is quite curious that most people tend to associate only the name of Jean-Louis Dupont to the *Bosman* ruling, as he has built a prestigious career in the field of sports law. However, one cannot understand the legal approach to the case without the background, expertise, political and intellectual interests of Luc Misson, one of the forgotten names of the *Bosman* case that this chapter wants to remember 20 years later.

2.5 Conclusion

This chapter has proposed a challenge: to analyse *Bosman* without referring to the facts or the legal grounds of the case. We have argued that *Bosman* needs to be understood as yet another stage of the process of transformation of European football. *Bosman* was not the starting point of what has been labelled by some as modern football. It was only an accelerator, if at all. As explained in this chapter, Jean-Marc Bosman was by no means alone. Professional football players throughout Europe had already challenged their employment conditions twenty years before him. England, France and Spain had modified their transfer systems years before *Bosman*. Similarly, EU institutions increasingly questioned the international transfer system in the late 1980s and early 1990s. The political climate in Brussels was very hostile towards UEFA. It was reaching a tipping point by the time

---

[77]Interview with Luc Misson (Liège, 6 June 2006).

[78]Ibid.

Bosman's case reached the European court. Also, professional clubs and leagues questioned the existing competition structures as they wanted a bigger share of European football's profits.

The common thread joining these dots is the commercial development of European football linked to the de-regulation of the audiovisual market in the continent. The interest of television operators to pay large sums of money to obtain football broadcasting rights put in motion a transformation in which *Bosman* is a stage, but not the origin. Finally, the persons that recognised these dynamics and managed to skilfully interpret the importance of European law in this context were Luc Misson and Jean-Louis Dupont.

The narrative has perhaps overemphasized the importance of the context leading up to *Bosman*. Here we may have been provocative in presenting the case as almost unavoidable. But this change of narrative looks to spur the informed debate on the 20th anniversary of the ruling: Can we understand *Bosman* somehow differently and from a different disciplinary framework?

We believe that the basis of the argument is correct though. It has been argued, especially from within UEFA, that Jean-Marc Bosman could have withdrawn his case, in a similar way to what happen years later in the *Oulmers-Charleroi* case. One would never know whether UEFA and FIFA would have reformed the players market without a ruling of the CJEU. It is safe to affirm, though, that the structures of European football were clearly reaching a point of no return. One way or another structures and regulations had to change to adapt to the economic, political and legal pressures of the different stakeholders.

References

Bent I, McIlroy R, Mousley K, Walsh P (2000) Football confidential. BBC Books, London

Dietschy P (2013) Making football global? FIFA, Europe, and the non-European football world, 1912-74. J Global Hist 8(2):279–298

García B (2007) UEFA and the European Union, from confrontation to co-operation? J Contemp Eur Res 2(3):202–223

García B, Meier HE (2012) Limits of interest empowerment in the European Union: the case of football. J Eur Integr 34(4):359–378

García B, Palomar Olmeda A, Pérez González C (2011) Spain: Parochialism or innovation? In: Niemann A, García B, Grant W (eds) The transformation of European football: towards the europeanisation of the national game. Manchester University Press, Manchester, pp 134–151

Geeraert A et al (2013) The governance network of European football: introducing new governance approaches to steer football at the EU level. Int J Sport Policy Polit 5(1):113–132

Giulianotti R (1999) Football, a sociology of the global game. Polity Press, Cambridge

Greenfield S, Osborn G (2001) Regulating football: commodification, consumption and the law. Pluto Press, London

Holt M (2006) UEFA, governance and the control of club competition in European football. Football Governance Research Centre, Birkbeck University

Holt M (2007) The ownership and control of elite club competition in European football. Soccer Soc 8(1):50–67

Lanfranchi P, Taylor M (2001) Moving with the ball, the migration of professional footballers. Berg, Oxford

Marples M (1954) A history of football. Secker & Warburg, London
McArdle D (2000) From boot money to Bosman: football, society and the law. Cavendish, London
Murray B (1994) Football, a history of the world game. Scholar Press, Aldershot
Niemann A et al (2011) The transformation of European football: Towards the Europeanisation of the national game. Manchester University Press, Manchester
Parrish R (2003) Sports law and policy in the European Union. Manchester University Press, Manchester
Platts C, Smith A (2010) Money, money, money? The development of financial inequalities in English professional football. Soccer Soc 11(5):643–658
Roderick M (2006) The work of professional football, a labour of love?. Routledge, Oxon
Tomlinson A (1983) Tuck up tight lads: structures of control within football culture. In: Tomlinson A (ed) Explorations in football culture. Leisure Studies Association Publications, Eastbourne, pp 165–186

Chapter 3
Bosman: A Legacy Beyond Sports

Mattias Derlén and Johan Lindholm

Abstract The 1995 *Bosman* case from the CJEU is one of the most famous judgments ever delivered by the Luxembourg court. It is well-known in sporting contexts, but this article takes the discussion beyond that area, demonstrating *Bosman's* importance in other areas of law by using network analysis. This illustrates that *Bosman* is an exceptional case, both in its own right and as a source of further cases, citing *Bosman* directly or indirectly. We also demonstrate that *Bosman* is primarily cited for four reasons: the jurisdiction of the CJEU in matters of preliminary rulings, the use of the fundamental freedoms against private entities, non-discriminatory obstacles on the internal market and the temporal effects of CJEU judgments. However, when analyzed further it becomes clear that the *Bosman* case contains few truly original contributions to EU law and largely builds on existing case law to draw important conclusions. Thus, the Court must have other reasons for citing *Bosman*. Given the characteristics of the case many such reasons are plausible. *Bosman* is well-written, well-reasoned, well-known and well-connected, making it an excellent source to use in future cases.

Keywords The *Bosman* case · Network analysis · Indegree centrality · Pagerank · Betweenness centrality · Embedded cases

---

M. Derlén · J. Lindholm (✉)
Department of Law, Umeå University, 901 87 Umeå, Sweden
e-mail: johan.lindholm@umu.se

M. Derlén
e-mail: mattias.derlen@umu.se

A. Duval and B. Van Rompuy (eds.), *The Legacy of* Bosman,
ASSER International Sports Law Series, DOI 10.1007/978-94-6265-120-3_3

Contents

3.1 Introduction

On 15 December 1995, the Court of Justice of the European Union (CJEU) issued its preliminary ruling in *Bosman*.[1] As made obvious by scholars engaged in the fields of law, policy, and economics – not least through the contributions in this volume – the *Bosman* decision has had a massive impact on sports in general and football in particular, not only in Europe, but around the world.[2] Because the public has a great interest in sports and *Bosman* represents one of the most significant restrictions of sport's self-governance, the ruling has probably received more public attention than any other CJEU decision, before or since.[3] While they may not be familiar with the finer legal points of the CJEU's decisions, many elementary school kids know what it means for a football player 'to do a Bosman'.[4]

However, this contribution does not concern *Bosman* and sports, but examines the ruling's impact on EU law more generally. As explained below, its impact has been significant in several ways. In this contribution we approach this question from the particular, but arguably very important perspective of the CJEU itself. As elaborated below, *Bosman* has a central position in the network of the CJEU's case

[1]Case C-415/93 *Union Royale Belge des Sociétés de Football Association and others v. Bosman and others*, ECLI:EU:C:1995:463.

[2]Binder and Findlay 2011; Késenne 2006; Kranz 1998; Goddard et al. 2012.

[3]Késenne 2006, p. 636; Forster and Pope 2004, pp. 129–131; Van den Bogaert 2013, p. 97.

[4]'I must be Belgium's most famous football player, but no one knows who I am.' Jean-Marc Bosman quoted in 'The Sad Saga of the Man Who Made Soccer Stars Rich'. Time Magazine, 16 February 2011.

law. In fact, an empirical approach based on network analysis reveals that it is in several regards one of the most central rulings (see Sect. 3.2).[5] One interesting aspect of the case that is revealed using this approach is that many of the decisions citing and being cited by *Bosman* have relatively little in common. In other words, *Bosman* connects a broad range of CJEU decisions through a web of citations. A more traditional, analytical approach reveals that the CJEU to this day refers to *Bosman* to support a wide range of legal rules and principles (see Sect. 3.3). These findings suggest that *Bosman*'s impact as a precedent is both broad and deep, but that its precedential value has less to do with the novelty of its findings and more with its more intangible qualities (see Sect. 3.4).

3.2 Measuring *Bosman*'s Importance—An Exceptional Case

3.2.1 The Starting Point—A Fickle Court

In recent years it has become commonplace to analyze complex phenomena using network analysis, even outside natural sciences, including in the social[6] and legal sciences.[7] In its most basic form, a network consists of a collection of related things (vertices), such as individuals, texts, amino acids, or websites, and connections between these things (edges). Once constructed, such networks can be analyzed to understand the organization and interconnectedness of large and complex phenomena.[8] In this chapter we use network analysis to examine the CJEU's entire body of case law (1954–2011) as a network constructed from citations (edges) between decisions (vertices).[9]

When studying the case law of the CJEU as a network we can observe that the Court treats important and non-important cases differently.[10] One generally expects the average judgment's relevance as a precedent to initially and gradually increase, as it is cited for the information it has on a particular issue, up to a peak, and then to decline as newer cases concerning the same subject matter are decided.[11]

As illustrated by the figure below, this holds true for the CJEU: the average case's importance builds gradually to a peak and then steadily declines. The turnover rate

[5]When it comes to the empirical approach, this contribution builds upon our previous studies, including most obviously Derlén and Lindholm 2014.

[6]Wasserman and Faust 1994.

[7]Fowler et al. 2007.

[8]Easley and Kleinberg 2010, pp. 1–7; Newman 2010, pp. 1–8.

[9]The dataset and the method are explained in greater detail in Derlén et al. 2013; Derlén and Lindholm 2014; Derlén and Lindholm 2015.

[10]Derlén and Lindholm 2016.

[11]Fowler and Jeon 2008, p. 25.

of cases at the CJEU is quite significant. A typical CJEU judgment reaches its peak value as a precedent after an average of only eight years,[12] after which the judgment will decline in importance as the Court moves on to citing other, newer cases. This lends empirical support to the claim that the Court in Luxembourg tends to cite cases in a chain, i.e. using recent cases as support for a position rather than citing the underlying, original cases.[13]

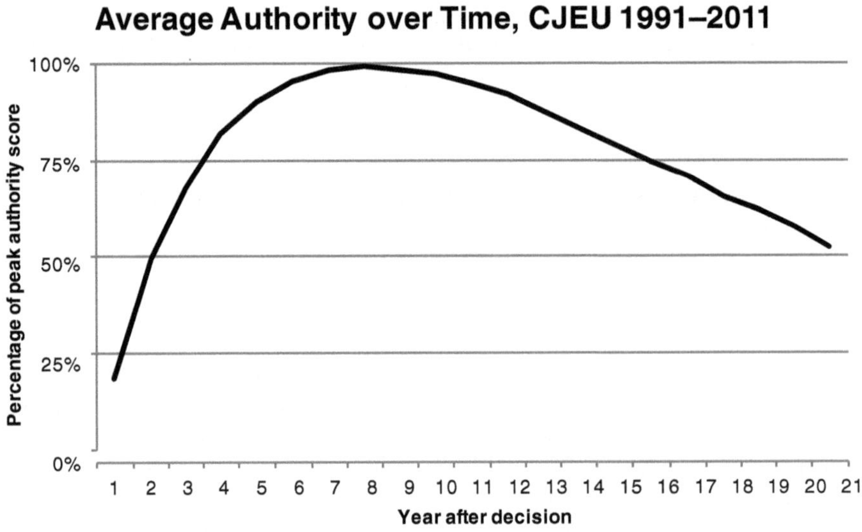

In comparison, important cases will withstand the passing of time better than non-important ones. They will typically rise faster and remain relevant for a longer time.[14] The discussion below will demonstrate that *Bosman* exhibits these characteristics. Furthermore, even within the category of important cases, *Bosman* remains exceptional.

3.2.2 Indegree Centrality

One central element of network analysis is trying to determine how close to the center of the network different vertices are. Network analysis includes a number of centrality measurements that seek to capture different types of such centrality.

One of the simplest and most intuitive centrality measurements is *indegree centrality*, which for our dataset is simply the number of times a decision has been

[12]This is significantly faster than the United States Supreme Court (circa twenty-seven years), see Fowler and Jeon 2008, p. 25.

[13]Derlén and Lindholm 2014, pp. 675–676.

[14]Derlén and Lindholm 2016.

cited.[15] As the figure below clearly demonstrates, the CJEU has cited *Bosman* consistently and continuously from day one. Citations were most frequent during the period between 2000 and 2005. Nevertheless, the CJEU continues to cite *Bosman* heavily.

In fact, the high frequency of CJEU citations has in recent years elevated *Bosman* to the most cited decision. In so doing it surpassed the CJEU's 1974 decision in *Dassonville*.[16] This is indicative of the significant influence *Bosman* has, considering that *Dassonville* had a twenty-one year advantage on *Bosman* and is the seminal decision on free movement of goods, an area of law developed predominantly through CJEU case law.[17]

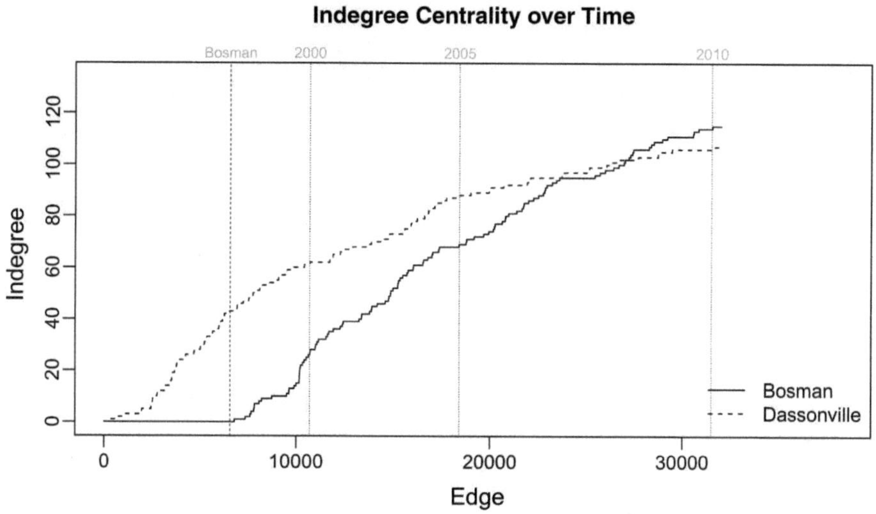

3.2.3 *Casting a Wider Net—PageRank and Betweenness Centrality*

As impressive as this is, in order to fully gage the impact of the *Bosman* decision on the development of CJEU case law we should take into account not only direct references, but also its sustained legacy through the decisions that continue

[15]Using network terminology, a vertex's indegree centrality is equal to its inward directed edges.

[16]Case 8/74 *Procureur du Roi v Benoît and Gustave Dassonville*, ECLI:EU:C:1974:82. According to the Eur-Lex database (eur-lex.europa.eu), the CJEU has at the time of writing cited *Bosman* in 143 other decisions and *Dassonville* in 119 other decisions. Derlén and Lindholm 2014.

[17]For an overview of the free movement of goods and the importance of the *Dassonville* judgment, see Derlén and Lindholm 2010.

to build upon it. While *Bosman* has contributed to the CJEU case law by being directly relied upon by an incomparable number of decisions (first generation), its indirect contribution in terms of decisions that cite decisions that cites *Bosman* (second generation) is so extensive that it is difficult to visualize. If one considers both its 'children' and 'grandchildren', *Bosman*'s progeny comprises a significant portion of the CJEU's collective body of case law.

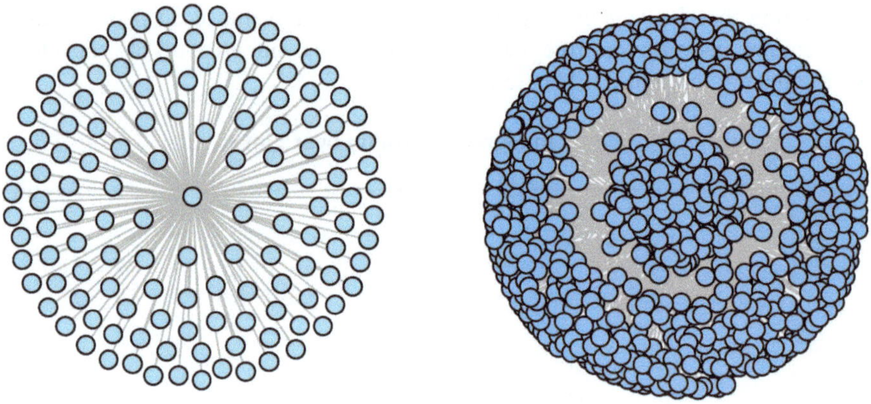

"First and Second Generation"

One method for capturing *Bosman*'s extended influence on the CJEU's case law is to consider its *PageRank*. PageRank is a network centrality measurement initially developed to determine the centrality of webpages, which famously forms the basis of Google's search engine.[18] Using PageRank, we calculate *Bosman*'s precedential value by considering not only how many cases cite *Bosman*, but also how important those cases are in terms of the case that cite them, and so on.[19] This approach captures the legally intuitive idea that not every reference is equally important in terms of influencing legal development and that greater weight should be placed on citations from influential decisions.

As revealed by the figure below, *Bosman*'s precedential power has not declined over time, thereby deviating from how the precedential value of cases typically

[18]Brin and Page 1998; Page et al. 1998. http://ilpubs.stanford.edu:8090/422/1/1999-66.pdf. Accessed 13 October 2015.

[19]PageRank is an example of a feedback centrality measurement. One of the crucial factors when using PageRank is how to set the so-called damping factor which, very simplified, affects how far back in a chain of citations weight will be given. For this and previous studies (see Derlén and Lindholm 2016) we use a damping factor of 0.5. This means that the Random Walker will on average take two steps backwards. The damping factor in the original PageRank algorithm is set higher (to 0.85, giving a 1-d=0.15 chance of a teleport, see Brin and Page 1998, p. 110). However, in a citation network it makes intuitive sense to use a lower damping factor, corresponding to an average path length of 2, see Chen et al. 2007, p. 8.

develops over time. In fact, *Bosman* reached its all-time highest value as precedent towards the end of the studied period. The development of *Bosman* is impressive even when compared with *Dassonville*; even that seminal case has a clear downward trend over time.[20] This confirms the conclusion drawn above based on indegree centrality: *Bosman*'s impact on CJEU case law is among the most influential CJEU decisions and there is little indication that its influence is waning.

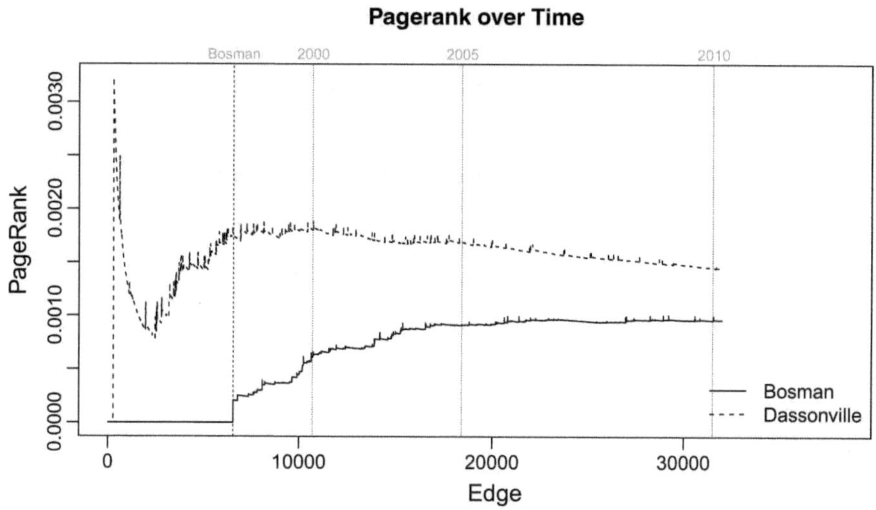

While indegree centrality and PageRank are fairly good measurements of *how big* of an impact individual decisions have on the case law network, they fail to reveal *what* has in fact been impacted. In this regard it has to be noted that Jacob warns against drawing far-reaching conclusions from *Bosman*'s central position in the CJEU citation network, since the Court cites the decision for a number of different reasons.[21]

We can empirically test Jacob's claim by considering *Bosman*'s *betweenness centrality*. Betweenness centrality seeks to capture the influence that a particular vertex exerts in a network due to its strategic position. It is done by calculating the shortest paths between all vertices in a network and then examining how many of these paths flow through a particular vertex. A vertex with high betweenness centrality is one that lies on many such shortest paths.[22] In a social network, a person

[20]The volatility of the early development of *Dassonville* is likely attributable to the very limited data size during the early years of the network.

[21]Jacob 2014, p. 52. While we tend to agree with Jacob's unsupported claim that *Bosman* is 'much better known as an authority in the sphere of economic mobility and competition in professional sports', we are unconvinced that the public's primary characterization of a decision is the touchstone of its relevance, particularly if it flies in the face of the practice of the highest legal institution.

[22]Freeman 1977.

that has a high betweenness centrality is important because that person brings other persons or groups of persons closer together. In a network based around information, like a case law network, a vertex with high betweenness centrality is important because a lot of information will flow through it.

Bosman has, with a comfortable margin, the highest betweenness centrality of all CJEU decisions[23] and, as illustrated by the figure below, it has consistently increased over time. The fact that *Bosman* has the highest betweenness centrality in the CJEU's case law network, which is an information network, suggests that it is strategically placed between otherwise loosely connected areas of law. For this reason, it can affect information transferred between them. This is also consistent with Jacob's claim that *Bosman* is cited for a variety of reasons.

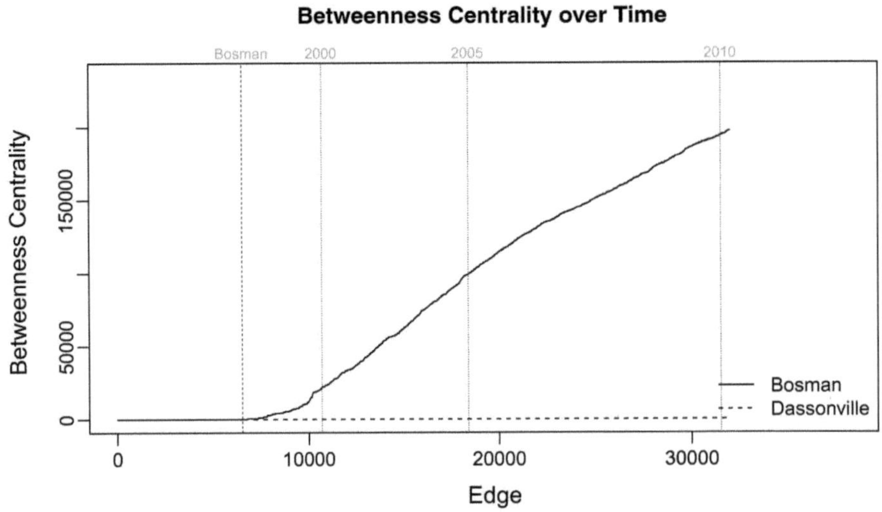

While we thus agree with Jacob's claim, we disagree with his conclusion. In our opinion, the fact that the CJEU has cited the *Bosman* decision for a variety of reasons speaks to its quality and importance, not against it. We do, however, agree with Jacob that quantitative empirical studies of law should be accompanied by more traditional legal analyses.

3.3 The Many Sides of *Bosman*

3.3.1 Introduction

A case-by-case examination reveals that *Bosman*'s impact on subsequent case law or, put differently, how it is used in later judgments, particularly pertains to four

[23] Derlén and Lindholm 2014, p. 683.

legal issues: (i) the Court's jurisdiction to hear a preliminary ruling; (ii) the application of fundamental freedoms to private entities; (iii) the existence of an obstacle to a fundamental freedom and justification of such obstacles; and (iv) the temporal effects of CJEU decisions.[24] As explored below, on each of these issues the Court's reasoning in *Bosman* has had a substantial impact on subsequent CJEU case law and, more generally, EU law.

3.3.2 The Relationship Between the CJEU and National Courts

In order to claim jurisdiction over the *Bosman* dispute and provide a preliminary ruling, the Court first had to dismiss the claim made by the sport governing bodies that it should refrain from answering the questions referred by the Belgian court on the grounds that they did not relate to the facts and issues of the case. The CJEU began by presenting the general principles governing the relationship between the CJEU and national courts when it comes to preliminary rulings and then concluded that it had jurisdiction, as the issues were not hypothetical and the national court had provided all the relevant information.[25]

Bosman is far from the only preliminary ruling case where one of the parties have tried to persuade the CJEU to decline jurisdiction. The Court in such cases frequently refers to *Bosman* in support of an approach that balances competing interests, but largely defers to the assessment of the referring national court[26]:

> According to settled case-law, it is solely for the national court before which the dispute has been brought, and which must assume responsibility for the subsequent judicial decision, to determine in the light of the particular circumstances of the case both the need for a preliminary ruling in order to enable it to deliver judgment and the relevance of the questions which it submits to the Court (see, in particular, Case C-415/93 Bosman [1995] ECR I-4921, para 59, and Case C-305/05 Ordres des barreaux francophones et germanophone and Others [2007] ECR I-5305, paragraph 18).
>
> Nevertheless, the Court has held that it cannot give a preliminary ruling on a question submitted by a national court where it is quite obvious that the ruling sought by that court on the interpretation or validity of European Union law bears no relation to the actual facts of the main action or its purpose, where the problem is hypothetical, or where the Court does not have before it the factual or legal material necessary to give a useful answer to the questions submitted to it (see Bosman, paragraph 61, and Case C-36/99 Idéal tourisme [2000] ECR I-6049, paragraph 20).

---

[24] The issues are presented below in the order that they are addressed in the *Bosman* ruling.

[25] Case C-415/93 *Union Royale Belge des Sociétés de Football Association and others v. Bosman and others*, ECLI:EU:C:1995:463, paras 56–67.

[26] This example is from Case C-194/08 *Susanne Gassmayr v Bundesminister für Wissenschaft und Forschung,* ECLI:EU:C:2010:386, paras 29–30 (regarding a Directive improving work conditions for pregnant women and new parents), but there are many others like it, see, e.g., Case C-379/98 *PreussenElektra v. Schleswag AG*, ECLI:EU:C:2001:160, para 39; Case C-112/00 *Eugen Schmidberger, Internationale Transporte und Planzüge v Republik Österreich*, ECLI:EU:C:2003:333, para 33.

This balanced approach is a primary reason for the CJEU citing *Bosman* and it appears that the Court particularly relies on this element of *Bosman* when it takes a generous stance towards national courts. Many of the decisions relying on this part of *Bosman* are quite important in their own right. It is also noteworthy that the facts and substantive issues of these cases vary markedly from each other and from *Bosman*.[27]

3.3.3 Fundamental Freedoms and Private Entities

For many, the most shocking aspect of *Bosman* was the restrictions it imposed on sport governing bodies' ability to regulate their own sport, particularly since these are private entities, not Member States. At the time of *Bosman*, it was well known and largely accepted that private entities could rely upon Treaty-based fundamental freedoms against Member States (the so-called vertical direct effect). Almost two decades had passed since the ruling in *Defrenne II*, where the CJEU declared that the Treaty provision ensuring equal pay for men and women could be relied upon by private entities against other private entities,[28] opening the door for the so-called horizontal direct effect of Treaty Articles. At the time of *Bosman*, and still to this day,[29] *Defrenne II* remained the only case where the CJEU gave a Treaty article 'full' horizontal direct effect.[30] In that context, the CJEU's conclusion that Jean-Marc Bosman could invoke the right to free movement of workers against football's governing bodies, as the latter determined the terms on which professional sportsmen can engage in gainful employment, was an important development.[31]

[27]Case C-379/98 *PreussenElektra v. Schleswag AG*, ECLI:EU:C:2001:160, para 38; Case C-261/95 *Rosalba Palmisani v Istituto nazionale della previdenza sociale (INPS)*, ECLI:EU:C:1997:351, para 18; Case C-302/97 *Klaus Konle v Republik Österreich*, ECLI:EU:C:1999:271, para 33; Case C-438/05 *International Transport Workers' Federation, Finnish Seamen's Union v Viking Line ABP, OÜ Viking Line Eesti*, ECLI:EU:C:2007:772, para 28; Case C-213/07 *Michaniki Ae V. Ethniko Simvoulio Radiotileorasis, Ipourgos Epikratias*, ECLI:EU:C:2008:731, paras 32–35; Case C-515/08 *dos Santos Palhota and others*, ECLI:EU:C:2010:589, para 20; Case C-62/14 *Peter Gauweiler and Others v German Bundestag*, EU:C:2015:400, para 28.

[28]Case 43/75 *Gabrielle Defrenne v Société anonyme belge de navigation aérienne Sabena*, ECLI:EU:C:1976:56.

[29]Some subsequent decisions have shown that individuals may under certain circumstances invoke the right to not be discriminated against private entities. This principle can sometimes be traced backed to *Bosman*, see Case C-281/98 *Roman Angonese v Cassa di Risparmio di Bolzano SpA*, ECLI:EU:C:2000:296, para 33, sometimes not, see, Case C-144/04 *Werner Mangold v. Rüdiger Helm*, ECLI:EU:C:2005:709.

[30]Because the provision concerns the right to equal remuneration regardless of gender the two entities must of course also be engaged in an employment relationship, but this concerns the Article's substantive scope, not its direct effect or invocability.

[31]Case C-415/93 *Union Royale Belge des Sociétés de Football Association and others v. Bosman and others*, ECLI:EU:C:1995:463, paras 69–87, 82–87.

The CJEU has subsequently relied upon *Bosman* in holding that private entities can under certain circumstances rely directly upon Treaty articles against other private entities. The approach used in *Bosman* has come to dominate much of the post-*Defrenne II* case law regarding invoking fundamental freedoms against private entities. *Bosman* also has had a more extended impact on EU law, particularly in three regards.

Firstly, in a number of influential decisions the CJEU has identified private entities that by merit of their position or regulatory activity can be expected to respect the Treaties in the same way as Member States.[32] This includes cases that, like *Bosman*, concern the right to free movement of persons, and more specifically the free movement of workers.[33] However, the Court has also relied on *Bosman* to conclude that private entities can base their claims against other private entities on fundamental freedoms, including the right to free movement of services.[34]

Secondly, the Court has subsequently expanded which private entities can incur obligations under the fundamental freedoms. *Bosman*'s progeny on this issue obviously includes other cases where the defendant was a sports governing body,[35] but has subsequently been extended to other, similarly positioned private entities, like bar associations[36] and trade unions.[37]

Thirdly and finally, the Court has also invoked *Bosman* in support of its conclusion that the general right not to be discriminated against on grounds of nationality can be invoked against an even more extensive class of private entities, including hospital systems[38] and private employers.[39]

[32]Schepel 2012, pp. 182–183.

[33]Case C-94/07 *Andrea Raccanelli v Max-Planck-Gesellschaft zur Förderung der Wissenschaften eV*, ECLI:EU:C:2008:425, para 44.

[34]Case C-309/99 *J. C. J. Wouters, J. W. Savelbergh and Price Waterhouse Belastingadviseurs BV v Algemene Raad van de Nederlandse Orde van Advocaten*, ECLI:EU:C:2002:98, para 120; Case C-341/05 *Laval un Partneri Ltd v Svenska Byggnadsarbetareförbundet, Svenska Byggnadsarbetareförbundets avdelning 1, Byggettan and Svenska Elektrikerförbundet*, ECLI:EU:C:2007:809, para 98; Case C-438/05 *International Transport Workers' Federation, Finnish Seamen's Union v Viking Line ABP, OÜ Viking Line Eesti*, ECLI:EU:C:2007:772, paras 33–34, 50.

[35]Cases C-51/96 and C-191/97 *Christelle Deliège v. Ligue Francophone de Judo et Disciplines Associées ASBL and others*, ECLI:EU:C:2000:199, para 47.

[36]Case C-309/99 *J. C. J. Wouters, J. W. Savelbergh and Price Waterhouse Belastingadviseurs BV v Algemene Raad van de Nederlandse Orde van Advocaten*, ECLI:EU:C:2002:98, para 120.

[37]Case C-341/05 *Laval un Partneri Ltd v Svenska Byggnadsarbetareförbundet, Svenska Byggnadsarbetareförbundets avdelning 1, Byggettan and Svenska Elektrikerförbundet*, ECLI:EU:C:2007:809, para 98; Case C-438/05 *International Transport Workers' Federation, Finnish Seamen's Union v Viking Line ABP, OÜ Viking Line Eesti*, ECLI:EU:C:2007:772, paras 33–34, 50.

[38]Case C-411/98 *Angelo Ferlini v Centre hospitalier de Luxembourg*, ECLI:EU:C:2000:530, para 50.

[39]Case C-281/98 *Roman Angonese v Cassa di Risparmio di Bolzano SpA*, ECLI:EU:C:2000:296, paras 32–33.

3.3.4 Obstacles and Justifications

Having concluded that Jean-Marc Bosman could invoke fundamental freedoms against the defendants, the Court considered the substantive scope of those freedoms. The CJEU put particular effort into determining whether the transfer rules, which are non-discriminatory measures, constitute obstacles to the free movement of workers under EU law, as well as the ability of sports governing bodies to justify such restrictions. In approaching these issues, the CJEU drew from a broad range of case law on fundamental freedoms, including several decisions concerning free movement of goods, free movement of services, and freedom of establishment.[40] The Court also acknowledged that sports governing bodies, despite being private entities, could rely on the justifications available to the Member States to justify such restrictions.[41]

This part of *Bosman* has subsequently been important for defining what constitutes a relevant obstacle to fundamental freedoms:[42]

> it is clear from the Court's case-law, in particular from the judgment in *Bosman*, cited above, that Article 48 of the Treaty prohibits not only all discrimination, direct or indirect, based on nationality but also national rules which are applicable irrespective of the nationality of the workers concerned but impede their freedom of movement.

The CJEU has subsequently relied upon *Bosman* in other cases concerning the free movement of workers.[43] However, the CJEU has also relied upon *Bosman*'s definition of obstacles in cases concerning other freedoms, such as the free movement of services, even though *Bosman* does not in fact deal with this freedom specifically.[44]

---

[40]Case C-415/93 *Union Royale Belge des Sociétés de Football Association and others v. Bosman and others*, ECLI:EU:C:1995:463, paras 92–104, 116–120, citing Case 81/87 *The Queen v H. M. Treasury and Commissioners of Inland Revenue, ex parte Daily Mail and General Trust plc*, ECLI:EU:C:1988:456; Case 143/87 *Christopher Stanton and SA belge d'assurances "L'Étoile 1905" v Institut national d'assurances sociales pour travailleurs indépendants (Inasti)*, ECLI:EU:C:1988:378; Joined Cases C-267/91 & 268/91 *Criminal proceedings against Bernard Keck and Daniel Mithouard*, ECLI:EU:C:1993:905; Case C-384/93 *Alpine Investments BV v Minister van Financiën*, ECLI:EU:C:1995:126; Case C-55/94 *Reinhard Gebhard v Consiglio dell' Ordine degli Avvocati e Procuratori di Milano*, ECLI:EU:C:1995:411.

[41]Case C-415/93 *Union Royale Belge des Sociétés de Football Association and others v. Bosman and others*, ECLI:EU:C:1995:463, para 86. The CJEU later changed direction, deciding that non-State actors cannot avail themselves of the public policy derogations. Case C-341/05 *Laval un Partneri Ltd v Svenska Byggnadsarbetareförbundet, Svenska Byggnadsarbetareförbundets avdelning 1, Byggettan and Svenska Elektrikerförbundet*, ECLI:EU:C:2007:809, para 84. For further discussion, see Odudu 2010.

[42]This example is from Case C-190/98 *Volker Graf v Filzmoser Maschinenbau GmbH*, ECLI:EU:C:2000:49, para 18.

[43]See Case C-212/06 *Government of Communauté française and Gouvernement wallon*, ECLI:EU:C:2008:178, para 44 (concerning benefits provided under a care insurance scheme); Case C-103/13 *Snezhana Somova v Glaven direktor na Stolichno upravlenie 'Sotsialno osiguryavane'*, EU:C:2014:2334, paras 36–37 (concerning old age pensions).

[44]Case C-438/05 *International Transport Workers' Federation, Finnish Seamen's Union v Viking Line ABP, OÜ Viking Line Eesti*, ECLI:EU:C:2007:772; Case C-97/09 *Ingrid Schmelz v Finanzamt Waldviertel*, ECLI:EU:C:2010:632, para 46.

3.3.5 Temporal Effects of CJEU Judgments

The final issue dealt with by the Court was the temporal effect of the judgment. In *Bosman*, football's governing bodies argued that an unlimited retroactive application of the decision's conclusions would have very serious consequences for the organization of football. After formulating the legal principles governing limiting temporal effects in exceptional cases, the Court concluded that in the circumstances of the particular case 'overriding considerations of legal certainty militate against calling in question legal situations whose effects have already been exhausted'.[45]

This part of the *Bosman* ruling typically receives little attention. It is, however, one of the prominent reasons for which the CJEU cites *Bosman*; the Court often relies on *Bosman* when a question of temporal limitation is raised.[46]

3.3.6 Summary and Conclusions

The findings above give some insight to *Bosman*'s high betweenness centrality. It is in part attributable to procedural issues relevant for cases regardless of the underlying substantive issue. While this does not, in our opinion, detract from *Bosman*'s precedential value, it does suggest that the case is not quite the unifier of areas of law that one could first expect.

However, we also find that *Bosman* has a broad and profound effect on the various areas of law linked to the completion of the internal market, including issues of application, scope, and substance. The unifying effect of *Bosman* is two-dimensional in the sense that it both relies on extensive case law concerning various

[45]Case C-415/93 *Union Royale Belge des Sociétés de Football Association and others v. Bosman and others*, ECLI:EU:C:1995:463, paras 139–146, para 144 quoted.

[46]Case C-292/04 *Wienand Meilicke, Heidi Christa Weyde and Marina Stöffler v Finanzamt Bonn-Innenstadt*, ECLI:EU:C:2007:132, para 36; Case C-313/05 *Maciej Brzeziński v Dyrektor Izby Celnej w Warszawie*, ECLI:EU:C:2007:33, para 55; Joined cases C-401/13 and C-432/13 *Vasiliki Balazs v Casa Judeţeană de Pensii Cluj (C-401/13) and Casa Judeţeană de Pensii Cluj v Attila Balazs* (C-432/13), EU:C:2015:26, para 52; Case C-242/09 *Albron Catering BV v FNV Bondgenoten and John Roest*, ECLI:EU:C:2010:625, para 35; Case C-73/08 *Nicolas Bressol e.a. and Céline Chaverot e.a. v Gouvernement de la Communauté française*, ECLI:EU:C:2010:181, para 90. The impact of *Bosman* in this context is even greater when later generations of the case are taken into account. For example, in Joined Cases C-359/11 and C-400/11 *Alexandra Schulz v Technische Werke Schussental GmbH und Co. KG and Josef Egbringhoff v Stadtwerke Ahaus GmbH*, EU:C:2014:2317, para 57, the CJEU does not refer to *Bosman*. It does however refer to Case C-92/11 RWE *Vertrieb AG v Verbraucherzentrale Nordrhein-Westfalen eV*, EU:C:2013:180, in which the discussion about temporal effects (paras 58–59) is, inter alia, based on Case C-402/03 *Skov Æg v Bilka Lavprisvarehus A/S and Bilka Lavprisvarehus A/S v Jette Mikkelsen and Michael Due Nielsen*, ECLI:EU:C:2006:6, and Case C-313/05 *Maciej Brzeziński v Dyrektor Izby Celnej w Warszawie*, ECLI:EU:C:2007:33, which in turn (para 50 and para 55, respectively) rely on *Bosman*.

fundamental freedoms (outward citations) and is being relied upon by subsequent cases concerning various fundamental freedoms (inward citations). If we were to follow the ripple effects that cases relying upon *Bosman* have had on CJEU case law, this impact is even greater.[47]

3.4 Explaining the Importance of *Bosman*—New Law or Good Law?

3.4.1 Introduction

It follows from the findings above that *Bosman* has been, from the moment of its delivery, an exceptionally influential precedent on several important issues and that it continues to be so still to this day. Why does the CJEU, twenty years after the ruling, continue to rely heavily on *Bosman* for a variety of legal rules and principles? Contrary to what one might assume, this is not immediately obvious from a traditional legal perspective: a careful examination of the parts of the ruling that the CJEU most frequently cites reveals that the decision's contribution to the law, compared to pre-existing case law, is relatively modest. *Bosman*'s main contribution is, in fact, how it relates to previous case law.

3.4.2 Placing Bosman in the Context of CJEU Case Law

One way of understanding *Bosman*'s connection to previous case law is to use a community detection algorithm and study the placement of *Bosman*. Network analysis includes several methods that can be used for grouping nodes into modules, an activity referred to as clustering.[48] We rely on the Random Walker to group cases into modules similar to areas of law.[49] The Random Walker measures the relative importance of cases and citations by distributing flow. The random

[47]Cases citing *Bosman* include well-known judgments like Case C-62/14 *Peter Gauweiler and Others v German Bundestag*, EU:C:2015:400; Case C-341/05 *Laval un Partneri Ltd v Svenska Byggnadsarbetareförbundet, Svenska Byggnadsarbetareförbundets avdelning 1, Byggettan and Svenska Elektrikerförbundet*, ECLI:EU:C:2007:809; Case C-438/05 *International Transport Workers' Federation, Finnish Seamen's Union v Viking Line ABP, OÜ Viking Line Eesti*, ECLI:EU:C:2007:772; Case C-224/01 *Gerhard Köbler v Republik Österreich*, ECLI:EU:C:2003:513; Case C-112/00 *Eugen Schmidberger, Internationale Transporte und Planzüge v Republik Österreich*, ECLI:EU:C:2003:333; Case C-379/98 *PreussenElektra v. Schleswag AG*, ECLI:EU:C:2001:160; Case C-281/98 *Roman Angonese v Cassa di Risparmio di Bolzano SpA*, ECLI:EU:C:2000:296.

[48]See generally Fortunato 2010; Girvan and Newman 2002; Leicht and Newman 2008.

[49]See further Derlén et al. 2013.

walk can, however, also be used to identify cases that are interrelated; cases among which the Random Walker spends relatively long time. To do so, we use the Map Equation[50] that exploits the known correlation between patterns in information and the ability to compress that information[51] to cluster nodes. The entire map is presented elsewhere.[52] Here we concentrate on the module in which the *Bosman* decision is clustered.[53] The module is illustrated below, with the top ten cases (as measured by PageRank) and the citations between them.

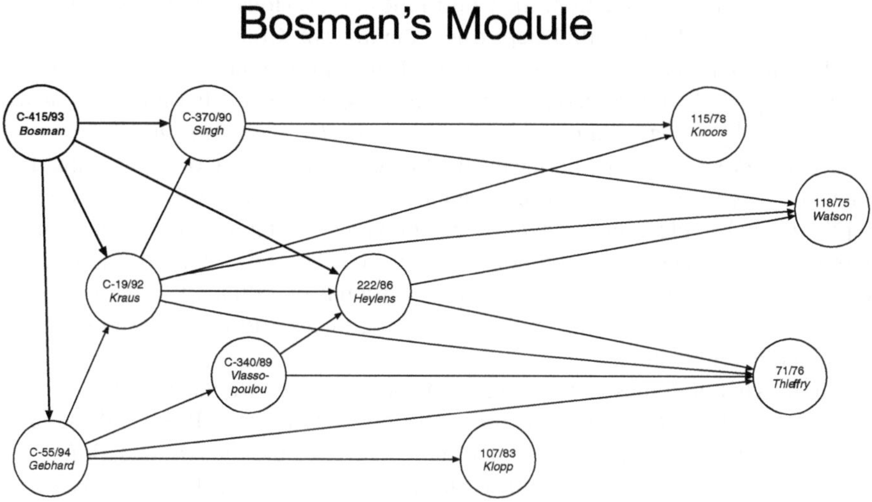

At first sight it seems surprising that the Random Walker and the Map Equation place *Bosman* in this module; most of the other decisions concern professional qualifications, often specifically concerning lawyers. However, at closer inspection we can see that *Bosman* has inserted itself firmly into the discussion concerning non-discriminatory obstacles in previous case law. As illustrated by the figure, many other, previous decisions, including *Kraus*, *Heylens* and *Thieffry*, are more structurally significant in the module.

It is worth noting that *Bosman* is the most recent case in the top ten of the module. In other words, the Map Equation does not place *Bosman* in a module where it serves other cases, but in a module where *Bosman* ties in to existing case law.

50 See generally Rosvall et al. 2009.

51 Shannon 1948.

52 Derlén et al. 2013.

53 The module, referred to as Professional Qualifications in our map, is one of the top 50 largest modules in the entire network, containing 24 nodes.

3.4.3 The Building Blocks of Bosman

In Sect. 3.3 we observed that *Bosman* is primarily cited for four reasons: the jurisdiction of the Court to answer a question for a preliminary ruling, the use of fundamental freedoms against private entities, non-discriminatory obstacles to the free movement, and the temporal effects of CJEU judgments. In all of these situations, *Bosman* builds upon previous case law.

First, regarding jurisdiction, the Court relies on previous judgments in all steps of the discussion. In the initial step, where the *Bosman* Court states that it is solely for the national court to determine the need for a preliminary ruling,[54] the CJEU relies on *Aprile*.[55] In the second step, where the Court states that it cannot answer irrelevant or hypothetical questions, it relies on *Meilicke* and *Furlanis*.[56]

Second, *Bosman* was by no means the first case where the Court found that fundamental freedoms can be invoked against certain private entities. As the Court explicitly makes clear in *Bosman*, it has previously established this principle in another sports-related decision. In 1974, the CJEU declared in *Walrave* that a sporting rule was directly discriminatory on grounds of nationality.[57] However, the Court goes further in *Bosman* by extending the direct effect to measures that are truly non-discriminatory.[58]

Third, when it comes to non-discriminatory obstacles we have already demonstrated above how *Bosman* builds upon previous judgments.[59] Besides those judgments it is also worth mentioning that the CJEU cites the *Masgio* and *Daily Mail* cases when discussing that Member States may not prevent their nationals from exercising EU fundamental freedoms.[60] Naturally, *Bosman* also plays a vital role in extending the market access approach to free movement of workers, but the case is firmly entrenched in previous case law.

[54]Case C-415/93 *Union Royale Belge des Sociétés de Football Association and others v. Bosman and others*, ECLI:EU:C:1995:463, para 59.

[55]Case C-125/94 *Aprile Srl, in liquidation v Amministrazione delle Finanze dello Stato*, ECLI:EU:C:1995:309.

[56]Case C-292/04 *Wienand Meilicke, Heidi Christa Weyde and Marina Stöffler v Finanzamt Bonn-Innenstadt*, ECLI:EU:C:2007:132; See also Case C-143/94 *Furlanis costruzioni generali SpA v Azienda nazionale autonoma strade (ANAS)*, ECLI:EU:C:1995:354.

[57]Case C-415/93 *Union Royale Belge des Sociétés de Football Association and others v. Bosman and others*, ECLI:EU:C:1995:463, paras 82–84, citing Case 36/74 *Walrave and Koch v. Union Cycliste Internationale*, ECLI:EU:C:1974:140, paras 17–19; See also Van den Bogaert 2002, p. 124.

[58]Van den Bogaert 2002, pp. 144–145; Schepel 2012, p. 182.

[59]See Sect. 3.4.2 above.

[60]Case C-10/90 *Maria Masgio v Bundesknappschaft*, ECLI:EU:C:1991:107; Case 81/87 *The Queen v H. M. Treasury and Commissioners of Inland Revenue, ex parte Daily Mail and General Trust plc*, ECLI:EU:C:1988:456.

Fourth and finally, the legal principles governing limitations on the temporal effects of rulings expressed in *Bosman* and, subsequently, cited had, as is clear from the judgment itself, previously been elaborated in *Blaizot*[61] and before that in *Denkavit.*[62] Many, albeit far from all, of the subsequent cases citing *Bosman* on these points of law do so in conjunction with some of these previous decisions.

3.4.4 Bosman as Good Law

As demonstrated above the CJEU continues to cite *Bosman,* to an incomparable extent, on issues where it could just as well cite many both prior and subsequent decisions. In fact, the *Bosman* case is somewhat of a rarity. Normally, CJEU cases have a relatively short lifespan and the Court tends to cite the most recent cases on a particular topic.[63] For very important cases the CJEU will refer back to the original case, where the rule or principle was first established. The previously discussed *Dassonville* case is an example of this.

However, *Bosman* is somewhere in-between. It is no longer recently decided, but it does not qualify as a truly original case either. This suggests that the *Bosman* decision has some specific quality, other than containing novel conclusions, that makes it attractive for the CJEU to cite. There are a number of possible, alternative, and interconnected explanations for this observation.

One obvious reason is that *Bosman* is *well-written.* Compared to many CJEU decisions, which tend to be succinct, cryptic, and sometimes outright enigmatic,[64] it is comparatively easy to read and follow the CJEU's reasoning in *Bosman.* One way that the Court contributes to making the decision more pedagogical is by breaking it down into fairly naturally connected parts. A well-written decision is presumably also a persuasive decision, making a reference to *Bosman* a natural option for the CJEU when seeking to persuade national courts and other audiences.

A second and similar reason is that *Bosman* is *well-reasoned.* Although it is somewhat counterintuitive, the *Bosman* decision's impact on CJEU case law can in part be due to the controversial nature of the case. The public interest in sports and the self-regulatory tradition of sport in general and football in particular forced the CJEU to address several generally important, but controversial issues under heavy scrutiny. The result is, in our opinion, an exceptionally well-reasoned and well-supported decision. Thus, the decision has qualities that can withstand the test of time, and causes it to still to this day be a highly relevant decision on a broad range of issues.

---

[61] Case 24/86 *Vincent Blaizot v University of Liège and others*, ECLI:EU:C:1988:43, paras 25–34.

[62] Case 61/79 *Amministrazione delle finanze dello Stato v Denkavit italiana Srl,* ECLI:EU:C:1980:100, paras 14–21.

[63] See Sect. 3.2 above.

[64] See also Derlén 2014, pp. 296–299.

A third possible reason is that *Bosman* is simply a *well-known* case, within and beyond the Court, not least because of the above mentioned controversial nature of the case. Thus, taken together with the qualities of the judgment itself, it would be natural if the decision is frequently top-of-mind for parties and the Court.

Finally, *Bosman* is clearly a *well-connected* case. *Bosman* cites twenty-one previous decisions, a fairly large but not exceptionally large amount. However, it is not the quantity, but the quality of the judgments cited that makes *Bosman* a particularly well-connected case.[65] In fact, it is the most embedded case in the network of CJEU case law, referring to many important previous decisions.[66] Thus, *Bosman* is undoubtedly a persuasive case, which is a reason in itself to cite it in support of legal arguments. In this regard *Bosman* is similar to the *Becker* case.[67] *Becker* is the third most important precedent in the network, as measured by PageRank, following directly after *Bosman*.[68] This is somewhat unexpected, as one of the main reasons to cite *Becker* is the direct effect of directives,[69] established earlier in *van Duyn*.[70] However, the CJEU has clearly preferred to cite *Becker*, rather than the original *van Duyn*. One reason for this might be that *Becker*, just like *Bosman*, is well-connected to previous case law.[71]

In conclusion, there are many reasons for the CJEU to cite *Bosman*, independent of the original discussions in the decision. It is a well-written, well-reasoned, well-known, and well-connected case, encompassing many different legal questions. This makes *Bosman* well placed to remain an important case for a long time.

References

Binder J, Findlay M (2011) The effects of the *Bosman* ruling on national and club teams in Europe. J Sport Econ 13(2):107–129

Brin S, Page L (1998) The anatomy of a large-scale hypertextual web search engine. Comput Netw ISDN Syst 30:107–117

Chen P, Xie H, Maslov S, Redner S (2007) Finding scientific gems with Google's PageRank algorithm. J Infometrics 1(1):8–15

[65]See Sect. 3.4.3 above for some examples of important cases cited by *Bosman*.

[66]Derlén and Lindholm 2014, pp. 683–686. We use Hub score, as developed by Kleinberg 1999, to measure the embeddedness of judgments in CJEU case law.

[67]Case 8/81 *Ursula Becker v Finanzamt Münster-Innenstadt*, ECLI:EU:C:1982:7.

[68]Derlén and Lindholm 2014, p. 678.

[69]See, among many other, Case C-425/12 *Portgás - Sociedade de Produção e Distribuição de Gás SA v Ministério da Agricultura, do Mar, do Ambiente e do Ordenamento do Território*, EU:C:2013:829, para 18; Case C-226/07 *Flughafen Köln/Bonn GmbH v Hauptzollamt Köln*, ECLI:EU:C:2008:429, para 31; Case C-363/05 *JP Morgan Fleming Claverhouse Investment Trust plc and The Association of Investment Trust Companies v The Commissioners of HM Revenue and Customs*, ECLI:EU:C:2007:391, para 58.

[70]Case 41/74 *Yvonne van Duyn v Home Office*, ECLI:EU:C:1974:133.

[71]*Becker* is the fourth most embedded case in the network, as measured by Hub score, see Derlén and Lindholm 2014, p. 685.

Derlén M (2014) Multilingual interpretation of CJEU case law: rule and reality. Eur Law Rev 39:295–315
Derlén M, Lindholm J (2010) Article 28 E.C. and rules on use: a step towards a workable doctrine on measures having equivalent effect to quantitative restrictions. Columbia J Eur Law 16:191–231
Derlén M, Lindholm J (2014) Goodbye *van Gend en Loos*, hello *Bosman*? Using network analysis to measure the importance of individual CJEU judgments. Eur Law J 20(5):667–687
Derlén M, Lindholm J (2015) Characteristics of precedent: the case law of the European court of justice in three dimensions. German Law J 16(5):171–196
Derlén M, Lindholm J (2016) Peek-a-boo, it's a case law system! Comparing the European court of justice and the United States supreme court from a network perspective. German Law J 17 (forthcoming)
Derlén M, Lindholm J, Rosvall M, Mirshahvalad A (2013) Coherence out of Chaos: mapping European union law by running randomly through the maze of CJEU case law. Europarättslig Tidskrift 2013:517–535
Easley D, Kleinberg J (2010) Networks, crowds, and markets. Cambridge University, Cambridge
Forster J, Pope N (2004) The political economy of sports organisations. Routledge, London
Fortunato S (2010) Community detection in graphs. Phys Rep 486:75–174
Fowler JH, Jeon S (2008) The authority of supreme court precedent. Soc Netw 30:16–30
Fowler JH, Johnson TR, Spriggs JF II, Jeon S, Wahlbeck PJ (2007) Network analysis and the law: measuring the legal importance of precedents at the U.S Supreme Court. Polit Anal 13:324–346
Freeman L (1977) A set of measures of centrality based on betweenness. Sociometry 40(1):35–41
Girvan M, Newman M (2002) Community structure in social and biological networks. Proc Natl Acad Sci USA 99(12):7821–7826
Goddard J, Sloane PJ, Wilson J (2012) The Bosman ruling and labor mobility in football (Soccer). In: Kahane LH, Shmanske S (eds) The Oxford handbook of sports economics. Oxford University Press, Oxford, pp 259–280
Jacob M (2014) Precedents and case-based reasoning in the European court of justice. Cambridge University Press, Cambridge
Késenne S (2006) The *Bosman* case and European football. In: Andreff W, Szymanski S (eds) Handbook on the Economics of Sport. Edward Elgar, Cheltenham, pp 636–642
Kleinberg J (1999) Authoritative sources in a hyperlinked environment. J ACM 46(5):604–632
Kranz A (1998) European Union law and football nationality restrictions: the economics and politics of the Bosman decision. Emory Int Law Rev 12:1091
Leicht E, Newman M (2008) Community structure in directed networks. Phys Rev Lett 100:118703
Newman M (2010) Networks. Oxford University Press, Oxford
Odudu O (2010) The public/private distinction in EU internal market law. RTD européen 46(4):826–841
Page L, Brin S, Motwani R, Winograd T (1998) The PageRank citation ranking: bringing order to the web. Technical report. Stanford University InfoLab
Rosvall M, Axelsson D, Bergstrom CT (2009) The map equation. Eur Phys J Spec Top 178:13–23
Schepel H (2012) Constitutionalising the market, marketising the constitution, and to tell the difference: on the horizontal application of the free movement provisions in EU Law. Eur Law J 18(2):177–200
Shannon C (1948) A mathematical theory of communication. Bell Syst Tech J 27(379–423):623–656
Van den Bogaert S (2002) Horizontality: the Court attacks? In: Barnard C, Scott J (eds) The law of the single European market: unpacking the premises. Hart Publishing, Oxford, pp 123–152
Van den Bogaert S (2013) From *Bosman* to *Bernard* C-415/93; [1995] ECR I-4921 to C-325/08; [2010] ECR I-2177. In: Anderson J (ed) Leading cases in sports law, T.M.C. Asser Press, The Hague, pp 91–106
Wasserman S, Faust K (1994) Social network analysis: methods and applications. Cambridge University Press, Cambridge

Chapter 4
Nationality Based Playing Quotas and the International Transfer System Post-Bosman

Simon Gardiner and Roger Welch

Abstract The European Court's ruling in the Bosman case resulted in the removal of post-contract restrictions on players moving to new clubs and the abolition of nationality quotas in so far as they impacted on players with EU nationality. This chapter charts the response to the Bosman ruling within football, with respect to the current FIFA rules on international transfers, and the continuing use of player quotas for non-EU players. The central focus of the chapter is the reintroduction of player quotas within Europe as a result of UEFA's 'home grown player rule'. We also discuss the proposal by FIFA for a 6 + 5 rule which, if ever implemented, would apply throughout the world. Our central contentions are that both the FIFA and UEFA rules on player quotas are incompatible with EU law, as is the current FIFA transfer system. The chapter concludes by suggesting that the best mechanism for resolving these issues lies in the adoption of the methodology of reflexive legal regulation using the method of EU social law as a paradigm.

Keywords Bosman · FIFA transfer rules · Nationality quotas · EU law

Contents

S. Gardiner (✉)
Leeds Beckett University, City Campus, Leeds LS1 3HE, UK
e-mail: s.gardiner@leedsbeckett.ac.uk

R. Welch
University of Portsmouth, Richmond Building, Portland Street,
Portsmouth PO1 3DE, UK
e-mail: roger.welch@port.ac.uk

A. Duval and B. Van Rompuy (eds.), *The Legacy of* Bosman,
ASSER International Sports Law Series, DOI 10.1007/978-94-6265-120-3_4

4.1 Introduction

Professional sport is subject to complex patterns of migration. These shift over a period of time with different sports in specific countries importing playing talent from a variety of other countries and regions. As greater distinctions have emerged between the commercial value of markets in a range of sports between countries, sporting rules providing player quotas based on nationality have emerged as a 'protectionist' mechanism to restrict supply and demand of players. These are of course in addition to legal rules that restrict immigration on basis of nationality through government initiated and imposed visa requirements.

Historically, the Union of European Football Association (UEFA)'s 3 + 2 rule that operated in the early 1990s, provided a good example of the imposition of a player quota system in professional football.

The *Bosman*[1] case resulted in major changes to the football transfer system. The first limb removed post-contract restrictions on employment opportunities imposed by the sporting rules regulating the transfer system and confirmed free agency. Although this part of the ruling only explicitly covers out of contract players, a threatened challenge to the legality under EU law of any form of transfer system led to the *Fédération Internationale de Football Association* (FIFA) adopting new rules for international transfers. The current rules on international transfers and their impact on freedom of movement will be discussed below.

The second limb of the ruling has had a significant impact on the legality and operation of playing quotas. Both limbs of the *Bosman* ruling were based on what is now Article 45[2] of the Treaty on the Functioning of the European Union (TFEU) establishing the rights of EU nationals to work on a non-discriminatory basis in any Member State. Bosman successfully argued that the 3 + 2 rule restricted the freedom of movement of players who are EU nationals as clubs with their 'full quota of foreign players' were likely to restrict new contracts to indigenous players. The Court of Justice of the European Union (CJEU), at the time of the ruling the European Court of Justice, agreed the rule offended the fundamental

[1]Case C-415/93 *Union Royale Belge des Sociétés de Football Association and others v. Bosman and others*, ECLI:EU:C:1995:463.

[2]This was previously Article 39 of the EC Treaty and at the time of the *Bosman* ruling was Article 48 of the EEC Treaty.

principle of EU law that all EC nationals must be treated on an equal basis.[3] The increased mobility of labour generated by the ruling has led to new patterns of migration on the part of professional sportsmen.

This chapter will chart the response to the *Bosman* ruling within football, with respect to the current FIFA rules on international transfers, and the continuing use of player quotas for non-EU players. The central focus of the chapter will be the reintroduction of player quotas within Europe as a result of UEFA's 'home grown player rule', which requires a specified number of players in a squad to have been developed by the club, or within the same football association, for a specified number of years as youth players. We will also discuss the proposal by FIFA for a 6 + 5 rule which, if ever implemented, would apply throughout the world. These specific regulatory regimes provide a case study of the operation of sporting rules providing player quotas which potentially could inform the operation of and the legality of quota systems in other team sports. As examples, quota systems are used or have been proposed, for example in basketball, cricket, handball, both codes of rugby and volleyball.[4]

The chapter will also discuss why player quotas have been incrementally reintroduced into football and other team sports and evaluate their legality in the context of the *Bosman* ruling and EU discrimination law. The underlying debate is the extent to which regulation of professional sports by sporting authorities should be subordinate to external legal regulation. These are issues which have been subject to developments in and challenges posed by EU law.

Whilst the main focus of this chapter is on player quotas, it is important to appreciate the interrelationship between the two limbs of *Bosman*. Nationality quotas clearly restrict freedom of movement if a player is unable to move to a club in a domestic league because he is a foreign national and a club already has its quota of foreign players. However, even if quota restrictions do not restrict the transfer of a particular player, he may still not be able to move to another club if his current club is demanding a transfer fee that the former is unable or unwilling to meet. The first limb of Bosman relaxes the system in that an out of contract player is able to move without a transfer fee being imposed. The current FIFA rules on international transfers further liberalise the system for players under contract. The chapter will consider the effectiveness of the latter and the extent to which player mobility is genuinely enhanced by the FIFA transfer rules.

Our central contention is that both the UEFA and FIFA rules on player quotas are in violation of EU law on freedom of movement. If this contention is correct then this will have repercussion for all quota systems used in professional sports where such sports are played in EU Member States. Quota systems will only be lawful if they can be justified and we will seek to demonstrate that the reasoning on justification which is set out in the *Bosman* ruling continues to be applicable,

---

[3]Blanpain and Inston 1996.

[4]Indeed, similar proposals have been mooted in other team sports. See FIVB ready to fight EU labor laws on '4 + 2' player rule. www.fivb.org/EN/ePublications/WorldVolleyNews/WV_News_26_E.pdf. Accessed 25 September 2015.

and therefore it remains very difficult for justification to be pleaded successfully. Similarly, if the FIFA international rules do not, in practice, enable players under contract to move to clubs in other countries then it can be argued these rules too fail to meet the requirements of EU law. The chapter will conclude by considering and discussing alternatives to the use of quota systems, and how the international transfer rules could be reformed, to enhance the ability of players of all nationalities, be they out of or under contract, to move between clubs in different countries.

4.2 The FIFA International Transfer Rules and Freedom of Movement

The *Bosman* ruling did and does not directly apply to players recruited from outside of the EU and EEA. Players from, as examples, European States outside of the EU/EEA, the Americas, most African countries, Asia and Australia are not protected by Article 45 TFEU. As a matter of historical record it should be noted that FIFA decided with effect from 1 April 1997 to change its rules to permit any player to move to other clubs within the EU on free transfers once their contracts expire. Thus a British club still has to pay a transfer fee to import a player from, for example, an Australian club. However, if it retains that player until his contract expires a transfer fee cannot be claimed unless that player negotiates a move to a club outside of the EU.

The view that *Bosman* had no implications for players who were still under contract was challenged by the European Commission in December 1998. Had this resulted in litigation before the European Court, this could have led to the transfer system being declared unlawful in its entirety. Indeed, writers such as Blanpain[5] have argued that any transfer system is a form of slavery in that players are shackled to clubs through the requirement that they can be registered with one club only and cannot play for another club until their registration has been released.[6]

This threat of litigation by the European Commission led to FIFA adopting new rules for the regulation of the international transfer system. These first came into force on 1 September 2001, and amended versions have applied since July 1 2005.

[5]Blanpain and Inston 1996.

[6]For background information in relation to the adoption of new international transfer rules by FIFA, see Caiger and O'Leary 1999; Pearson 2015, pp. 220–238; Tsatsas, Anelka's costly walk-out case has a hole in it. The Guardian, 23 July 1999; Gardiner and Welch 2007. On the applicability of Article 39, see Report from the Commission to the European Council of 10 December 1999, COM (1999) 644 with a view to safeguarding current sports structures and maintaining the social function of sport within the Community framework - The Helsinki Report on Sport; See also European Parliament Report of 18 July 2000, A5-0208/2000 on the Commission report to the European Council with a view to safeguarding current sports structures and maintaining the social function of sport within the Community framework – The Helsinki Report on Sport. For reference to the Commission's views on the compatibility of the transfer system with EU law, see Speech by Mrs. Viviane Reding of 13 March 2001, 01/117.

It must be emphasised that the FIFA rules apply only to international transfers where a player has negotiated a move to club in a different national association to the one in which he currently plays.[7]

Under these rules, transfer systems still apply to players under the age of 23, although even with regard to such players the intention was that negotiated transfer fees would be replaced by compensation calculated by applying criteria set out in Annex 4 to the rules. The transfer system is loosened up for players over 23 by enabling a player to terminate his contract and move to another club once the protected period of his contract has expired. This protected period is three seasons in the case of a contract signed by a player before his 28th birthday, and two seasons in the case of a contract signed after a player's 28th birthday. The rules specify that a player's contract may not last for longer than five years.

Under Article 17 of the FIFA rules, once the protected period has expired, a player is able to terminate his contract in order to join a new club provided compensation is paid to his current club. This compensation should be at least equal to the remaining value of the player's contract plus any transfer fee that the club paid for the player (the value of this fee decreases over the period of time that the contract has lasted). If there is unilateral breach without just cause during the protected period his club will again be entitled to claim compensation, but sporting sanctions will also be applied against the player. Sporting sanctions may also be applied where contracts are terminated outside of the protected period but such termination is not in accordance with the strict requirements of Article 17 (see the *Webster* case, below).[8]

The FIFA rules further enhance player mobility by enabling players to terminate their contracts if they have a due cause or a 'sporting just' cause. The former position is in accordance with general contract law principles to be found in common law countries if a club has committed a serious breach of contract which enables the player to establish constructive dismissal, so that it is the club that, in law, is deemed responsible for terminating the contract. However, there is no automatic correlation between the notion of a 'sporting just cause' and a club acting in breach of contract. For the purposes of international transfers only, Article 15 of the FIFA rules stipulates that sporting just cause includes failure to involve an 'established Professional' in less than 10 % of a club's official matches. However, the meaning of sporting just cause is otherwise not defined, and there is clearly scope for different interpretations at the level of national courts where national associations have embraced the concept of contract termination for 'sporting just' cause. It is of interest to note that the English Premiership and Football League

[7]FIFA Regulations on the Status and Transfer of Players. http://www.fifa.com/mm/document/affederation/administration/66/98/97/regulationsstatusandtransfer_en_1210.pdf. Accessed 28 September 2015. Although the rules do not cover domestic transfer, some of the rules are required to be transposed into domestic systems. Examples include permitting a player to terminate a contract for sporting just cause, and to negotiate a transfer to a new club in a different national association during the last six months of his current contract.

[8]Sporting sanctions include a ban on a player playing for his new club for up to four months. The maximum ban that can be imposed in 12 months, but this only applies where the club has induced the player to act in breach of his employment contract.

rules have yet to do this even though the FIFA rules specify that all national associations should make provision for such termination in their national rules.

4.3 The FIFA Rules in Practice

As is so often the case the devil is in the detail, and even when the protected period has expired, or the player wishes to terminate for sporting just cause, he may not terminate his contract during a season. Indeed, a player only has 15 days after the last official match of the season to notify his club that he has decided to terminate his contract with it.

The practical significance of these restrictions is demonstrated by the findings of FIFA's Dispute Resolution Chamber (DRC) in the *Webster* case. Andy Webster terminated his contract with the Scottish football club, Hearts FC at the end of the 2005–2006 season and then agreed to move to Wigan FC. Hearts successfully argued that Article 17 did not apply, even though the protected period of Webster's contract had expired, as he had failed to give the requisite 15 days' notice. In fact, Webster gave notice within 15 days of the Scottish Cup Final, which he argued by custom and practice constituted the last match of the Scottish season. The DRC disagreed but, on the basis that this constituted a minor breach of the rules, only banned him from the first two matches of the following season. With respect to compensation, the DRC rejected Hearts' claim of £5 million and awarded the club £625,000. This figure was arrived at by reference to the residual value of Webster's contract with Hearts. The basis for awarding this lower amount of compensation was approved by the Court of Arbitration for Sport (CAS).[9]

The *Webster* case was initially hailed as the 'new Bosman' in so far as it confirms the right of a player to change clubs irrespective of whether his current club is prepared to release him from his contract. However, the case also demonstrates the narrow nature of the freedom of movement provided by Article 17 in that it limits the window of opportunity for contract termination to 15 days. This is particularly problematic given prohibitions, contained in the rules of national associations, on under-contract players from talking to or being approached by other clubs. For example, in Britain, players can only approach clubs in domestic leagues after their contracts have expired. Where a player is seeking to move to a club in a different national association, the FIFA rules permit the player to negotiate a contract with a new club where the player is in the final six months of his contract.

The way in which the FIFA rules have not led to the intended relaxation of the transfer system is particularly illustrated by the decision of the CAS in *Matuzalem*.[10] The CAS granted Shaktar Donetsk compensation of 11,258,934 Euros plus interest in circumstances where it accepted that the player had terminated his contract in accordance with Article 17 of the FIFA rules outside the

[9]CAS 2007/A/1298/1299/1300 *Wigan Athletic FC/Heart of Midlothian/Webster*.

[10]CAS 2008/A/1519–1520 *Matuzalem/Shaktar Donetsk/Real Zaragoza/FIFA*.

protected period of his contract. In calculating this compensation, the CAS took into account a number of factors including the conduct of the player in accepting a salary increase at a time when he knew he was looking to move to another club.

The CAS's approach to Article 17 is encapsulated by Para 63 of its judgment where it states: '… a termination of a contract without just cause, even if this occurs outside of the Protected Period and following the appropriate notice period, remains a serious violation of the obligation to respect an existing contract and does trigger the consequences set out in Article 17 para 1 FIFA Regulations. In other words, Article 17 FIFA Regulations does not give to a party, neither a club nor a player, a free pass to unilaterally breach an existing agreement at no price or at a given fix price.'

It is clear from this dictum that the CAS does not perceive Article 17 as providing for the right of a player to buy out his contract as this concept would be commonly understood. Rather, the Article does enable a player to secure his release from being registered as a player with a particular club, but only if the relevant compensation is paid and this may well be a very substantial sum of money which is in excess of the direct financial loss suffered by a club as a result of the player's termination of his contract. Despite criticisms, from among others by FIFPro, the footballers' international trade union, *Matuzulem* has been followed by the CAS in subsequent case law.[11] It is FIFPro's position that compensation should be wholly based on the residual value of a player's contract.

As things stand, the failure of the FIFA rules to result in a significant relaxation of the transfer system has led to renewed calls from FIFPro for further external intervention. FIFPro has criticised how the enhanced player mobility, which the FIFA rules were intended to bring about, has in practice been circumvented by restrictive interpretations and the levels of compensation that a player or his new club are required to pay if a player decides to terminate his contract outside of the protected period. Consequently, FIFPro warned FIFA and UEFA that it was seriously contemplating mounting a legal challenge to the transfer system in the CJEU, and in September 2015 lodged a formal competition complaint with the European Commission with specific reference to the FIFA international transfer rules.[12] FIFPro also supports findings of an EU Report, published in January 2013, which urges the overhaul of the football transfer system.[13]

---

[11]See CAS 2009/A/ 1880 *Essam El-Hadaray v FIFA & Al-Ahly Sporting Club*. For further discussion, see Parrish 2015.

[12]Players' union Fifpro to take transfer system to European courts. The Guardian, 17 December 2013. http://www.theguardian.com/football/2013/dec/17/players-union-fifpro-transfer-system-european-courts. Accessed 8 September 2015; Football transfer system must change, says world players' union. BBC Sport, 17 December 2013. http://www.bbc.com/sport/0/football/25418135. Accessed 8 September 2015. For details of the formal complaint lodged in 2015, see http://www.fifpro.org/en/news/fifpro-takes-legal-action-against-fifa-transfer-system. Accessed 8 September 2015.

[13]Report by the KEAN European Affairs and the Centre for the Law and Economics of Sport of January 2013, the Economic and Legal Aspects of Transfers of Players. http://ec.europa.eu/sport/library/documents/cons-study-transfers-final-rpt.pdf. Accessed 21 October 2015. For further in-depth critiques of the FIFA transfer rules, see Parrish 2015; see Pearson 2015, pp. 220–238.

Part of the rationale for the reintroduction of player quotas is the need for a genuine competitive balance between clubs. The aforementioned 2013 Report on the transfer system also seeks to address this issue by recommending that FIFA and national football associations to ensure stronger controls over financial transactions. The Report also proposes the introduction of a 'fair-play levy' on transfer fees of an amount to be agreed by the sport/s governing bodies and clubs to ensure fund redistribution from rich to less wealthy clubs.

At the end of this chapter we set out our arguments for the adoption of reflexive law methodology to resolve ongoing controversies concerning both the transfer system and player quotas. Essentially, if freedom of movement for players, irrespective of their nationality, is to be genuinely meaningful then it is necessary to combine a further liberalisation of the transfer system with rules on international transfers that do not discriminate against a player on the basis of his nationality.

4.4 Nationality Quotas and *Bosman*

The history of nationality quotas in football needs to be understood. In the past, restriction on foreign players (with no real distinction between EU national foreigners and non-EU national foreigners) was common before the *Bosman* ruling for many years. The CJEU case of *Dona v Mantero*[14] was a key development. National footballing rules in Italy stating that only players affiliated to the Italian Football federation could play in professional matches, were held to be contrary to fundamental freedom of movement provisions. Essentially, these would be only players who were Italian born or eligible to play for the Italian national side through other specific grounds, e.g. Italian ancestory.

In 1978 in response to the ruling, UEFA entered an agreement with the European Commission to abolish the restrictions on the number of foreign players who were EU nationals, which a club could have under contract. UEFA also agreed that no more than two such players would be allowed to take part in a match (the restriction would not apply to players who had been resident for five years in the territory of the relevant association). Subsequently, the so-called 3 + 2 Rule was developed by UEFA in light of a gentleman's agreement with the European Commission in 1991. This rule restricted the number of foreign players, that is, players who were not nationals of the domestic leagues in which they played, who could be included on a team-sheet in a UEFA competition to three. An additional two foreign players could be included if they had played in a country for an uninterrupted period of five years. Such players were deemed to be assimilated into the relevant domestic league. Nationality was defined in terms of whether the player was eligible for selection for the national team of the country

[14]Case C-13/76 *Gaetano Donà v Mario Mantero*, ECLI:EU:C:1976:115.

team in which the club was located. The allowance supported by the Commission also provided for the top divisions in the national leagues to operate the policy. It is also important to stress that this was not a limit but a threshold that could be exceeded and led to different configurations of the application of the rule around the European domestic leagues.[15] For instance, in English football, players from Wales, Scotland, Northern Ireland and the Irish Republic were not counted as foreigners within the rule.

The facts of the *Bosman* case do not need repeating. But for the purposes of this chapter, the key question that the CJEU was asked by way of a preliminary ruling, was

> Are Articles 48 (now Article 45 TFEU), 85 and 86 of the Treaty of Rome of 25 March 1957 to be interpreted as … (ii) prohibiting the national and international sporting associations or federations from including in their respective regulations provisions restricting access of foreign players from the European Community to the competitions which they organize?

In the Advocate General (AG)'s Opinion, AG Lenz was clear on the application of what is now Article 45 TFEU, in that the freedom of movement provisions for workers is to give them:

> The right, 'subject to limitations justified on grounds of public policy, public security or public health', to accept offers of employment actually made, to move freely within the territory of Member States[16] … No deep cogitation is required to reach the conclusion that the rules on foreign players are of a discriminatory nature. They represent an absolutely classic case of discrimination on the ground of nationality. Those rules limit the number of players from other Member States whom a club in a particular Member State can play in a match. Those players are thereby placed at a disadvantage with respect to access to employment, compared with players who are nationals of that Member State.[17]

The AG's Opinion dismissed the argument that team player quotas could have the same exemption that national team players and eligibility provisions have been accepted as having.[18] Additionally he discussed a number of potential justifications. The first justifying argument posited was that a player's nationality is paramount in football, where 'the identification of the spectators with the various teams is guaranteed only if those teams consist, at least as regards a majority of the players, of nationals of the relevant Member State'.[19] AG Lenz counters this

---

[15]For more details, see Van den Bogaert 2005.

[16]Opinion of Advocate General Lenz in Case C-415/93 *Union Royale Belge des Sociétés de Football Association and others v. Bosman and others*, ECLI:EU:C:1995:293, para 132.

[17]Ibid., para 135.

[18]Ibid., para 137, support for this view was found as Advocate General Lenz argued in the *Walrave* judgment that the Court was of the opinion that the prohibition of discrimination under Article 48 does not affect 'the composition of sport teams, in particular national teams'. In *Donà*, on the other hand, it held that that prohibition was not infringed if foreign players were excluded 'from participation in certain matches for reasons which are not of an economic nature, which relate to the particular nature and context of such matches and are thus of sporting interest only, such as, for example, matches between national teams from different countries'.

[19]Ibid., para 141.

claim by providing multifarious examples of the cosmopolitan make up of teams that was evident as emerging even in the pre-*Bosman* period within the array of European national leagues. Ultimately, he accepted the view that, 'the great majority of a club's supporters are much more interested in the success of their club than in the composition of the team'.[20]

The second justifying argument is that the rules supporting quotas are necessary 'to ensure that enough players are available for the relevant national team'[21] and their absence would adversely affect 'the development of young players'.[22] AG Lenz believed that nothing had been demonstrated that the development of young players in a Member State would be adversely affected if the rules on foreign players were dropped. This deduction on his part seems to have been incorrect and will be discussed further later.

The third argument is that 'the rules on foreigners serve the purpose of ensuring a certain balance between the clubs, since otherwise the big clubs would be able to attract the best players'.[23] However AG Lenz, foretelling what has become an on-going discourse around quotas and competitive balance, stated:

> I am of the opinion that there are other means of attaining that objective without affecting the right of freedom of movement. Moreover, the rules are in any case only to a very limited extent appropriate to ensure a balance between the clubs. The richest clubs are still in a position to afford the best — and thus as a rule the most expensive — foreign stars. At the same time, such clubs have the opportunity to engage the best native players, without any comparable rule setting the limits.[24]

Similarly the CJEU doubted the case for nationality quotas inevitably boosting competitive balance, in that:

> Although it has been argued that the nationality clauses prevent the richest clubs from engaging the best foreign players, those clauses are not sufficient to achieve the aim of maintaining a competitive balance, since there are no rules limiting the possibility for such clubs to recruit the best national players, thus undermining that balance to just the same extent.[25]

The CJEU's striking out of the 3 + 2 rule has had, as stated above, a significant impact upon patterns of migration of professional footballers inter and intra Europe. However, it is vital to understand that the *Bosman* ruling coincided with significant changes to the economic contours of European football with unprecedented amounts of new money coming into football (and to a lesser degree other sports). This has come from the vast increase in the value of media rights and the symbiosis between sport and newly developed telecommunication technologies,

[20]Ibid., para 143.

[21]Ibid., para 141.

[22]Ibid.

[23]Ibid.

[24]Ibid., para 147.

[25]Case C-415/93 *Union Royale Belge des Sociétés de Football Association and others v. Bosman and others*, ECLI:EU:C:1995:463, para 107.

the increased attractiveness of sport to commercial sponsors, operationalising of merchandising opportunities and the cognizance and exploitation of a range of commercially related sports rights.

This represents the 'brave new world' with the commercialisation and commodification of contemporary sport, notably football, that the *Bosman* ruling is located within and to a significant degree is representative of.[26]

4.5 Nationality Quotas Post-*Bosman*

In the years since the *Bosman* ruling was delivered, clubs within EU Member States have had a wide number of nationalities to select a team from. As stated above, there is a clear interface here with the ongoing relaxation of transfer rules as required first by the *Bosman* ruling and more recently by the European Commission. Indeed the only real restrictions will be derived from a Member State's individual immigration rules. For example European footballers, who are not nationals of EU Member States (and the EEA states of Liechtenstein, Iceland and Norway), and players from outside of Europe are still required to be in possession of a work permit if they are to play for a club in the English Premier and Football Leagues. Similarly, the regulations of national sporting associations may still impose quotas on the fielding of non-EU foreign players. The latter position is widespread around Europe although it does not apply in the English Leagues.[27]

However, with respect to such quotas, yet further player mobility was generated by the CJEU ruling in *Kolpak*.[28] The facts of *Kolpak* are straightforward. Kolpak was a Slovakian goalkeeper for the German Handball club, TSV Ostringen eV Handball. According to the rules of the DHB, the German Handball Federation clubs were prohibited from fielding more than 2 non-EU nationals. The CJEU was asked to give a preliminary ruling on whether, under Article 38 of the European Association Agreement between Slovakia and the EU, Slovakian workers were entitled to general equality of treatment with nationals of the relevant Member State.

Applying its reasoning in *Bosman*, the CJEU ruled that nationals of third countries who were parties to European Association Agreements were entitled to be treated in the same way as national players for the purposes of a sport's rules. In short, they could not be considered ineligible for team selection because there was

---

[26]See García B in this book for further analysis of this commodification.

[27]See Colucci M (2008) Quota For Foreign Football Players allowed to Play in a Club: a Comparative Analysis at National Level. Available at https://www.idmarch.org/document/Fu%C3%9Fball-Bundesliga/3IV7-show/QUOTA+FOR+FOREIGN+FOOTBALL+PLAYERS+ALLOWED+TO+PLAY+IN+A+CLUB+A+COMPARATIVE+ANALYSIS+AT+NATIONAL+LEVEL+%28Updated+to+30+of+May+2008%29. Accessed on 28 September 2015.

[28]C-438/00 *Deutscher Handballbund eV v Maros Kolpak*, ECLI:EU:C:2003:255.

already the specified quota of non-EU nationals selected for the game. Similarly, in *Simutenkov*,[29] a case involving a Russian national playing professional football in Spain, the CJEU ruled that he was protected by a non-discriminatory provision contained in an agreement on partnership and cooperation signed between the EU and the Russian Federation in 1994.

Essentially, nationals of a number of countries that have entered into agreements with the EU containing non-discrimination clauses which can be interpreted as taking direct effect, must be treated on an equal basis with nationals of the Member State in which they have secured employment. Thus quota restrictions on 'foreign players' do not apply to them as such restrictions constitute 'working conditions' for the purposes of non-discrimination clauses in relevant agreements. Not all agreements between individual countries and the EU will contain such provisions, but, in addition to football, the *Kolpak* case has had an effect on sports such as both codes of rugby and cricket; games which *Bosman* has only minimally impacted upon as they are not widely played professionally in Europe. Such players have become commonly known as 'Kolpak' players.

The 'Cotonou Agreement' between the EU and the African, Caribbean and Pacific Group of States (ACP) concerning the objectives of sustainable development and poverty reduction has had a significant impact. For example, a number of players have been signed by rugby league sides from countries such as Fiji, Tonga and Samoa. In rugby union and cricket, a significant number of South Africans have taken advantage of the ruling to play for professional clubs in England. In English county cricket, in comparison to say Australian players, South African cricketers can no longer be subject to rules which restrict the number of overseas players that can play for a county to one in any given season. As a response to a concern that many county teams are fielding significant number of players not eligible to play for the England national team, the governing body for cricket, the England and Wales Cricket Board (ECB), has linked the central payments made to counties to the number of English qualified players who represent the county. This in effect means that every game a 'Kolpak' player plays instead of an English qualified player, a county receives over a £1000 less from the ECB.[30]

Prior to the ruling in *Kolpak*, there had been some speculation that the CJEU was going to extend Article 45 TFEU to nationals of associate countries. Such radical change was not given effect and Article 45 TFEU remains inapplicable to such nationals. Thus, they have no rights to enter a Member State to take up employment, or to move from Member State to Member State in order to do so.[31] A trans-

---

[29]Case C-265/03, *Igor Simutenkov v Ministerio de Educación y Cultura and Real Federación Española de Fútbol*, ECLI:EU:C:2005:213.

[30]For more, see Boyes 2005. Note a stricter interpretation by the EU Commission of the Cotonou Agreement has led to narrower work permit criteria based on need for past international record of recipients. See Brett O, ECB wins overseas player battle. BBC Sport, 26 October 2009. http://news.bbc.co.uk/sport2/hi/cricket/counties/8325975.stm. Accessed 28 September 2015.

[31]Boyes 2003, p. 72; Hendrickx 2003, p. 12; Van den Bogaert 2004, p. 267.

fer to a club in another Member State will still be subject to that country's immigration rules. Presumably, national laws requiring work permits, on the expiry of a non-national's contract, still apply to nationals of countries with associate status. Moreover, a number of the European countries, to which *Kolpak* applied, are now EU Member States and their nationals will be protected fully by Article 45 TFEU.

4.6 Why Are Quotas Back on the Agenda?

Whilst *Kolpak* has not had the dramatic effect that some anticipated, its consequences combined with those of *Bosman* have resulted in ongoing and significant controversy. As is not unusual in the context of discrimination law there has been a backlash with arguments at various levels in football that the legacy of *Bosman*, compounded by *Kolpak*, is to damage the fortunes of national teams and prevent the emergence of home-grown talent. In a range of professional team sports within the EU, the player squads have become increasingly cosmopolitan with newly emerging patterns of player migration developing. However, it should be stressed again that professional sport has been an employment sector that has historically involved complex patterns of international migration.[32]

In the last few years, a number of sports and in particular football, have moved to re-introduce player quotas. In April 2005, UEFA introduced its 'home grown players' rule for European cup competitions and recommended that national associations adopt similar rules for their own domestic leagues.[33] In May 2008, FIFA formally proposed a '6 + 5 rule' based on a quota of six national players in any given team.[34] Although the UEFA rule predates the FIFA proposal we shall consider the two rules out of chronological order on the basis that, on the face of it, FIFA's proposals are more problematic legally.

But first it is necessary to address the major question as to why there has been increasing concern from the football authorities over the impact of *Bosman* and the subsequent case law of the CJEU. The following can be identified as the *perceived* problems that European law and particularly the *Bosman* ruling has created for football. They are interesting to consider in the context of the analysis of AG Lenz.

[32]Lanfranchi and Taylor 2001.

[33]See the current UEFA Regulations for the Champions League Competition. http://www.uefa.com/multimediafiles/download/regulations/uefa/others/82/68/51/826851_download.pdf. Accessed 28 September 2015.

[34]Fifa backs Blatter on quota plan. BBC Sport, 30 May 2008. http://news.bbc.co.uk/sport2/hi/football/europe/7421348.stm. Accessed 28 September 2015.

First, aggregation of playing talent within a small elite of clubs in European football, notably those who have been able to qualify for participation in the UEFA Champions League on a regular basis, has led to a real challenge to the crucial sporting characteristic of unpredictability of outcome as a distortion of sporting competition and dominance of these clubs due to their control of the top playing talent whose nationality is largely irrelevant.

Secondly, the freedom of movement provisions have led to the top talent from EU Member States moving to the economically powerful leagues in European football, notably England's Premier League, Spain's La Liga and Italy's Serie A. This influx into the economically powerful leagues has resulted in diminished opportunities for young emerging indigenous talent within those Member States. This can be supported by research that demonstrates that foreign players employed by English, Spanish, Italian, German and French clubs in each countries' top league, made up 42.4 % of all players during the 2007–2008 season rising to 46.59 % of all players in the 2013–2014 season. In the English Premier League, the number of foreign players in these two respective seasons has moved from 59.5 % to 62.9 %.[35]

Thirdly, this migration has been at the expense of young domestic talent in the top European leagues. Contrary to the view expressed by AG Lenz in *Bosman* discussed above that it was unlikely that the migration of foreign players would increase to the extent that the chances of domestic players would be seriously diminished,[36] it is argued that, in fact, this is just what has occurred.[37] It is also argued that young domestic players have also been unable or unwilling to move to other Member States in meaningful numbers as a balancing tendency to differing degrees in different countries.

Fourthly, this migration has manifested itself in a smaller pool of eligible players to pick for the national teams of Member States. Consequently national teams throughout Europe have been weakened. This is a widely held belief. However, one research study suggests that over a thirty-year period from 1977 to 2007, the performance of the England national team has improved in the post-*Bosman* years.[38]

Fifthly, Member States from which playing talent has migrated are increasingly impoverished in terms of the performance of their club teams. Beyond the new dynamic that has emerged since *Bosman* within the EU, the *Kolpak* and

---

[35]Professional Football Players' Observatory (PFPO), Annual Review of the European Football Players. http://www.football-observatory.com. Accessed 28 September 2015. This research identified that European wide, non-European players now represent 50 % of the total number of foreign players). See also 'Fewer club-trained players, more expatriate footballers in the big five European leagues 2009'. http://www.fifa.com/world-match-centre/news/newsid/109/649/7/index.html. Accessed 28 September 2015.

[36]Case C-415/93 *Union Royale Belge des Sociétés de Football Association and others v. Bosman and others*, ECLI:EU:C:1995:463, para 145.

[37]This argument is fundamentally the basis of recent proposals found in the Report of the FA Chairman's England Commission of May 2014. For a more detailed analysis, see Winnie 2014.

[38]Huxtable 2008.

Simutenkov[39] cases have applied non-discrimination provisions to a wider range of countries beyond the EU's borders. Moreover, Europe, as the powerhouse of world football, has also become a focus for migration patterns of player talent into Europe from around the world. Subject to any quota system operated by a particular football association and national immigration rules, significant numbers of foreign non-EU national players have been able to secure employment within European football leagues. This has both caused impoverishment in national leagues world-wide and impacted adversely upon national sides. It has also created exploitation and the trafficking of playing talent away from many, mainly developing, countries.[40]

Lastly, in the context of the pan-European UEFA competitions, especially the Champions League, economic impact includes less competitive balance in competitions, an increased link between money and sporting success and fewer opportunities for local-trained players to play.[41]

The above arguments are regarded as undermining the rationales of *Bosman* and *Kolpak* and, essentially, the re-introduction of playing quotas in some guise is seen as righting the wrongs of the effects of the rulings. With reference to these arguments, the chapter will now examine the legality of FIFA's and UEFA's proposals for player quotas.

4.7 FIFA 6 + 5 Rule

This proposal, agreed at the FIFA Congress in May 2008, essentially provides that at the beginning of each match, each club must field at least six players who are eligible to play for the national team of the country of the club.[42] However, there are no restrictions proposed on the number of non-eligible players under contract with the club (although restrictions on size of squads that may be permitted in individual leagues will have to be taken into account).[43] This restriction applies to

[39]Case C-265/03 *Igor Simutenkov V Abogado del Estado, Real Federacion Espanola de Futbol and Ministerio Fiscal* ECLI:EU:C:2005:213, involved a Russian national playing professional football in Spain, where the CJEU ruled that he was protected by a non-discriminatory provision contained in an agreement on partnership and cooperation signed between the EU and the Russian Federation in 1994.

[40]Backe Madsen and Johansson 2008.

[41]University of Liverpool and Edge Hill University (2013) Study on the Assessment of UEFA's Home-Grown Player Rule. Study for the European Commission EAC/07/2012.

[42]Yes in principle to 6 + 5 rule. FIFA.com, 5 February 2008. http://www.fifa.com/about-fifa/news/y=2008/m=2/news=yes-principle-rule-684707.html. Accessed 28 September 2015.

[43]The English Premier League has been criticised on squad sizes operated by many clubs, e.g. it is reported in 2008–2009 season, Liverpool FC had a first team squad of 62 players, see Jackson J, Uefa slam 'ridiculous' Big Four squad sizes. The Guardian, 29 March 2009. http://www.theguardian.com/football/2009/mar/29/uefa-liverpool-squad-sizes-premier-league. Accessed 28 September 2015.

the starting line-up of the team, and coaches will be able to modify the ratio of national players in the team during the game with up to three permitted substitutions all of whom can be non-eligible players.

It should be noted, that at the time of writing, the 6 + 5 proposal has been deferred.[44] However, given FIFA's insistence that it is both preferable to UEFA's rule and compatible with EU law it can be anticipated that the 6 + 5 rule or something akin to it will resurface in the future.[45] It is also the case that the proposal both reflects and feeds current political debates concerning the pros and cons of economic migration – in particular, perspectives that see economic migration as a problem which has a damaging impact on indigenous populations. Thus it remains pertinent to examine the history of the proposed rule and legal arguments for and against its compatibility with EU law.

FIFA claims the proposal is needed for all the reasons stated above, but, additionally, because 'the universal development of football over the last century would not continue if there were increasing inequalities between continents, countries and protagonists in football'.[46] There has been political support for FIFA's proposal[47] and significant support for it within the football family.[48] However, most academic evaluation has been that within Europe such player quotas would clearly be contrary to Article 45 TFEU in terms of being a form of discrimination ruled unlawful by the CJEU decisions in *Dona*,[49] *Bosman*, *Kolpak* and *Simutenkov*.[50]

An alternative analysis is presented by a FIFA commissioned report by the Institute for European Affairs (INEA).[51] As with the partly-UEFA funded, Independent European Sport Review (the Arnaut Report),[52] the INEA Report

---

[44]BBC sport reported that the FIFA congress in June 2010 decided to abandon the proposal, see Fifa scraps plans for 'home-grown' player rule. BBC Sport, 10 June 2010. http://news.bbc.co.uk/sport2/hi/football/8733164.stm. Accessed 28 September 2015. However, there has been no official confirmation of this by FIFA or indeed by other interested parties such as FIFPRo.

[45]Sepp Blatter urges Europe to back his '6 plus 5' local talent rule. ESPN FC, 12 August 2015. http://www.espnfc.co.uk/fifa-world-cup/story/2561968/sepp-blatter-urges-europe-to-revive-his-6-plus-5-rule. Accessed 28 September 2015.

[46]FIFA Congress supports objectives of 6 + 5. FIFA.com, 30 May 2008. www.fifa.com/about-fifa/news/y=2008/m=5/news=fifa-congress-supports-objectives-783657.html. Accessed 28 September 2015.

[47]UK All Party Parliamentary Football Group, English Football and its Governance. http://www.publications.parliament.uk/pa/cm201011/cmselect/cmcumeds/writev/792/fg83.htm. Accessed 28 September 2015.

[48]Mourinho voices support for FIFA's "6 + 5" rule. ESPN FC, 30 May 2009. http://www.espnfc.com/story/632412. Accessed 28 September 2015.

[49]Case C-13/76 *Gaetano Donà v Mario Mantero*, ECLI:EU:C:1976:115.

[50]Boucher 2007, pp. 18–19; Anderson 2009; Majani 2009, pp. 19–25; Williams and Haffner 2008, pp. 1017–1019.

[51]Expert Opinion by the Institute for European Affairs of 24 Ocober 2008, regarding the Compatability of the "6 + 5 Rule" within European Community Law.

[52]Arnaut J (2006) Independent European Sport Review, UK Presidency of the EU 2005.

exemplifies a recognised way of presenting a lobbying position on the development of the EU's sports policy. However, unlike the Arnaut Report, which was the culmination of significant consultation amongst a range of stakeholders in European sport and which provides a well-argued and constructed case for greater recognition of the 'specificity of sport' by the EU, the INEA Report is somewhat more limited. Arguably, it provides a badly structured, repetitive and somewhat simplistic justification for the 6 + 5 proposal. Most football fans understand the significance of the 'Hand of God' in determining an outcome—it is not difficult to identify the 'hand of FIFA' in the Report's recommendations.

The argument present by the INEA Report is as follows. The 6 + 5 proposal is portrayed as being axiomatically for the good of football as a response to the detrimental impact of the *Bosman* ruling in the years subsequent to it. The major problems the ruling has created for football, as perceived by the authors of the Report, have been summarised above. The 6 + 5 proposal is consequently presented as being a purely sporting rule outside the 'soft law' regulatory involvement of the EU in sport and a 'sporting response' to the perceived current ills within football and thus not contrary to European competition law. This argument is very unlikely to succeed given the CJEU rulings in *Meca-Medina* and *Motoe*.[53] Taken together these rulings enable the CJEU to consider the compatibility with EU law of any rules, which a sport's regulatory body have deemed 'pure' sporting rules that impact on a person's ability to participate in that sport or have other economic consequences.[54]

Similarly, the INEA Report contends that the proposal is not discriminatory under Article 45 TFEU. However, the central legal barrier to the implementation of FIFA's proposal is that it is clearly likely to constitute direct discrimination. As held by the CJEU in *Commission v Italy*,[55] direct discrimination cannot be justified and can be legitimated only by reference to one of the express derogations in Article 45(3) TFEU on grounds of public policy, public security or public health or through secondary legislation. It is difficult to see how the 6 + 5 rule, any more than the original pre-*Bosman* 3 + 2 rule, could permit derogation under any of these headings and therefore should be ruled as inherently unlawful.

There are arguments, developed initially in the *Cassis de Dijon* case,[56] that there can be an 'unwritten justification' of direct discrimination in circumstances of 'pressing reasons of public interest', and that the 6 + 5 rule should be regarded in this light by the CJEU.[57] However, it is debatable whether the interests

[53]Case C-519/04 P *David Meca-Medina and Igor Majcen v. Commission*, ECLI:EU:C:2006:492; Case C-49/07 *Motosykletistiki Omospondia Ellados NPID (MOTOE) v Elliniko Dimosio*, ECLI:EU:C:2008:376.

[54]For further discussion, see Weatherill 2006, pp. 647, 652, 657; Weatherill 2009.

[55]Case C-283/99 *Commission v Italy*, ECLI:EU:C:2001:307.

[56]Case 120/78 *Rewe-Zentrale AG v Bundesmonopolverwaltung für Branntwein*, ECLI:EU:C:1979:42.

[57]Conzelmann 2008, p. 26, who cites Case C-2/90 *Commission of the European Communities v Kingdom of Belgium (Wallonian Garbage)*, ECLI:EU:C:1992:310 and Case C-379/98 *PreussenElektra v. Schleswag AG*, ECLI:EU:C:2001:160 in support of this position.

of sport could ever be seen in this way. By way of analogy, it is useful to have regard to the CJEU rulings in *Viking*[58] and *Laval*.[59] These cases concern conflict between national law on rights to strike and the freedoms of establishment and to provide services. In these rulings, despite accepting that rights to strike have the status of fundamental rights within the EU, the CJEU gave priority to protecting the freedoms established by the EU Treaty.[60] If a similar approach is taken to freedom of movement under Article 45 TFEU, and the symbiotic relationship this has with EU discrimination law then, even if the 6 + 5 rule does genuinely further the interests of professional football (and potentially other sports), it is unlikely to pass the test of 'pressing public interest'. The needs of sport are surely of less significance to the public interest than the exercising of *fundamental* rights to strike by trade unions and their members to protect pay, conditions and job security.

The INEA Report also argues that the 6 + 5 rule should be seen as indirect rather than direct discrimination and thus can be justified as a proportionate means to deal with the above problems. The Report argues that the rule is not based on a nationality of the player but to the 'entitlement to play for the national team concerned'.[61] This seems a very weak argument. Whilst nationality is the primary requirement for eligibility for the national teams, it does not give an automatic right to be able to play for such teams. For example, some players who have become naturalised in a certain country based on a stipulated period of residency, but who have previously played for another national team, are not eligible due to FIFA restrictions.

One sporting rule that the European Commission has consistently seen as legitimate is the right to select national athletes for national team competitions.[62] Therefore, it is clear that a non-national cannot play for a national side. So given that the 6 + 5 rule will disadvantage all non-nationals it would appear to be directly discriminating against that group. Whilst it is true there is no formal

---

[58]Case C-438/05 *International Transport Workers' Federation and Finnish Seamen's Union v. Viking Line ABP and OÜ Viking Line Eesti*, ECLI:EU:C:2007:772.

[59]Case C-341/05 *Laval un Partneri Ltd v Svenska Byggnadsarbetareförbundet, Svenska Byggnadsarbetareförbundets avdelning 1, Byggettan and Svenska Elektrikerförbundet*, ECLI:EU:C:2007:809.

[60]For a thorough discussion of these cases, see Davies 2008, pp. 126–148.

[61]Expert Opinion by the Institute for European Affairs of 24 October 2008, regarding the Compatability of the "6 + 5 Rule" within European Community Law, p. 136.

[62]Commission White Paper of 11 July 2007, COM (2007) 391 final - White Paper on Sport, para 4.2; re-affirmed in the Communication from the Commission to the European Parliament, the Council, the European Economic and Social Committee and the Committee of the Regions of 18 January 2011, COM(2011) 12 final Developing the European Dimension in Sport. However note the continued interest of restrictions of access to individual competitions within Member States for non-nationals. See T.M.C. Asser Instituut, Edge Hill University and Leiden University (2010) Study on the Equal Treatment of Non-Nationals in Individual Sports Competitions NO. EAC/19/2009.

restriction on the number of non-nationals a club can employ, in practice it is likely that clubs will adopt the view that it is less commercially viable to employ any more non-nationals. Applying the classic test for direct discrimination used in English law the point (albeit one that cannot be pre-determined) will be reached when it can be said that 'but for' a player's nationality he would have been seen as a suitable player for a club to recruit.[63]

If the 6 + 5 rule is not directly discriminatory, but can correctly be seen as indirect discrimination, then justification is available. However, it is argued below that justification of the rather less discriminatory UEFA rule should fail on the basis of proportionality. If this view were to coincide with that adopted by the courts then justification of the FIFA rule must surely be impossible. In this respect, the view that the FIFA rule should be supported because the UEFA 'proposal to ensure that a certain number of home-grown players are included in a squad of 25 simply does not go far enough'[64] is rather ironic in that it is being favoured as more effective because it operates in a more discriminatory manner. A basic tenet of European law is that the more discriminatory a policy is, the more difficult it becomes to justify it as a proportionate response.[65]

Ultimately, it is difficult to discern any fundamental difference between the 6 + 5 rule and the 3 + 2 rule rejected in *Bosman*—the latter is really the former in a new guise. Similarly, the problems that *Bosman* is regarded as having created were entirely predictable and indeed intended consequences of the ruling. It was always clear that best leagues attract the best players and will continue to do so. This is part of the logic of EU social law that workers can move to other Member States where they can enjoy the best rewards for their labour. There is no rational basis for excluding footballers from this. In a sense it is a case of *Bosman* there and back again. As is substantiated below, in examining the arguments advanced for justifying both the FIFA and UEFA rules the reasons for rejecting these as identified by AG Lenz in *Bosman* remain pertinent and cogent.

Moreover, the philosophical basis of EU law on freedom of movement is that EU nationals are able to move between Member States irrespective of the perceived problems this causes for national economies or the job security of national workers. If reducing unemployment is (correctly) not regarded as justifying national quotas it is difficult to see how invoking the specificities of sport will be seen as anything other than an attempt at special pleading. On a global basis, the FIFA proposal underestimates the barrier to the international mobility of footballers erected by national immigration laws. In Britain, for example, work permits are effectively

---

[63]This test was first formulated by the House of Lords in *James v Eastleigh Borough Council* [1990] 2 AC 751.

[64]UK All Party Parliamentary Football Group, English Football and its Governance. http://www.publications.parliament.uk/pa/cm201011/cmselect/cmcumeds/writev/792/fg83.htm. Accessed 28 September 2015.

[65]See the principle of proportionality as propounded by the CJEU in Case 170/84 *Bilka-Kaufhaus Gmbh v Weber von Hartz*, ECLI:EU:C:1986:204.

only available to top internationals from top national teams, and even where a player has a work permit he is still required to obtain a new one before he can transfer to another club.[66] The idea that foreign players are swamping the English and other European Leagues seems a peculiarly European case of xenophobia.

It should be noted that the international players union, the Fédération Internationale des Associations de Footballeurs Professionnels (FIFPro), although supporting the sporting aims behind the FIFA proposal, accepts that, as professional players are employees, both national and EU law provisions will be infringed.[67] The European Parliament and the European Commission have indicated clearly that they regard the 6 + 5 rule as directly discriminatory and contrary to Article 45 TFEU. This is within the development of a European sports law policy that has applied the values of equality and equal treatment that have been generally and expressly determined by the CJEU.[68]

4.8 Home-Grown Player Rule

However, both FIFPro and the European Commission have indicated some approval for UEFA's rules on home grown players, though FIFPro has emphasised the need to protect young players, including those from Africa, in that the rule could have the unintended consequence of an influx of trainee players between 14 and 16 into the major European leagues.[69] Alternatively Miettinen and Parrish have argued that the UEFA rules may offend EU law in that they cannot be justified by reference to normal principles 'on the grounds that they are disproportionate, unfit for the purposes they are relied upon or pursue economic as well as legitimate and justifiable non-economic objectives'.[70]

The UEFA plan was first proposed in 2005. The rule requires clubs participating in the Champions League and the UEFA Cup (now the Europa Cup) to have a minimum number of home-grown players, i.e. players who, regardless of their nationality, have been trained by their club or by another club in the same national association for at least three years between the age of 15 and 21. This was set at 4

[66]For current position, see https://www.gov.uk/government/organisations/uk-visas-and-immigration. Accessed 28 September 2015.

[67]For FIFPro's view on the 6 + 5 rule and the home grown players rule, see http://www.fifpro.org/en/?mod=one&id=16627. Accessed 28 September 2015.

[68]Joined Cases 117/76 and 16/77 *Albert Ruckdeschel & Co. and Hansa-Lagerhaus Ströh & Co. v Hauptzollamt Hamburg-St. Annen; Diamalt AG v Hauptzollamt Itzehoe*, ECLI:EU:C:1977:160.

[69]Conzelmann 2008.

[70]Miettinen and Parrish 2007.

players in a maximum squad of 25 in the first season of application – 2006–2007. This rose to 8 out of the maximum squad of 25 players in the 2008–2009 season.[71]

The perceived legitimacy of this policy has led to a number of domestic leagues around Europe introducing similar restrictions to their playing squads. In England, the Football League introduced restrictions, which started in the 2009–2010 season, which require 4 players in match day squad to have been registered by a domestic club for 3 years before their 21st birthday.[72] In fact, for most Football League clubs this will merely be reflecting the status quo that has existed for many years with clubs already complying with this requirement. More significantly, in terms of the potential practical impact, the Premier League has adopted similar rules with effect from season 2010–2011.[73]

Any policy or rule that is intrinsically liable to affect migrant workers more than national workers and thus impede access to the labour market and freedom of movement constitutes indirect discrimination. It is clear that UEFA's rule falls into this category but, as such, will be lawful if it can be justified. Using the terminology of the test developed in cases such as *Gebhard*[74] and wider employment law cases such as *Bilka-Kaufhaus*,[75] firstly, the suitability of the measure for securing the attainment of its objectives needs to be established, and secondly, that the measure does not go beyond what is necessary in order to attain the objective. Therefore, for justification of the UEFA rule to be established, the objectives secured by the rule must not be outweighed by the discriminatory impact of it and there must be no other means by which these objectives can be met just as effectively.[76]

With respect to potential justification, it is important to take into account that the rule has received positive response from a number of quarters. Like the European Commission and FIFPro, the European Parliament has been supportive and,

> Expresses its clear support for the UEFA measures to encourage the education of young players by requiring a minimum number of home-grown players in a professional club's

[71]UEFA, Regulations of the UEFA Champions League 2008/2009. http://www.uefa.com/multimediafiles/download/regulations/uefa/others/70/22/60/702260_download.pdf. Accessed 28 September 2015. See also Geey D (2014) UEFA and its Amended Home Grown Player Rule' on impact of Financial Fair Play Rules on makeup and size of playing squad. www.danielgeey.com/uefa-and-its-amended-home-grown-player-rule. Accessed 28 September 2015.

[72]Clubs vote for 'home-grown' rule. BBC Sport, 18 December 2008. http://news.bbc.co.uk/sport2/hi/football/7789808.stm. Accessed 28 September 2015.

[73]Conn D, Home grown doesn't mean English but rule will help. The Guardian, 2 September 2010. Premier League squads may be up to 25 senior players and must include no more than 17 players who are not home grown. A player is home grown if he has spent 3 seasons with any English or Welsh club. However, there are no restrictions on the number of players in a squad below the age of 21.

[74]Case C-55/94 *Gebhard v Consiglio dell'Ordine degli Avvocati e Procuratori di Milano*, ECLI:EU:C:1995:411; [1996] 1 CMLR 603.

[75]Case 170/84 *Bilka-Kaufhaus Gmbh v Weber von Hartz*, ECLI:EU:C:1986:204.

[76]For a comprehensive discussion of applying these principles to the home-grown player rule, see Downward et al. 2014, pp. 493–510.

> squad and by placing a limit on the size of the squads … [it] believes that such incentive measures are proportionate and calls on professional clubs to strictly implement this rule.[77]

The Arnaut Report contended that the measure would: encourage training programmes in order to promote, develop, nurture and educate new talents; promote the local nature of clubs, so fans identify more with their team; maintain competitive balance by reducing the importance of money; reduce the tendency towards 'hoarding' of players; and widen the pool of talent within an association eligible to represent the national team.[78] The Report went on to suggest rather optimistically that, 'the purpose and nature of this rule is such that it would qualify for an exception under EU competition law'.[79] Equally, however, if this is not the most appropriate legal instrument to provide security for this system, the authors also consider that guidelines could be very useful on the matter to confirm the compatibility of the rule with European Community law.

The White Paper on Sport reaffirms this position:

> Acceptance of limited and proportionate restrictions (in line with EU Treaty provisions on free movement and European Court of Justice rulings) to the principle of free movement in particular as regards: the right to select national athletes for national team competitions; the need to limit the number of participants in a competition; the setting of deadlines for transfers of players in team sports … rules requiring that teams include a certain quota of locally trained players could be accepted as being compatible with the Treaty provisions on free movement of persons if … indirect discrimination effects resulting from them can be justified as being proportionate to a legitimate objective pursued, such as to enhance and protect the training and development of talented young players.[80]

The White Paper highlighted the need for further consideration and, in 2008, the Commission published a Report accepting that the home grown player rules 'seem(s) to comply with the principle of free movement of workers … even though they might lead to indirect discrimination on the basis of nationality, the UEFA rules have been endorsed by the Commission, subject to a review of their practical consequences by 2012'.[81]

An academic assessment of the home grown player rule published in April 2013, provides an extensive legal and economic analysis.[82] There is an acceptance that the rule 'amounts to an indirectly discriminatory rule because even though the

---

[77]European Parliament resolution of 29 March 2007, (2006/2130(INI)) on the future of professional football in Europe, p. 34.

[78]Arnaut J (2006) Independent European Sport Review, UK Presidency of the EU 2005, para 6.58.

[79]Ibid., para 6.59.

[80]Commission White Paper of 11 July 2007, COM (2007) 391 final - White Paper on Sport, action 9 of the Pierre de Coubertin Action Plan, p. 6.

[81]Commission Press Release of 28 May 2008, IP/08/807 UEFA's rules on home-grown players receive green light from the Commission. http://europa.eu/rapid/press-release_IP-08-807_en.htm. Accessed 28 September 2015.

[82]University of Liverpool and Edge Hill University (2013) Study on the Assessment of UEFA's Home-Grown Player Rule. Study for the European Commission EAC/07/2012.

Rule is neutral in terms of nationality, national workers are placed at an advantage over migrant workers'.[83] The Report also accepts that UEFA's claim that there is a sporting justification for the rule promoting competitive balance but that '[The] neutrality or very limited positive effect of the Rule in terms of improving competitive balance and the training and development of young European Union players must be balanced against the impact the Rule has on restricting a player's freedom of movement'.[84] Two main recommendations are made. Firstly, the impact of the home grown player rule needs continued monitoring and position should be reviewed in three years' time. Secondly, 'rather than adopting a negative position on the Rule, the European Commission should extend an invitation to UEFA to consult with key stakeholders on whether alternative measures, that do not carry discriminatory effects, can deliver more substantial benefits for European football'.[85]

4.9 Alternative Sporting Measures

The focus on alternative measures is a key issue in this area. The authors' view is that the reality of the home grown player rule, like the 6 + 5 rule, is that it is protectionist in nature. Most fundamentally, even if the rule is seen as justifiable in political and footballing contexts, it still has to satisfy the legal requirement of proportionality, and the above arguments fail to take into account that there are alternative ways of securing the legitimate interests of professional football.

Although outside the focus of this chapter, the alternatives can be divided into sporting rules, firstly that impact upon the labour market with the focus on sports men and women, and secondly, that impact upon the product market.

Labour market sporting rules include: contractual restraints on the player including the length of a player's employment contract; training compensation to provide greater club incentives for youth development, restricting the transfer of minors; and, squad size limits.

Product markets policies include: cost control measures such as salary caps and/or transfer fee caps; UEFA's Financial Fair Play Regulations; club licensing schemes; and, greater revenue sharing which is designed to equalize the financial muscle of clubs around Europe.[86]

---

[83]Ibid., para 6.

[84]Ibid., para 11.

[85]Ibid.

[86]Uefa introduces tough penalties for spendthrift clubs. BBC Sport, 27 May 2010. http://news.bbc.co.uk/sport2/hi/football/europe/8709871.stm. Accessed 28 September 2015. It should be noted that the EU Report on the transfer system also calls for full implementation of UEFA's Financial Fair Play rule along with stronger 'solidarity mechanisms' to enhance youth development and the protection of minors.

It should be noted that the 2013 EU Report on the transfer system (see above) also calls for full implementation of UEFA's Financial Fair Play rule along with stronger 'solidarity mechanisms' to enhance youth development and the protection of minors.

Similarly, as indicated above, the Report on the home grown player rule urges UEFA to consider alternatives and the suggestion is that:

> Before the rule can categorically be described as compatible with EU free movement law, less restrictive alternatives should first be examined, particularly those that do not carry discriminatory effects and are not located within the labour market.[87]

It is indeed the product market interventions that we believe need to be considered urgently and are likely to pass the test of legal justification discussed above. As made clear by AG Lenz in *Bosman*, redistribution of income provides the most effective and fairest way of ensuring that the vast sums of money secured by large clubs are shared with their smaller brethren.[88] This both increases the potential for competitive balance and provides income for the development and enhancement of youth academies and the establishment of national scouting networks. Rather than preventing clubs from fielding foreign players is it not much better to encourage the provision of the requisite financial and physical resources for the identification and development of young local talent?[89]

It may be the case at present for it to be commercially more attractive to attract youth talent from other clubs who are classified as 'home-grown' rather than investing in potentially costly infrastructure. Indeed, in the context of post-*Bosman* transfer systems, youth academies are increasingly seen as not commercially viable.[90] This is because once a player has reached the age of 23 or 24 and is out of contract, free agency applies with no right for a transfer fee or compensation from the former employing club. This is despite the money that club may have invested in training that player in his youth. However, in this regard it could be possible for clubs to enter into a collective agreement with one another to reserve a share of the income from broadcasting rights and the like for clubs that agree to invest in youth academies. Such an agreement would also meet the aspirations of football fans who, typically, enjoy seeing their club field a mixture of international stars and players with local connections and thus a genuine commitment to the club.

Other possibilities that may constitute a more proportionate response to solve the perceived problems in football include salary caps; though these have been

---

[87]University of Liverpool and Edge Hill University (2013) Study on the Assessment of UEFA's Home-Grown Player Rule. Study for the European Commission EAC/07/2012.

[88]Case C-415/93 *Union Royale Belge des Sociétés de Football Association and others v. Bosman and others*, ECLI:EU:C:1995:463, para 233.

[89]Lynam 2009.

[90]Conn D, Clubs leave lost youth behind as academies fail English talent. The Guardian, 9 September 2009. http://www.theguardian.com/football/david-conn-inside-sport-blog/2009/sep/09/chelsea-fifa-premier-league-academies. Accessed 28 September 2015.

rejected by FIFPro and operate artificially to restrict the income that professional players can earn. It may be only the big stars who can become millionaires through playing the 'beautiful game', but this is a dream that many young footballers from working class backgrounds have and why should it be denied to them. Such restrictions do not exist in other parts of the entertainment industry such as music and acting so why should they in professional sport.[91] It is also important to take account of UEFA's Financial Fair Play Regulations, which are designed to equalize the financial muscle of clubs around Europe.[92] This does not impose a formal salary cap but should restrain clubs from paying salaries to players that they cannot afford.

FIFPro has suggested as an alternative that there be a cap on transfer fees.[93] This seems rather more attractive: it will contribute to the restoration of competitive balance and prevent the richer clubs gazumping attempts by smaller clubs to sign star players. Admittedly, it will reduce the signing on fee that such players will earn but this is preferable to a permanent restriction on their incomes.

Arguably the weakest argument for the UEFA rule, and indeed FIFA's 6 + 5 rule, is the view that it will increase the number of players eligible for national teams by increasing the pool of national talent. The best clubs will always recruit the best national players and there should always be sufficient numbers of these to provide the squads for international competitions. As AG Lenz observed, the fortunes of the Scottish team are hardly affected by the fact that their best players often choose to play in the English Premier League. Indeed, as he also commented, the importing of foreign internationals into a domestic league has a tendency to improve the skills of domestic players rather than have a negative impact on their development.[94] Moreover, any player, whether or not a national of the country where the club is located, can become a 'home grown player' after playing in a domestic league for a three year period between the ages of 15 and 21.[95]

As well as the issue of proportionality, it is also necessary to take into account the unintended effect the home grown player rule could have on the supply and trafficking of young players from developing countries, particularly Africa, largely carried out by un-licensed agents and outside of regulatory frameworks.[96]

[91]Fort and Quirk 1995, pp. 1265–1299; Harris 2002, p. 120.

[92]Uefa introduces tough penalties for spendthrift clubs. BBC Sport, 27 May 2010. http://news.bbc.co.uk/sport2/hi/football/europe/8709871.stm. Accessed 28 September 2015.

[93]Miettinen and Parrish 2008.

[94]Case C-415/93 *Union Royale Belge des Sociétés de Football Association and others v. Bosman and others*, ECLI:EU:C:1995:463, paras 145–146.

[95]The Spanish national, Cesc Fabregas, whilst he played for Arsenal can be cited as an illustration. The link therefore between being a home grown player and being eligible for the national side is not certain. Conversely, and somewhat ironically, some nationally eligible players, such as the former English international, Owen Hargreaves, who was an apprentice player at Bayern Munchen, are not 'home grown players'.

[96]Note recent CAS case concerning the upholding of FIFA Players' Status Committee judgment against the Danish FA and FC for registering minor players from Nigeria—CAS 2008/A/1485 *FC Midtjylland v. FIFA*; See also Backe Madsen and Johansson 2008.

As things stand, FIFA has estimated that there are around half a million transfers of minors in football per year.[97] This is movement of young people on a very significant scale and the home grown player rule could exacerbate the problem. The rule may be designed to encourage the development of young local talent, but in practice it could lead to abuse of the notion of what a home grown player actually is.

FIFA has recently modified its transfer regulations so that young players under 18 can now move to a club in a different region or country as long as the family relocates to it for non-football reasons, such as a parent changing jobs.[98] There is evidence that in the past, parents have in fact been provided with 'manufactured' jobs by clubs in the local area.[99] The new regulation does however require a sub-committee of the FIFA Players' Status Committee to vet all transfers of minors,[100] but it can be anticipated that new circumventions of the system will be devised. Thus, it is at least feasible that clubs will manipulate the nature of the home-grown player, and the UEFA rule will contribute to rather than prevent exploitative trafficking. In this context, it is worth reiterating that the EU report on the transfer system calls for effective measures to deal with the issue of trafficking of young players.

4.10 Similar Rules in Other Sports

Team sports other than football have of course been subject to the same issues around how to respond to EU law challenges provided by the *Bosman* ruling to sporting rules that operate as player restraints. Different sports have a variety of player quotas in national and pan-European competitions and a number of sports have moved to introduce rules requiring playing squads containing a number of locally trained players. For example, in April 2014 the European Commission issued a 'Reasoned Opinion' that requires the Spanish Association of Basketball Clubs, to 'change its rules on the composition of basketball teams, as the current

[97]Scott M and Gibson O, Fifa cracks down on child transfers. The Guardian, 5 September 2005. http://www.theguardian.com/football/2009/sep/05/uefa-fifa-child-footballer-transfers. Accessed 28 September 2015.

[98]FIFA Regulations on the Status and Transfer of Players. http://www.fifa.com/mm/document/affederation/administration/66/98/97/regulationsstatusandtransfer_en_1210.pdf. Accessed 28 September 2015.

[99]Scott M, Chelsea facing legal threat over signing boy of 11. The Guardian, 5 September 2009. http://www.theguardian.com/football/2009/sep/05/chelsea-legal-threat-alleged-player-poaching. Accessed 28 September 2015. Chelsea FC were under FIFA imposed transfer ban over Chelsea's illegal recruitment of the teenage forward Gaël Kakuta from Lens, overturned by agreement between parties before formal appeal hearing by CAS.

[100]For further details see, http://www.fifa.com/mm/document/affederation/administration/regulations_on_the_status_and_transfer_of_players_en_33410.pdf. Accessed 28 September 2015.

quotas for locally trained players lead to indirect discrimination towards players from other Member States'.[101] The European Commission established that in some competitions, rules required between 40 % and 88 % of the players to be locally trained and that the sporting justifications of encouraging the recruitment and training of young payers and promotion competitive balance, did not pass the test of 'appropriateness and proportionality'.[102]

4.11 The Regulatory Future

We have sought to substantiate through the above arguments that tensions between the traditional autonomy of sporting regulatory bodies and external legal intervention, particularly through rulings of the CJEU and the resultant juridification of sporting rules, has generated uncertainty and in the context of discrimination law renewed resistance – particularly in professional football.

As we have also demonstrated, similar tensions continue to exist in the context of the FIFA international transfer system, and these have now resulted in formal legal action by FIFPro through its competition complaint to the European Commission with regard to the FIFA transfer rules (see above). It can certainly be contended that the ways in which the FIFA transfer rules have been restrictively interpreted along with the implementation of home-grown player rules in both European and domestic competitions have created a position where players under contract, and to a significant extent out of contract, do not possess the freedom of movement that EU law requires.

FIFPro still favours resolution through collective agreement, and this accords with our own contentions that the best mechanism for resolving all of the problems identified above lies in the adoption of the methodology of reflexive legal regulation using the method of EU social law as a paradigm.[103] The advantage of reflexive law is that it enables a set of principles to be provided, which must be adhered to as a minimum, but the detailed implementation of a system of regulation is delegated to relevant bodies be they (as examples) national legislators or governing bodies of particular sports. A system of reflexive law can provide a

---

[101] Spanish Basketball clubs call for reform after EC Opinion. World Sport Law Report, April 2014. http://www.e-comlaw.com/world-sports-law-report/article_template.asp?ID=1644. Accessed 28 October 2015.

[102] Ibid.

[103] The origin of this term lies in legal sociology, and its essence is that intervention through external regulation should both reflect the norms established by those historically involved in the internal regulation of the activities in question and impose modifications to those norms which can be enforced by legal means. Our arguments are fully elaborated in Gardiner and Welch 2007. See also Branco-Martins R (2003) European Sport's First Collective Labour Agreement EFFC, p. 1. Available at http://www.worldcat.org/title/european-sports-first-collective-labour-agreement/oclc/717822012?referer=di&ht=edition. Accessed 28 September 2015; Gardiner et al. 2009; Downward et al. 2014, pp. 506–507 on the value of using social dialogue.

compromise between ensuring that particular standards are complied with and respecting the autonomy of those concerned with operating a particular system or activity and who understand the specificities involved.

The advantage of EU social law is that it requires the involvement of the relevant social partners. Under Article 154 TFEU, the European Commission must engage in dialogue with the social partners as to the content of any proposed Directive. Moreover, Article 155 TFEU permits the relevant social partners to conclude their own collective agreements, which, if the social partners so request, may then be given legal force through an EU Directive.

FIFPro has agreements with both FIFA and UEFA for social dialogue. This provides the basis for a collective agreement regulating football to be entered into in the future. Through such a collective agreement, or in its absence a directive derived from social dialogue, EU law could require national football associations to adopt a modified and more flexible version of the FIFA transfer rules which would be incorporated into their more detailed national rules reflecting national preferences.

One possible variation to the current FIFA rules would be, on the expiry of a contract's protected period or where the contract is terminated for sporting just cause, to permit a player to terminate his contract *during* a season if a player has negotiated a move to a club which is in a different league, and which is thus not in competition with his current club. The normal rules relating to such a player being cup-tied could continue to apply as far as domestic or European cup competitions are concerned. Such a change should also reduce the complexities involved in the implementation of Article 17 of the FIFA Rules, as demonstrated by the *Webster* case (see above). Another change to the current rules could be to place an absolute limit on the compensation that is to be paid to a club, where a player exercises a right to buy out his contract, to the actual financial loss incurred by that club.

Perspectives on national quotas are inevitably coloured by attitudes to the international mobility of labour in general. In the case of the authors, for example, we see football as a global sport with a global audience and would like to see footballers being able to play for any club in the world irrespective of their nationalities. This is of course subject to the need to protect young players from trafficking or exploitation, but again we are of the view that these sorts of abuses are more the product of immigration rules rather than being prevented by them. Our preferred solution to problems such as maintaining a competitive balance between clubs and encouraging local talent, would be through a combination of a cap on transfer fees and redistribution of income to assist clubs in establishing and maintaining effective local academies.

However, personal political perspectives notwithstanding, if something like the home grown player rule was the result of a collective agreement involving FIFPro, UEFA and FIFA, or at least EU legislation based on dialogue between these social partners, then this would put such a rule on a legitimate basis with the detail of the rule and the justifications for it being the product of rigorous bargaining replacing or underlying legislative processes.

This would reflect the appeal from sports bodies for legal certainty and greater precision of the regulatory environment. Most importantly, as any such rule would then have a clear legal foundation, it would pre-empt or at least limit the impact of the vicissitudes of litigation before the European Court.

4.12 Conclusions

In the wake of *Bosman* and the challenge to the transfer system threatened by the European Commission it appeared that out of contact players had an absolute right to negotiate a transfer to a new club irrespective of their nationality. The only restriction in the context of the latter being that non-EU players are subject to a country's immigration rules. Furthermore, players under contract had the right unilaterally to terminate their contracts once the protected period in a contract had expired.

So what of *the legacy of Bosman*? As things have turned out, the liberalisation promised by the FIFA international transfer rules have proved to be more smoke and mirrors than a reform of substance, and the enhancement of player mobility has consequently been ephemeral and illusory. On the other hand, the other change of note since *Bosman*, the imposition of player quotas through UEFA's home grown player rule, has clearly impacted on a players' abilities to move to a new club, even where a player is out of contract. In our view, this rule is in contravention of *Bosman*, and the purported justifications of it fail to meet the criteria of proportionality. The ongoing problem is that of legal uncertainty where ascertaining (or not) the correct legal position is subject to the vagaries of piecemeal litigation.

We agree with the recommendation, advocated in the EU Report on the home-grown players' rule, for what amounts to a moratorium for an agreed period of time such as three years, during which no reference would be made by the social partners or the European Commission to the CJEU (it is not possible, of course, to prevent litigation by an individual player). In light of the above arguments on reflexive legal regulation, we would also contend that the best use of this time-frame would be for FIFA, UEFA and FIFPro to use the EU Treaty provisions on EU social law to conclude a collective agreement, or agree the basis of a directive, which would create a reformed international transfer system which genuinely enhances player mobility and provides a genuine competitive balance between clubs. Ideally, such a system would not require the use of nationality quotas and thus would be free of any taint of discrimination.

References

Anderson C (2009) Player contracts: new FIFA regulations on the transfer of minors. World Sports Law Rep 7(11):3
Backe Madsen L, Johansson JM (2008) Den Forsvunne Diamanten (The Lost Diamond). Tiden Norsk Forlag, Norway
Boucher P (2007) Kicking off. Employment Law 18–19
Boyes S (2003) In the shadow of Bosman: the regulatory Penumbra of sport in the EU. Nottingham Law J 12(2):72
Boyes S (2005) Caught behind or following-on? Cricket, the European Union and the 'Bosman effect'. Entertainment Sports Law J 3(1):1–10
Caiger A, O'Leary J (1999) In my opinion: Footballer's contracts. Sports Law Bull 2(5):2
Conzelmann R (2008) Models of the promotion of home grown players for the protection of national representative teams. Int Sports Law J 3–4:26–30
Davies ACL (2008) One step forward, two steps back? The *viking* and *laval* cases in the ECJ. Ind Law J 37(2):126–148
Downward P, Parrish R, Pearson G, Semens A (2014) An assessment of the compatibility of UEFA's home grown player rule within article 45 TFEU. Eur Law Rev 39(4):493–514
Fort R, Quirk J (1995) Cross-subsidization, incentives, and outcomes in professional team sports leagues. J Econ Lit 33(3):1265–1299
Gardiner S, Welch R (2007) The contractual dynamics of team stability versus player mobility: who rules 'the beautiful game'? Entertainment Sports Law J 5:1
Gardiner S, Parrish R, Siekmann R (2009) EU, sport, law & policy regulation, re-regulation and representation. T.M.C. Asser Press, The Hague
Harris P (2002) Salary caps. Sport Law J 10(1):120
Hendrickx F (2003) The European non-EU player and the Kolpak case. Int Sports Law J 2003(2):12–15
Huxtable F (2008) Player quotas: the good, the bad and the illegal. Soccer Investor
Lanfranchi P, Taylor M (2001) Moving with the ball: the migration of professional Footballers. Berg, Oxford
Lynam I (2009) Player contracts: '6 + 5': analysis of whether the proposal is 'fit for purpose'. World Sports Law Rep 7:5
Majani F (2009) An excavation into the legal deficiencies of the FIFA 6 Plus 5 rule and the UEFA home-grown players rule in the eyes of the European Union law. Int Sports Law J 2009(1–2):19–25
Miettinen S, Parrish R (2007) Nationality discrimination in community law: an assessment of UEFA regulations governing player eligibility for European Club competitions (the home-grown player rule). Entertainment Sports Law J 5:2
Miettinen S, Parrish R (2008) The sporting exception in European union law. T.M.C. Asser Press, The Hague
Parrish R (2015) Article 17 of the FIFA regulations on the status and transfer of players: compatibility with EU law. Maastricht J Eur Comp Law 22(2):256–283
Pearson G (2015) Sporting justifications under EU free movement and competition law: the case of the football "transfer system". Eur Law J 21(2):220–238
Van den Bogaert S (2004) And another uppercut from the European court of justice to nationality requirements in sports regulations. Eur Law Rev 29(2):267–275
Van den Bogaert S (2005) Practical regulation of the mobility of sportsmen in the EU post Bosman. Kluwer Law International, The Hague
Weatherill S (2006) Anti-doping revisited—the demise of the rule of "purely sporting interest"? Eur Competition Law Rev 27(12):645–657
Weatherill S (2009) Article 82 EC and sporting 'conflict of interest': the judgment in Motoe. Int Sports Law J 2009(1–2):3–7
Williams R, Haffner A (2008) FIFA quotas ruled offside? New Law J 158:1017–1019
Winnie D (2014) Limiting non-EU players entering english football. World Sports Law Rep 12:10

Chapter 5
The FIFA Regulations on the Status and Transfer of Players: Transnational Law-Making in the Shadow of Bosman

Antoine Duval

Abstract This chapter retraces the emergence of a new FIFA transfer system in the wake of the *Bosman* ruling. It purposes to show the complexity and plurality of the legal game surrounding the regulation of global football. After the *Bosman* ruling many believed it was a comeback of the state in the self-regulatory sphere of sports regulation. Yet, the legal interaction between EU law and the private rules of FIFA regulating the transfers of football players across borders is more intricate. As we will show, the FIFA Regulations on the Status and Transfer of Players (FIFA RSTP) put in place after the *Bosman* ruling were negotiated under the shadow of an EU Competition law investigation triggered by the EU Commission. These negotiations involving a wide range of actors ended in 2001 with an agreement signed between the EU Commission and UEFA and FIFA. Thereafter, a reformed transnational system was put in place by FIFA to regulate international transfers of football players and enshrined in the FIFA RSTP. This legislative story illustrates the public-private nature of transnational law-making in the sporting world. Instead of perceiving these transnational rules as purely self-regulatory or purely subjected to national or European law, this case study demonstrates that we need to better grasp the fact that in reality both orientations are in tension and impossible to disentangle.

Keywords FIFA · FIFA RSTP · Bosman · Lex sportiva · Sports law · EU law · Legal pluralism · Court of arbitration for sport · Arbitration

A. Duval (✉)
European and International Sports Law, T.M.C. Asser Institute,
The Hague, The Netherlands
e-mail: a.duval@asser.nl

A. Duval and B. Van Rompuy (eds.), *The Legacy of* Bosman,
ASSER International Sports Law Series, DOI 10.1007/978-94-6265-120-3_5

Contents

5.1 Introduction

Law has entered an uncertain transnational age. The collection of 'new' legal concepts encapsulating this widely shared feeling is in itself revealing. Scholarly contributions looking at transnational law,[1] global law[2] or global administrative law[3] embody the perception of this shift in the academic field. In this context, sport has been often identified as a social field prone to impersonate these changes.[4] The emergence of a *lex sportiva*, a transnational law of sport produced by the Sports Governing Bodies (SGBs) and/or the Court of Arbitration for Sport (CAS), is being actively discussed in academic circles.[5] In this chapter, I argue that this new legal theoretical perspective must be taken into account when analysing the *Bosman*[6] ruling of the Court of Justice of the European Union (CJEU) and its

---

[1]For an overview on the concept, see Zumbansen 2012b, pp. 898–925. For a more programmatic approach to it, see Zumbansen 2012a, pp. 53–86. In the sporting context, see Latty 2007.

[2]For a recent contribution, see Walker 2014. For an early use of the concept, see Teubner 1997b. In the sporting context, see Casini 2010.

[3]For a general outline, see Kingsbury et al. 2005, pp. 15–62. In the sporting context, see Casini 2015.

[4]Gunther Teubner mentions "the emergence of a *lex sportiva internationalis*", see Teubner 1997a, p. 4. Similarly, François Rigaux had drawn previously on the example of sport (and more particularly football) to discuss the emergence of non-statal legal orders, see Rigaux 1989, pp. 283–291.

[5]For a comprehensive overview of the question, see Latty 2007. See also, amongst a growing literature: Casini 2011; Foster 2010; Duval 2013.

[6]Case C-415/93 *Union Royale Belge des Sociétés de Football Association and others v. Bosman and others*, ECLI:EU:C:1995:463.

aftermath. In other words, the legal and political effects of the *Bosman* ruling must be understood as a specific move in a complex transnational political and legal game. To illustrate this point, this chapter focuses on the evolution of the regulation of the transfer system in football after *Bosman.*

Football is an ideal social practice to study the impact of globalization[7] or 'glocalization'.[8] Indeed, the FIFA World Cup is one of the rare occurrences of a shared global social event cutting through the localisms and offering a common cultural reference point. In a global public sphere at its inception, football is probably one of the few already existing common grounds. Professional football is per se a cosmopolite activity: fans often support foreign teams or local teams composed of foreign players. Meanwhile, football has become a truly transnational industry, workers are constantly on the move and transfers are for a substantial share made on a transnational basis.[9] The world of football is coming close to a cosmopolitan utopia or nightmare, depending on one's point of view. This progressive dis-embedding of football from its national and local context prompts a number of social challenges. How, if any, should the solidarity between the different leagues and clubs be maintained? How to avoid that young players be trafficked from one country to another? How to ensure that foreign players joining leagues situated in countries where labour protections are weak get paid? How to balance the interests of rich European clubs and their fans with those of poor non-European clubs and their fans? All these questions (and many others) raise significant practical difficulties that national states have been unable or unwilling to tackle. FIFA has unilaterally ceased the opportunity to fill this global governance gap. Its legitimacy, however, is not, to say the least, uncontested, but it remains the only 'sheriff in town' providing a transnational set of rules and institutions. It is to some extent necessary to re-embed football's labour market and tackle the negative externalities resulting from its rapid transnationalization.[10]

Professional football players are usually contracted under a fixed-term contract. A player can leave his club only after paying (himself or usually his future club) compensation. This operation is commonly known as a transfer. As such there is nothing unusual in compensating your contractual partner when breaching a contractual agreement. Yet, three aspects are specific in the case of football players. First, the compensation owed is usually substantially higher than the one due in case of a contractual breach by a normal worker. Second, the player in breach

[7]For a sobering view on the impact of globalization on football, see Taylor 2006. But see contra Frick 2009; Eliasson 2009; Milanovic 2005; and Croci and Ammirante 1999.

[8]Giulianotti and Robertson 2004.

[9]In 2014, 13,090 international transfers were recorded by FIFA TMS, FIFA's subsidiary company tasked with the supervision of the transfer market. See International transfers break $4bn mark - FIFA TMS Annual Report. FIFA.com, 28 January 2015. http://www.fifa.com/governance/news/y=2015/m=1/news=international-transfers-break-4bn-mark-fifa-tms-annual-report-2512285.html. Accessed 1 October 2015.

[10]On the dialectic between dis-embedding and re-embedding of economic markets, see the classical work by Polanyi 2011.

moving to a club situated in another country risks a temporary ban from exercising his profession and his new club a temporary transfer ban issued by FIFA if no compensation is paid. Third, if the player moving is under 23, in general a training compensation will be due to the clubs having contributed to his training. These specific features are enshrined in the FIFA Regulations on the Status and Transfer of Players (RSTP) applying to all international transfers. As it will be discussed in greater detail below, these regulations constitute a parallel transnational labour law applicable exclusively to professional football players and their employers. The RSTP relies on a very potent private system of adjudication and enforcement guaranteeing its efficacy.

Paradoxically, the current shape taken by this system circumventing conventional national labour laws stems from the *Bosman* ruling of the CJEU. Many have sought to portray this intervention as a comeback of the state (and law) in football. This article will argue that this comeback has been at best light-touch. In slightly pompous academic terms, the *Bosman* case was rather an exercise in 'reflexive law'.[11] Thus, this article suggests that the Court's decision must be understood neither as deregulatory nor regulatory: it is rather counter-democratic.[12] Accordingly, I will show that the *Bosman* ruling was instrumental in providing the impetus for the negotiation of the current transfer system. The ruling offered a window of opportunity to launch a complex transnational law-making process involving a multiplicity of actors. This process, triggered by the European Commission, took place in the shadow of EU competition law and was concluded with a seemingly soft agreement that paved the way to the introduction of the FIFA RSTP as we know it. Arguably, it constitutes a remarkable example of the complexity and entanglement of the new transnational public/private law-making processes at play in a globalizing world.[13] The recent decision of FIFPro, the global football players' union, to launch a new complaint against the RSTP before the European Commission may re-start this legislative process.[14] In this context, a clearer understanding of the legal and political dynamics underlying the introduction of the RSTP in the first place will certainly be of great use to navigate the upcoming challenges for the various actors concerned.

The first part of this chapter will provide a review of the *Bosman* ruling in so far as it relates to the transfer system and study the doctrinal displacements, which have opened the way for the transnational legislative process leading up to the adoption of the FIFA RSTP (2.). The second part will be dedicated to this transnational legislative process and its legal foundations in the procedural finesses of EU

---

[11]In a nutshell, for Gunther Teubner 'law, is 'reflexive' insofar as the legal system itself 'stimulates' processes of social self-regulation.' Teubner 1983, p. 277.

[12]On the notion of counter-democracy, see Rosanvallon 2008.

[13]For a broader take on this entanglement, see Zumbansen and Callies 2010.

[14]On the new complaint, see FIFPro legal action against FIFA transfer system. FIFPro.com, 18 September 2015. http://www.fifpro.org/en/news/fifpro-takes-legal-action-against-fifa-transfer-system. Accessed 1 October 2015.

competition law enforcement (3.). Finally, the third part will scrutinize the practical outcome of this process. In other words, it will explore the fundamental institutional structures putting the RSTP to work (4.).

5.2 The Impact of *Bosman* on the Transfer System

Jean-Marc Bosman is a well-known figure in Europe and beyond. His name stands for the man that revolutionized football.[15] The decision of the CJEU bearing his name is particularly famous for having put an end to the nationality restrictions in football, and thus de facto Europeanising the beautiful game.[16] However, simultaneously, the CJEU also held that the transfer regulations of the Union of European Football Associations (UEFA), insofar as they concerned out-of-contract players, were contrary to EU free movement law. This is the main legal mark left by the CJEU on the transfer system in force in football. In a move that proved to be decisive for its future shape, Advocate General (AG) Lenz also considered the compatibility of the transfer system with EU competition law.

5.2.1 The Transfer System in the Bosman Ruling

Jean-Marc Bosman's story, in a nutshell,[17] was mainly about what is known in England as the retain system. At the end of his contract of employment with his former club, Royal club liégeois, Bosman was not considered free to sign for any club willing to employ him as any normal worker would. Instead an interested club had to pay a specific fee to Royal club liégeois in order to obtain the transfer certificate necessary to field the player. This duty to buyout the right to contract with an out-of-contract player was considered 'an obstacle to freedom of movement for workers'[18] by the CJEU. Even though the UEFA rules at that time stipulated that 'the business relationship between the two clubs is to exert no influence on the activity of the player, who is to be free to play for his new club',[19] the 'new club must still pay the fee in issue, under pain of penalties which may include its being struck off for debt, which prevents it just as effectively from signing up a

[15] As Stephen Weatherill puts it, the ruling 'changed everything'. See Weatherill 2010, pp. 480–487.

[16] See on this aspect the chapter by Simon Gardiner and Roger Welch in this volume. See also on the Europeanization of football: Niemann et al. 2011.

[17] On the broader social context of the case see the chapter by Borja Garcia in this volume.

[18] Case C-415/93 *Union Royale Belge des Sociétés de Football Association and others v. Bosman and others*, ECLI:EU:C:1995:463, para 100.

[19] Ibid., para 101.

player from a club in another Member State without paying that fee'.[20] In other words, even if the player was in principle allowed to play for his new club, the pending threat over a club's head in the form of a fine or ban was sufficient to significantly impact on a club's willingness to recruit a player, and thereby to restrict thc right to free movement of the latter. This reasoning is important, as it is transposable to in-contract players subjected to the compensation (and sanctions in case of non-payment) imposed by the FIFA RSTP. The Court found that, something not obvious at that time, a restrictive but non-discriminatory practice could be contrary to the free movement rights of workers.[21]

Yet, this was not the end of story. The CJEU also recognized that such a restriction could be justified if it was aimed at attaining a legitimate objective and a proportionate means to do so. In this context, it famously recognized that:

> In view of the considerable social importance of sporting activities and in particular football in the Community, the aims of maintaining a balance between clubs by preserving a certain degree of equality and uncertainty as to results and of encouraging the recruitment and training of young players must be accepted as legitimate.[22]

This is a crucial formula,[23] which opens a world of opportunities for FIFA or UEFA to justify their regulatory choices. Nevertheless, in the *Bosman* case, the rules submitted to the control of the CJEU were deemed disproportionate, and therefore held contrary to EU law. On the one hand, the transfer rules for out-of-contract players were judged inadequate to attain the objective of maintaining financial and competitive balance between football clubs, as they 'neither preclude the richest clubs from securing the services of the best players nor prevent the availability of financial resources from being a decisive factor in competitive sport, thus considerably altering the balance between clubs'.[24] On the other hand, the CJEU recognized that 'the prospect of receiving transfer, development or training fees is indeed likely to encourage football clubs to seek new talent and train young players'.[25] But, as the fees in question were 'by nature contingent and uncertain and are in any event unrelated to the actual cost borne by clubs of training both future professional players and those who will never play professionally', thus '[t]he prospect of receiving such fees cannot, [...], be either a decisive factor in encouraging recruitment and training of young players or an adequate means of financing such activities, particularly in the case of smaller clubs'.[26] In addition to

[20]Ibid.

[21]O'Keeffe and Osborne 1996.

[22]Case C-415/93 *Union Royale Belge des Sociétés de Football Association and others v. Bosman and others*, ECLI:EU:C:1995:463, para 106.

[23]The role of legal formulas in the jurisprudence of the CJEU is highlighted for example by Azoulai 2011.

[24]Case C-415/93 *Union Royale Belge des Sociétés de Football Association and others v. Bosman and others*, ECLI:EU:C:1995:463, para 107.

[25]Ibid., para 108.

[26]Ibid.

this, the CJEU considered, referring to the thoroughly argued opinion submitted by AG Lenz in the Bosman case,[27] that 'the same aims can be achieved at least as efficiently by other means which do not impede freedom of movement for workers'.[28]

Despite UEFA and FIFA's initial resistance,[29] the ruling was implemented and restrictions bearing on out-of-contract players were lifted. Still, it was uncertain whether the CJEU's decision would have further impact on the structure and functioning of the transfer system. In fact, this impact would later materialise due to a publicly often-overlooked element of the decision: the opinion of AG Lenz.

5.2.2 The Transfer System in the AG's Opinion

At the time of the *Bosman* ruling, sport was not a competence of the EU. Thus, a re-regulation of the football players' market by the EU, though theoretically conceivable under its internal market competences, was very unlikely. To implement the judgement, the Commission was also deprived of the possibility to use a classical infringement procedure under Article 260 TFEU, as it would have done in the case of a Member State restricting the free movement of EU citizens. Instead, the only tool available to directly, and decisively, influence the decisions of FIFA and UEFA, was (and still essentially is) EU competition law. In other words, the competition rules were 'lurking in the background'[30] of the *Bosman* ruling. In that regard the Commission could rely on the opinion of AG Lenz. The CJEU, for its part, decided to decline responding to the question of the national court on the compatibility of the transfer rules with Articles 101 and 102 TFEU (then 85 and 85 EC).[31]

The role of the AG at the CJEU is often underestimated. The draft judgment he delivers will not necessarily influence the Court immediately, but it is far from a meaningless message-in-a-bottle either. Instead, many of the doctrinal shifts taken by the CJEU over the years are grounded on arguments found in these opinions. This is especially true of the Bosman case. AG Lenz delivered a powerful opinion, which is acknowledged by the Court in its ruling.[32] Until today, this opinion pro-

---

[27]Opinion of Advocate General Lenz in Case C-415/93 *Union Royale Belge des Sociétés de Football Association and others v. Bosman and others*, ECLI:EU:C:1995:293, para 226.

[28]Case C-415/93 *Union Royale Belge des Sociétés de Football Association and others v. Bosman and others*, ECLI:EU:C:1995:463, para 109.

[29]For a comprehensive summary of the post-Bosman political and legal "battle" over the transfer system, see Irving 2002.

[30]Weatherill 2003, p. 67.

[31]Case C-415/93 *Union Royale Belge des Sociétés de Football Association and others v. Bosman and others*, ECLI:EU:C:1995:463, para 138.

[32]The *Bosman* ruling crucially refers to the Opinion of the Advocate General Lenz at *Bosman*, para 99 and para 110 of the judgment.

vides the core of the analytical frame used for the application of EU law to sport. In one aspect it was even going further than the decision itself: it considered the application of EU competition law to the transfer system. AG Lenz defined football clubs as undertakings and the football federations as associations of undertakings (national federations) or associations of associations of undertakings (UEFA and FIFA).[33] The rules imposed by UEFA or the national federations were labelled decisions of associations of undertakings or agreements between undertakings (the clubs).[34] He concluded that the transfer rules concerned were having a substantial effect on trade between the Member States.[35] His longest-lasting achievement was to provide a cognitively convincing case that these rules were restricting competition. He was persuaded that 'those rules replace the normal system of supply and demand by a uniform machinery which leads to the existing competition situation being preserved and the clubs being deprived of the possibility of making use of the chances, with respect to the engagement of players, which would be available to them under normal competitive conditions'.[36] This is so, because '[i]f the obligation to pay transfer fees did not exist, a player could transfer freely after the expiry of his contract and choose the club which offered him the best terms'.[37] In other words, as 'a transfer takes place only if a transfer fee is paid, the tendency to maintain the existing competition situation is inherent in the system'.[38] Therefore, the 'competition which is restricted by those rules is that between the clubs'.[39] This analytical blueprint proved extremely influential in the later challenge by the Commission of the FIFA RSTP on the basis of EU competition law.

AG Lenz did not stop here. He also laid the ground to the justificatory framework that he transposed analogically from the free movement realm to the EU competition law assessment. He recognized that '[i]f a rule which at first sight appears to contain a restriction of competition is necessary in order to make that competition possible in the first place, it must indeed be assumed that such a rule does not infringe Article [101(1)]'.[40] However, he added that 'only restrictions of competition which are indispensable for attaining the legitimate objectives pursued by them do not fall within Article [101(1)]'.[41] He was suggesting introducing a form of 'European rule of reason'[42] into the structure of Article 101 TFEU, an

[33]Opinion of Advocate General Lenz in Case C-415/93 *Union Royale Belge des Sociétés de Football Association and others v. Bosman and others*, ECLI:EU:C:1995:293, para 255–256.

[34]Ibid., para 258–259.

[35]Ibid., para 260.

[36]Ibid., para 262.

[37]Ibid.

[38]Ibid.

[39]Ibid., para 263.

[40]Ibid., para 265.

[41]Ibid., para 269.

[42]Ibid., paras 266–269. Coining the notion of 'European Rule of Reason', see Monti 2002, p. 1086.

introduction that would later come true in *Wouters*[43] and would explicitly be endorsed in the sporting context in *Meca-Medina.*[44] AG Lenz's opinion has had far-reaching consequences for the world of football. It left its fingerprints on the solution adopted in the *Bosman* case and inspired the European Commission to pro-actively use EU competition law as a source of political and legal leverage to obtain a reform of the FIFA RSTP.

5.3 Transnational Law-Making in the Shadow of EU Competition Law: The 2001 Agreement Between UEFA, FIFA and the Commission

Bosman was not the end, but rather the beginning of a new era in the history of the regulation of transfers in international football.[45] In the immediate aftermath of the ruling, the Commission was sanguine about its intentions to enforce the decision. Federations were to 'take immediate action to amend the existing transfer system and to stop discriminating on the grounds of nationality'.[46] The Commission quickly hit the wall of the federations' political power,[47] however, and the transfer system reform lingered for years. Instead a long and complex negotiated process to impose a new international transfer system followed, a process triggered by the Commission's decision to decisively challenge FIFA's rules under EU competition law. This process resulted in the 2001 agreement between UEFA, FIFA and the Commission, defining key principles applicable to the transfer system.

5.3.1 The Commission's Crusade Against FIFA's RSTP

In 1997 FIFA adopted a new RSTP and notified it to the Commission to obtain its green light as regard its compatibility with EU competition law.[48] The new regulations

43 Case C-309/99 *J. C. J. Wouters, J. W. Savelbergh and Price Waterhouse Belastingadviseurs BV v Algemene Raad van de Nederlandse Orde van Advocaten*, ECLI:EU:C:2002:98.

44 Case C-519/04 P *David Meca-Medina and Igor Majcen v. Commission*, ECLI:EU:C:2006:492.

45 Highlighting this 'Pandora's box' effect of *Bosman*, see Stephen Weatherill's chapter in this volume.

46 Commission Press Release, IP/95/1411 First reaction by Commissioners Padraig Flynn and Karel van Miert. http://europa.eu/rapid/press-release_IP-95-1411_en.htm. Accessed 25 August 2015. See also Van Miert 1996.

47 The then commission in charge of the competition investigation, Karel Van Miert, gave a vivid and bitter account of his encounter with the sporting world in his memoirs on his years at the European Commission. See Van Miert 2000, pp. 164–165.

48 For a succinct history of FIFA's transfer regulations, see De Weger 2008, pp. 3–6. On the 1997 RSTP, see Zimmerman 2015, pp. 49–51.

abolished transfer fees for out-of-contract players, but the Commission was of the opinion that the transfer fees for in-contract players were also restricting competition. Henceforth, exactly three years after the *Bosman* ruling, it sent a statement of objections to FIFA on 15 December 1998. Under Article 14(3) of Regulation 17/62, which defined the procedure applicable at that time in competition proceedings, the statement of objections was officially signalling the intention to adopt a prohibition decision finding an infringement of EU competition law.

The statement remains unpublished and unavailable to the public. Nevertheless, in its preliminary guidelines on the application of the competition rules to sport,[49] the Commission referred to the grounds raised to challenge FIFA's transfer regulations. It pointed out that with the new FIFA regulations, '[t]he clubs have agreed to refrain from hiring their players freely (in other words without having to pay fees) and have together decided who is responsible for fixing and paying the fee'.[50] Thus, the clubs 'have […] given up the freedom to hire players by transfer without a fee or in return for a fee that is calculated objectively on the basis of the costs incurred by the old club in training/promoting the players'.[51] They 'have also abandoned the possibility of hiring players who unilaterally terminate their contract'.[52] The Commission concluded that '[t]he fact that the above rules apply to all international transfers of players within the European Union […], and that the fees are extremely high, and indeed exorbitant in the case of the best players, would appear sufficient to demonstrate that their purpose and effect is significantly to restrict and/or distort competition on the market in professional football matches staged by the first-division clubs in the Community and the EEA'.[53] Furthermore, as far as free movement rights are concerned, the Commission held that 'the ban on transfers following a unilateral termination of a contract by a player in cases where the player has fulfilled all obligations under national employment law, as well as the standard employment contract between players and clubs […] represent a violation of Article [45 TFEU] because such measures can restrict the right of free movement of young athletes'.[54] The avowed objective of the Commission in opening this investigation was 'for FIFA to withdraw its ban on the transfer of players who have unilaterally terminated their contract, provided that they have fulfilled their contractual obligations'.[55]

[49]European Commission, Preliminary guidelines on the application of the competition rules to sport, O/99/59. See also the summary of the statement of objections included in Commission Decision of 28 May 2002, Affaire IV/36 583-SETCA-FGTB/FIFA (the rejection decision of the complaint submitted by the Belgium unions SETCA and FGTB) paras 27–35. http://ec.europa.eu/competition/antitrust/cases/dec_docs/36583/36583_54_3.pdf. Accessed 25 August 2015.

[50]European Commission, Preliminary guidelines on the application of the competition rules to sport, O/99/59, para 30.

[51]Ibid.

[52]Ibid.

[53]Ibid.

[54]Ibid.

[55]Ibid.

With this statement of objection, the Commission was clearly walking into the footprints of AG Lenz. The reasoning used, as regards the economic effect of the transfer system and its restrictive effect on competition, is similar to the one developed in the opinion under *Bosman*, though it extends beyond out-of-contract players. The CJEU itself came very close of putting the FIFA RSTP 1997 to the EU law test in the *Balog*[56] case, but it was removed from the Court's registrar after a last-minute amicable settlement between FIFA and the player.[57] The pressure was slowly mounting on FIFA to change its transfer system, but this did not lead to the rules being declared contrary to EU competition law. Instead of a vertical and hierarchical pattern of law enforcement, as we know it from a classical positivist model of law, what happened was a horizontal, network-like and complex instance of negotiation to define (and design) a new FIFA RSTP that would be deemed compatible with the requirements imposed by EU competition law. This is a remarkable example of the shift of legal practice from a vertical to a horizontal paradigm.[58]

5.3.2 Legislating in the Shadow of EU Competition Law: Towards the 2001 Agreement

One specific characteristic of EU competition law is that it does not fit well the classical top-down syllogistic paradigm of law enforcement. Instead, the Commission when enforcing EU competition law has often recourse to informal settlements or commitment decisions.[59] In this context, the meaning of the law and its practical impact in a particular case is negotiated with the alleged wrongdoer. It is not the intention of this article to engage in an in depth review of this enforcement practice. The 2001 agreement between FIFA, UEFA and the Commission is just an early illustration of this shift. I argue that when the Commission uses EU competition law to police emerging transnational private regulations, it will most likely engage in a new form of transnational law-making process in the shadow of the EU competition law.[60]

[56]Case C-264/98 *Balog* OJ C 278 [1998], p. 28. Removal from the register on 16 June 2001: OJ C 173, p. 32.

[57]Agreement reached between FIFA and Tibor Balog on 28 March 2001. FIFA.com, 28 March 2001. http://www.fifa.com/about-fifa/news/y=2001/m=3/news=agreement-reached-between-fifa-and-tibor-balog-march-2001-77073.html. Accessed 24 August 2015.

[58]For a theoretical account of this shift, see Ost and Van de Kerchove 2002. For his part, Antoine Garapon has coined this shift a move from the jurisdictional paradigm to a relational paradigm in law enforcement, see Garapon 2013, pp. 39–49.

[59]On the (exponential) use of settlements in EU competition law enforcement see (amongst a fastly growing literature): Wills 2006; Mehta and Tierno Centella 2008; Vallery 2008; Ibañez Colomo 2013; Dunne 2014.

[60]This view resonates, not only linguistically, with the political science framework advanced by Arnout Geeraert in his chapter included in this book.

5.3.3 The Negotiation

As far as the investigation of FIFA's transfer system is concerned, the negotiation phase started with a bang. It is the decision of Mario Monti, then EU Commissioner responsible for competition, to stop playing cat and mouse with FIFA, and his threat of adopting a negative decision that could involve a hefty fine, that a new type of legislative process was set in motion.[61] It was, indeed, the 'ultimate weapon'[62] used to push FIFA to change its transfer rules.

The words employed by Commission officials to describe the ensuing process are informative to capture its nature. Monti, in an early speech after making his threat, spoke of the fact that 'FIFA, UEFA and FIFPRO are currently preparing new transfer rules, and proposals of a very general character have been discussed with them at an informal level'.[63] He clearly indicated that the Commission would 'collaborate with FIFA in the search for a new system which is compatible with the rules of the Treaty'.[64] Another Commissioner Ms. Reding in charge of the education and culture portfolio at that time, talked of a 'fructuous dialogue', 'cooperation', and of the readiness of the European Commission to condone a new transfer system compatible with EU law.[65] Later on, the same Commissioner, in a speech

---

[61]In his words: "In the absence of any structured and clear proposals from FIFA for new regulations bringing the transfer rules into line with Article [101], a negative decision will be prepared". Speech by Mario Monti of 17 April 2000, SPEECH/00/152 on Sport and Competition. http://europa.eu/rapid/press-release_SPEECH-00-152_en.htm. Accessed 24 August 2015.

[62]"Après une période raisonnable d'attente et en l'absence de propositions concrètes de la FIFA, les services de la Commission ont continué d'instruire l'affaire en vue de faire adopter par la Commission une décision d'interdiction des dispositions réglementaires de la FIFA contestées. Cependant, cette voie était vue comme l'arme ultime de la Commission pour amener la FIFA à amender son règlement de 1997 et ses circulaires interprétatives de façon à les rendre compatibles avec le droit communautaire." See the summary of the statement of objections included in Commission Decision of 28 May 2002, Affaire IV/36 583-SETCA-FGTB/FIFA (the rejection decision of the complaint submitted by the Belgium unions SETCA and FGTB) para 38.

[63]Speech by Mario Monti of 17 April 2000, SPEECH/00/152 on Sport and Competition. http://europa.eu/rapid/press-release_SPEECH-00-152_en.htm. Accessed 24 August 2015.

[64]Ibid.

[65]"La Commission européenne veut le partenariat entre la Communauté européenne et le mouvement sportif. Mais pour qu'un dialogue fructueux soit possible, il faut que les deux parties y soient ouverts. Le cas des règles de transfert de la FIFA actuellement sous instruction en est un bon exemple. Comme vous le savez, la Commission européenne est prête à homologuer un nouveau système de transferts respectueux tant de la spécificité du sport (et notamment de l'équilibre compétitif entre les clubs) que du respect du droit communautaire. Il me semble évident que le système existant ne satisfait ni l'un ni l'autre. Dans ces circonstances, c'est à vous de faire le prochain pas dans la voie de la coopération que je souhaite suivre: c'est à vous d'être les innovateurs. Je peux vous assurer que la Commission européenne est prête à prendre en compte toute proposition constructive. Personne, à la Commission européenne, ne souhaite recourir à des décisions d'interdiction. Mais celles-ci deviendraient inévitables en l'absence d'alternatives acceptables et viables." Speech by Viviane Reding of 30 June 2000 at the UEFA Congress, SPEECH/00/250 Renforcer le dialogue entre la Commission européenne et le monde du sport pour renforcer la fonction sociale du sport. http://europa.eu/rapid/press-release_SPEECH-00-250_fr.htm. Accessed 24 August 2015.

to the European Parliament, indicated that the Commission 'has patiently waited for the FIFA to present alternatives to the present system, so that a mutually satisfactory and equitable solution can be reached by consensus'.[66] Since when is EU competition law applied by consensus? Nevertheless, the investigation of the Commission into the FIFA RSTP is recurrently qualified as an instance of 'dialogue with the world of football'.[67]

This lead to the creation of a joint FIFA/UEFA Task Force devising a reform proposal, which was submitted to the European Commission in October 2000.[68] FIFPro, however, did not endorse this proposal. In response, the Commission emphasized that it was 'hopeful that a satisfactory solution can be found through this dialogue that has been set up recently with FIFA and the other interested parties in a constructive spirit and announced that it would continue the dialogue with the interested parties with a view to reaching a solution as soon as possible'.[69] The negotiations spilled over into early 2001. At that point, the Commission was hopeful 'that a compromise to the benefit of clubs, players and fans could be found soon provided that the football world demonstrates common sense and political will'.[70] Again, taking the words of the Commission at face value, it was in 'search for a compromise'.[71] One does not come closer to admitting that the enforcement of EU competition law is subject to a complex multi-stakeholder (political) negotiation with no real veto player in sight.[72] On 14 February 2001, the Commissioners Monti, Reding and Diamantopoulou and the Presidents of FIFA and of UEFA 'firmly cemented an agreement on a significant number of issues related to the FIFA rules on the international transfers of footballers'.[73] Nevertheless, 'technical discussions' were still on-going with FIFA and UEFA.[74] It was not before early

[66]Statement by Viviane Reding to the European Parliament of 7 September 2000, SPEECH/00/290 Commission's investigation into FIFA's transfer rules. http://europa.eu/rapid/press-release_SPEECH-00-290_en.htm. Accessed 24 August 2015.

[67]Ibid., 'Both Mario Monti and myself have engaged ourselves in dialogue with the world of football'.

[68]See Parrish 2003, pp. 142–143.

[69]Commission Press Release of 6 December 2000, IP/00/1417 Football transfers: Commission underlines the prospect of further progress. http://europa.eu/rapid/press-release_IP-00-1417_en.htm. Accessed 25 August 2015.

[70]Commission Press Release of 24 January 2001, MEMO/01/19 Spokesperson's statement on football transfers discussions. http://europa.eu/rapid/press-release_MEMO-01-19_en.htm. Accessed 25 August 2015.

[71]Ibid.

[72]Meier and García 2013.

[73]Commission Press Release of 14 February 2001, IP/01/209 Joint statement by Commissioners Monti, Reding and Diamantopoulou and Presidents of FIFA Blatter and of UEFA Johansson. http://europa.eu/rapid/press-release_IP-01-209_en.htm. Accessed 25 August 2015.

[74]Commission Press Release of 16 February 2001, IP/01/225 Outcome of technical discussion with FIFA/UEFA on Transfer systems. http://europa.eu/rapid/press-release_IP-01-225_en.htm. Accessed 25 August 2015.

March 2001 that they 'finalised their discussions on revised FIFA Regulations on international football transfers'.[75]

As this collage of the official press releases and communications from the side of the Commission shows, one could witness an instance of legislative, political, or diplomatic, negotiations between the football world and the EU institutions.[76] The 2001 agreement is a particular instance of a complex post-national rulemaking involving private and public, national and transnational organisations and challenging the perception of a vertical, top-down relationship between the EU, FIFA and UEFA. The scenario leading up to the adoption of the FIFA RSTP fits a legal pluralist narrative of the relationship between the EU law and the private transnational rules of FIFA (also known as *lex fifa*[77]), rather than a classic top-down hierarchical primacy of EU law, as it is often presented.

5.3.4 The Agreement

The final agreement as such was formalised through an exchange of letters between FIFA President Blatter and the EU Commissioner for competition Monti.[78] Its legally binding nature remains vague and subject to speculation.[79] But, in any case, the agreement would probably not bind the CJEU and the FIFA RSTP remains challengeable in front of national courts on the basis of EU law.[80] The judicial road is a difficult one, however, it is both long and costly, and arguably, after Bosman's sad precedent,[81] not an attractive option for a player hoping to

[75]Commission Press Release of 5 March 2001, IP/01/314 Outcome of discussions between the Commission and FIFA/UEFA on FIFA Regulations on international football transfers. http://europa.eu/rapid/press-release_IP-01-314_en.htm. Accessed 25 August 2015.

[76]FIFA also pushed strongly for a political involvement of the Member States, see 'FIFA reiterates call for special status for sport. FIFA.com, 6 December 2000. http://www.fifa.com/about-fifa/news/y=2000/m=12/news=fifa-reiterates-call-for-special-status-for-sport-75581.html. Accessed 24 August 2015. This pressure resulted in the so-called 'Nice Declaration': Conclusions of the Presidency of the European Council of 7–9 December 2000 (Nice), Annex IV – Declaration on the specific characteristics of sport and its social function in Europe, of which account should be taken in implementing common policies.

[77]Franck Latty was the first to my knowledge to make use of the concept of *lex FIFA*, see Latty 2011.

[78]Commission Press Release of 5 March 2001, IP/01/314 Outcome of discussions between the Commission and FIFA/UEFA on FIFA Regulations on international football transfers. http://europa.eu/rapid/press-release_IP-01-314_en.htm. Accessed 25 August 2015.

[79]On this question, see Egger and Stix-Hackl 2002, pp. 90–91.

[80]Ibid., p. 91.

[81]Van den Bogaert 2015.

stay active in the football world.[82] The agreement had the merit, in the eyes of FIFA and UEFA, to de facto foreclose any challenge of the FIFA transfer system for at least the years following its conclusion. In the nearly 15 years since then, no serious challenge to the FIFA RSTP has been launched, in spite of FIFPro's continuous critical stance to it. One year after the conclusion of the agreement, the Commission decided to close the case it had opened against the FIFA RSTP, citing the agreement as a game-changer justifying that the RSTP be now deemed in compliance with the competition rules.[83]

The agreement as such is based on a number of principles that must be 'fully reflected in the FIFA Regulations to be amended'.[84] The principles in question are the following:

- in the case of players aged under 23, a system of training compensation should be in place to encourage and reward the training effort of clubs, in particular small clubs;
- creation of solidarity mechanisms that would redistribute a significant proportion of income to clubs involved in the training and education of a player, including amateur clubs;
- international transfer of players aged under 18 to be allowed subject to agreed conditions; the football authorities will establish and enforce a code of conduct to guarantee the sporting, training and academic education to be provided:
- creation of one transfer period per season, and a further limited mid-season window, with a limit of one transfer per player per season;
- minimum and maximum duration of contracts of respectively 1 and 5 years;
- contracts to be protected for a period of 3 years up to 28; 2 years thereafter;
- the system of sanctions to be introduced should preserve the regularity and proper functioning of sporting competition so that unilateral breaches of contract are only possible at the end of a season;
- financial compensation can be paid if a contract is breached unilaterally whether by the player or the club;
- proportionate sporting sanctions to be applied to players, clubs or agents in the case of unilateral breaches of contract without just cause, in the protected period;

[82]FIFPro which is currently actively looking for a player willing to challenge the current FIFA RSTP has not found anyone ready to take this risk. See Duff, FIFA's New Headache: Plot to End 125-Year-Old Transfer Rules. Bloomberg, 21 August 2015. http://www.bloomberg.com/news/articles/2015-08-21/fifa-s-new-headache-plot-to-end-125-year-old-transfer-rules. Accessed 23 August 2015.

[83]The summary of the statement of objections included in Commission Decision of 28 May 2002, Affaire IV/36 583-SETCA-FGTB/FIFA (the rejection decision of the complaint submitted by the Belgium unions SETCA and FGTB), para 51: 'Les nouvelles règles adoptées par le Comité exécutif de la FIFA, le 5 juillet 2001, semblent être en mesure de donner une réponse satisfaisante au grief que vous avez formulé portant sur le point 2 de la circulaire n° 616 de la FIFA du 4 juin 1997'.

[84]Commission Press Release of 5 March 2001, IP/01/314 Outcome of discussions between the Commission and FIFA/UEFA on FIFA Regulations on international football transfers. http://europa.eu/rapid/press-release_IP-01-314_en.htm. Accessed 25 August 2015.

- creation of an effective, quick and objective arbitration body with members chosen in equal numbers by players and clubs and with an independent chairman;
- arbitration is voluntary and does not prevent recourse to national courts.

This agreement is the tangible outcome of the 'football transfers talks'[85] as the then Commission President Prodi would qualify what was still formally a Commission investigation based on its duty to enforce EU competition law. It was not directly endorsed by FIFPro, which started legal proceedings in a Belgium Court to challenge the legality of the new FIFA rules. Yet, after FIFA offered to associate FIFPro in the implementation of the new RSTP, the players' union abandoned its confrontational stance in order to move to a more accommodating position.[86] Through its decisive competence to open and close an EU competition law investigation, the Commission created a new political space to police and polish the transnational private rules applicable to sport.[87] The Commission can force different parties to come to the table, as well as it can decide when the negotiation game needs to stop. Before the procedural reforms introduced by Regulation 2003/1 this was mainly done through informal settlements, as exemplified by the agreement with FIFA and UEFA.[88] Nowadays, such a settlement would be most likely procedurally more burdensome, as a formal commitment procedure has been introduced.[89] Nevertheless, it would potentially also be possible to open informal legislative negotiations before opening an investigation and entering into the formalized bout of the procedure. The way competition law operate in the football context is not without recalling the idea of a regulatory competition law.[90] Though, in the present context, the Commission plays a rather passive regulatory role and its intervention takes a more reflexive turn. Since the early 2000, the Commission has been weary to reproduce its legislative adventure with the FIFA RSTP in other sporting contexts. As some commentators have pointed out, it may have felt politically bruised from this episode.[91] This long retreat might be about

[85]Commission Press Release of 6 March 2001, IP/01/320 Commission President Prodi welcomes outcome of football transfers talks. http://europa.eu/rapid/press-release_IP-01-320_en.htm. Accessed 25 August 2015.

[86]On FIFPro's position and internal dissensions during (and after) the negotiations, see Dabscheck 2004 and Dabscheck 2006.

[87]This is also recognized by political scientists, see for example the contribution by Arnout Geeraert in this book.

[88]Idot 1999.

[89]See Council Regulation (EC) of 16 December 2002, No 1/2003 on the implementation of the rules on competition laid down in Articles 81 and 82 of the Treaty [2003] OJ L 1/1, Article 9.

[90]See Ibáñez Colomo 2010 and Dunne 2014.

[91]In other words: 'In the sports sector, the Commission has been busier than the Court since *Bosman* and there is here a discernible feel that the Commission intends to draw a line under its adventures, and, moreover, with a sigh of relief. Neither Mr Monti nor Ms Reding, Commissioners for Competition and Culture respectively, have gathered much popular approval for their engagement with the sports sector and, at times of potentially radical institutional change within the Union's architecture, it would be unrealistic to suppose that such perceptions do not colour choice of priorities.' See Weatherill 2003, p. 60.

to end. The acute governance crisis faced by the SGBs, as well as a renewed interest in implicating the Commission, through its competition law enforcement arm, to challenge and check the transnational rules of various sports, will most likely lead to a replay of similar dynamics of transnational law-making in the field of sport in the coming years.[92]

The impact of this agreement can only be understood by accounting for the transnational legal context in which the *lex sportiva* (or in the present case *lex FIFA*) operates. Thus, it has served as a blueprint for the adoption of the highly successful—in terms of its practical impact on the football labour market—FIFA RSTP.

5.4 The FIFA RSTP's Successful Autonomous Afterlife

The first fully-fledged FIFA RSTP[93] came to life shortly before *Bosman*, in 1994, as FIFA promoted a centralization of the management and regulation of international transfers in football.[94] However, in its current form the RSTP's structure was decisively influenced by the 2001 Agreement with the Commission. The ambition of this part is not to offer a description of the content of the rules applying to international transfers. Instead, it aims at describing how the autonomous system operates institutionally. In theoretical terms, the focus will be on the operation of the Hartian secondary rules of the RSTP. The practical success of the RSTP is undeniable. The FIFA Dispute Resolution Chamber (DRC) and Player Status Committee (PSC) are dealing with a mounting number of cases.[95] In fact, these bodies, on the basis of the RSTP, decide an important share of the disputes arising out of international transfers and contracts in football.[96] The implementation of these decisions is largely dependent on a close-knit network of private power connecting FIFA with the national federations. Overall, the RSTP's institutional system functions very much as an autonomous, post-national, system of dispute resolution for transnational labour conflicts in football.

[92]In favour of such a revival, see Van Rompuy 2015.

[93]In this section, if not otherwise indicated we refer to the 2015 version of the FIFA RSTP.

[94]De Weger 2008, p. 3.

[95]The FIFA Annual Reports recorded more than 1600 claims lodged in front of the PSC and DRC in 2013, 2014 and 2015.

[96]This is has been confirmed to us by FIFPro's legal counsel Will Van Megen (email on file with the author). However, Will Van Megen also pointed out that in certain countries, where trustworthy national dispute resolution bodies are in place, litigants prioritize them (citing Germany, France, England, Denmark, Italy and the Netherlands).

5.4.1 The Autonomous Judicial System

Three institutions play a crucial role in the judicial system giving flesh to the FIFA RSTP: the DRC, the PSC and the Court of Arbitration for Sport (CAS). The former two are internal to FIFA's structure. As any other members of a FIFA Committee, the members of the PSC are designated by the FIFA Executive Committee based on the procedure set out in Article 34.3 of the FIFA Statutes. Both the president and the vice-president of the PSC are members of the FIFA Executive Committee.[97] The DRC, however, is composed in a paritary fashion. As provided by Article 4 of the Rules Governing the Procedures of the Players' Status Committee and the Dispute Resolution Chamber, the 24 members of the DRC are 'made up of an equal number of player and club representatives' and 'shall be appointed by the FIFA Executive Committee on the proposal of the players' associations and the clubs or leagues'.[98]

The PSC is competent to deal with employment disputes involving a coach and an association or a club, disputes between clubs that do not fall in the DRC's competence, and disputes linked to the issuing of an International Transfer Certificate (ITC).[99] The DRC, for its part, deals with disputes between clubs and players in relation to the maintenance of contractual stability where there has been an ITC-request, employment-related disputes between a club and a player of an international dimension and disputes relating to training compensation and the solidarity mechanism.[100] Both the PSC and the DRC adjudicate in the presence of at least three members unless the case is of such a simple nature that it can be dealt with by a single-judge.[101] The single judge of the PSC is the Chairman of the PSC or a person appointed by him or her, while the members of the DRC designate amongst themselves one single judge of the DRC for the players and one for the clubs. If the single judge of the DRC is faced with a case involving 'fundamental issues', he or she must refer it to the chamber. The decisions of the DRC and the PSC may be appealed to the CAS provided the procedural delay to do so is respected.[102]

The 2001 agreement was clear: 'arbitration is voluntary and does not prevent recourse to national courts'. The purely voluntary nature of arbitration and the

[97]The current composition of the PSC. http://www.fifa.com/aboutfifa/organisation/bodies/standingcommittees/committee=1882032.html. Accessed 23 August 2015.

[98]The current composition of the DRC. http://www.fifa.com/about-fifa/committees/committee=1889876/index.html. Accessed 23 August 2015.

[99]The scope of jurisdiction of the FIFA PSC is provided in Article 23.1. FIFA RSTP read in conjunction with Articles 22 and 24 FIFA RSTP.

[100]The scope of jurisdiction of the FIFA DRC is provided in Article 24.1. FIFA RSTP read in conjunction with Articles 22 FIFA RSTP.

[101]The competence of the single judge is set out in details at Article 23.4. FIFA RSTP for the PSC and Article 24.2 FIFA RSTP for the DRC.

[102]See Articles 23.4 and 24.2 FIFA RSTP in conjunction with Article 67 FIFA Statutes.

creation of an option to have recourse to national courts was one of the *sine qua non* demands of the Commission during the 2001 negotiations. In fact, Article 22 FIFA RSTP stipulates that FIFA is competent to hear claims based on the RSTP, '[w]ithout prejudice to the right of any player or club to seek redress before a civil court for employment-related disputes'. Yet, in practice this seems to be a mere façade, as very few disputes arising out of international transfers or out of international football players' contract are dealt with by national courts.[103] There are three main reasons for this. First, players and clubs are prone to refer their disputes to the DRC or the PSC as both are theoretically adjudicating at a relatively swift pace[104] and cheap price.[105] Moreover, in a transnational context, the DRC and the PSC also have the advantage of circumventing the risk (and the fear) of a biased, potentially xenophobic national court, which would be inclined to rule against the foreign club or player. Thus, the FIFA DRC is often used as a vehicle for players claiming their outstanding wages against their former clubs.[106] Finally, and more importantly, the jurisdiction of the DRC and the (Single Judge of the) PSC is often triggered by the request for an ITC. The reception of an ITC is a necessary requirement for any football player to register with a new club located in a different national football association.[107] In case there is a pending contractual dispute between the player and his former club, the former association must refuse to provide the ITC and the player and/or his new club will have to turn to the PSC to

[103]Zimmerman 2015, p. 77.

[104]Article 25.1 FIFA RSTP: 'As a rule, the single judge and the DRC judge shall adjudicate within 30 days of receipt of a valid request and the Players' Status Committee or the Dispute Resolution Chamber shall adjudicate within 60 days.' This rule is, however, not truly respected in practice. DRC cases have in recent years taken up to two or three years to be resolved. Thus, this advantage on paper should be relativized.

[105]Article 25.2 FIFA RSTP: 'The maximum cost of proceedings before the Players' Status Committee, including the single judge, as well as before the DRC, including the DRC judge, in relation to disputes regarding training compensation and the solidarity mechanism shall be set at CHF 25,000 and shall normally be paid by the unsuccessful party. The allocation of costs shall be explained in the decision. Proceedings before the DRC and the DRC judge relating to disputes between clubs and players in relation to the maintenance of contractual stability as well as employment-related disputes between a club and a player of an international dimension are free of charge.'

[106]Zimmerman 2015, pp. 89–94.

[107]Article 9.1 FIFA RSTP: 'Players registered at one association may only be registered at a new association once the latter has received an International Transfer Certificate (hereinafter: ITC) from the former association. The ITC shall be issued free of charge without any conditions or time limit. Any provisions to the contrary shall be null and void. The association issuing the ITC shall lodge a copy with FIFA. The administrative procedures for issuing the ITC are contained in Annexe 3, Article 8, and Annexe 3a of these regulations.'

obtain a provisory registration.[108] Henceforth, if no proceedings have been initiated at the national level, the DRC will be automatically seized to adjudicate the contractual dispute.[109] The parties can always reject this, and insist that a national judge decides the labour dispute, but this will lead to competing jurisdictions with an uncertain and costly parallel process in front of both the DRC and the national courts.[110] Moreover, if a party turns first to the national courts, its case will be refused by the DRC to avoid any temptation of forum shopping.[111] Due to these factors, an important share of the transnational labour disputes arising out of the football employment field are concentrated in the hands of FIFA's dispute resolution bodies. Even if *de jure* players and clubs have the possibility to bring their disputes in front of national courts,[112] de facto their careers are too short to be wasted on intricate and uncertain legal battles. Instead, they prefer to turn massively to the DRC and the PSC to deal with these matters. The success of this private ordering is reminiscent of Lisa Bernstein's famous study of private dispute resolution mechanisms prevalent amongst diamonds dealers in New York.[113] Indeed, the football world too has 'developed an elaborate, internal set of rules, complete with distinctive institutions and sanctions, to handle disputes among industry members'.[114]

Eventually, clubs and players wishing to challenge the decisions adopted by the DRC and the PSC must do so in front of the CAS. At the time of the 2001 Agreement, FIFA had in mind the creation of a special Arbitration Tribunal for

---

[108]Article 8.2.7 Annex 3 of FIFA RSTP: 'The former association shall not deliver an ITC if a contractual dispute on grounds of the circumstances stipulated in Annexe 3, Article 8.2 para 4 b) has arisen between the former club and the professional player. In such a case, upon request of the new association, FIFA may take provisional measures in exceptional circumstances. If the competent body authorises the provisional registration (cf. Article 23 para 3), the new association shall complete the relevant player registration information in TMS (cf. Annexe 3, Article 5.2 para 6). Furthermore, the professional player, the former club and/or the new club are entitled to lodge a claim with FIFA in accordance with Article 22. FIFA shall then decide on the issue of the ITC and on sporting sanctions within 60 days. In any case, the decision on sporting sanctions shall be taken before the delivery of the ITC. The delivery of the ITC shall be without prejudice to compensation for breach of contract.'

[109]'FIFA is competent to hear:
a) disputes between clubs and players in relation to the maintenance of contractual stability (Articles 13–18) where there has been an ITC request and a claim from an interested party in relation to said ITC request, in particular regarding the issue of the ITC, sporting sanctions or compensation for breach of contract'. Article 22.a) FIFA RSTP. See also De Weger 2008, pp. 16–17.

[110]On this question of the concurrent jurisdiction of a national court and the DRC, see Zimmerman 2015, pp. 77–81.

[111]Ibid., pp. 108–110.

[112]For a famous example, see Case C-325/08, *Olympique Lyonnais v Olivier Bernard and Newcastle United FC*, ECLI:EU:C:2010:143.

[113]Bernstein 1992.

[114]Ibid., p. 115.

Football.[115] However, in light of the costs incurred to do so, it decided to introduce instead an arbitration clause in favour of the CAS in its statutes in 2002.[116] Under the existing jurisprudence of the Swiss Federal Tribunal, each club or player that participates in DRC or PSC proceedings, without raising any direct objection regarding to the CAS arbitration clause or the jurisdiction of the DRC and the PSC, is bound by a CAS arbitration clause.[117] The Swiss Court found that by requesting jointly with his new club an ITC, the player 'admitted the application of the specific regulation adopted by the Respondent federation [FIFA] and he submitted to the procedure foreseen by the regulations to decide the disputes in connection with the filing of a request for an ITC'.[118] Thus, '[i]t must be acknowledged with the CAS that the Appellant could not without violating the rules of good faith submit a request for an ITC to FIFA (or at least participate in such a request in his favour) and invoke the specific provision of the RSTP […] whilst refusing to participate in the procedure instituted by the same provision to resolve the disputes in connection with such a request […]'.[119] This is close to a catch-22 situation: On the one hand, the player should not claim an ITC from the Single Judge of the PSC if he does not want to be subjected to the jurisdiction of the DRC and the CAS on the merit of the dispute; but, on the other hand, if he does not do so he will not be able to play for his new club.[120] Accordingly, the FIFA RSTP's judicial system is crowned by the CAS, which from its apex exercises a decisive function in interpreting the RSTP.[121] In fact, the window of opportunity to challenge CAS awards is so narrow in front of the Swiss Federal Tribunal that it is generally reasonable to consider the CAS the ultimate arbiter in matters concerning the FIFA RSTP.[122]

The Commission's wish to leave the way open to national courts was well intended. It was aimed at ensuring the protection of the due process rights of the

---

[115]See Revised FIFA Regulations for the Status and Transfer of Players. FIFA.com, 24 August 2001, pp. 18–19. http://www.fifa.com/mm/document/affederation/administration/ps_769_en_68.pdf. Accessed 25 August 2015. See also Zimmerman 2015, pp. 132–133.

[116]See Arbitration Tribunal for Football (TAF) – Court of Arbitration for Sport (CAS). FIFA.com, 10 December 2002. http://www.fifa.com/mm/document/affederation/administration/tas_827_en_63.pdf. Accessed 25 August 2015.

[117]See ATF, 4A_548/2009 *X. v. Y. & Fédération Internationale de Football Association (FIFA)* [2010]. Translation by Charles Poncet. http://www.swissarbitrationdecisions.com/sites/default/files/20%20janvier%202010%204A%20548%202009.pdf. Accessed 25 August 2015.

[118]Ibid., para 4.2.2.

[119]Ibid.

[120]In other words: 'Es zeigt sich, dass Fussballspieler bei internationalen Klubwechseln, die stets ein Gesuch um Ausstellung eines internationalen Freigabescheins zur Folge haben, sich der im Regelwerk der FIFA vorgesehenen Gerichtsbarkeit der FIFA und des CAS nicht entziehen können'. See Zimmerman 2015, p. 159.

[121]This is vividly clear from the importance of the CAS jurisprudence in interpreting the scope of Article 17 on the termination of a contract without just cause. See Zimmerman 2015 and Czernota 2013.

[122]Rigozzi 2010.

persons affected by the RSTP. Yet, it is also inadequate to deal with an entirely transnational field of socio-economic relations in which stakeholders are in search of a specialized, impartial and a-national judge. Whether the CAS as an institution is truly independent from the SGBs remains debatable.[123] In fact, if the Commission were to enter new negotiations over FIFA's transfer system, this would be a potential point for improvement of the current framework. In any case, the efficacy of FIFA's RSTP is grounded in the popularity and insularity of the dispute resolution mechanisms that give flesh to its normative potential.

5.4.2 The Autonomous Normative System

Labour law and contract law are traditionally the monopoly of the nation state. At the EU level, the proposal for a unified European Civil Code has been highly controversial, and many refuse to engage in a European-wide harmonisation of civil law rules.[124] Similarly, the development of a European labour law is embryotic at best, and littered with opt-outs on part of the Member States. In this context, the FIFA RSTP appears as a transnational legal alien. It is a private corpus of norms applying autonomously to a very specific set of transnational economic relations: international football transfers and labour contracts. As such it is (almost) irrelevant whether these norms are recognized as legitimate by national legal orders, they take precedence by being effective in practice.

In the case of football transfers, if the player or the club decide to launch a proceeding with the DRC or the PSC, the traditional primacy of national law will be supplemented by the practical primacy of the FIFA RSTP. The decision of these bodies, which might entail a temporary ban on the exercise of one's profession or a hefty fine, will be based mainly if not exclusively on the rules provided by the FIFA RSTP deriving from the 2001 Agreement. This is clearly stated at Article 25.6 FIFA RSTP stipulating that:

> The Players' Status Committee, the Dispute Resolution Chamber, the single judge or the DRC judge (as the case may be) shall, when taking their decisions, apply these regulations whilst taking into account all relevant arrangements, laws and/or collective bargaining agreements that exist at national level, as well as the specificity of sport.

The same is true for the CAS, as Article 66.2 FIFA Statutes foresees that the 'CAS shall primarily apply the various regulations of FIFA and, additionally, Swiss law'. In DRC, PSC and CAS practice, which is not entirely consistent due to the absence of a doctrine of *stare decisis*, this usually means that FIFA's RSTP prevails over national law unless there is a legal lacuna.[125] In the words of FIFA's

[123]Duval and Van Rompuy 2016.

[124]Famously, Legrand 1997, pp. 44–63.

[125]For a comprehensive assessment of the question of the law applicable in front of the DRC and CAS, see Zimmerman 2015, pp. 111–129 and 162–184.

official commentary to the RSTP, Article 25.6 leaves to the competent body a 'certain amount of discretion'[126] as to the law applicable in a specific case. In practice, the CAS in its jurisprudence has not hesitated to set aside national laws to the privilege of the FIFA RSTP.[127] This view is supported in the literature in the name of the necessity to preserve the equality before the law and to secure legal certainty.[128]

This is made legally possible with the complicity of Swiss arbitration law. Before the adoption of the 2001 FIFA RSTP, the FIFA (and UEFA) transfer rules were imposed by the sheer private power of FIFA. But after the *Bosman* case, the sporting federations understood the risk of being challenged successfully in national (and European) courts. Thus, they made use of the very liberal Swiss laws applying to international arbitration in order to isolate their decision-making procedures and rules from the purview of the Courts via the proxy of the CAS.[129] The Swiss Private International Law Code (PILA) foresees in its Article 187.1 that in case of an international arbitration the parties are free to choose the law applicable to their dispute.[130] In CAS proceedings parties usually submit to CAS's own arbitration rules, which includes, for appeal proceedings (e.g. appeals against FIFA DRC or PSC decisions), a choice of law provision. Article R.58 of the CAS Code 2013 stipulates that:

'The Panel shall decide the dispute according to the applicable regulations and, subsidiarily, to the rules of law chosen by the parties or, in the absence of such a choice, according to the law of the country in which the federation, association or sports-related body which has issued the challenged decision is domiciled or according to the rules of law the Panel deems appropriate. In the latter case, the Panel shall give reasons for its decision.'

In fact, when reviewing decisions adopted by the FIFA DRC and PSC, the CAS has usually prioritized the application of the FIFA RSTP over any other national law potentially applicable. In the famous *Webster* case, the CAS considered that FIFA's choice of law clause (Article 60.2. FIFA Statutes) 'underlines the primary application of the various FIFA regulations'[131] and is supported by Article R.58

---

[126]FIFA Commentary on the Regulations for the Status and Transfer of Players 2006, p. 77.

[127]See, for example, TAS 2005/A/983 & 984 *Club Atlético Peñarol c. Carlos Heber Bueno Suarez, Cristian Gabriel Rodriguez Barrotti & Paris Saint-Germain* [2006].

[128]Zimmerman 2015, p. 127: 'Es ist anzustreben, dass für alle Teilnehmer des verbandsrechtlich organisierten Fussballs dieselben Voraussetzungen gelten. Dies führt bei Streitigkeiten zu einer besseren Vorhersehbarkeit und schliesslich auch zu grösserer Rechtssicherheit.'

[129]On this strategy and its limits under EU law, see Duval 2015a, b.

[130]It states: 'The arbitral tribunal shall decide the case according to the rules of law chosen by the parties or, in the absence thereof, according to the rules of law with which the case has the closest connection.' See also Zimmerman 2015, pp. 165–166.

[131]CAS 2007/A/1298 *Wigan Athletic FC v/Heart of Midlothian* and CAS 2007/A/1299 *Heart of Midlothian v/Webster & Wigan Athletic FC* & CAS 2007/A/1300 *Webster v/Heart of Midlothian* [2008], para 78.

CAS Code.[132] Furthermore, 'the Panel finds that article 25(6) of the FIFA Status Regulations [RSTP] and the reference in article 17(1) to the 'law *of the country concerned*' are not, properly speaking, choice-of-law clauses'.[133] Instead, Article 25(6) FIFA RSTP 'must be deemed a general reminder to the decision-making bodies of FIFA (PSC, DRC, Single Judge and DRC Judge) that in making their decisions under the FIFA regulations they must not apply those regulations in a vacuum but must account for the applicable contractual arrangements, collective agreements and national law'.[134] In other words, in case of an appeal against a decision of the FIFA DRC or PSC, 'the *"applicable regulations"* for the purposes of Art. R58 of the Code are, indisputably, FIFA's regulations because the appeal and the counterclaim are directed against a decision by FIFA, which was passed applying FIFA's rules and regulations'.[135] Concretely, the 'voluntary and express submission of an employment dispute to the FIFA dispute-resolution mechanism, despite the option to proceed before the Turkish courts, constitutes a choice by the parties for the dispute to be decided in accordance with the FIFA Statutes and Regulations'.[136] Only an unlikely express choice of law by the parties against the FIFA RSTP could potentially lead the CAS to apply a different set of rules.[137] This autonomist approach of the CAS to the law applicable in disputes related to the enforcement by FIFA's internal bodies of the RSTP is justified in the literature by the need to foster a uniform approach to the applicable law in order to ensure that all football players and clubs worldwide are faced with the same rights and obligations and that disputes be resolved in a similar way.[138] Furthermore, this would be supported by the fact that the parties would voluntarily submit to the

[132]Ibid., para 79.

[133]Ibid., para 85.

[134]Ibid., para 86.

[135]CAS 2006/A/1180 *Galatasaray SK v. Ribéry & OM* [2007], para 7.6.

[136]Ibid, para 7.8.

[137]See CAS 2007/A/1274 *M. v. Ittihad Club* [2007], para 11 and CAS 2009/A/1880 *FC Sion v. FIFA & Al-Ahly Sporting Club* and CAS 2009/A/1881 *E. v. FIFA & Al-Ahly Sporting Club* [2010], para 10.

[138]Zimmerman 2015, p. 181: 'Damit kann sichergestellt werden, dass für alle Teilnehmer im internationalen Fussball weltweit die gleichen Voraussetzungen gelten und dass sämtliche sich daraus ergebenden Streitigkeiten nach den gleichen Rechtsregeln beurteilt werden.' Similarly, in TAS 2005/A/983 and 984 *Club Atlético Peñarol c. Carlos Heber Bueno Suarez, Cristian Gabriel Rodriguez Barrotti & Paris Saint-Germain* [2006], para 24: 'La Formation arbitrale considère à cet égard que le sport est par nature un phénomène transcendant les frontières. Il est non seulement souhaitable, mais indispensable que les règles régissant le sport au niveau international aient un caractère uniforme et largement cohérent dans le monde entier. Pour en assurer un respect au niveau mondial, une telle réglementation ne doit pas être appliquée différemment d'un pays à l'autre, notamment en raison d'interférences entre droit étatique et réglementation sportive. Le principe de l'application universelle des règles de la FIFA—ou de toute autre fédération internationale—répond à des exigences de rationalité, de sécurité et de prévisibilité juridique. Tous les membres de la famille mondiale du football sont ainsi soumis aux mêmes règles, qui sont publiées. L'uniformité qui en résulte tend à assurer l'égalité de traitement entre tous les destinataires de ces normes, quel que soit le pays où ils se trouvent.'

jurisdiction of the DRC and PSC.[139] Yet, this latter argument, though formally valid, ignores the fact that in reality the players and the clubs have little practical choice. If they are to obtain quickly and incontestably the necessary ITC to field a player, they must turn to the Single Judge of the PSC.

Thanks to the accommodating stance of Swiss arbitration law towards the use of transnational private rules in international arbitration, the CAS is in practice disregarding national law when adjudicating on disputes based on the FIFA RSTP.[140] Consequently, the FIFA RSTP is very much the only source of law applying to disputes linked with international transfers and contracts of football players (and coaches). It constitutes the key transnational body of norms recognized (in the sense of Hart's rule of recognition) as valid by the officials settling disputes between the actors engaged in these activities. In this context, the body of CAS precedents regarding the interpretation of the text of the FIFA RSTP has a decisive influence on the dispute resolution bodies of FIFA, which adjust their decision-making and their interpretation of the various rules (be it anti-doping rules or the RSTP) to the reasoning used by the CAS.[141]

Since 2001, the FIFA RSTP has been through a number of reforms[142] but the core of its normative structure and interpretation remains largely influenced by the wording and spirit of the original 2001 Agreement.[143] In the absence of international rules imposed conjointly by national states, the football world has developed, in the shadow of *Bosman* and Swiss arbitration law, a specific 'global law without the state'.[144] A global law which is not the product of a global democracy but of a messy, invisible, political process involving a plurality of actors representing a conflicting set of interests. This obviously raises burning questions of legitimacy,[145] which go way beyond the scope of the present article. To point out the prevalence of this peculiar and influential set of private rules is already an important step in critically engaging with this particular dimension of the problem.

---

[139]Zimmerman 2015, p. 182: 'Dafür spricht auch der Umstand, dass die Parteien sich bewusst an die FIFA und an den CAS gewandt haben, obwohl sie auch berechtigt gewesen wären, ihre Streitsach vor ein Zivilgericht zu bringen.'

[140]Steingruber 2010.

[141]On the development of arbitral precedents (referring specifically to the CAS), see Kaufmann-Kohler 2007, pp. 365–366. See also more comprehensively, Maisonneuve 2011, pp. 441–533.

[142]There are eight different versions of the Regulations in total (2001, 2005, 2008, 2009, 2010, 2012, 2014, 2015).

[143]A spiritual connection highlighted by the latest CAS award in the *Mutu* saga, CAS 2013/A/3365 and 3366 *Juventus FC & A.S. Livorno Calcio S.p.A. v. Chelsea FC* [2015]. See my blog on this decision, Duval, Interpreting the FIFA Transfer Regulations with a little help from EU Law. Asser.nl, 27 March 2015. http://www.asser.nl/SportsLaw/Blog/post/the-cas-and-mutu-episode-4-interpreting-the-fifa-rstp-with-a-little-help-from-eu-law. Accessed 26 August 2015.

[144]Teubner 1997b.

[145]I share the view that '[a]s the sites and trajectories of transnational governance continue to span more and more regulatory areas, the combined question of '*who's in charge and to whose benefit?*' has to move into the center of an interdisciplinary engagement.' See Zumbansen 2014, p. 2.

Finally, one key particularity that is instrumental in securing the efficacy and attractiveness of this private dispute resolution system is FIFA's capacity to enforce the decision reached by its organs or the CAS.

5.4.3 The Autonomous Enforcement System

Lisa Bernstein in her fascinating account of the self-regulatory patterns of New York's diamond dealers emphasized the enforcement power derived from the capacity of the community to exclude law-infringing members. She pointed out that '[w]hat is unique about the diamond industry is not the importance of trust and reputation in commercial transactions, but rather the extent to which the industry is able to use reputation/social bonds at a cost low enough to create a system of private law enabling most transactions to be consummated and most contracts enforced completely outside the legal system'.[146] More precisely, 'the DDC [the Diamond's Dealers Club] has the ability to bring unique pressures on the losing party to pay: it can put him out of business almost instantaneously by hanging his picture in the clubroom of every bourse in the world with a notice that he failed to pay his debt'.[147] In a slightly different and remarkably transnational fashion, a similar process is at play as far as the enforcement of decisions taken by the DRC, the PSC or the CAS is sought. Indeed, one of the reasons why the DRC and PSC are so popular amongst players and clubs alike is that they can rely on FIFA's private enforcement power to secure the claims derived from the final decisions of those bodies (be it a CAS award or a DRC/PSC decision) without relying on the national legal system of the place where the player or club concerned is located.[148] According to some, this enforcement mechanism would fail in less than one per cent of cases.[149] In fact, it is perceived as 'significantly more effective, quicker and less expensive than the recognition and enforcement of an arbitral award under the NYC [New York Convention]'.[150]

FIFA, through its position at the apex of a networked pyramid of associations in charge of regulating football, has put in place a system to enforce claims derived from disputes dealt with by the DRC and PSC (and ultimately CAS). In a nutshell, FIFA provides for additional 'sporting' sanctions against non-complying clubs or players. This is made possible through the disciplinary power of FIFA as an association. Article 64.1 of the FIFA Disciplinary Code (2011 edition) foresees that:

[146]Bernstein 1992, p. 138.

[147]Ibid., p. 149.

[148]This is clearly hinted at by De Weger 2008, p. 39, and Zimmerman 2015, p. 202.

[149]See Haas 2014, p. 13.

[150]Ibid.

'1. Anyone who fails to pay another person (such as a player, a coach or a club) or FIFA a sum of money in full or part, even though instructed to do so by a body, a committee or an instance of FIFA or a subsequent CAS appeal decision (financial decision), or anyone who fails to comply with another decision (non- financial decision) passed by a body, a committee or an instance of FIFA, or by CAS (subsequent appeal decision):

a) will be fined for failing to comply with a decision;
b) will be granted a final deadline by the judicial bodies of FIFA in which to pay the amount due or to comply with the (non-financial) decision;
c) (only for clubs:) will be warned and notified that, in the case of default or failure to comply with a decision within the period stipulated, points will be deducted or relegation to a lower division ordered. A transfer ban may also be pronounced;
d) (only for associations) will be warned and notified that, in the case of default or failure to comply with a decision within the period stipulated, further disciplinary measures will be imposed. An expulsion from a FIFA competition may also be pronounced.

The CAS has endorsed the applicability of this mechanism to the enforcement of CAS awards.[151] More precisely, these sanctions are to be implemented by the national associations, which themselves are exposed to sanctions if they do not abide by the decision of the disciplinary committee.[152] The sanctions include painful bans for players and relegations for clubs, as well as pecuniary penalties and transfer bans.[153] The Swiss Federal Tribunal has also expressly sanctioned its compatibility with Swiss law.[154] The Court considered that a Swiss association

[151]CAS 2005/A/957 *Clube Atlético Mineiro v. Fédération Internationale de Football Association (FIFA)* [2006], para 26: 'At the same time, the Panel remarks that, pursuant to Article 61.1 of the FIFA Statutes, "the Confederations, Members and Leagues shall agree… to ensure that members, affiliated Players and officials comply with the decisions passed by the CAS". In other words, all subjects affiliated to FIFA, including clubs and players, are bound to comply with awards issued by CAS. Therefore, although CAS is assuredly not "a body of FIFA", its awards are to be considered, under the FIFA Statutes and from its perspective, to have the same effect as a decision issued by a body of FIFA. As a result, the failure to comply with a CAS award, in addition to the possible enforcement proceedings available at State level, exposes a party affiliated with FIFA also to a possible disciplinary proceeding, in accordance with Article 70 FDC. Any different interpretation would seriously impair the efficiency and effectiveness of the FIFA disciplinary system: appeal to the CAS is intended to secure an external review of the FIFA decisions, and cannot be construed as a way to obtain per se, even on the basis of frivolous appeals, an immunity from the disciplinary sanctions for non-compliance with obligations imposed by FIFA rules.'

[152]Article 64.2 FIFA Disciplinary Code: 'If a club disregards the final time limit, the relevant association shall be requested to implement the sanctions threatened." See also Zimmerman 2015, p. 193.

[153]See Articles 64.1, 3 and 4 FIFA Disciplinary Code.

[154]ATF, 4P.240/2006, 5 January 2007. See also FIFA Circular 1080, 13 February 2007.

can rightfully impose disciplinary sanctions on its members to enforce its decisions as, and this is the potentially controversial statement, these do not replace the state monopoly on mandatory enforcement.[155]

However, this power of sanction against a player is not without limits. In its widely commented *Matuzalem* decision,[156] the Swiss Federal Tribunal found that a worldwide lifelong ban imposed on a player as the result of its non-compliance with a CAS decision condemning him (jointly with his new club) to pay 11,858,934 million € to his former club was disproportionate, amounted to a violation of his personality rights, and was therefore contrary to Swiss substantive public policy.[157] The Court considered that the 'measures taken by such sport federations which gravely harm the development of individuals who practice the sport as a profession are licit only when the interests of the federation justify the infringement of privacy'.[158] In that regard, '[t]he threat of an unlimited occupational ban based on Art. 64(4) of the FIFA Disciplinary Code constitutes an obvious and grave encroachment in the Appellant's privacy rights'.[159] Furthermore, '[s]hould payment fail to take place, the award under appeal would lead not only to the Appellant being subjected to his previous employer's arbitrariness but also to an encroachment in his economic freedom of such gravity that the foundations of his economic existence are jeopardized without any possible justification by some prevailing interest of the world football federation or its members'.[160] Thus, under Swiss law, FIFA is not entirely free to use its disciplinary power to exclude permanently non-compliant members from the football world. However, the

[155]Ibid., para 4.2: 'Der angefochtene Schiedsspruch betrifft keine Zwangsvollstreckung, sondern Sanktionen auf vereinsrechtlicher Grundlage. Es ist im schweizerischen Vereinsrecht anerkannt, dass die Verletzung von Mitgliedschaftspflichten Sanktionen wie Vereins- oder Verbandsstrafen zur Folge haben kann (RIEMER, Berner Kommentar, N. 205 ff. zu Article 70 ZGB; vgl. auch DERSELBE, Sportrechts-Weltmacht Schweiz, Causa Sport 2004, S. 106 f.). Wenn ein privater Verein (wie vorliegend die Beschwerdegegnerin) zur Erreichung seines Zwecks Regeln und Bestimmungen aufstellt, denen sich seine Mitglieder unterwerfen, ist es grundsätzlich zulässig, dass er Sanktionen vorsieht, um die Verpflichtungen der Mitglieder abzusichern. Das ist auch in privatrechtlichen Verträgen denkbar; zu erwähnen ist etwa die Vereinbarung einer Konventionalstrafe. Die Mitglieder unterwerfen sich solchen Sanktionsmöglichkeiten freiwillig, auch wenn wie die Beschwerdeführerin mit einer gewissen Berechtigung geltend macht bei der dominanten Stellung, wie sie die Beschwerdegegnerin im Fussball einnimmt, die Möglichkeit des Austritts für einen Fussballclub, der an Meisterschaften mitspielen möchte, kaum in Frage kommt. Dass die innerhalb einer Vereinsstruktur vorgesehene Sanktionierungsmöglichkeit vollstreckungsähnliche Wirkung zeitigen kann, weil das betroffene Mitglied angehalten wird, seinen Verpflichtungen nachzukommen, ist bei genügender statutarischer Grundlage nicht zu beanstanden und bringt die vereinsrechtlichen Sanktionen nicht in Konflikt mit dem Zwangsmonopol des Staates.'

[156]ATF 4A_558/2011, 2 March 2012. See Levy 2012; Steingruber 2012; Burger 2012.

[157]ATF 4A_558/2011, 2 March 2012, para 4.3.5.

[158]ATF 4A_558/2011, 2 March 2012, para 4.3.3. Translation by Charles Poncet. http://www.swissarbitrationdecisions.com/sites/default/files/27%20mars%202012%204A%20558%202011.pdf. Accessed 26 August 2015.

[159]Ibid., para 4.3.5.

[160]Ibid.

existing mechanisms remain very intrusive, insofar as a temporary ban in a short career span is extremely detrimental for any professional player. Likewise, relegation is economically deadly for any high-level professional club and the mere threat of it should be enough to trigger compliance with a decision of the system.

In this context, if national courts were to decide to challenge this private enforcement system, they will most likely face the raw political power and leverage of FIFA.[161] Nevertheless, this potential threat has not stopped a German court from recently challenging the system in a case involving a training compensation due on the basis of the FIFA RSTP.[162] In that case, a small German club, which spent only a very short time at a professional level, was unlucky enough to have hired a young Argentinean player for which it was found by the DRC[163] and the CAS[164] to owe a training compensation to his former Argentinean clubs (Excursionistas and River Plate) of a total of 157 000€. The club refused to pay and resisted FIFA's calls to comply with the decisions. It was then, initially, sanctioned with a point deduction ordered by FIFA and imposed by the national federation (in fact by the regional federation as the club had been relegated in the meanwhile) followed by relegation. Yet, instead of paying an amount, which apparently it had not the economic capacity to pay, the club decided to challenge the decisions of the regional federation in front of the German courts. Though unsuccessful at first instance,[165] the club obtained in appeal that the decision of the federation be set aside due to the incompatibility of the original CAS award it was implementing with EU free movement law. The decision is now under appeal in front of the Bundesgerichtshof (BGH), Germany's highest civil court. In any event, if the Court were to decide that in this specific case the decision of FIFA should not have been implemented by the local federation, it remains that this will be based on a very specific facts constellation, in which a CAS panel openly disregarded well-established EU case law. This challenge arose because the claimant had nothing to lose. SV Wilhelmshaven was a semi-professional (and then amateur) club with no means to pay the compensation. This would probably not occur if the claimant were a professional Bundesliga club. Indeed, no established club would risk being relegated, and therefore most likely going bankrupt, even if it could challenge *ex-post facto* that relegation in front of national courts. The BGH's decision remains extremely interesting, its practical impact on the enforcement system of the FIFA RSTP, however, will probably be relatively minor.

161 On this power, see Meier and García 2015.

162 OLG Bremen, 2 U 67/14, 30 December 2014. See Duval, SV Wilhelmshaven: a Rebel with a cause! Challenging the compatibility of FIFA's training compensation system with EU law. Asser.nl, 24 February 2015. http://www.asser.nl/SportsLaw/Blog/post/sv-wilhelmshaven-a-rebel-with-a-cause-challenging-the-compatibility-of-fifa-s-training-compensation-system-with-eu-law. Accessed 26 August 2015. Orth 2015.

163 DRC Decision 128921a and 128921b of 5 December 2008.

164 CAS 2009/A/1810 and 1811 *SV Wilhelmshaven v. Club Atlético Excursionistas & Club Atlético River Plate*, [2009].

165 LG Bremen, 12 O 129/13, 25 April 2014.

The FIFA RSTP's system has had a very successful autonomous life of its own. This is mainly due to the fact that it offers a relatively cheaper, faster and surer way to deal with transnational football labour disputes. In an utterly transnationalized field of social life, it is not surprising that the actors have recourse to denationalized institutions to settle their disputes. They provide for a neutral playing field to solve conflicts and decide difficult distributive questions. As pointed out earlier, this does pose acute question of fairness and distributive justice that can be captured more broadly under the umbrella term of legitimacy (be it input or output). Why are the CAS, the DRC or the PSC the right institutions to decide these questions? Why is the FIFA RSTP the fundamental text to which they deem necessary to refer to decide these questions? How representative and legitimate are the people drafting and interpreting the FIFA RSTP? How representative and legitimate are the people adjudicating the FIFA RSTP? All those questions deserve an answer, which this chapter is not capable to provide. For the purpose of this piece, it is sufficient to note that the *Bosman* ruling has shaped this system in various ways. First, it has radically denationalized football's labour market and rendered international transfers ubiquitous. This dis-embedding of football's labour market from its national cradles stressed, in a Polanyian double-movement,[166] the need for a re-embedding at a more appropriate level: the global level. Second, *Bosman* bequeathed the Commission with the legal weapons to stir the legislative process that led to the adoption of the new FIFA RSTP. It is this RSTP that nowadays guides the actions of the myriad of actors involved in the transfer market, be it players, agents, club managers or football officials. To sum up, it legally defines and constructs the reality of the football transfer market as we experience it (often with excitement) in our daily life.

5.5 Conclusion: The Long Shadow of Bosman and the Future of the FIFA RSTP

The FIFA RSTP in its current form is not the end of history. Neither is this chapter an a-critical endorsement of its merits. My primary aim was to show that *Bosman* had indirectly engendered the institutionalization of a private regulatory system produced in collaboration between the Commission and the fuzzy social field referred to as the football family, and that this system has a tremendous effect on the practices it purports to shape.

The aftermath of the *Bosman* ruling was populated by doomsayers predicting the imminent death of football.[167] Football is still alive and kicking, and *Bosman* did not trigger the deregulatory wave that some may have hoped for. Instead it

[166] On this double movement, see Polanyi 2011. For another use of Polanyi's double movement in a transnational legal context, see Teubner 2010a, b, p. 2.

[167] Then UEFA President Lennard Johansson went on record claiming that the EU was trying "to kill club football in Europe", quoted by García 2007, p. 202.

generated an atypical re-regulation, involving a peculiar negotiation between the Commission, FIFA, UEFA and FIFPro, of which the new FIFA RSTP is the main outcome. In my view, *Bosman* should stand in the people's mind for an attempt at democratization in place of deregulation. The judgment imposed on football's private regulators a duty to justify their political choices and to adopt a more inclusive law-making process. The corruption scandals that rock FIFA currently are there to remind us of the necessity of this duty, and of how much this is still unfinished business. I contend that the position of the CJEU and the Commission regarding SGBs is counter-democratic in essence.[168] It provides affected actors access to a forum that allows them to ask for justifications for measures taken by the executive or legislative branch of the SGBs. It creates a deliberative space where it was dramatically (and still often is) missing. As pointed out in this case study, the Commission is also directly involved in the production of FIFA's rules, and has a crucial legislative co-responsibility. Thus, in the world of football, *Bosman*'s main legacy is the adoption of an institutionalized FIFA RSTP that leaves less space for the exercise of discretionary and arbitrary power than its predecessors. EU law and the Commission served as potent irritants to reflexively push through this institutionalization.

Since September 2015, FIFA's RSTP is facing anew a legal challenge from the player's side.[169] This can put in motion a similar legislative dynamic as the one outlined in the present chapter. Since the adoption of the 2001 FIFA RSTP, many authors have argued that it constitutes a disproportionate restriction of competition and free movement.[170] This article does not intend to take a side in this debate. Nonetheless, if the Commission decides to investigate FIFA over the RSTP, and, hence, re-open the legislative process, it (and we) should be fully aware of its legislative role and put the emphasis on an inclusive (and transparent) process of consultation, duly balancing the input of the various affected actors. To this end, it could also for example tie the closure of its investigation to the conclusion of a collective agreement on the new FIFA transfer rules (at least insofar as they apply to the European territory) in the sectorial social dialogue committee for professional football.[171] This committee is supposed to be representative of the broad

---

[168] Rosanvallon 2008, p. 8: 'By "counter-democracy" I mean not the opposite of democracy but rather a form of democracy that reinforces the usual electoral democracy as a kind of buttress, a democracy of indirect powers disseminated throughout society—in other words, a durable democracy of distrust, which complements the episodic democracy of the usual electoral-representative system.' A (very) long version of this argument can be found in my Phd thesis, see Duval 2015a, b. http://cadmus.eui.eu/bitstream/handle/1814/36997/2015_Duval.pdf?sequence=1. Accessed 25 August 2015.

[169] See FIFPro legal action against FIFA transfer system. FIFPro.org, 18 September 2015. http://www.fifpro.org/en/news/fifpro-takes-legal-action-against-fifa-transfer-system. Accessed 25 August 2015.

[170] Weatherill 2003; Egger and Stix-Hackl 2002; Blanpain 2003; Drolet 2006; Coppo 2011; Pearson 2015; Parrish 2015.

[171] On the (limited) output of the social dialogue committee since its introduction, see the chapter by Richard Parrish in this volume.

range of actors operating on the football labour market, and as such could be an appropriate institution to carefully balance the different interests affected by the RSTP. In doing so, the Commission would delegate the legislative power it derives from its position as the enforcer of EU competition law to a more representative body of the social field concerned.[172] In any eventuality, the Commission will play a crucial role in deciding, or not, to trigger a new legislative process. The recent inflation of transfers[173] and CAS's controversial interpretation of Article 17 of the FIFA RSTP might well speak for such an intervention.[174] Yet, this intervention should be reflexive and not destructive. In other words, geared towards insuring that new rules be produced and applied in a fashion that is inclusive of the plurality of actors and interests affected by the RSTP's daily legal operation.

Finally, the fact that a transnational legal system plays a decisive role in solving disputes arising out of a specific field of human activity is not unproblematic as far as our concept of law is concerned.[175] This necessarily points towards the much-discussed issue of the pluralism of law in a global, transnational, context[176] and the progressive shift from a pyramidal to a network paradigm of law.[177] Thus, this case study challenges the idea that the state is still in control (and at the centre) of all law-making in our globalizing world.[178] This, in turn, does not mean that the state (or the EU for that matter) is irrelevant. The role of Swiss law for example is crucial in ensuring the legal bite of FIFA's RSTP and providing it with the legal certainty needed to operate. Thus, we are dealing with complex transnational 'assemblages'[179] rather than clear-cut radically autonomous global legal orders. Conversely, the question of the legitimacy of this transnational body of rules cannot be tackled with the usual democratic regression to a *pouvoir constituant*. Yet, those rules exist in practice, and are probably here to stay in the absence of a global state. They are needed to stabilize normative expectations and ensure the functioning of football's transnational labour market. Thus, the RSTP's impact on a number of actors necessitates a critical engagement with its legitimacy and, from a normative standpoint, an assessment of the legal and political tools available to challenge it. In this regard, as mentioned above, the EU has a fundamental

---

[172]Thus participating in the societal constitutionalization of the field by enhancing its internal democratization and reflexivity. On the need to push for the constitutionalization of the functional legal fields, regimes, systems arising under the pressure of globalization, see Teubner 2012.

[173]See Commission Press Release of 7 February 2013, IP/13/95 Commission blows the whistle over inflated football transfer fees and lack of level playing field. http://europa.eu/rapid/press-release_IP-13-95_en.htm Accessed 26 August 2015.

[174]Parrish 2015, pp. 256–282.

[175]On the need to rethink our concept of law in a transnational age, see Von Daniels 2010.

[176]In this regard in Zumbansen 2010, p. 187: 'Transnational law is another name for transnational legal pluralism for an (inherently interdisciplinary) inquiry into the nature of legal regulation of problems, which have long been extending beyond the confines of jurisdiction.'

[177]Ost and Van de Kerchove 2002.

[178]In Saskia Sassen's words, it is to some extent 'losing control', see Sassen 1996.

[179]See Sassen 2006.

democratizing role to play. In a political game radically re-shuffled by globalization, new counter-powers must be imagined to match the shift of power towards transnational and private institutions.[180] The control imposed by the *Bosman* ruling on FIFA's transfer rules should be re-interpreted in this light as an instance of political re-empowerment of (European) citizens over disembedded transnational rules and institutions.

References

Azoulai L (2011) The 'retained powers' formula in the case law of the European Court of Justice: EU law as total law? Eur J Legal Stud 4(2):192–219

Beck U (2005) Power in the global age: a new global political economy. Polity Press, Cambridge

Bernstein L (1992) Opting out of the legal system: extralegal contractual relations in the diamond industry. J Legal Stud 21(1):115–167

Blanpain R (2003) The legal status of sportsmen and sportswomen under international, European and Belgian national and regional law. Kluwer Law International, The Hague

Burger L (2012) For the first time, the Supreme Court sets aside an arbitral award on grounds of substantive public policy. ASA Bull 30(3):603–610

Casini L (2010) Il Diritto Globale dello Sport. Giuffrè editore

Casini L (2011) The making of a lex sportiva by the court of arbitration for sport. Ger Law J 12(5):1317–1340

Casini L (2015) The emergence of global administrative systems: the case of sport. Glocalism J Cult Polit Innov 1:1–18

Coppo G (2011) Contractual stability and EU competition law. Eur Sports Law Policy Bull 1:291–309

Croci O, Ammirante J (1999) Soccer in the age of globalization. Peace Rev 11(4):499–504

Czernota PA (2013) FIFA transfer rules and unilateral termination without "just cause". Berkeley J Entertainment Sports Law 2(1):1–47

Dabscheck B (2004) The globe at their feet: FIFA's new employment rules—I. Sport Soc Cult Commer Media Polit 7(1):69–94

Dabscheck B (2006) The globe at their feet: FIFA's new employment rules—II. Sport Soc Cult Commer Media Polit 9(1):1–18

De Weger F (2008) The jurisprudence of the FIFA dispute resolution chamber. T.M.C. Asser Press, The Hague

Drolet J-C (2006) Extra time: are the new FIFA transfer rules doomed? Int Sports Law J 2006(1–2):66–73

Dunne N (2014) Commitment decisions in EU competition law. J Compet Law Econ 10(2):399–444

Duval A (2013) Lex sportiva: a playground for transnational law. Eur Law J 19(6):822–842

Duval A (2015a) La Lex Sportiva face à L'Union européenne: Guerre et Paix dans l'espace juridique transnational. PhD Thesis, European University Institute, Florence

Duval A (2015b) The court of arbitration for sport and EU law: chronicle of an encounter. Maastricht J Eur Comp Law 22(2):224–255

Duval A, Van Rompuy B (2016) Protecting athletes' right to fair trial through EU competition law: the Pechstein case. In: Takács T, Lazić V, Van Rompuy B (eds) Paulussen C., Fundamental rights in international and European law: public and private law perspectives. T.M.C. Asser Press, The Hague, pp 245–278

---

[180]This is the key lesson one can draw from the scholarship of the late Ulrich Beck, see Beck 2005.

Egger A, Stix-Hackl C (2002) Sports and competition law: a never-ending story? Eur Compet Law Rev 23(2):81–91

Eliasson A (2009) The European football market, globalization and mobility among players. Soccer Soc 10(3–4):386–397

Foster K (2010) Lex sportiva: transnational law in action. Int Sports Law J 2010(3–4):20–25

Frick B (2009) Globalization and factor mobility the impact of the “Bosman-ruling” on player migration in professional soccer. J Sports Econ 10(1):88–106

Garapon A (2013) Michel Foucault, visionnaire du droit contemporain. Raisons politiques 52:39–49

García B (2007) UEFA and the European Union: from confrontation to co-operation? J Contemp Eur Res 3(3):202–223

Giulianotti R, Robertson R (2004) The globalization of football: a study in the glocalization of the ‘serious life’. Br J Sociol 55(4):545–568

Haas U (2014) The enforcement of football-related arbitral awards by the Court of Arbitration for Sport (CAS). Int Sports Law Rev 1:12–29

Ibáñez Colomo P (2010) On the application of competition law as regulation: elements for a theory. Yearb Eur Law 29(1):261–306

Ibañez Colomo P (2013) Three shifts in EU competition policy: towards standards decentralization, settlements. Maastricht J Eur Comp Law 20(3):363–384

Idot L (1999) A propos des engagements en droit de la concurrence: quelques réflexions sur la pratique communautaire et française. Cahiers de Droit Européen 4:569–610

Irving JG (2002) Red card: the battle over European football’s transfer system. Univ Miami Law Rev 56:667–725

Kaufmann-Kohler G (2007) Arbitral precedent: dream, necessity or excuse? Arbitr Int 23(3):357–378

Kingsbury B, Krisch N, Steward RB (2005) The emergence of global administrative law. Law Contemp Probl 68:15–62

Latty F (2007) La Lex Sportiva: Recherche Sur Le Droit Transnational. Martinus Nijhoff Publishers, Leiden

Latty F (2011) La Lex FIFA. In: Maisonneuve M (ed) Droit et Coupe du Monde, Economica, pp 9–27

Legrand P (1997) Against a European civil code. Mod Law Rev 60(1):44–63

Levy R (2012) Swiss federal tribunal overrules CAS award in a landmark decision: FIFA vs Matuzalem. Int Sports Law J 2012(1–2):35–38

Maisonneuve M (2011) L’arbitrage des litiges sportifs. La Librairie Générale de Droit et de Jurisprudence, Paris

Mehta K, Tierno Centella M-L (2008) Settlement procedure in EU cartel cases. Compet Law Int 4:11–18

Meier HE, García B (2013) Abandoning hopes for veto power: institutional options for sport governing bodies in the European Union. Int J Sport Policy Polit 5(3):421–443

Meier HE, García B (2015) Protecting private transnational authority against public intervention: FIFA’s power over national governments. Public Adm 93(4):890–906

Milanovic B (2005) Globalization and goals: does soccer show the way? Rev Int Polit Econ 12(5):828–850

Monti G (2002) Article 81 EC and public policy. Common Mark Law Rev 39(5):1057–1099

Niemann A, Garcia B, Grant W (2011) The transformation of European football: towards the Europeanisation of the national game. Manchester University Press, Manchester

O’Keeffe D, Osborne P (1996) L’affaire Bosman: un arrêt important pour le bon fonctionnement du Marché unique européen. Revue du Marché Unique Européen 1:17–44

Orth JF (2015) Entscheidungsvollzug in der Verbandspyramide und Ausbildungsentschädigung. Sport und Recht 2:51–56

Ost F, Van de Kerchove M (2002) De la pyramide au réseau? Pour une théorie dialectique du droit. Publications des Facultés Universitaires Saint Louis, Bruxelles

Parrish R (2003) Sports law and policy in the European Union. Manchester University Press, Manchester
Parrish R (2015) Article 17 of the FIFA regulations on the status and transfer of players. Compatibility with EU law. Maastricht J Eur Comp Law 22(2):256–282
Pearson G (2015) Sporting justifications under EU free movement and competition law: the case of the football 'transfer system'. Eur Law J 21(2):220–238
Polanyi K (2011) The great transformation: the political and economic origins of our time. Beacon Press, Boston
Rigaux F (1989) Les situations juridiques individuelles dans un système de relativité générale: cours général de droit international privé. Martinus Nijhoff Publishers, Leiden
Rigozzi A (2010) Challenging awards of the Court of Arbitration for Sport. J Int Dispute Settl 1(1):217–265
Rosanvallon P (2008) Counter-democracy. Politics in an age of distrust. Cambridge University Press, Cambridge
Sassen S (1996) Losing control? Sovereignty in an age of globalization. Columbia University Press, New York
Sassen S (2006) Territory—authority—rights: from medieval to global assemblages. Princeton University Press, Princeton
Steingruber AM (2010) Sports arbitration: determination of the applicable regulations and rules of law and their interpretation. Int Sports Law J 3–4:54–68
Steingruber AM (2012) Matuzalem: CAS award set aside on the ground on public policy: de facto unlimited prohibition to work as a football player as a violation of public policy. Int Sports Law J 2012(1–2):9–44
Taylor M (2006) Global players? Football, migration and globalization, c. 1930–2000. Hist Soc Res 31(1):7–30
Teubner G (1983) Substantive and reflexive elements. Mod Law, Law Soc Rev 17(2):239–285
Teubner G (1997a) 'Global Bukowina': legal pluralism in the world society. In: Teubner G (ed) Global law without the state. Darmouth, Aldershot, pp 3–22
Teubner G (ed) (1997b) Global law without the state. Dartmouth, Aldershot
Teubner G (2010a) Constitutionalising polycontexturality. Soc Legal Stud 20(2):210–229
Teubner G (2010b) Societal constitutionalism and the politics of the common. Finnish Yearb Int Law 21:2–15
Teubner G (2012) Constitutional fragments: societal constitutionalism and globalization. Oxford University Press, Oxford
Vallery A (2008) Les procédures de règlement négocié de la Commission européenne en matière de concurrence: entre flexibilité et sécurité juridique. In: De Walsche A, Levi L (eds) Mélanges en hommage à Georges Vandersanden. Bruylant, Bruxelles, pp 734–770
Van den Bogaert S (2015) Bosman: one for all…. Maastricht J Eur Comp Law 22(2):174–179
Van Miert K (1996) L'arrêt "Bosman": la suppression des frontières sportives dans le Marché unique européen. Revue du Marché Unique Européen 1:5–9
Van Miert K (2000) Mijn Jaren in Europa. Lannoo, Tielt
Van Rompuy B (2015) The role of EU competition law in tackling abuse of regulatory power by sports associations. Maastricht J Eur Comp Law 22(2):179–208
Von Daniels D (2010) The concept of law from a transnational perspective. Ashgate Publishing Limited, Surrey
Walker N (2014) Intimations of global law. Cambridge University Press, Cambridge
Weatherill S (2003) "Fair play please!": recent developments in the application of EC law to sport. Common Mark Law Rev 40(1):51–93
Weatherill S (2010) Bosman changed everything: the rise of EC sports law. In: Maduro M, Azoulai L (eds) The past and future of EU law. Hart Publishing, Oxford, pp 480–487
Wills WPJ (2006) Settlements of EU antitrust investigations: commitment decisions under Article 9 of Regulation No 1/2003. World Compet 29(3):345–366
Zimmerman M (2015) Vertragsstabilität im internationalen Fussball. Dike Verlag, Zürich/St. Gallen

Zumbansen P (2010) Transnational legal pluralism. Transnatl Legal Theory 1(2):141–189

Zumbansen P (2012a) Defining the space of transnational law: legal theory, global governance and legal pluralism. In: Handl G, Zekoll J, Zumbansen P (eds) Beyond territoriality: transnational legal authority in an age of globalization. Martinus Nijhoff Publishers, Leiden, pp 53–86

Zumbansen P (2012b) Transnational law evolving. In: Smits J (ed) Elgar encyclopedia of comparative law. Edward Elgar, Cheltenham, pp 898–925

Zumbansen P (2014) The incurable constitutional itch: transnational private regulatory governance and the woes of legitimacy. Osgoode legal studies research paper series, Paper No. 18 10:6:1–28

Zumbansen P, Callies G-P (2010) Rough consensus and running codes. Hart Publishing, Oxford

Chapter 6
EU Competition Law and Organisational Rules

Katarina Pijetlovic

Abstract This chapter addresses the application of EU competition law to organisational rules in the sports sector, including the judgments that were passed by the CJEU on this topic, as well as the relevant European Commission decisions. Internal market cases are also discussed in a separate section to the extent necessary. They are important for the understanding of competition law due to the high level of convergence between the two areas in their application to the rules of sports governing bodies. The 2006 Meca-Medina case deserves special attention in this regard because it confirmed that the Wouters test that introduced regulatory ancillarity in the EU competition law analytical framework applies to organisational rules in the sport industry. Implicitly and retrospectively, Meca-Medina also validated the Commission's approach in ENIC and Mouscron cases. Finally, the Commission Staff Working Document contains Annex I on Sport and EU Competition Rules that provided a useful general guidance and will be examined in detail.

Keywords Meca-Medina · Organisational rules · Regulatory rules · EU competition law · Wouters · White Paper on Sport

Contents

K. Pijetlovic (✉)
Department of Law, Liverpool Hope University, Liverpool, UK
e-mail: pijetlk@hope.ac.uk

A. Duval and B. Van Rompuy (eds.), *The Legacy of* Bosman,
ASSER International Sports Law Series, DOI 10.1007/978-94-6265-120-3_6

6.1 Introduction

The relationship between EU competition law and organisational (regulatory) rules in sport was originally formed in 1970s in the *Walrave* and *Donà* cases decided under free movement law. Therein, the Court of Justice of the European Union (CJEU) famously held that sport is subject to EU law 'only in so far as it constitutes economic activity [...]'.[1] This has been reiterated by the Court on several occasions later on, most notably in *Bosman, Deliège and Lehtonen*.[2] The required economic effect referred to in these cases presents a generally applicable jurisdictional threshold on the competences of EU institutions to act, as well as a constitutional limitation regarding the applicability of EU competition law. Apart from certain rules of the game (*lex ludica*)[3] and sport as a purely amateur pursuit, it is hard to imagine a rule passed by sport governing bodies that is completely devoid of economic effect in practice. All sporting rules and practices that *do* produce required economic effect may become subject to a compatibility analysis under the Treaty, including its competition articles.

Regardless of the constitutional competence to decide on the application of the competition articles to organisational rules in the sports sector, in *Bosman and*

[1]Case 36/74 *Walrave and Koch v. Union Cycliste Internationale*, ECLI:EU:C:1974:140, para 4; Case C-13/76 *Gaetano Donà v Mario Mantero*, ECLI:EU:C:1976:115, para 12.

[2]Case C-415/93 *Union Royale Belge des Sociétés de Football Association and others v. Bosman and others*, ECLI:EU:C:1995:463, para 73; Cases C-51/96 and C-191/97 *Christelle Deliège v. Ligue Francophone de Judo et Disciplines Associées ASBL and others*, ECLI:EU:C:2000:199, para 41; Case C-176/96 *Jyri Lehtonen and Castors Canada Dry Namur-Braine ASBL v. Fédération royale belge des sociétés de basket-ball ASBL (FRBSB)*, ECLI:EU:C:2000:201, para 42.

[3]As defined by Foster 2006, p. 421. The rules of the game are, e.g. offside in football, the dimensions of a tennis court, and the number of fielded players.

Deliège the Court avoided any discussion on the application of Articles 101 and 102 TFEU to sporting rules that produce economic effect. The two cases were decided *exclusively* under internal market provisions. Advocate Generals (AGs), however, did not leave us completely empty handed and both addressed this issue in their respective Opinions. Whereas AG Lenz in *Bosman* focused exclusively on weighing pro and anti-competitive features of the restrictive clauses and utilised an emerging commercial ancillarity as a method for a compatibility assessment, AG Cosmas in *Deliège* alluded to the possibility of using certain non-economic interests as a justification for the rules that restrict competition.

Three years after AG Cosmas' Opinion, the CJEU in *Wouters*[4] accepted purely non-economic public interest justifications under Article 101(1) TFEU for agreements restrictive of the freedom of action. This case introduced the so-called regulatory ancillarity in the application of competition law and paved the way for the seminal judgement in *Meca-Medina*,[5] which to date remains the only case on the organisational rules in sport decided by the Court under the EU antitrust provisions.

Prior to the passage of the Court's judgement in *Meca-Medina* a lot of uncertainty still surrounded the application of EU competition law to legal issues involving organisational rules of sport. *Meca-Medina* not only enhanced legal certainty, but also provided a modified analytical framework for such rules and practices by adopting the *Wouters* test in its entirety. It is therefore important to distinguish organisational rules from the rules intended to regulate revenue-producing activities of the sporting bodies. The former involves activities on the market in which clubs and federations exploit their performances and commercial rights through, for instance, the sale of tickets and media rights for sports events, merchandising, as well as via activities on the supply market for buying and selling of players. Examples of organisational rules, on the other hand, include rules of the game, rules concerning selection criteria for sports competitions, 'at home and away from home' rules, rules preventing multiple ownership in club competitions, rules concerning the composition of national teams, anti-doping rules and rules concerning transfer windows.

In 2007 the EU Commission published the White Paper on Sport accompanied by a Commission Staff Working Document.[6] It summarised the EU competition law approach to the sports sector and provided examples of organisational rules in sport that are likely to infringe, as well as organisational rules likely not to infringe the competition provisions.

However, as emphasised by both the Court in *Meca-Medina* and by the Commission in the White Paper on Sport, there can be no automatic exclusion of

---

[4]Case C-309/99 *J. C. J. Wouters, J. W. Savelbergh and Price Waterhouse Belastingadviseurs BV v Algemene Raad van de Nederlandse Orde van Advocaten*, ECLI:EU:C:2002:98.

[5]Case C-519/04 *P David Meca-Medina and Igor Majcen v. Commission*, ECLI:EU:C:2006:492.

[6]Commission White Paper of 11 July 2007, COM (2007) 391 final - White Paper on Sport; Commission Staff Working Document of 11 July 2007, COM (2007) 391 final - The EU and Sport: Background and Context - Accompanying document to the White Paper on Sport.

any organisational sporting rule that produces economic effect from the scope of the Treaty. Their compatibility with EU competition provisions can only be made on a case-by-case basis within the analytical framework provided by Annex I of the Commission Staff Working Document that, among others, includes the *Meca-Medina* test. This contextual approach to regulatory rules is further complemented by the notion of the specificity of sport, included in Article 165(1) TFEU by the Lisbon Treaty amendments that entered into force on 1 December 2009.

This article states that '[t]he Union shall contribute to the promotion of European sporting issues, while taking account of the *specific nature of sport*, its structures based on voluntary activity and its *social and educational function*' [emphasis added]. Prior to the passage of the Lisbon Treaty amendments, the sport-related public interest based on the specificity of the industry and its social and educational function was already taken into consideration and accepted by both the Court and the Commission in many internal market cases. This is significant for competition law as well due to the high level of convergence with the free movement area[7] and virtually uniform compatibility tests for organisational rules in sport.

Against this general background, this chapter explains the evolution of the law and policy concerning the application of Articles 101 and 102 TFEU to organisational rules in the sport sector.

6.2 Sporting Rules in Internal Market Jurisprudence

6.2.1 Purely Sporting Rules: Walrave [1974] and Donà [1976]

Apart from sporting rules that do not constitute an economic activity and therefore do not fall within the scope of the Treaty according to para 4 of *Walrave*, the CJEU set out the test for the so-called purely sporting rules. In para 8 of *Walrave* it made an exception for a directly discriminatory sporting rule on selection of athletes for national representative teams. Specifically, with regard to discrimination based on nationality as prohibited under Articles 18, 45 and 56 TFEU, the Court stated that such prohibition 'does not affect the composition of sport teams, in particular national teams, the formation of which is a question of purely sporting interest and as such has nothing to do with economic activity.'[8] It further added in para 9 that 'this restriction on the scope of the provisions in question must however remain limited to its proper objective.' Accordingly, the Treaty would not apply to economic sporting activities as long as the motive for the proportionate rules was non-economic, or in other words, 'purely sporting'.

---

[7]Baquero Cruz 2002; Mortelmans 2001.

[8]Case 36/74 *Walrave and Koch v. Union Cycliste Internationale*, ECLI:EU:C:1974:140, para 8.

Two years later in *Donà*[9] a football agent challenged the strict nationality and residence preconditions for participation in all non-amateur matches imposed by the Italian Football Federation. The challenged rules limited the right to participate in matches (as professional or semi-professional players) almost exclusively to Italian nationals. In para 14 of *Donà*, the Court modified and restricted the rule in para 8 of *Walrave*. The exception to prohibition on direct discrimination for the composition of national teams was reformulated and substituted with the exclusion of foreign players 'from participation in certain matches for the reasons which are not of an economic nature, which relate to the particular nature and context of such matches and are thus of sporting interest only'. Matches between national teams were mentioned only as an example of the kind of exclusion of players that fall under this category of sporting exception.

As acknowledged by AG Lenz in *Bosman*, *Donà* represents a limitation on para 8 in *Walrave*. The Court rightly did not make a reference to that paragraph because it was aware that the question of the composition of sport teams may well be dominated by non-sporting motives. AG Lenz concluded that neither the basis nor the extent of the 'exception' can be deduced with certainty from these two judgments.[10]

Purely sporting rules are therefore the rules that are exempted, since they: (1) produce the required economic effect, (2) are based on non-economic, purely sporting motives, (3) relate to the particular nature and context of certain matches, and (4) are proportionate. According to some authors, the 'purely sporting' rules exception 'does not apply to sports teams, or to general rules on team composition, but only to nationality rules in national team sports'.[11] It is indeed difficult to think of any other rule that would in practice align with the strict demands of this exception. However, as a matter of legal and judicial construction, such possibility exists and the Court has been citing this exception in its other judgments outside the context of nationality discrimination.[12]

6.2.2 *Objectively Justified Rules: Bosman [1995], Lehtonen [2000], and Bernard [2010]*

Unlike purely sporting and inherent rules (discussed below), objectively justified rules in sport constitute restrictions under internal market law. Such restrictions

[9]Case C 13/76 *Gaetano Donà v Mario Mantero*, ECLI:EU.C.1976:115.

[10]Opinion of Advocate General Lenz in Case C-415/93 *Union Royale Belge des Sociétés de Football Association and others v. Bosman and others*, ECLI:EU:C:1995:293, paras 138–139.

[11]Parrish and Miettinen 2008, p. 100.

[12]Case C-519/04 *P David Meca-Medina and Igor Majcen v. Commission*, ECLI:EU:C:2006:492, para 25; Case C-415/93 *Union Royale Belge des Sociétés de Football Association and others v. Bosman and others*, ECLI:EU:C:1995:463, para 76.

can, however, be justified under the generally applicable objective justification framework as set out in *Kraus* and *Gebhard*.[13] Accordingly, those rules that (1) pursued a legitimate aim compatible with the Treaty and were justified by pressing reasons of public interest, and (2) are compatible with the principle of proportionality do not breach the provisions on free movement of persons.[14] Importantly, the assessment of sporting rules under the *Gebhard*-style framework involves a sensitive application of EU law to sport,[15] and the recognition of the specificity of the sports industry. Unlike in ordinary cases, in sport cases the Court uses an alteration of the test for both directly and indirectly discriminatory rules.[16] The Court was asked to consider the legality of organisational rules in sports under Article 45 TFEU in *Bosman*, *Lehtonen*, and *Bernard*.[17]

The facts of the *Bosman* case are well-known; it involved a directly discriminatory '3+2' rule passed by Union of European Football Associations (UEFA) that placed quota on clubs in fielding foreign players and non-discriminatory transfer fee rules which restricted the professional activities of football players. With regard to the latter, in view of the considerable social importance of football in the EU, the Court acknowledged encouraging the recruitment and training of young players and maintaining the competitive balance between clubs as legitimate objectives.[18] Conversely, it brushed aside the attempts to justify quotas on the basis of their alleged necessity to maintain the traditional link between each club and their country, to create a sufficient pool of top national players to be fielded in national representative team, and to maintain competitive balance between clubs. The fact that the quota rule was drawn up in collaboration with the Commission did not shield it from judicial scrutiny or provide any guarantees as to its compatibility with the Treaty, as the Commission does not have the power to authorise rules and practices contrary to the Treaty. Quotas were abolished by the Court, whereas the transfer fees for the expired contracts were found unsuitable for the attainment of the said objectives and also failed the proportionality test.

The Court considered that in the light of its answers under Article 45 TFEU, it was unnecessary to address the questions on interpretation of Articles 101 and 102 TFEU that were also referred to it for a preliminary ruling. However, AG Lenz in *Bosman*, entertained the arguments of the respondent that referred to the 'rule of

[13]Case C-55/94 *Reinhard Gebhard v Consiglio dell'Ordine degli Avvocati e Procuratori di Milano*, ECLI:EU:C:1995:411; Case C-19/92 *Dieter Kraus v Land Baden-Württemberg*, ECLI:EU:C:1993:125.

[14]Ibid., paras 37 and 32.

[15]Parrish and Miettinen 2008, p. 73.

[16]Discriminatory measures normally can only benefit from the exhaustive list of Treaty-based exceptions such as public policy, public health, and public security, but not from an open list of justifications available to non-discriminatory measures. Sport is an exception to this rule.

[17]Case C-325/08, *Olympique Lyonnais v Olivier Bernard and Newcastle United FC*, ECLI:EU:C:2010:143.

[18]Case C-415/93 *Union Royale Belge des Sociétés de Football Association and others v. Bosman and others*, ECLI:EU:C:1995:463, para 106.

reason', a concept applied in the US under Article 1 of the Sherman Act. While he acknowledged that Europe does not have the 'rule of reason' doctrine and instead uses Article 101(3) TFEU as a platform for exemption analysis, he nevertheless found a functional equivalent that existed at the time in the form of the *DLG* case[19] on commercial ancillarity, a precursor to *Wouters* case that contained the same basic approach to assessment of legality of restrictions as the core competition test applied to sporting rules today.[20]

In *Lehtonen*, the transfer of a basketball player did not take place within the specified time period, i.e. within the so-called 'transfer window' passed by the International Basketball Federation. A player that was not employed within the specified period could not play for his team in competitions for that season. Citing *Bosman*, the Court reiterated in para 50 of *Lehtonen* that being fielded is the 'essential purpose of a professional player's activity' and the rules prohibiting fielding restrict the chances of being employed. Because they affected labour market access as opposed to the exercise of economic activity, transfer windows were not inherent rules, but instead restrictions to free movement that fell to be examined under the objective justification framework.[21] The Court found them justified on non-economic grounds, namely the need for proper organisation of the game because mid-season transfers could substantially alter the sporting strength and, therefore, the competition between teams in the course of a championship.[22] Nevertheless, transfer windows in this particular case were found to be disproportionate and in breach of Article 45 of the Treaty because they were opened substantially longer for the players from outside the EU.[23] The instruction from Annex I of the Commission Staff Working Document is that, had the transfer periods in *Lehtonen* been proportionate, they would have been justified not only under free movement law, but also under Articles 101(1) and 102 TFEU.[24] Objectively justified sporting rules under internal market law satisfy the inherency test under competition law and *vice versa*.[25]

The questions on the interpretation of EU competition law provisions were considered inadmissible due to the insufficient factual information provided by the referring national court. Similarly to AG Lenz in *Bosman*, AG Alber in *Lehtonen*

---

[19]Case C-250/92 *Gøttrup-Klim e.a. Grovvareforeninger v Dansk Landbrugs Grovvareselskab AmbA (DLG)*, ECLI:EU:C:1994:413.

[20]Opinion of Advocate General Lenz in Case C-415/93 *Union Royale Belge des Sociétés de Football Association and others v. Bosman and others*, ECLI:EU:C:1995:293, paras 269–270.

[21]Case C-176/96 *Jyri Lehtonen and Castors Canada Dry Namur-Braine ASBL v. Fédération royale belge des sociétés de basket-ball ASBL (FRBSB)*, ECLI:EU:C:2000:201, paras 47–50.

[22]Ibid., paras 51–55.

[23]Ibid., paras 56–58. It was nevertheless left for the national court to ascertain whether there were any objective reasons that could justify this difference in the transfer windows (see para 59).

[24]Commission Staff Working Document of 11 July 2007, COM (2007) 391 final—The EU and Sport: Background and Context—Accompanying document to the White Paper on Sport, Annex I, para 2.2.1.6.

[25]Pijetlovic 2015, pp. 228–233.

considered the rule *prima facie* restrictive, but adopted the reasoning from *DLG* to support the reasoning that necessary and proportionate rules may be saved from being labelled as restrictions.[26]

In *Bernard*, a trainee footballer was required to pay damages for the loss suffered by the club that trained him as a method of compensation for signing his first professional contract with another club and, consequently, breaching his contractual obligations. The Court utilised the obstacle approach to find that the compensation scheme in *Bernard*, while constituting neither a prohibition on signing a contract with a club in another Member State nor discrimination on the basis of nationality, nevertheless discourages the player from exercising his right of free movement by making it less attractive.[27] Referring to the *Bosman* case by taking into account the considerable social importance of sporting activities, in particular football, in the EU, the Court accepted the objective of encouraging recruitment and training of young players as legitimate.[28] The social importance of sport played a crucial role in legitimating this objective and it would probably not be accepted as such in (m)any other employment sectors. Unlike in *Bosman*, the compensation fees in *Bernard* were deemed capable of attaining the said objective.[29] Thereafter, the Court referred for the first time to Article 165(1) TFEU; it set out the standard of application of the proportionality principle in the objective justification framework, according to which account must be taken of the specific characteristics of sport and its social and educational function.[30] The same standard of application of proportionality test, it is submitted, applies in the interpretation and application of EU competition law to sport.

6.2.3 Inherent Rules: Deliège [2000]

The concept of inherent rules originated in *Deliège* where the Court was asked to determine the compatibility with Article 56 (and Articles 101 and 102) TFEU of selection rules of the governing body for judo in Belgium limiting the number of participants in the high-level international competitions that do not involve national teams competing against each other. The question forwarded to the CJEU by the Tribunal de Première de Namur was whether it was contrary to those articles to 'require professional or semi-professional athletes, or persons aspiring to professional or semi-professional activity, to be authorised by their federation in

[26]Opinion of Advocate General Alber in Case C-176/96 *Jyri Lehtonen and Castors Canada Dry Namur-Braine ASBL v. Fédération royale belge des sociétés de basket-ball ASBL (FRBSB)*, ECLI:EU:C:1999:321, paras 107–108.

[27]Case C-325/08, *Olympique Lyonnais v Olivier Bernard and Newcastle United FC*, ECLI: EU:C:2010:143, paras 23–37.

[28]Ibid., para 39.

[29]Ibid., paras 41–45.

[30]Ibid., para 40.

order to be able to compete in international competition which does not involve national teams competing against each other'.[31]

The Court first dismissed the applicability of the purely sporting rule exception and recognised that unlike in *Bosman the rules challenged in Deliège* 'do not determine the conditions governing *access* to the labour market by professional sportsmen and do not contain nationality clauses limiting the number of nationals of other Member States who may participate in a competition'.[32] The selection rules at issue in the main proceedings were, therefore, considered as non-discriminatory rules affecting the exercise of an economic activity rather than discriminatory market access rules.[33] The Court proceeded to specify that the challenged rules could not in themselves constitute an obstacle on the freedom to provide services under Article 56 TFEU because limiting the number of participants 'is *inherent* in the conduct of an international high-level sports event, which necessarily involves certain selection rules or criteria being adopted'.[34] The sport organisations must further be able to demonstrate that selection rules are based on objective criteria independent from the personal circumstances of the athletes.[35]

Although the Court did not explicitly mention that the inherent rules should be proportionate, such requirement follows from para 65 of the judgment:

> [...] the adoption, for the purposes of an international sports tournament, of one system for selecting participants rather than another must be based on a large number of considerations unconnected with the personal situation of any athlete, such as the nature, the organisation and the financing of the sport concerned.

Accordingly, the discriminatory rule would be considered disproportionate and would fail the inherency test. The preference of one system over another is left to sporting bodies and organisers[36] as long as the selection is made on the basis of objective factors unconnected with the athletes' personal situation. The proportionality of such a system is not questioned by the Court as it is deemed proportionate by default.

Only non-discriminatory rules that do not relate to market access can satisfy the inherency test under the free movement provisions.[37] Therefore, the inherent rules

[31]Cases C-51/96 and C-191/97 *Christelle Deliège v. Ligue Francophone de Judo et Disciplines Associées ASBL and others*, ECLI:EU:C:2000:199, para 22.

[32]Ibid., para 61.

[33]Under the '*Säger* formula' this would have been enough to find a breach. Para 12 of Case C-76/90 *Manfred Säger v Dennemeyer & Co. Ltd*, ECLI:EU:C:1991:331 provides that Article 56 TFEU requires: '*not only the elimination of all discrimination against a person providing services on the ground of his nationality but also the abolition of any restriction, even if it applies without distinction to national providers of services and to those of other Member States, when it is liable to prohibit or otherwise impede the activities of provider of services established in another Member State where he lawfully provides similar services*'. See on this point Parrish and Miettinen 2008.

[34]Cases C-51/96 and C-191/97 *Christelle Deliège v. Ligue Francophone de Judo et Disciplines Associées ASBL and others*, ECLI:EU:C:2000:199, para 64 (emphasis added).

[35]Ibid., para 65.

[36]Ibid., paras 67–68.

[37]Parrish and Miettinen 2008.

exception includes rules that, based on legitimate objectives,[38] do not constitute restrictions because they derive from the need, and their restrictive effects are, inherent in the organisation of sport, and are proportionate. The Commission in its Communication on Sport did not differentiate between competition and internal market law when it examined the compatibility of sporting rules with any EU law against the inherency and proportionality tests.[39]

The questions on the interpretation of EU competition law provisions in *Deliège* were similar to those expressed in *Lehtonen* in claiming them inadmissible due to insufficient factual information provided by the referring national court. AG Cosmas in *Deliège* referred to and followed the approach of AG Lenz in *Bosman*.[40]

6.2.4 Final Remarks

The distinctions made in internal market cases between purely sporting, inherent, and objectively justified rules do not apply in the analytical structure of competition law to organisational rules in sport. It is submitted that the different types of sporting rules identified in internal market law cases should all be dealt with under a single objective justification test, since it is able to accommodate every type of organisational rule and yet produce the same result. This would also bring clarity in cases where a legal claim is raised under both internal market and competition provisions of the Treaty. This judicial route naturally stems from the analytical framework provided by the *Meca-Medina/Wouters* test, discussed in Sect. 6.7, which mirrors the objective justification test under internal market law.

6.3 Applicability of Articles 101 and 102 TFEU in the Sporting Sector

Articles 101 and 102 TFEU provide a primary tool to control behaviour by undertakings that produce anti-competitive effects. The underlying objectives of these articles are of economic nature and include protecting undistorted competition on

[38]This criterion is specifically mentioned only in relation to competition provisions (in *Meca-Medina* case) but it applies to free movement as well. In *Deliège* the objective of the challenged rules was to make competitions workable by allowing only a limited number of selected participants.

[39]The Communication from the Commission to the European Parliament, the Council, the European Economic and Social Committee and the Committee of the Regions of 18 January 2011, COM(2011) 12 final Developing the European Dimension in Sport, para 4.2.

[40]Opinion of Advocate General Cosmas in Joined Cases C-51/96 and C-191/97 *Christelle Deliège v. Ligue Francophone de Judo et Disciplines Associées ASBL and others*, ECLI:EU:C:1999:147, paras 110–112.

the market, achieving optimal allocation of resources, increasing consumer welfare and aiding in creation of the European internal market.[41] During the various stages of integration the EU increasingly moved from a purely economic constitution designed for a market-oriented system to a constitutional model inclusive of wider socio-cultural concerns. This is reflected in both the application of EU competition articles by the EU institutions as well as in the development of EU sports law and policy. The application of antitrust law to organisational rules in the sporting sector inevitably raises questions on the interrelationship and balance between economic and social dimensions of the Union's policy and can become a relatively complex issue.

Article 101(1) TFEU prohibits agreements between undertakings, decisions by associations of undertakings or concerted practices, which are considered capable of affecting trade between Member States and that have as their object (i.e., subjectively intend) or effect (i.e., objectively cause)[42] the prevention, restriction, or distortion of competition within the internal market. Article 102 TFEU prohibits the abuse of market power by undertakings in a dominant position in one or more relevant markets. The thrust of this policy is not to prohibit the acquisition and existence of power per se, but is directed at controlling the unilateral behaviour of a dominant firm(s). In essence, three related enquiries must be conducted when determining the existence of an abuse of a dominant position,[43] namely relevant market determination, dominance on the relevant market and establishing the abuse of that dominant position.

According to settled case law, Articles 101 and 102 TFEU are not mutually exclusive, but may be applied simultaneously.[44] Already in its early judgment of *Continental Can* the CJEU held that Articles 101 and 102 TFEU seek to attain the same aim of maintaining effective competition within the common market.[45] The agreements between two or more undertakings containing restrictive clauses might create or reinforce a position of dominance which is, or may become, subject to abuse. Such agreements may be deemed incompatible with both Article 101 and 102 TFEU.

---

[41]For more details, see Craig and De Búrca 2011, p. 959.

[42]For the concept of 'effects on trade', see Case C-56/65 *Societe Technique Miniere v. Maschinenbau Ulm (STM)*, ECLI:EU:C:1966:38, para 7; Case 56/64 *Consten and Grundig*, ECLI:EU:C:1966:41, para 27. See also European Commission Guidelines of 27 April 2004, on the effects on trade concept contained in Articles 81 and 82 of the Treaty [2004] OJ C 101/81.

[43]The Court has laid down the definition of the concept of dominant position in Case 27/76 *United Brands v. Commission*, ECLI:EU:C:1978:22, para 65.

[44]See Case 85/76 *Hoffmann-La Roche*, ECLI:EU:C:1979:36, para 116; Case 66/86 *Ahmed Saeed Flugreisen and Silver Line Reisebüro GmbH v Zentrale zur Bekämpfung unlauteren Wettbewerbs e.V.*, ECLI:EU:C:1989:140, para 37; Joined Cases C-395/96 P and C-396/96 P *Compagnie Maritime Belge Transports SA, Compagnie Maritime Belge SA and Dafra-Lines A/S v Commission*, ECLI:EU:C:2000:132, para 33.

[45]Case 6/72 *Europemballage Corporation and Continental Can Company Inc. v. Commission*, ECLI:EU:C:1973:22, para 11; See also Case T-51/89 *Tetra Pack Rausing SA v. Commission*, ECLI:EU:T:1990:41, para 22.

It has been recognised that national and international sporting associations, clubs and independent athletes can constitute 'undertakings'.[46] Sporting federations can, in addition, also constitute an 'association of undertakings'[47] or an 'association of associations of undertakings'.[48] Their rules can amount to 'agreements or decisions,'[49] distort competition within the relevant market and affect trade between Member States within the meaning of Articles 101 and 102 TFEU.[50] Article 102 TFEU does not include the concept of 'association of undertakings', but applies to unilateral conduct of one or more dominant 'undertakings'. The General Court has held that even where a sports federation, such as FIFA, is not active on a particular market, it may be considered an 'undertaking' under

---

[46]For national and international sporting associations as undertakings see Case T-193/02, *Laurent Piau v Commission*, ECLI:EU:T:2005:22, paras 69–72; Commission Decision of 27 June 2002, COMP IV/37.806—ENIC/UEFA, para 25; Opinion of Advocate General Lenz in Case C-415/93 *Union Royale Belge des Sociétés de Football Association and others v. Bosman and others*, ECLI:EU:C:1995:293, points 255 et seq; Commission Decision of 27 Ocober 1992, in IV/33.378 and IV/33.384—Distribution of package tours during the 1990 World Cup [1992] OJ L 326/31, paras 47 and 52–53. For individual athletes as undertakings see Cases C-51/96 and C-191/97 *Christelle Deliège v. Ligue Francophone de Judo et Disciplines Associées ASBL and others*, ECLI:EU:C:2000:199, paras 56–57. According to AG Lenz in *Bosman*, para 263, football players employed by a football club do not constitute undertakings, as they are workers and not providers of services. See Commission Staff Working Document of 11 July 2007, COM (2007) 391 final - The EU and Sport: Background and Context - Accompanying document to the White Paper on Sport, Annex I, para 2.1.3 clarifies that '*even if athletes are employed by a sport club, they may be considered undertakings insofar as they carry out economic activities independent thereof, e.g., by entering into sponsoring agreements*'.

[47]Case T-193/02, *Laurent Piau v Commission*, ECLI:EU:T:2005:22, paras 69–72, where the General Court held that '*69. [...] FIFA's members are national associations, which are groupings of football clubs for which the practice of football is an economic activity. These football clubs are therefore undertakings within the meaning of Article [101 TFEU] and the national associations grouping them together are associations of undertakings within the meaning of that provision. 70. The fact that the national associations are groupings of 'amateur' clubs, alongside 'professional' clubs, is not capable of calling that assessment into question. [...] 72. Since the national associations constitute associations of undertakings and also, by virtue of the economic activities that they pursue, undertakings, FIFA, an association grouping together national associations, also constitutes an association of undertakings within the meaning of Article [101 TFEU].*' See also Opinion of Advocate General Lenz in Case C-415/93 *Union Royale Belge des Sociétés de Football Association and others v. Bosman and others*, ECLI:EU:C:1995:293, paras 255–257; Commission Decision of 23 July 2003, COMP/C.2-37.398 – Joint Selling of the Commercial Rights of the UEFA Champions League [2003] OJ L 291/25.

[48]Ibid., UEFA Champions League, para 106.

[49]Case T-193/02, *Laurent Piau v Commission*, ECLI:EU:T:2005:22, para 75. Rules drawn up unilaterally by sporting associations consisting of undertakings will usually constitute decisions by an association of aundertakings (see Commission Decision of 27 June 2002, COMP IV/37.806—ENIC/UEFA, para 26, for a rule drawn up by the UEFA Executive Committee, and Case C-519/04 *P David Meca-Medina and Igor Majcen v. Commission*, ECLI:EU:C:2006:492, para 45 for a rule drawn up by the International Olympic Committee and implemented by the International Swimming Federation).

[50]For general guidance see European Commission Guidelines of 27 April 2004, on the effect of trade concept contained in Articles 81 and 82 of the Treaty [2004] OJ C 101/7.

Article 102 TFEU to the extent that it represents the emanation of its members that are active on that market.[51] Furthermore, when they directly engage in an economic activity, sporting federations usually acquire a status of an undertaking in a monopolistic position,[52] whereas clubs organised in a league may be held collectively dominant within the meaning of Article 102 as interpreted by the relevant case law.[53] Rules adopted by international sporting organisations would normally affect trade between Member States due to their scope of application. Additionally, rules of national sports associations usually affect only the territory of their respective country, but in the light of the high degree of internationalisation and mobility in professional sport, those rules may also affect trade between Member States.[54]

The scope of Articles 101(1) and 102 TFEU is very broad since no actual and direct effect on trade is required and *prima facie* any agreement and any abuse of a dominant position may be covered by these provisions. However, there are a number of exceptions available. Two exceptions that are of particular importance for the topic of this chapter are the economic efficiency defence and the judicially developed ancillary restraints doctrine.

6.4 Exceptions Under Articles 101 and 102 TFEU

6.4.1 Economic Efficiency Defence Under Articles 101(3) and 102 TFEU

Agreements, decisions or practices that are incompatible with Article 101(1), but satisfy the conditions under Article 101(3) of the Treaty, are valid and enforceable with no prior decision to that effect being required.[55] The rationale behind this provision is that certain agreements may have both pro-competitive and

[51]Case T-193/02, *Laurent Piau v Commission*, ECLI:EU:T:2005:22, paras 112 and 116.

[52]Commission Staff Working Document of 11 July 2007, COM (2007) 391 final - The EU and Sport: Background and Context - Accompanying document to the White Paper on Sport, Annex I, para 2.1.4 recognises that: '*sports associations usually have practical monopolies in a given sport and may thus normally be considered dominant in the market of the organisation of sport events under Article [102] EC.*'.

[53]For discussion on the concept of collective dominance in the sporting context see Case T-193/02, *Laurent Piau v Commission*, ECLI:EU:T:2005:22, paras 113–115; Opinion of Advocate General Lenz in Case C-415/93 *Union Royale Belge des Sociétés de Football Association and others v. Bosman and others*, ECLI:EU:C:1995:293, para 285.

[54]For more on the application of basic elements of EU competition law in sporting sector, see Commission Staff Working Document of 11 July 2007, COM (2007) 391 final - The EU and Sport: Background and Context - Accompanying document to the White Paper on Sport, discussed in Sect. 6.6.

[55]Council Regulation (EC) of 16 December 2002, No 1/2003 on the implementation of the rules on competition laid down in Articles 81 and 82 of the Treaty [2003] OJ L 1/1, Article 1(2).

anti-competitive features. The dual nature of economic effects usually involves complex economic analysis weighting the beneficial and harmful effects in order to determine whether the agreement qualifies for the exemption. Accordingly, those agreements, decisions or practices that fulfil the four conditions outlined in this provision would benefit from an exemption. Two positive conditions state that an agreement must improve the production or distribution of goods or promote technical or economic progress, and at the same time allow consumers a fair share of the resulting benefits. Two negative conditions require that an agreement cannot contain any restrictions that are not essential to the attainment of the objectives under agreement (i.e. disproportionate restrictions) and cannot lead to the elimination of competition in respect of a substantial part of the product in question. Balancing of anti-competitive and pro-competitive effects is conducted exclusively within the framework laid down by Article 101(3),[56] and there is no scope in this provision for non-competition arguments that cannot be translated into economic efficiencies.[57] The approach of the EU Commission is that under Article 101(3), public policy objectives may be taken into account only if they can be subsumed under one of its four conditions,[58] so as a supplement to economic benefits that the agreement generates.[59]

A company holding a dominant position may benefit from an exemption under Article 101(3) of the Treaty when its conditions are fulfilled.[60] In the *Piau* case decided in the sporting context, the General Court held that if the conduct of a

---

[56]See European Commission Guidelines of 27 April 2004, on application of Article 81(3) of the Treaty [2004] OJ C 101/97, para 11; European Commission Guidelines of 14 January 2011, on the applicability of Article 101 of the Treaty on the Functioning of the European Union to horizontal co-operation agreements [2011] OJ C11/1, para 20. See also Case T-65/98 *Van den Bergh Foods Ltd v Commission*, ECLI:EU:T:2003:281, para 107; Case T-112/99 *Métropole télévision (M6), Suez-Lyonnaise des eaux, France Télécom and Télévision française 1 SA (TF1) v Commission*, ECLI:EU:T:2001:215, para 74, where the General Court held that it is only in the framework of Article 101(3) that the pro- and anti-competitive aspects of a restriction may be weighed.

[57]See also Semmelmann 2008, p. 15. The Commission has accepted arguments on the basis of environmental protection in Case IV/F 1/36/718 - *CECED* [2000] OJ L 187/47. In Case 26/76 *Metro SB-Großmärkte GmbH & Co. KG v Commission*, ECLI:EU:C:1977:167, para 43, the Court has accepted that '*the establishment of supply forecasts for a reasonable period constitutes a stabilising factor with regard to the provision of employment which, since it improves general conditions of production, […] comes within the framework of the objectives to which reference may be had pursuant to Article [101(3)]*'. The stabilising effect of an agreement on employment may translate into cost savings and other efficiency gains.

[58]European Commission Guidelines of 27 April 2004, on the application of Article 81(3) of the Treaty [2004] OJ C 101/97, para 42. So far, the other policy objectives have been considered under the first condition. See also Commission White Paper of 28 April 1999, on Modernisation of the rules implementing Articles 81 and 82 of the EC Treaty, Commission Programme No 99/027 1999/OJ C 132/1, which in para 56 states that Article 101(3) is meant to '*provide a legal framework for the economic assessment of restrictive practices and not to allow the application of the competition rules to be set aside because of political considerations*'.

[59]See Sect. 6.4.2.

[60]European Commission Guidelines of 27 April 2004, on the application of Article 81(3) of the Treaty [2004] OJ C 101/97, pp. 97–118, para 106.

dominant company satisfies all the conditions of Article 101(3) such conduct should not be classified as an abuse under Article 102 of the Treaty.[61]

Unlike Article 101 TFEU, Article 102 TFEU does not contain an exemption provision. However, the Commission outlined in its 2005 Discussion Paper the conditions under which a dominant company may also rely on the efficiency defence in cases of abusive exclusionary conduct. These conditions, which reproduce the four cumulative criteria of Article 101(3) TFEU, were later confirmed in the Commission Guidance reflecting the overall reform and the uniform approach towards Article 102 TFEU and shifting the focus from the form-based towards a more effects-based analysis.[62] By mirroring the cartel exemption provision, the efficiency defence amounts to a functional and analytical equivalent of Article 101(3) TFEU in the framework of Article 102 TFEU.

6.4.2 Regulatory Ancillarity

Ancillary restraints (restrictions on competition that are directly related and objectively necessary for the implementation of the main non-restrictive transaction and are proportionate to it) fall outside of the ambit of Article 101(1) TFEU.[63] The *STM*, *Metro* and *DLG* cases[64] involved 'commercial ancillarity' restraints because the restrictions on competition were ancillary to a legitimate *commercial* purpose.[65]

The exception that is relevant for organisational rules in sport was introduced by the CJEU in *Wouters*[66] and it was characterised by Monti as a 'European-style rule of reason'[67] and by Whish, perhaps more accurately, as a 'regulatory ancillarity'.[68] The judgment does not really introduce the rule of reason in Article 101(1) because balancing of the pro- and anti-competitive effects of restrictions involves economic

[61]Case T-193/02, *Laurent Piau v Commission*, ECLI:EU:T:2005:22, para 119.

[62]Communication from the Commission of 24 February 2009, Guidance on the Commission's enforcement priorities in applying Article 82 of the EC Treaty to abusive exclusionary conduct by dominant undertakings [2009] OJ C 45/7, para 30.

[63]European Commission Guidelines of 27 April 2004, on the Application of Article 81(3) of the Treaty [2004] OJ C 101/97, paras 28–31; Case T-112/99 *Métropole télévision (M6), Suez-Lyonnaise des eaux, France Télécom and Télévision française 1 SA (TF1) v Commission*, ECLI:EU:T:2001:215, para 104.

[64]Case C-56/65 *Societe Technique Miniere v. Maschinenbau Ulm (STM)*, ECLI:EU:C:1966:38; Case 26/76 *Metro SB-Großmärkte GmbH & Co. KG v Commission*, ECLI:EU:C:1977:167; Case C-250/92 *Gøttrup-Klim e.a. Grovvareforeninger v Dansk Landbrugs Grovvareselskab AmbA (DLG)*, ECLI:EU:C:1994:413.

[65]As termed by Whish 2009, p. 126.

[66]Case C-309/99 *J. C. J. Wouters, J. W. Savelbergh and Price Waterhouse Belastingadviseurs BV v Algemene Raad van de Nederlandse Orde van Advocaten*, ECLI:EU:C:2002:98, para 97.

[67]Monti 2002, pp. 1087–1088.

[68]As termed by Whish 2009, p. 126.

arguments on both sides, whereas *Wouters* introduces a balancing between EU competition law objectives and non-economic public interests that do not necessarily need to be a part of the Union's objectives. Accordingly, certain types of agreements or decisions that restrict the commercial behaviour of undertakings do not violate the prohibition in Article 101(1) TFEU, if, because of their *context and objectives*, the restrictions in those agreements or decisions are *inherent* and *proportionate* to the realisation of non-competition objectives.[69] In the case law on regulatory ancillarity[70] the exception was applied only in cases of regulatory restrictions imposed by collective private bodies (and public legal persons when engaging in economic activity and not exercising powers which are typical of public authority) in the public interest, whether at national, European or global level. The Court has so far applied this framework only to rules having a public law character and deemed necessary for the proper organisation and ethical conduct of a certain profession. It is submitted that these facts do not imply that the framework developed under that case law cannot be used to accommodate other kinds of non-competition objectives, in particular those under policy-linking clauses of the Treaty, the importance of which has been enhanced by the Lisbon amendments.[71] To allow a reliance on the public interest defence for agreements concluded by private parties that do not derive their powers from public laws, especially private collective bodies such as the *Fédération Internationale de Football Association* (FIFA) and UEFA, is necessary in an area where no responsible public authority vested with powers to enforce the laws protecting those public interests exists.[72] It represents a constitutional fine-tuning of the Union's competition law in view of the increase in private governance and self-regulation of certain sectors and the corresponding decrease in the private/public divide in EU law.

It is worth mentioning that in the *ENIC* case concerning the UEFA rule prohibiting multiple ownership of clubs the Commission applied the *Wouters* test and recognised its necessity. The foregoing considerations present one of the reasons why the principle of convergence ought to be formally adopted within competition and internal market provisions to the extent possible.[73] The Court has anyhow

---

[69]Case C-309/99 *J. C. J. Wouters, J. W. Savelbergh and Price Waterhouse Belastingadviseurs BV v Algemene Raad van de Nederlandse Orde van Advocaten*, ECLI:EU:C:2002:98, para 97; Case C-519/04 *P David Meca-Medina and Igor Majcen v. Commission*, ECLI:EU:C:2006:492, para 42.

[70]Ibid.; Case C-1/12 *Ordem dos Técnicos Oficiais de Contas v Autoridade da Concorrência (OTOC)*, ECLI:EU:C:2013:127, and Case C-136/12 *Consiglio nazionale dei geologi v Autorità garante della concorrenza e del mercato and Autorità garante della concorrenza e del mercato v Consiglio nazionale dei geologi (CNG)*, ECLI:EU:C:2013:489. See also Commission Decision of 27 June 2002, COMP IV/37.806 — ENIC/UEFA.

[71]Pijetlovic 2015, p. 153. The EU for the first time has a duty to mainstream the policy objectives under Article 7 TFEU after the Lisbon amendments: '*The Union shall ensure consistency between its policies and activities, taking all of its objectives into account and in accordance with the principle of conferral of powers*'.

[72]However, the General Court held that where there is public authority with powers, for example, in relation to product safety, it is not for private undertakings to take the initiative to eliminate the products which are not safe. See Case T-30/89 *Hilti AG v Commission*, ECLI:EU:T:1991:70, para 118.

[73]Pijetlovic 2015, pp. 215–235.

made some competition decisions on the basis of single market considerations, which at that time, due to misunderstandings and lack of any references to convergence, attracted a lot of criticism.[74]

The framework established by *Wouters* can accommodate any other policy objectives in accordance with Article 7 TFEU and, at the same time, stay faithful to the already established and persistently defended paradigms that balancing of anti-competitive and pro-competitive effects is conducted exclusively within the framework of Article 101(3) TFEU. Only economic efficiencies are to be taken into account in the exemption provision which includes public policy objectives that can be translated into an economic efficiency argument.[75]

Namely, an agreement or decision that restricts competition, but genuinely pursues a public policy objective under some of the policy-linking clauses[76] or outside their scope,[77] that is not protected by a public regulation,[78] and that fulfils the *Wouters* criteria could thus escape the scope of Article 101(1) TFEU. Should the outcome of the *Wouters* test be different, the agreement or decision would have to satisfy the four conditions of Article 101(3). If the public policy objective that it pursues can be transposed into economic benefits, it should be taken into account also in the framework of the exemption provision, although it is likely to fail the indispensability requirement in the cases where it already failed to satisfy the proportionality under *Wouters*. This is the true face of the European-style rule of reason and to interpret the exemption provision as suitable for purely non-competition arguments would have the effect of completely blurring the distinction between the different paragraphs of Article 101.[79]

Under Article 102 TFEU, the EU Courts and the Commission normally use the concept of objective justification coupled with the proportionality test[80] instead of

---

[74]See, for example, discussion on Case 56/64 *Consten and Grundig*, ECLI:EU:C:1966:41, Jones and Sufrin 2011, pp. 204–209.

[75]Monti 2002, p. 1057 and pp. 1090–1091; Faull and Nikpay 2007, para 3.406; Case T-17/98 *Matra Hatchette v Commission*, ECLI:EU:C:2000:70, para 139; Joined Cases C-403/08 and C-429/08) *Football Association Premier League Ltd and others v QC Leisure and others and Karen Murphy v Media Protection Services Ltd*, ECLI:EU:C:2011:631.

[76]Such as clauses related to environmental protection in Article 11 TFEU, consumer protection in Article 12 TFEU, achieving high level of employment in Article 147(2) TFEU, respect for cultural diversities in Article 167(4) TFEU, health protection in Article 168(1) TFEU, competitiveness of the Union's industry in Article 173(3) TFEU, and regional development under Article 175 TFEU.

[77]See Case C-309/99 *J. C. J. Wouters, J. W. Savelbergh and Price Waterhouse Belastingadviseurs BV v Algemene Raad van de Nederlandse Orde van Advocaten*, ECLI:EU:C:2002:98, Case C-519/04 *P David Meca-Medina and Igor Majcen v. Commission*, ECLI:EU:C:2006:492, and Case C-250/92 *Gøttrup-Klim e.a. Grovvareforeninger v Dansk Landbrugs Grovvareselskab AmbA (DLG)*, ECLI:EU:C:1994:413.

[78]Case T-30/89 *Hilti AG v Commission* [1991] ECR II-1439, ECLI:EU:T:1991:70, para 118.

[79]Pijetlovic 2015, p. 156.

[80]Case T-65/89 *BPB Industries Plc and British Gypsum Ltd v Commission*, ECLI:EU:T:1993:31, para 94; Case T-30/89 *Hilti AG v Commission* [1991] ECR II-1439, ECLI:EU:T:1991:70, paras 102–119; Case 311/84 *Centre belge d'études de marché - Télémarketing (CBEM) v SA Compagnie luxembourgeoise de télédiffusion (CLT) and Information publicité Benelux (IPB)*, ECLI:EU:C:1985:394, para 26.

the ancillary restraints doctrine, although both concepts perform exactly the same function. It would appear from the decisional practice of the Commission, as well as from the Commission's Guidance,[81] that objective justifications may include non-economic objectives and amount to an equivalent of public policy justification under Article 101(1) TFEU. A dominant undertaking that engages in an abusive, but objectively justified and proportionate conduct will be, as a matter of technicality, considered as not having committed an abuse in the first place.[82]

It is submitted that the objective justification defence has been replaced by the *Wouters* test when applying Article 102 TFEU to regulatory acts of collective bodies that pursue a public policy interest. With regard to organisational rules in sport, this submission is no longer debatable. The Commission in its Staff Working Document was unequivocal that *Meca-Medina*, that fully embraced *Wouters* test in regard to Article 101(1) TFEU, provides guidance as regards the methodological approach towards assessing a sporting rule under *both* Articles 101 and 102 TFEU.[83]

6.5 Commission Investigation in *FIA* [2001] and Court's Decision in *MOTOE* [2008]

A case concerning the conflict of interest between the regulatory and commercial functions of a sport association involved the *Fédération Internationale d'Automobile* (FIA), the international association for motor sport. FIA is the organiser and promoter of motor sport championships, including Formula One. It issued licences to any party wishing to participate in international motor sport events authorised by FIA, including track owners, vehicle manufacturers, organisers of motor sport events and drivers. License holders were allowed to organise or enter only those events authorised by FIA. Entering or organising events not authorised by FIA would lead to the loss of their license and the end of any commercial activity in motor sport. This way, FIA was able to exercise control over everyone and everything needed to stage a rival championship that could compete with FIA's events.

The Commission found evidence that the competing GTR Organisation was forced out of the market by FIA's rules and that the GTR series were replaced

[81]Communication from the Commission of 24 February 2009, Guidance on the Commission's enforcement priorities in applying Article 82 of the EC Treaty to abusive exclusionary conduct by dominant undertakings [2009] OJ C 45/7.

[82]On the last point, see Opinion of Advocate General Jacobs in Case C-53/03 *Synetairismos Farmakopoion Aitolias & Akarnanias (Syfait) and Others v. GlaxoSmithKline plc and GlaxoSmithKline AEVE, formerly Glaxowellcome AEVE*, ECLI:EU:C:2004:673, para 72.

[83]Commission Staff Working Document of 11 July 2007, COM (2007) 391 final - The EU and Sport: Background and Context—Accompanying document to the White Paper on Sport, Annex I, para 2.1.1; Case C-250/92 *Gøttrup-Klim e.a. Grovvareforeninger v Dansk Landbrugs Grovvareselskab AmbA (DLG)*, ECLI:EU:C:1994:413.

by the FIA GT Championship. Furthermore, FIA claimed media rights to all events incorporating the FIA name, which were then transferred to International Sportsworld Communicators (ISC). In addition, Formula One teams were forced by the terms of the tripartite Concorde Agreement to assign all broadcasting rights in the Formula One championship to FIA, which were later transferred to Formula One Administration Ltd (FOA), a commercial rights holder. The same agreement also prevented Formula One teams from racing in any other series comparable to Formula One for a considerably long period of time. The promoters' rights were taken directly by FOA, which had been given the power by the FIA to determine who can and cannot be a promoter of a grand prix. It is also interesting to note that the vice-president of FIA, Bernie Ecclestone, was in control of both FOA and ISC.

An agreement between FOA and a number of broadcasters and promoters involved in the Formula One championship was reinforcing the existing hurdles for those who wished to stage a series competing with Formula One. The promoters' contracts prevented circuits used for Formula One races from being used for competing races, while the agreements with broadcasters placed a massive financial penalty, ranging from between 33 to 50 % of the price paid, if they televised anything deemed by FOA to be a competitive threat to Formula One.[84]

In 1999, the Commission issued a Statement of Objections. It came to the preliminary conclusion that the rules described were contrary to Articles 101(1) and 102 TFEU as they gave FIA control to block the organisation of races that competed with the events FIA promoted or organised, in particular Formula One from which it derived the biggest commercial benefit. The Commission also objected to certain terms of the contracts between the FOA and broadcasters. Finally, the Commission objected to FIA rules according to which FIA automatically acquired media rights to all motor sport events, even if they were promoted by a different promoter. The core of all of the objections was directed at the conflict between the FIA's legitimate role as the regulator of international motor sport and its commercial interests.[85]

In 2001 the Commission closed the case after reaching a settlement with FIA's president Max Mosley and the CEO of FOA Bernie Ecclestone. The settlement provided that FIA would:

> limit its role to that of a sport regulator without influence over the commercial exploitation of the sport and thus removing any conflict of interest (through the appointment by FIA of a 'commercial rights holder' for 100 years in exchange for a one-off fee); guarantee access to motor sport to any racing organisation and to no longer prevent teams to participate in and circuit owners to organize other races provided the requisite safety standards are met; waive its TV rights or transfer them to the promoters concerned; and remove the anticompetitive clauses from the agreements between FOA and broadcasters.[86]

[84] Commission Press Release of 30 June 1999, IP/99/434 Commission opens formal proceedings into Formula One and other international motor racing series.

[85] Commission Press Release of 26 January 2001, IP/01/120 Commission welcomes progress towards resolving the long-running FIA/Formula One case.

[86] Commission Staff Working Document of 11 July 2007, COM (2007) 391 final - The EU and Sport: Background and Context - Accompanying document to the White Paper on Sport, Annex I, para 2.2.2.1.

Later in 2001, after consultation with all the interested parties, the Commission closed its investigation in the *FIA* case satisfied that the agreed amendments will alleviate competition concerns.[87] In 2003 it ended its monitoring of FIA's compliance with the 2001 settlement.[88]

It is important to compare this case with *MOTOE* in which the restrictions on competition were enabled through the grant of special or exclusive rights by the Greek government. In *MOTOE*, Article 49 of the Greek Road Traffic Code provided that a license to organise motorcycling events would be issued to the organisers by the Minister for Public Order or the authorities empowered by him only after the organiser secures the consent from the official representative of the *Fédération Internationale de Motocyclisme* (the International Motorcycling Federation) in Greece. Accordingly, the power to grant consent for the organisation of motorcycling events was given to ELPA (*Elliniki Leskhi Aftokinitou kai Periigiseon* - Automobile and Touring Club of Greece), a legal person and a non-profit association which organized the same kinds of events in Greece. MOTOE (Greek Motorcycling Federation) planned to organise a motorcycling competition in Greece, but ELPA rejected its application for no objective reason and, therefore, failed to obtain authorisation from the competent ministry. Subsequently, MOTOE claimed pecuniary damages from the government in the Greek national court relying on Articles 102 and 106(1) TFEU. Article 49 of the Greeks Road Traffic Code conferred on ELPA a position of monopoly power over the organisation of motorcycle events in Greece which as such does not breach Article 102 of the Treaty unless that power is being abused. MOTOE claimed that ELPA abused its monopolistic position by refusing to grant the consent needed for authorisation of its planned event.

There was no doubt that ELPA was dominant on the markets for the organisation of motorcycling events and for their commercial exploitation by means of sponsorship, advertising and insurance contracts. Granting special or exclusive rights to an undertaking to control whether and under which conditions other undertakings can gain access and engage in activities on the relevant market entails such conclusion. ELPA's monopoly to grant the necessary consent was statutory and, therefore, the examination of Article 106 TFEU was needed. The classification of ELPA as an undertaking entrusted with the operation of 'services of general economic interests' for the purposes of Article 106(2) TFEU was dismissed on the following ground: the undertaking's economic activities related to the organisation and commercial exploitation of motorcycling events were not conferred by an act of entrustment by the public authority, an element needed for the application of this provision. The power to grant consent to applications for authorisation to organise motorcycling events, although stemming from an act of public authority, could not be classified as an economic activity. Consequently, Article 106(2) TFEU was held inapplicable to this part of ELPA's activities.[89]

---

[87]Commission Press Release of 30 October 2001, IP/01/1523 Commission closes its investigation into Formula One and other four-wheel motor sports.

[88]Commission Press Release of 31 October 2003, IP/03/1491 Commission ends monitoring of FIA/Formula One compliance with 2001 settlement.

[89]Case C-49/07 *Motosykletistiki Omospondia Ellados NPID (MOTOE) v Elliniko Dimosio*, ECLI:EU:C:2008:376, paras 44–47.

The Court then turned its attention to Article 106(1) TFEU in conjunction with Article 102 TFEU. The mere creation or reinforcement of a dominant position through the grant of special or exclusive rights within the meaning of Article 106(1) TFEU was not in itself considered incompatible with Article 102 TFEU. However, it held that:

> a Member State will be in breach of the prohibitions laid down by those two provisions if the undertaking in question, merely by exercising the special or exclusive rights conferred upon it, is led to abuse its dominant position or where such rights are liable to create a situation in which that undertaking is led to commit such abuses (*Höfner and Elser*, cited above, paragraph 29; *ERT*, cited above, paragraph 37; Case C–179/90 *Merci convenzionali porto di Genova* [1991] ECR I-5889, paragraphs 16 and 17; and Case C-323/93 *Centre d'insémination de la Crespelle* [1994] ECR I-5077, paragraph 18). In this respect, it is not necessary that any abuse should actually occur (see, to that effect, Case C-55/96 *Job Centre* [1997] ECR I-7119, paragraph 36). In any event, Articles [102 TFEU and 106(1) TFEU] are infringed where a measure imputable to a Member State, and in particular a measure by which a Member State confers special or exclusive rights within the meaning of Article [106(1) TFEU], gives rise to a risk of an abuse of a dominant position (see, to that effect, *ERT*, cited above, paragraph 37; *Merci convenzionali porto di Genova*, cited above, paragraph 17; and Case C-380/05 *Centro Europa 7* [2008] ECR I-0000, paragraph 60).[90]

The judgment in *MOTOE*, paras 49 and 50, clearly indicates that the Court will consider Article 106(1) in conjunction with Article 102 breached where the dominant position creates the mere possibility for an undertaking to commit an abuse. The concept of abuse is interpreted broadly, covering 'a risk of an abuse of a dominant position'. The key question is the discretion that a Member State leaves for the regulatory bodies to abuse the conferred powers. Should an undertaking be under an obligation to engage in abusive practices, the Member State is to be held responsible for such practices, and conversely, if an undertaking has discretion not to abuse its special powers the Member State will not be held responsible for the committed abuses.[91]

This is reminiscent of the approach to oligopolistic markets and even to a substantive assessment of concentrations than to the well-established approach to Article 102 TFEU under which abuse has to take place in order to find violation. On the facts of the case, ELPA was the sole organizer of motorcycling events and, in addition, was in charge of giving consent to other undertakings to organise and commercially exploit motorcycling events. Such powers granted to ELPA an apparent advantageous position over its competitors, whereby it could restrict access to the relevant market for all other operators.[92]

---

[90]Ibid., paras 49 and 50.

[91]For an analytical comment on *MOTOE* that details this point see Miettinen 2009, pp. 137–149.

[92]Case C-49/07 *Motosykletistiki Omospondia Ellados NPID (MOTOE) v Elliniko Dimosio*, ECLI:EU:C:2008:376, para 51. In Case C-41/90 *Klaus Höfner and Fritz Elser v Macrotron GmbH*, ECLI:EU:C:1991:161, para 29, it was held that the state measure within the meaning of Article 106(1) will be unlawful where by exercising exclusive rights conferred on it an undertaking cannot avoid abusing dominant position. In Case C-203/96 *Chemische Afvalstoffen Dusseldorp BV and Others v Minister van Volkshuisvesting, Ruimtelijke Ordening en Milieubeheer*, ECLI:EU:C:1998:316, para 61, the Court held that Article 106(1) in conjunction with Article 102 will be breached where the Member State '*adopts any law, regulation or administrative provision which enables an undertaking on which it has conferred rights to abuse its dominant position*'.

The final word of the Court was that:

> [...] a rule, which gives a legal person such as ELPA the power to give consent to applications for authorisation to organise motorcycling events *without that power being made subject by that rule to restrictions, obligations and review*, could lead the legal person entrusted with giving that consent to distort competition by favouring events which it organises or those in whose organisation it participates. [...].[93]

Although paras 49 and 50 considered the mere existence of a conflict of interest in breach of Article 106(1) in conjunction with 102, this breach could have been avoided if the power granted to ELPA were subject to an appropriate standard of control. In this case there was no such control mechanism upon ELPA's activities and Greece lost the case. Nevertheless, as concerns the more general principle derived from the *MOTOE* judgment, a justification for the inevitable abuse could be found. Miettinen concluded that, 'as a consequence of *MOTOE*, it could be argued that since all undertakings that are endowed with regulatory powers are placed in a dominant position, regardless of whether they abuse that position they must be subject to 'restrictions, obligations and review.''[94]

Much like *MOTOE*, *FIA* was a case of sporting 'conflict of interest' examined under the TFEU competition rules. In both cases the central issue was the conflation of regulatory and commercial functions in one body, which ultimately led to the blocking of competing organisations and preventing market access. Both cases involved sporting bodies which abused organisational rules to protect their private interests rather than acting on behalf of public interests. None of the cases involved the specificity of sport in any form. Unlike *MOTOE*, in *FIA* there was no element of state involvement, as the powers delegated stemmed not from an act of a public authority, but from its own rules and a web of private agreements. Whereas in *MOTOE* the requirement on the Member State was to create a system of safeguards against abuse (by ELPA's refusal to grant the consent necessary for the issuance of license) of the dominant position it enabled, in *FIA* the mere fact that the body was issuing licenses was not a problem. Rather, it was the restrictions on competition that those licenses entailed under the disputed rules.[95] The safeguard against an unjustified refusal of licenses as in the *FIA* case was the

---

[93]Case C-49/07 *Motosykletistiki Omospondia Ellados NPID (MOTOE) v Elliniko Dimosio*, ECLI:EU:C:2008:376, para 51.

[94]Miettinen 2009, p. 147.

[95]This is evident from the Statement of Objections and from section 6 of the Notice of 13 June 2001 published pursuant to Article 19(3) of Council Regulation No 17), concerning Cases COMP/35.163—Notification of FIA Regulations, COMP/36.638—Notification by FIA/FOA of agreements relating to the FIA Formula One World Championship, COMP/36.776—GTR/FIA & others [2001] OJ C 169/5, which says that '*the notified agreements as amended will remove those barriers which had prevented in the past the use of FIA licensed products and circuits or the participation of FIA licensees in different disciplines or in competing events in the same discipline. The proposed changes to the notified agreements will, for example, result in the availability of racetracks in Europe for rival series to use, even if these circuits already host FIA Formula One championship events.*'.

obligation to insert a new clause ensuring that a legal recourse against FIA's decisions would be available not only within their organizational structure, but also before national courts.

6.6 Commission Decisions in *Mouscron* [1999] and *ENIC* [2002]

Several years prior to the seminal *Meca-Medina* judgement, in *ENIC*[96] and in the unpublished *Mouscron* decision[97] the Commission directly applied para 97 of *Wouters* in its positive assessment of the UEFA rule on multi-club ownership and the 'home and away rule', respectively.

In *Mouscron*, the organisation of a sport on a territorial basis was brought into question. The UEFA 'home and away rule', according to which each club must play its home matches at its own ground, was challenged on the basis of Article 102 by the French Communauté Urbaine de Lille after UEFA refused to allow the Belgian club Excelsior Mouscron to play its home match against the French club Metz in Lille. The Commission rejected the complaint; it considered the rule indispensable for the organisation of national and international competitions in view of ensuring equality of chances between clubs. Furthermore, the rule was also found to be proportionate.

In *ENIC* ethical considerations on multi-club ownership prevented the Commission to find the rule restrictive under competition law and, instead, it was considered 'inherent'. Specifically, the rule stated that no two or more clubs participating in a UEFA club competition may be directly or indirectly controlled by the same entity or managed by the same person. According to the Commission the rule was designed to 'ensure the uncertainty of the outcome and to guarantee that the consumer has the perception that the games played represent honest sporting competitions [...]'.[98] Additionally, the public's perception of integrity is an essential precondition to keep the consumer's confidence and interest, as well as marketability of sporting competitions. Otherwise, as an inevitable consequence over time, '[c]lubs would be less capable of extracting value from ancillary activities and investment in clubs would lose value'.[99] The rule was held proportionate, since it did not prevent capital investment in football clubs, but merely prohibited

---

[96]Commission Decision of 27 June 2002, COMP IV/37.806—ENIC/UEFA. See also Commission Press Release of 27 June 2002, IP/02/942 Commission Closes Investigation into UEFA Rule on Multiple Ownership of Football Clubs.

[97]Commission Decision of 3 December 1999, COMP/E3/36.85—Lille/UEFA (the *Mouscron* case); Commission Press Release of 9 December 1999, IP/99/965 Limits to Application of Treaty Competition Rules to Sport: Commission Gives Clear Signal; See also European Commission, XXIXth Report on Competition Policy 1999, pp. 166–167.

[98]Commission Decision of 27 June 2002, COMP IV/37.806—ENIC/UEFA, para 28.

[99]Ibid., para 32.

more than one club with the same ownership, management or control from participating in the same UEFA competition.[100]

6.7 *Meca-Medina* [2006]: The Ultimate Test for Regulatory Rules in Sport

All judgements of the CJEU prior to and after *Meca-Medina* that dealt with organisational rules in sport were taken solely under provisions on freedom of movement of workers and services. The first time that the Court directly addressed the application of competition provisions to regulatory rules in sport was in the *Meca-Medina* judgment of 2006. This decision confirmed the applicability of the analytical structure developed in *Wouters* to regulatory rules in sport. For this reason, the case deserves special attention.

6.7.1 Factual Background

The case involved two professional swimmers who were found to have breached the sport's anti-doping rules adopted by the International Olympic Committee (IOC). They tested positive for nandrolone and were suspended for a period of four years by the Doping Panel of the International Swimming Federation that implemented the rules for their discipline.[101] Contesting the anti-doping rules, the applicants asserted that they were in breach of Articles 101 and 102, and Article 56 on freedom to provide services:

> [...] First of all, the fixing of the limit at 2 ng/ml is a concerted practice between the IOC and the 27 laboratories accredited by it. That limit is scientifically unfounded and can lead to the exclusion of innocent or merely negligent athletes. In the applicants' case, the excesses could have been the result of the consumption of a meal containing boar meat. Also, the IOC's adoption of a mechanism of strict liability and the establishment of tribunals responsible for the settlement of sports disputes by arbitration (the CAS and the ICAS) which are insufficiently independent of the IOC strengthens the anti-competitive nature of that limit. [...].[102]

---

[100]Ibid., para 34.

[101]The appeal against the suspension was first launched before the Court of Arbitration for Sport which confirmed the decision of the doping panel but later, when scientific experiments showed that nandrolone's metabolites can be produced endogenously by the human body at a level which may exceed the accepted limit when certain foods have been consumed, they reduced the sanctions to two years. In 2001, however, the applicants launched the complaint with the Commission whose decision they appealed against before the General Court, and finally the decision of the General Court was brought before the Court.

[102]Case C-519/04 *P David Meca-Medina and Igor Majcen v. Commission*, ECLI:EU:C:2006:492, paras 16–17.

6.7.2 Judgment of the Court: Scope of the Treaty

As a starting point the Court reiterated the principles developed in its previous case law. The orthodox rule that originated in para 4 of *Walrave* provides that 'sport is subject to Community law only in so far as it constitutes an economic activity [...]'.[103] Rules of 'purely sporting' interest having nothing to do with economic activity are excluded from the scope of the Treaty.[104] The Court cited paras 14 and 15 of *Donà* and held that freedom of movement provisions 'do not preclude rules or practices justified on non-economic grounds which relate to the particular nature and context of certain sporting events' and are limited to their proper objective.[105] Such a restriction on the scope of the freedom of movement provisions 'cannot be relied upon to exclude the *whole* of a sporting activity from the scope of the Treaty'.[106] This was established in identical language 11 years before *Meca-Medina* by the Court's answer to the arguments raised by the German Government in *Bosman* that sport such as football is not an economic activity, that it is akin to culture and should be treated as such, and to UEFA's arguments in that case calling for an exception due to the particular nature of sport. The Court said it was addressing 'the question of application of Article [45 TFEU] to rules laid down by sporting associations' that UEFA and German government were contesting.[107]

In *Meca-Medina* and *Bosman* the Court stated the obvious: the sporting activity in question and sport regulations cannot altogether be excluded from the scope of the Treaty. The restriction on the scope of the Treaty concerning the rules that fulfilled the requirements for the exception introduced in *Walrave* and *Donà* cannot be relied on to argue that the sporting activity governed by those rules falls outside of the scope of the Treaty. There is no such thing as a general exception for sports under the Treaty.

In the para 27 of *Meca-Medina* the Court used the new language that resulted in giving that paragraph the false reputation of severely limiting the scope of the purely sporting exception that originated in paras 8 and 9 of *Walrave*. Having set out its position from the previous case law, it said that:

> In the light of all these considerations, it is apparent that the mere fact that a rule is purely sporting in nature does not have the effect of removing from the scope of the Treaty the person engaging in the activity governed by that rule or the body which has laid it down.[108]

---

[103]Ibid., para 22.

[104]Ibid., para 25 (citing Case 36/74 *Walrave and Koch v. Union Cycliste Internationale*, ECLI:EU:C:1974:140, para 8).

[105]Ibid., para 26.

[106]Ibid., para 26 (citing Case C-415/93 *Union Royale Belge des Sociétés de Football Association and others v. Bosman and others*, ECLI:EU:C:1995:463, para 76, and Cases C-51/96 and C-191/97 *Christelle Deliège v. Ligue Francophone de Judo et Disciplines Associées ASBL and others*, ECLI:EU:C:2000:199, para 43, emphasis added).

[107]Case C-415/93 *Union Royale Belge des Sociétés de Football Association and others v. Bosman and others*, ECLI:EU:C:1995:463, para 69.

[108]Case C-519/04 P *David Meca-Medina and Igor Majcen v. Commission*, ECLI:EU:C:2006:492, para 27.

All the Court does here is re-state what is already clear 'in the light of the above considerations': if a certain rule is purely sporting, it does not mean that person engaged in the activity governed by that rule cannot rely on the Treaty in regard to any other rule that governs that activity, and it does not mean that a body that adopted a rule considered purely sporting will be removed from the scope of the Treaty in regard to other organisational rules it lays down. In either case, the fact that the Court uses the language of 'it is apparent' would imply that it does not change anything in regard to the previous case law. Weatherill thought that a possible interpretation of the decision in *Meca-Medina* would hold that the so-called rule of 'purely sporting interest', originating in *Walrave and Koch*, has now been eliminated as a basis for immunising sports rules which have an economic effect from review under EU law.[109]

Thereafter, the Court overruled the decision of the General Court by finding an error in the interpretation of law. It held that:

> *even if those rules do not constitute restrictions on freedom of movement because they concern questions of purely sporting interest and, as such, have nothing to do with economic activity, that fact means neither that the sporting activity in question necessarily falls outside the scope of Articles [101 TFEU] and [102 TFEU] nor that the rules do not satisfy the specific requirements of those articles.* However, in para 42 of the contested judgment, the [General Court] held that the fact that purely sporting rules may have nothing to do with economic activity, with the result that they do not fall within the scope of Articles [45 TFEU] and [56 TFEU], means, also, that they have nothing to do with the economic relationships of competition, with the result that they also do not fall within the scope of Articles [101 TFEU] and [102 TFEU]. In holding that rules could thus be excluded straightaway from the scope of those articles solely on the ground that they were regarded as purely sporting with regard to the application of Articles [45 TFEU] and [56 TFEU], without any need to determine first whether the rules fulfilled the specific requirements of Articles [101 TFEU] and [102 TFEU], as set out in paragraph 30 of the present judgment, the [General Court] made an error of law.[110]

Therefore, the rules found to be purely sporting for the purpose of freedom of movement provisions are not by virtue of that fact also excluded from the assessment under competition law provisions. They have to satisfy the requirements of both sets of the Treaty rules separately. A generous approach of the General Court to the scope of sporting autonomy was quashed and tighter legal requirements for compatibility of the rules of governing bodies with EU law were set by the Court. Weatherill saw the overruling of the General Court judgment not as a criticism to the convergence thesis, but as the Court pointing out the inadequacy of the General Court analysis.[111] Indeed, the Court had merely reminded us that the two sets of provisions protect different freedoms of action and include different elements and that those differences deserve recognition.

---

[109]Weatherill 2008, p. 345.

[110]Case C-519/04 P *David Meca-Medina and Igor Majcen v. Commission*, ECLI:EU:C:2006:492, paras 31–33 (emphasis added).

[111]Weatherill 2008, p. 342.

The Court's position can be explained by reference to the constitutional limitations, and presumptions in Article 101 TFEU. Namely, the constitutional limitations on the action of the Union institutions operate generally, but their specific influence might be different in different substantive Treaty provisions. For example, with regard to the principle of subsidiarity in Article 5 of the Treaty on the European Union (TEU) purely internal situations fall outside the scope of internal market rules and, therefore, are not under the Union's competence.[112] Nevertheless, the EU competition rules may apply even if the situation is purely internal, as long as there is a required effect on competition. Similarly, the notion of appreciability delimits the respective competences between Member States and the Union with regard to competition provisions, but it has no real counterpart in the internal market area. Hence, restrictions on competition which do not produce an appreciable effect on trade between Member States are not subject to EU law with respect to competition provisions, but it may be examined under the free movement articles. Therefore, para 31 of *Meca-Medina* works in reverse too and the Court could have produced equal effect by saying:

> even if those rules do not constitute restrictions on competition because they do not produce appreciable (economic) effect on trade between Member States and, as such, are not a subject of Union competence under competition provisions, that fact means neither that the (sporting or other) activity in question necessarily falls outside the scope of the free movement provisions nor that the rules do not satisfy the specific requirements of those articles.

The formalistic application, in which the effect of fundamental Union principles under one article could determine the outcome under another would deprive those other Treaty articles of their proper function. Thus, the competence to act is generally not transplantable from competition to internal market articles and vice versa. Neither specific exceptions, nor general constitutionally-based limitations can produce a generic effect of excluding a subject matter of the scope of the Treaty articles.

The language in para 31 of *Meca-Medina* can be further explained by the difference in presumptions. With regard to cases that involve the specificity of sport, the internal market does not have the equivalent of the hard-core restrictions in Article 101(1) TFEU. In sports cases, both directly discriminatory and merely restrictive rules are treated within the same analytical framework. However, under Article 101(1), if a rule constitutes a '*per se*' or hard-core restriction by object, it is not open to the parties to argue that it in fact does not amount to a restriction and the presumption of a breach of that provision is conclusive, as opposed to rebuttable. In that case, a rule that has satisfied all the requirements for the category II exception under the free movement provisions cannot benefit from the attempt at that exception under Article 101(1) to which it would otherwise be

[112] Case 175/78 *The Queen v Vera Ann Saunders*, ECLI:EU:C:1979:88; See also Joined cases C-225/95, C-226/95 and C-227/95 *Anestis Kapasakalis, Dimitris Skiathitis and Antonis Kougiagkas v Greece*, ECLI:EU:C:1998:332.

entitled but for the hard-core restrictions and conclusive presumptions of the breach. A party may rely on Article 101(3), but not on any of the judicially-developed exceptions available for ancillary restraints analysis under Article 101(1) TFEU. Conversely, if there is no conclusive presumption under the competition provisions and the rule has already been regarded under internal market articles as 'purely sporting', this interpretation can be transposed to competition law cases with no further analysis required. The para 31 in *Meca-Medina* should be read in this light. Once there is a rebuttable presumption under EU competition law articles and the 'required economic effect' is established under both sets of provisions, all other conditions for an exception are the same.[113]

6.7.3 Judgment of the Court: The Test

Finally, the Court directed its attention to the application of Article 101(1) TFEU. Relying on its previous ruling in *Wouters*, the Court emphasised the need for a contextual approach:

> Not every agreement between undertakings or every decision of an association of undertakings which restricts the freedom of action of the parties or of one of them necessarily falls within the prohibition laid down in Article [101(1) TFEU]. For the purposes of application of that provision to a particular case, account must first of all be taken of the overall context in which the decision of the association of undertakings was taken or produces its effects and, more specifically, of its objectives. It has then to be considered whether the consequential effects restrictive of competition are inherent in the pursuit of those objectives (*Wouters and Others*, paragraph 97) and are proportionate to them.[114]

The fact that the doping rule was intended to safeguard the objective of fair play and ethics in sports did not exclude it from the scope of competition rules; the economic effects that it produced had to be considered in the light of the *Wouters* inherency test and the requirement of proportionality. The rule was found to restrict athletes' freedom of action, but to the extent that the general objective was to provide a level playing field and preserve integrity of sporting competition and the sanctions were necessary to ensure compliance with the doping ban, the restrictions were deemed inherent. The Court also found that athletes did not demonstrate that the controversial rule was disproportionate and upheld the previous finding of the Commission on this point.

So the athletes lost. Of particular importance is that they did not lose because the rules were of 'purely sporting' interest, but because these rules satisfied the test laid down by the Court in para 42.[115]

---

[113]Pijetlovic 2015, pp. 222–223.

[114]Case C-519/04 P *David Meca-Medina and Igor Majcen v. Commission*, ECLI:EU:C:2006:492, para 42.

[115]Weatherill 2008, p. 345.

According to that test, an organisational sporting rule or practice that is found to restrict the freedom of action under Article 101(1) or 102 may not breach those provisions to the extent that the rule in question pursues a legitimate objective, its restrictive effects are inherent in the pursuit of that objective and are proportionate to it. The process of assessing the compatibility of the rules under the internal market objective justification test, therefore, involves essentially the same analytical points as the test under para 42 of *Meca-Medina.*

In *Meca-Medina*, just as in *Wouters*, the Court applied a moderate intensity proportionality test.[116] This intensity would usually vary depending on the restriction in question. It does not follow from *Meca-Medina* that the Court has given any special consideration to sport in this regard.

6.7.4 Final Remarks

The *Meca-Medina* judgment hit closer to the core of sporting autonomy than any other judgment prior to it. Needless to say, it was not welcomed by the sporting bodies. In particular, the IOC and the two largest football governing bodies (FIFA and UEFA) considered it as an attack on their authority and an unnecessary intrusion into the scope of their sporting autonomy. UEFA's Director of Legal Affairs commented on the judgment in *Meca-Medina* saying that it has opened up a possibility for almost any sports sanction for any offence (e.g. doping, match-fixing, gambling, bad conduct, etc.) to be described as representing a condition 'for engaging in' sporting activity and be challenged under EU competition law.[117] However, the fact that sporting rules would be scrutinised under the competition provisions does not mean that they are necessarily found in breach of those provisions. Justified and proportionate rules withstand any legal challenge. But the concerns of the sporting bodies seem to disregard of this fact. *Meca-Medina* has opened a door for new possibilities to challenge most of the organisational sport rules and could arguably lead to a substantial increase in litigation.

6.8 Annex I Framework for Analysis of Organisational Rules in Sport

6.8.1 General Structure

This general framework is set out in the 2007 Commission Staff Paper, Annex I entitled Sport and EU Competition Rules. In para 2.1.2 of Annex I the Commission

[116]Lavrijssen 2010, pp. 636–659.

[117]Infantino 2006, pp. 3–4.

divided the approach to organisational rules in sport into four distinct steps. Step 1 includes an enquiry on the nature of the body that adopted the rule, for instance, whether the sports association that adopted the rule is to be considered an undertaking or an association of undertakings. As explained below in Annex I, these may include individual athletes, sport clubs and national and international sporting associations. Whereas this step essentially comprises an applicability test, Step 2 contains the regulatory ancillarity test and raises the question on the existence of restrictions on competition within the meaning of Article 101(1) TFEU and/or an abuse of a dominant position under Article 102 TFEU. The answer to this question depends on the outcome of the *Meca-Medina/Wouters* test. The rule or practice adopted by an undertaking or association of undertakings which is found to satisfy the cumulative criteria of the *Meca-Medina/Wouters* test is considered compatible with Articles 101 and 102 TFEU. Should the rule or practice fail to meet *any* of the criteria, it would breach Article 101(1) and/or would constitute an abuse contrary to Article 102 TFEU. Nevertheless, another condition has to be satisfied to finally reach this conclusion: Step 3 refers to the requirement that any restriction or abuse, if found, must have an appreciable effect on trade between Member States in order to breach EU competition rules. Step 4 represents the exemption stage of analysis. It is a final, but relatively insubstantial, lifeline for a restrictive or abusive sporting rule with an appreciable effect on intra-Union trade. It examines whether a restrictive rule fulfils the conditions of Article 101(3) TFEU or the equivalent economic efficiency test under Article 102 TFEU as described in Sect. 6.4.1. It must be acknowledged that it is highly unlikely that a rule of a sporting organisation pursuing a non-competition goal that cannot be translated into economic efficiencies or a rule that has failed the *Meca-Medina/Wouters* test on the point of proportionality would satisfy the requisite economic conditions.[118] That outlines yet another *raison d'être* of the *Wouters* test in the sporting context, for without it, the broad scope of Article 101(1) would most likely render virtually any organisational rule of sport that restricts the freedom of action and relies on the non-competition justification incompatible with the entire Article 101 TFEU.

6.8.2 Organisational Rules not Likely to Infringe Articles 101 and 102 TFEU

In Annex I the EU Commission, as a matter of general guidance, provided a list of examples of rules likely not to infringe the competition articles. Due to a very high

[118]Commission Staff Working Document of 11 July 2007, COM (2007) 391 final - The EU and Sport: Background and Context - Accompanying document to the White Paper on Sport, Annex I, para 2.1.6, says that '*such a justification is most likely to apply where a rule is not inherent in the organisation or proper conduct of sport so as to justify the application of* Wouters *but where the beneficial effects of a rule outweigh its restrictive effects.*'.

degree of convergence between internal market and competition law analytical structures and their respective identical outcomes with regard to the legality of rules, the list was partly generated from internal market case law. Annex I specifies that the legitimate objectives of sporting rules would normally relate to the 'organisation and proper conduct of competitive sport'.[119] The following types of rules constitute examples of organisational sporting rules that, based on their legitimate objectives, are unlikely to violate competition law, provided that the restrictions contained in such rules are inherent and proportionate to the objectives pursued:

- *Rules of the game* (e.g., the rules fixing the length of matches or the number of players on the field) typically do not have any economic effect and would fall under para 4 of *Walrave*;
- *Rules concerning selection criteria for sport competitions*, such as in *Deliège* discussed in Sect. 6.2.3 in internal market context, would produce identical results under competition provisions due to the virtually identical test;
- *'At home and away from home' rules* such as in *Mouscron* decision (discussed in Sect. 6.6);
- *Rules preventing multiple ownership in club competitions* such as in *ENIC*, discussed in Sect. 6.6;
- *Rules concerning the composition of national teams*, such as in *Walrave* case (discussed in Sect. 6.2.1);
- *Anti-doping rules* such as in *Meca-Medina* case (discussed in Sect. 6.7);
- *Rules concerning transfer periods*, also referred to as 'transfer windows', such as in *Lehtonen* case (discussed in Sect. 6.2.2) and;
- *Licensing systems for sport clubs/teams* in professional league competitions are also likely to satisfy the *Meca-Medina/Wouters* test. Such rules are intended to ensure the financial stability of clubs/teams (and, thus, the regularity of sport competitions) and the availability of proper and safe sport facilities. These rules are considered inherent in and necessary for the organisation of sport, but the proportionality will be carefully reviewed where they may interfere with business decisions of clubs/teams. The break-even requirement in UEFA's Club Licencing and Financial Fair Play Regulations is currently facing a legal challenge before the CJEU in the *Striani* case.[120]

---

[119] Ibid., para 2.1.5.

[120] Case C-299/15 *Daniele Striani and Others v Union européenne des Sociétés de Football Association (UEFA) and Union Royale Belge des Sociétés de Football-Association (URBSFA)*, ECLI:EU:C:2015:519, lodged on 19 June 2015. Read more in Van Rompuy B (2015) The Brussels Court Judgment on Financial Fair Play: A Futile Attempt to Pull off a Bosman, http://www.asser.nl/SportsLaw/Blog/post/the-brussels-court-judgment-on-financial-fair-play-a-futile-attempt-to-pull-off-a-bosman-by-ben-van-rompuy#_ftnref5. Accessed 10 July 2015.

6.8.3 *Organisational Rules that May Infringe Articles 101 and 102 TFEU*

The Commission also composed a list of rules with a higher likelihood of causing problems concerning compliance with competition law; nonetheless, it added that some of them could be justified under certain conditions of Article 101(3) or Article 102 TFEU. It must be emphasised that some of the rules mentioned in this category are capable of passing the *Meca-Medina/Wouters* assessment:

- *Rules protecting sports associations from competition* have been evaluated for their compatibility with EU competition law in the *FIA* case and in the Court's *MOTOE* case, discussed in Sect. 6.5. Motor sports, especially Formula One, are more akin to business than to sport.[121] The restrictive organisational rules in those cases were intended to protect private commercial interests. There are, however, some other sports governing bodies that prohibit the formation of alternative leagues by the member clubs or condition the entry to the organisational market upon fulfilment of certain criteria, but that might be justifiable on the basis of public interest objectives. Such clauses may pass *Meca-Medina/Wouters* and the internal market objective justification tests, but will be subject to a strict proportionality analysis. An example of such a rule is Article 49 of UEFA Statutes that can be justified on the basis of solidarity mechanisms that enable the fulfilment of the socio-cultural functions of football and work to preserve a certain financial and sporting balance between clubs and an effective and proper organisation of sport. Elsewhere I argued that certain UEFA conditions implementing Article 49 of its Statutes would have to be amended to pass the proportionality test.[122]
- *Rules excluding legal challenges of decisions by sports associations before national courts.* The denial of access to ordinary courts, which may facilitate anti-competitive agreements or conduct was addressed in the *FIA* case, discussed in Sect. 6.5 and in the *FIFA* case. One of the Commission's objections in *FIA* related to the lack of possibility to challenge FIA decisions outside the FIA structure. FIA was forced to insert a new clause clarifying that anyone subject to its decisions can challenge them before national courts as a safeguard against unjustified refusals of licenses. Similarly, throughout negotiations with FIFA on transfer rules in case of valid contracts, the Commission insisted that arbitration would be voluntary and would not prevent recourse to national courts, which led to FIFA modifying its transfer rules to this end.[123] Sporting associations usually

[121]Cygan 2007, p. 76.

[122]Pijetlovic 2015, pp. 290–301.

[123]Commission Staff Working Document of 11 July 2007, COM (2007) 391 final - The EU and Sport: Background and Context—Accompanying document to the White Paper on Sport, para 2.2.2.2; See also Report from the Commission - XXXIst Report on Competition Policy 2001, SEC/2002/0462 final, para 220.

do have arbitration clauses in their commitment agreements with players. Some of them contain clauses that facilitate anti-competitive practices, such as the ones imposed by tennis governing bodies.[124]

- *Rules concerning nationality clauses for sport clubs/teams*, such as quota requirements in *Bosman*. Today it is clear that these directly discriminatory rules will infringe free movement provisions and, therefore, any economic justifications they could produce under the economic efficiency defence will not have an effect on their illegality under internal market provisions. Whereas the rules challenged under both internal market and competition law must pass both tests to be considered legal, it is sufficient that they violate only one set of provisions to be considered void and unenforceable. On the other hand, indirectly discriminatory rules, such as UEFA's home-grown players rule, might be able to satisfy the internal market objective justification criteria and, therefore, survive the *Meca-Medina/Wouters* test.[125]
- *Rules regulating the transfer of athletes between clubs* (except transfer windows), such as transfer fees in *Bosman* discussed in Sect. 6.2.2, also belong to the more problematic category of organisational rules. However, some of these rules are capable of satisfying *Meca-Medina/Wouters* test as we saw in *Bernard*, a case that concerned compensation fees for young players. *Bosman* did not address the legality of transfer fees for players who are still under contract. In 1998 the Commission issued a statement of objections concerning FIFA's Regulations for the Status and Transfer of Players, but closed the investigation in 2002 following FIFA's commitments to modify its transfer rules for in-contract players.[126] The main commitments were inclusions of certain measures to support the training of players (e.g. training compensation for young players and a solidarity mechanism), establishing a transfer period per season, specification of contractual arrangements between players and clubs (e.g. regulating duration of contracts, and specifying when breaches of contracts are possible, including sanctions), and ensuring that arbitration is voluntary and does not prevent recourse to national courts in case of disputes.
- *Rules regulating professions ancillary to sport* were assessed under EU competition law in the *Piau* case in the context of the activity of players' agents. The General Court considered it an economic activity involving the provision of services which does not fall within the scope of the specific nature of sport.[127] In order to acquire a licence, players' agents were required to have impeccable reputation, pass a written examination and take out professional liability insurance policy or deposit a bank guarantee. This constituted a barrier to access to that

---

[124]Pijetlovic 2013, pp 161–186.

[125]University of Liverpool and Edge Hill University (2013) Study on the Assessment of UEFA's Home-Grown Player Rule. Study for the European Commission EAC/07/2012.

[126]Report from the Commission - XXXIst Report on Competition Policy 2001, SEC/2002/0462 final, para 220; See also Commission Press Release of 5 June 2002, IP/02/824 Commission closes investigations into FIFA regulations on international football transfers.

[127]Report from the Commission - XXXIst Report on Competition Policy 2001, SEC/2002/0462 final, para 73.

economic activity. However, because (1) the contested FIFA rules sought to protect players and their short careers for incompetent representation in transfer negotiations by raising professional and ethical standards for the occupation, (2) the compulsory license system did not eliminate the effective competition and it is based on qualitative rather than quantitative selection criteria appropriate for the attainment of the first objective, and (3) there existed no collective organisation of players' agent and no generalised national rules, the restrictions on competition brought about by the compulsory licence system could enjoy an exemption decision under Article 101(3) TFEU.[128] It followed from these considerations that an abuse of a dominant position under Article 102 TFEU could also not be established.[129]

In 2009 the Commission funded an independent study on sport agents. The main concerns identified were of an ethical nature, including financial crime and exploitation of young players.[130]

6.8.4 Comment

Both of the lists in Annex I are non-exhaustive and were composed exclusively on the basis of existing case-law. Even though there is a lot of fluidity, it can be concluded that the overall difference between the lists is whether the organisational rule protects public or private interests, and whether the specific nature of sport is involved. We saw in *Piau* that even where the rules protected public interests, but were not connected to the notion of the specificity of sport, the General Court did not refer to the possibility of regulatory ancillarity, but simply concluded that restrictions existed. Protecting private interests, the lack of connection to the specific nature of sport or direct discrimination (other than the purely sporting rules within the meaning of paras 14 and 15 of *Donà*), will eliminate the possibility of passing *Meca-Medina/Wouters* test. As a matter of law, such rules may nevertheless benefit from commercial ancillarity or the Article 101(3) exemption and the equivalent defences under Article 102 TFEU. It would not influence the outcome if the claimant also brought action under internal market provisions.

Some important outstanding issues that have not been subject to either a Commission or a Court's decision are uncompensated player release rules, salary caps and the home-grown players rule. The Commission pays due caution to the fact that regardless of the tentative classification of items on the two lists, an individual

[128]Ibid., paras 102–104.

[129]Ibid., para 119.

[130]Study by KEA European Affairs, the Centre for the Law and Economics of Sport and the European Observatoire of Sport and Employment of November 2009 commissioned by the European Commission, DG for Education and Culture on Sports Agents in the European Union. http://ec.europa.eu/sport/library/studies/study-sports-agents-in-eu.pdf. Accessed 10 July 2015.

analysis of every challenged organisational sporting rule on a case-by-case basis is indispensable. In its Communication on Sport the Commission further emphasises that through dialogue with sports stakeholders it will continue its efforts to explain on a theme-per-theme basis the relation between EU law and sporting rules.[131] The sports governing bodies nonetheless need to be careful not to take the Commission's opinion as a final say on the legality of their rules. The fact that a rule is drafted in collaboration with the Commission does not shield it from judicial scrutiny or provide any guarantees as to its compatibility with EU law. The Commission does not have the power to authorise rules and practices that are contrary to the Treaty.

References

Baquero Cruz J (2002) Between competition and free movement: the economic constitutional law of the european community. Hart Publishing, Oxford

Craig P, De Búrca G (2011) EU law, 5th edn. Oxford University Press, Oxford

Cygan A (2007) Competition and free movement issues in the regulation of formula one races. In: Bogusz B, Cygan A, Szyszczak E (eds) The regulation of sport in the European Union. Edward Elgar, Cheltenham, pp 74–94

Faull J, Nikpay A (2007) The EC law of competition, 2nd edn. Oxford University Press, Oxford

Foster K (2006) Lex sportiva and lex ludica: The CAS's jurisprudence. In: Blackshaw I, Siekmann R, Soek J (eds) The court of arbitration for sport 1984–2004. T.M.C. Asser Press, The Hague, pp 420–440

Infantino G (2006) Meca-Medina: a step backwards for the European sports model and the specificity of sport? Sports Law Adm Practice 13:3–4

Jones A, Sufrin B (2011) EU competition law, 4th edn. Oxford University Press, Oxford

Lavrijssen S (2010) What role for national competition authorities in protecting non-competition interests after Lisbon? Eur Law Rev 35:636–659

Miettinen S (2009) Policing the boundaries between regulation and commercial exploitation: lessons from the *MOTOE* Case. In: Gardiner S et al (eds) EU, sport, law and policy. T.M.C. Asser Press, The Hague, pp 137–149

Monti G (2002) Article 81 and public policy. Common Market Law Rev 39:1057–1099

Mortelmans K (2001) Towards convergence in the application of the rules on free movement and on competition? Common Market Law Rev 38:613–649

Parrish R, Miettinen S (2008) Sporting exception in European Union law. T.M.C. Asser Press, The Hague

Pijetlovic K (2013) Fundamental rights of athletes in the EU post-Lisbon. In: Kerikme T (ed) Protecting human rights in the EU: controversies and challenges of the charter of fundamental rights. Springer, Heidelberg, pp 161–186

Pijetlovic K (2015) EU sports law and breakaway leagues in football. Springer/T.M.C. Asser, The Hague

Semmelmann C (2008) The future role of the non-competition goals in the interpretation of article 81 EC. Global Antitrust Rev 1:15–47

Whish R (2009) Competition law, 6th edn. Oxford University Press, Oxford

Weatherill S (2008) Anti-doping revisited—the demise of the rule of 'purely sporting interest? In: Weatherill S (ed) European Union sports law: collected papers. T.M.C. Asser Press, The Hague, pp 335–352

[131]The Communication from the Commission to the European Parliament, the Council, the European Economic and Social Committee and the Committee of the Regions of 18 January 2011, COM(2011) 12 final Developing the European Dimension in Sport.

Chapter 7
EU Control of State Aid to Professional Sport: Why Now?

Ben Van Rompuy and Oskar van Maren

Abstract In the aftermath of the *Bosman* judgment, the application of the free movement and antitrust rules to the sports sector rapidly intensified and deepened. Until very recently, however, the application of the EU State aid rules remained an anomaly in the story of 'European sports law'. This chapter aims to explain why the public financing of sports infrastructure and professional sports clubs only in recent years started to attract State aid scrutiny. Considering the general policy dynamics of European State aid control, it is argued that the late appearance of enforcement efforts is not as remarkable as it may appear. The extension of the reach of State aid control to new sectors or new forms of aid has typically been the result of external constraints on the European Commission's independent agenda-setting abilities. In the case of sport, it was primarily the case law of the EU courts that triggered the sudden surge in formal investigations and decisional practice.

Keywords State aid law and policy · Sport · Professional football clubs · Sports infrastructure · European commission · Enforcement discretion · Prioritisation · Complaint handling

B. Van Rompuy (✉)
T.M.C. Asser Instituut, The Hague, The Netherlands
e-mail: b.van.rompuy@asser.nl

B. Van Rompuy
Vrije Universiteit Brussel, Ixelles, Belgium

O. van Maren
T.M.C. Asser Instituut, The Hague, The Netherlands
e-mail: o.van.maren@asser.nl

A. Duval and B. Van Rompuy (eds.), *The Legacy of* Bosman,
ASSER International Sports Law Series, DOI 10.1007/978-94-6265-120-3_7

Contents

7.1 Introduction

In *Walrave and Koch v UCI* (1974) and *Donà v Mantero* (1976), the Court of Justice of the European Union (CJEU) established that sport is subject to EU law in so far as it constitutes an economic activity.[1] Yet it was only after the landmark judgment in *Bosman* (1995) that the application of EU law to sport rapidly intensified and also deepened.[2] EU trade law entered the sports arena first, but EU competition law soon followed. In *Bosman*, as well as in its subsequent sports-related judgments, the CJEU confined itself to the application of the free movement rules.[3] It was therefore the European Commission who initiated the application of the EU antitrust rules to the sports sector. The Commission's enforcement practice, which mainly focused on commercial activities related to sport (such as the sale of sports media rights), was first and foremost the consequence of the growing commercialisation of professional sport and developments in the European audiovisual sector since the mid-1990s. Yet the Court's message in *Bosman*, namely that sporting practices should fall for assessment under EU law, but not necessarily

[1]Case 36/74 *Walrave and Koch v. Union Cycliste Internationale*, ECLI:EU:C:1974:140, para 8.

[2]Case C-415/93 *Union Royale Belge des Sociétés de Football Association and others v. Bosman and others*, ECLI:EU:C:1995:463.

[3]Despite the guidance on the application of the competition rules from the Advocate Generals in their Opinions. See e.g. Opinion of Advocate General Lenz in Case C-415/93 *Union Royale Belge des Sociétés de Football Association and others v. Bosman and others*, ECLI:EU:C:1995:293; Opinion of Advocate General Cosmas in Joined Cases C-51/96 and C-191/97 *Christelle Deliège v. Ligue Francophone de Judo et Disciplines Associées ASBL and others*, ECLI:EU:C:1999:147; Opinion of Advocate General Alber in Case C-176/96 *Jyri Lehtonen and Castors Canada Dry Namur-Braine ASBL v. Fédération royale belge des sociétés de basket-ball ASBL (FRBSB)*, ECLI:EU:C:1999:321.

condemnation and with due regard to sector-specific needs, endured. When the CJEU finally put an organisational sporting rule to the test under Article 101 TFEU in *Meca-Medina* (2006), it repeated that same message.[4] Professional sports associations lost the antitrust safe harbour for 'purely sporting' rules (as opposed to economic rules) they once believed they had.

So in the aftermath of *Bosman*, a growing body of 'European sports law' emerged, shaped by individual judgments and decisional practice applying the internal market and the antitrust rules to the sports sector.[5] Until very recently, the application of the EU State aid rules remained an anomaly in this story. At first blush, this might seem surprising. In most EU Member States national or local public authorities have for decades directly or indirectly funded the sports sector, mainly through public support for sports infrastructure or individual sports clubs. In so far as professional football and other clubs are the beneficiaries, there are no compelling arguments why they should be exempted from the State aid rules.[6] Moreover, it is settled case law that the scope of the State aid rules is defined by reference to the effects and not the social, educational or cultural objectives of the support measure in question.[7]

For a long time the European Commission maintained that it first needed to acquire sufficient experience based on individual cases before it could determine and clarify how the EU State aid rules should apply to (professional) sport.[8] Only since 2011, formal decisional practice started to emerge regarding the public financing of sports infrastructure projects such as football stadiums. And in 2013, the Commission launched high-profile investigations into aid measures granted to various top Spanish and Dutch football clubs, including Real Madrid and Barcelona.

---

[4]Case C-519/04 *P David Meca-Medina and Igor Majcen v. Commission*, ECLI:EU:C:2006:492. The Court clarified that the EU antitrust rules apply to a wider range of sporting rules than the General Court and the Commission had assumed, but at the same time it demonstrated great willingness to accommodate the specific characteristics of sport in the application of those rules. See e.g. Van Rompuy 2015, pp. 179–208.

[5]See e.g. Weatherill 2010, pp. 480–487; Van den Bogaert 2010, pp. 488–498.

[6]Since they engage in economic activities, professional sports clubs are considered to be undertakings under the competition rules. See e.g. references in Commission Decision 2003/778/EC of 23 July 2003, COMP/C.2-37.398—Joint selling of the commercial rights of the UEFA Champions League [2003] OJ L 291/24, para 106; Case T-193/02, *Laurent Piau v Commission*, ECLI:EU:T:2005:22, paras 69–72.

[7]See e.g. Case 173/73, *Italy v Commission*, ECLI:EU:C:1974:71, para 13.

[8]See e.g. European Parliament, Answer given by Mr Monti on behalf of the Commission to written Question E-1860/2003, 10 July 2003; European Parliament, Answer given by Mr Monti to written question E-2261/2003, 13 August 2003; Commission Staff Working Document of 11 July 2007 - The EU and Sport: Background and Context - Accompanying document to the White Paper on Sport, COM (2007) 391 final, Sect. 3.2.2; European Commission, Report from the 3rd meeting of the Expert Group on Sustainable Financing of Sport (XG FIN), January 2013. http://ec.europa.eu/sport/news/2013/20130111-eu-expert-group-fin_en.htm. Accessed 1 December 2015; European Ombudsman, 'State Aid and European football clubs? Summary of recommendation by the European Ombudsman following a complaint against the EU Commission', 17 December 2013.

The latter cases, which are still pending, concern land swaps/sale of State property (Spain, the Netherlands), tax advantages (Spain), and bank loans, guarantees or debt waivers (Spain, the Netherlands).

This chapter aims to explain why until very recently public support measures for professional sport have blissfully remained under the radar of EU state aid control. In other words, it narrowly focuses on one central question: why is the European Commission only now committed to enforcement—twenty years after *Bosman*?

The chapter is structured as follows. The first section briefly introduces the EU's State aid regime and then discusses how external constraints on its independent agenda-setting abilities have pushed the Commission to extent the reach of State aid control to new forms of aid or to new sectors. It will also be explained that a common pattern of gradual formalization of criteria first developed in precedent decisions enables the Commission to extract compliance from Member State governments and eschew political conflict. The second section will explain what triggered the sudden surge of decisional practice on State aid measures for sports infrastructures and how it accelerated the formalization process of sector-specific State aid rules. The third section will turn to State aid to professional sports clubs where the Commission still has to adopt individual precedent decisions. Also here it will be discussed what prompted the enforcement action *vis-à-vis* the Dutch and Spanish football clubs in 2013. The third and final section draws conclusions.

7.2 EU State Aid Policy-Making

Before turning to the emerging development of State aid control in the sports sector, it is essential to have a good understanding of the European Commission's policy- and decision-making environment. The Commission has the exclusive competence to exercise a priori control over State aid granted by the Member States (including national, regional, and local public authorities). This comes from the need to maintain a level playing in the single market, in particular by preventing subsidy races where Member States might outbid each other, and thus to ensure that the positive effects of State aid outweigh its negative effects in terms of distortion of competition. One of the most distinctive features of EU State aid control is closely tied to this function: it pits the Commission directly against Member State governments, rather than undertakings, and is therefore politically highly sensitive. The constant resistance the Commission encountered from the Member States in its endeavour to make the rules effective explains why a robust system of EU State aid control took more than three decades to develop.[9]

This section will first briefly introduce the Treaty rules on State aid and the procedural regime (2.1). It will then discuss how the absence of a formal regulatory

[9]For a detailed historical account, see Piernas López 2015.

framework opened up a regulatory space the Commission was able to fill. To eschew political conflict about individual State aid decisions, the Commission constantly sought to establish norm-interpreting administrative guidelines specifying the criteria for assessing the compatibility of particular types of State aid measures with the internal market (2.2).

7.2.1 The Treaty State Aid Rules

Articles 107–109 TFEU set out the core provisions on State aid. Article 107(1) TFEU establishes a general prohibition:

> Save as otherwise provided in this Treaty, any aid granted by a member State or through State resources in any form whatsoever which distorts or threatens to distort competition by favouring certain undertakings or the production of certain goods shall, in so far as it affects trade between Member States, be incompatible with the internal market.

The prohibition is neither absolute nor unconditional.[10] Article 107(1) TFEU only comes into play when all of the following elements are fulfilled: (1) there is an intervention by the State through State resources; (2) that confers an advantage to an undertaking or the production of certain goods; (3) that is selective; and (4) that is capable of distorting competition and affecting trade between Member States.

When a measure qualifies as State aid, the Member State concerned must prove that the conditions for the application of one the derogations apply. Article 107(2) TFEU contains automatic exemptions and Article 107(3) TFEU lists categories of aid that *may* be declared compatible with the internal market. The latter provision confers a wide discretion on the European Commission. Only the Commission has the competence (subject to control by the EU courts) to determine whether or not certain aid merits derogation from the general prohibition.[11] In the field of sport, but also more generally, Article 107(3)(c) concerning 'aid to facilitate the development of certain economic activities or of certain economic areas' is the most important discretionary exemption.

Article 108(3) TFEU obliges the Member States in principle to notify the Commission of any new aid they wish to grant to one or more undertakings.[12] The Member States are not allowed to put the proposed measure into effect until the Commission has approved it. Once the Commission receives a notification or

[10]Quigley 2015, pp. 193–194.

[11]According to settled case law, national courts do not have the power to declare a State aid measure compatible with the internal market. See e.g. C-354/90, *Fédération Nationale du Commerce Extérieur des Produits Alimentaires and Syndicat National des Négociants et Transformateurs de Saumon v French Republic*, ECLI:EU:C:1991:440, para 14.

[12]An exception to this rule applies when certain aid has been exempted from prior notification and approval. See Sect. 2.2.

decides to examine an aid measure that has been implemented absence prior approval (unlawful aid),[13] it will carry out a preliminary assessment and determine whether the measure constitutes State aid and, if so, whether the measure is compatible with the internal market. Should the Commission have doubts regarding the compatibility of an aid measure it can decide to launch a formal investigation pursuant to Article 108(2) TFEU. This procedure ends with a final decision finding that the aid is incompatible (prohibition decision) or compatible (positive decision) with the internal market.[14] If the Commission adopts a negative decision in cases of unlawful aid, the Member State must recover the aid from the beneficiary in order that it forfeits the advantage, which it had enjoyed over its competitors on the market, and re-establishes the situation existing before the granting of the unlawful aid.

7.2.2 *The Development of the State Aid Regime and Compliance*

EU State aid policy evolved slowly, but progressively in an environment characterized by the European Commission's exclusive competence to control State aid tempered by Member States political power.[15] While the Member States governments had agreed, in principle, on the need for supranational State aid control, each of them had an incentive to deviate from the State aid discipline, especially in times of economic crisis.[16] It was only in the mid-1980s that the Commission, empowered by judgments of the CJEU and the preparation of the Single Market,[17] established a rigorous enforcement regime. The Commission started to oblige

[13]Either on its own initiative or on the basis of a complaint. Since unlawfulness refers to procedural issues only (non-notification), it is still possible that the measure may be assessed as compatible and the aid therefore be approved. The qualification as unlawful aid may, however, have important consequences under national law. National courts are in principle required to suspend the payment of unlawful aid, or even order its recovery. See Commission notice of 4 April 2009 on the enforcement of State aid law by national courts [2009] OJ C 85/1.

[14]The Commission may also attach to a positive decision conditions subject to which aid may be considered compatible (conditional decision). Council Regulation (EU) 2015/1589 of 13 July 2015 laying down detailed rules for the application of Article 108 of the Treaty on the Functioning of the European Union [2015] OJ L 248/9, Article 9.

[15]Smith 1998, pp. 58–60.

[16]Piernas López 2015. For example, in a 1980 Notice, the Commission voiced concern that, in the wake of recurrent economic crises, 'the extent of the tendency towards non-notification or late notification would appear in some cases to indicate the possible existence of a general decision not to respect the provisions in question'. European Commission, 'The notification of State aids to the Commission pursuant to Article 93(3) of the EEC Treaty: the failure of the Member States to respect their obligations [1980] OJ C 252/2.

[17]See e.g. Aydin 2014; Piernas López 2015.

Member States to recover illegally granted State aid.[18] Moreover, by encouraging competitors to complain about alleged unlawful aid, the Commission increasingly obtained information independently from national governments, which in turn stimulated their compliance with the requirement to notify new aid measures.[19]

7.2.2.1 Towards a Rule-Based System

It took until 1998, however, for the Commission and the Council of Ministers to agree upon secondary legislation for State aid control. The Commission had originally sought to persuade the Council to adopt regulations on State aid procedures and on the exemption of certain categories of regional aid, but the Council blocked the proposals in 1966 and 1972. In response, the Commission gave up on this strategy and opted for a soft law approach.[20] It gradually introduced an array of policy frameworks, communications, and guidelines to clarify and codify its own standards for assessing certain categories of aid under the Treaty exceptions to the general prohibition of State aid. Formally these rules only bind the Commission, but the Commission managed to make its soft law practically binding for the Member States.[21] First, it enforces soft law indirectly through individual State aid decisions. Although Member States are entitled to draw up new State aid measures that do not match the compatibility criteria set out in the soft law instruments, following investigation the Commission will ask them to modify those measures or face potential recovery decisions. The mere threat of a long procedure and a negative decision is often sufficient to discourage Member States from notifying potential inadmissible aid in the first place.[22] Second, the Commission seeks the widest possible approval from the Member States before the adoption of soft law instruments. Yet, once the majority of Member States accepts the rules, it can force explicit approval onto others. If a Member State refuses to accept the adoption of e.g. new guidelines, the Commission may threaten to open formal investigations into all its existing State aid measures in that particular Member State falling under the new rules.[23]

---

[18]In its *Kohlengesetz* judgment, the CJEU established that the Commission was competent under Article 108(2) TFEU to require recovery of unlawful aid. Case 70/72, *Commission of the European Communities v Federal Republic of Germany (Kohlengesetz)* ECLI:EU:C:1973:87. Based on this judgement, the Commission announced in a 1983 Communication that it had 'decided to use all measures at its disposal to ensure the Member States' obligations under Article [108 TFEU] are respected'. Commission, Communication [1983] OJ C 318/3.

[19]Smith 1998, pp. 64–65.

[20]Cini 2001.

[21]Stefan 2012; Blauberger 2009, pp. 719–737.

[22]Blauberger 2009, pp. 729–732.

[23]For example, when all Member States except Germany accepted the revised guidelines on national regional aid, the Commission opened a formal investigation into all German regional aid schemes. European Commission, 'State aid: 24 Member States accept new regional aid guidelines (2007–2013); Commission Press Release of 27 June 2006, IP/06/851 State aid, Commission opens formal investigation against Germany. Once Germany finally approved the revised rules, the Commission closed the investigation. Blauberger 2009, pp. 729–730.

The development of a rules-based regime enabled the Commission to insulate itself from intense political pressures from the Member States.[24] Indeed, in a policy area that brings the Commission into direct conflict with national governments, an ad hoc approach would be unworkable. As one Commission official noted:

> Experience has shown that aid levels tend to rise if there are no hard-and-fast rules but only a vaguely formulated policy. There is nothing easier for the state aid controller than to allow a few percent more this time, a few percent more next time, and so on. The Commission needs rules to discipline itself. Rules are the best safeguard against political decisions which, if they were to proliferate, would destroy all state aid control.[25]

By appealing to rules set out in soft law instruments, precedents and the principle of equal treatment of Member States, the Commission garners substantial leverage to resist lobbying efforts in individual cases.[26] At the same time, the articulation of specific rules allows for more transparency and legal certainty and speeds up decision taking.[27]

As the scope of State aid control expanded to new forms of aid or to new sectors not covered by existing rules, the Commission gradually filled up regulatory gaps by adopting new frameworks and guidelines. Over time this practice resulted in a rather complex system of soft rules. A common pattern emerged: the translation of Commission practice in individual 'precedent' decisions into operational exemption criteria; the codification of those criteria in frameworks and guidelines; and the constant updating, clarification and/or tightening of the criteria on the basis of a changing policy context.[28]

7.2.2.2 From Mature Soft Law to Hard Law

Over the course of the 1990s, the widening scope of State aid control, more systematic notifications by the Member States and more frequent complaints had generated an expanding workload. The Commission found it increasingly difficult to direct its already stretched resources to the most distortive cases.[29] As a consequence, the Commission reconsidered its position towards 'hard' State aid law. It submitted two draft regulations to the Council of Ministers: (1) an Enabling Regulation,[30] approved by the Council in 1998, empowering the Commission to exempt certain categories of aid from the notification obligation; and (2) a procedural regulation,

---

[24] Smith 1998; Cini 2001.

[25] Rawlinson 1993, pp. 57–58.

[26] Smith 1998, p. 62.

[27] Rawlinson 1993, pp. 56–58.

[28] Cini 2001, p. 200.

[29] Blauberger 2009, pp. 732–733; Smith 1998, pp. 73–75.

[30] Council Regulation (EC) No 994/98 of 7 May 1998 on the application of Articles 92 and 93 of the Treaty establishing the European Community to certain categories of horizontal State aid [1998] OJ L 142/1.

adopted in 1999, codifying the procedural rules in State aid.[31] Based on the Enabling Regulation, the Commission adopted a series of Block Exemption Regulations (BERs) for State aid in areas where it gained sufficient case experience to define clear compatibility criteria. State aid measures meeting these conditions are considered unproblematic and therefore do not require the Commission's prior approval. Hence, in those areas covered by a BER a 'hardening' of soft law occurred: soft State aid rules were crystallized into hard law.[32]

Without abandoning recourse to soft law, the Commission has in more recent years continued to transform mature soft law into hard law. In 2008, the Commission consolidated the five existing BERs (covering aid to SMEs, research and development aid in favour of SMEs, employment aid, training aid and regional aid) into one single General Block Exemption Regulation (GBER) with simplified and harmonised conditions of application.[33] The GBER nearly tripled the number of block-exempted measures compared to the previous regulations. In the context of its programme for State aid Modernization,[34] the Commission proposed to further expand the scope of the GBER so it could better focus its *ex ante* scrutiny on cases with the biggest impact on the internal market. It estimates that the new GBER, which was adopted in 2014, exempts about 70 percent of all aid measures from *ex ante* control.[35]

7.2.3 The Articulation of Sector-Specific Rules: The Example of the Film and Audiovisual Sector

The previous section described how the formulation of operational exemption criteria for particular categories of aid—and their codification into soft law and, more recently, hard law - enabled the Commission to manage conflicts about admissible State aid. By clarifying the applicable standards and mobilizing private actors to come forward with evidence of violations of those rules, the Commission in turn extracted compliance from Member State governments. For aid measures not yet covered by existing rules, however, Member States could still claim ignorance (or simply decide to take the risk to grant the aid without the Commission's prior

[31] Council Regulation (EC) No 659/1999 of 22 March 1999 laying down detailed rules for the application of Article 93 of the EC Treaty [1999] OJ L 83/1.

[32] Blauberger 2009.

[33] Commission Regulation (EC) No 800/2008 of 6 August 2008 declaring certain categories of aid compatible with the common market in application of Articles 87 and 88 of the Treaty (General block exemption Regulation) [2008] OJ L 214/3.

[34] European Commission, Communication on State Aid Modernisation (SAM) (COM/2012/0209 final), 8 May 2012.

[35] Commission Press Release of 21 May 2014, IP/587/2014 State aid: Commission exempts more aid measures from prior notification.

approval).[36] The Commission, for its part, has generally sought to preserve its policy effectiveness in core sectors by minimizing confrontation with governments in peripheral sectors.[37] Accordingly, more often than not, external constraints on its independent agenda-setting abilities, such as rulings by the EU courts, complaints by third parties or the wider EU political agenda, pushed the Commission's Directorate General (DG) for Competition to extend the reach of State aid control to certain sectors it was not (yet) prepared to address, whether because of resource constraints or because of the politically sensitive attitude of the Member States.

To exemplify the process of event-driven policy formalisation in EU State aid control, this section will discuss the Commission's articulation of sector-specific State aid rules for films and audiovisual works. This example is particularly insightful because of the interesting parallels between State aid control practice in the film and audiovisual sector and the sports sector. Both sectors are characterized by a dual economic and cultural/societal nature and can lay claim on shaping European and national cultures and identities. Apart from macro-economic reasons (e.g. in terms of the number of jobs provided and the structural links to tourism or local and regional development) also social, cultural and educational returns are invoked to legitimise measures to support the cinema or sports sector. This makes State aid control complex and controversial. Not only industry stakeholders loudly trumpet the 'exceptional characteristics' of these sectors to justify special treatment under EU law. Also the Member States have encouraged the Commission to develop a sector-specific approach through various Council Declarations, Resolutions, and the inclusion of Treaty provisions on culture and sport.[38] Regarding cultural aspects, these expressions have immediate bearing on State aid control. In addition to a new discretionary exemption for State aid to promote culture (Article 107(3)(d) TFEU), the Maastricht Treaty also introduced a constitutional requirement to 'take cultural aspects into account' in all Union action. While there is no formal cross-sectional clause for sport, the reference to the specific

---

[36]Nicolaides 2002, p. 260. Yet the Commission has consistently upheld the principle that, in view of the mandatory nature of its review of State aid, neither the lack of any precedent involving the application of the State aid rules in similar cases nor the alleged lack of clarity in its policy can results in a legitimate expectation that the aid is lawful. See e.g. Commission Decision of 13 Mei 2013 on the aid scheme implemented by France for headquarters and logistics centres [2013] OJ L23/1, para 78.

[37]Smith 2001, p. 231.

[38]On cinematographic and other audiovisual works, see e.g. Council Resolution of 12 February 2001 national aid to the film and audiovisual industries [2001] OJ C73/3; Council Resolution of 21 January 2002 on the development of the audiovisual sector [2002] OJ C 32/4; Recommendation of the European Parliament and of the Council of 16 November 2005 on film heritage and the competitiveness of related industrial activities [2005] OJ L323/57 On sport, see e.g. Treaty of Amsterdam amending the Treaty on European Union, the Treaties establishing the European Communities and certain related acts - Declarations adopted by the Conference - Declaration on sport [1997] OJ C 340/136; European Council in Nice—December 7,8 and 9 2000—Annex IV to the conclusions of the Presidency: 'Declaration on the specific characteristics of sport and its social function in Europe, of which account should be taken in implementing common policies'.

nature of sport and its social and educational function in Article 165(1) TFEU does further support the need to give weight to these considerations also in State aid control.[39]

The Commission's State aid control practice in the film and audiovisual sector started to take shape following a 1998 decision on a French aid scheme for film production.[40] Until that decision, only a handful of aid schemes for the audiovisual sector had been notified to the Commission. In those early cases, the Commission's attention was limited to possible breaches of the principle of non-discrimination and the free movement rules. As long as a notified aid measure did not discriminate on grounds of nationality, it was considered compatible with the internal market.[41] This all changed when the Commission received a complaint about the exclusionary effects of the French aid scheme, which contained provisions rendering the amount of aid conditional on the use of French technical facilities, cast and crew. After the French authorities agreed to modify those provisions, the Commission approved the aid. In its decision, the Commission set out four specific compatibility criteria to assess aid to audiovisual production under the cultural derogation of Article 107(3)(d) TFEU: (1) the Member States must ensure that the content of the aided production is cultural (according to verifiable national criteria); (2) the producer must be free to spend at least 20 percent of the film budget in other Member States without any reduction of aid; (3) the aid intensity must be limited to 50 percent of the total budget of the film (except in case of low budget films); and (4) aid supplements for specific filmmaking activities are not allowed.[42] Because the French authorities had insisted on an equal treatment, the Commission undertook to review the schemes in place in other Member States under the criteria adopted in the French decision.[43] Pressure from the French government thus seized control of the Commission's State aid policy agenda.

[39]The CJEU has already recognized this with regard to the application of the EU free movement and competition rules. See e.g. Case C-325/08, *Olympique Lyonnais v Olivier Bernard and Newcastle United FC*, ECLI:EU:C:2010:143, para 40; Joined Cases C-403/08 and C-429/08) *Football Association Premier League Ltd and others v QC Leisure and others and Karen Murphy v Media Protection Services Ltd*, ECLI:EU:C:2011:631, para 101.

[40]Commission Decision of 24 June 1998 on State Aid N3/98 (France) Soutien à la production cinématographique.

[41]Pauwels et al. 2007. See e.g. Commission Decision 89/441/CEE of 21 December 1988 on aid granted by the Greek Government to the film industry for the production of Greek films [1989] OJ L208/38; European Commission, Sixteenth Report on Competition Policy (1987) p. 159; European Commission, Nineteenth Report on Competition Policy (1990) pp. 167–169; European Commission, XXIIth Report on Competition Policy (1993) pp. 248–249.

[42]Commission Decision of 24 June 1998 on State Aid N3/98 (France) Soutien à la production cinématographique.

[43]For this purpose, the Commission launched an inquiry requesting information from all Member States about their aid schemes for the audiovisual sector, the vast majority of which were not notified.

By 2000, the Commission reviewed and authorized the aid measures of four other Member States.[44] The Commission's review, however, faced considerable opposition. Several Member States, and specifically the ministers of culture, felt that it was intruding in a national policy domain, attacking their prerogative to define cultural policies and as such undermining the principle of subsidiarity.[45] The rising controversy led the Commission to shift the conflict from the review of individual measures to the design of soft rules.

In its 2001 Communication on certain legal aspects relating to cinematographic and other audiovisual works, the so-called Cinema Communication, the Commission consolidated its policy so far. In addition to the general legality principle,[46] it set out the four specific compatibility criteria developed in the French decision, which would remain valid until 2004.[47] Some minor changes were made in view of the Member States' concerns.[48] The validity of the assessment criteria was extended in 2004, 2007, and 2009 until the successor regime, the 2013 Cinema Communication, entered into force in November 2013.[49] In the latest Communication, the Commission for the first time revised the assessment criteria in view of a number of sector developments and trends in the design of national film support schemes. The new audiovisual State aid assessment framework, adopted after three rounds of public consultations, covers State aid for a wider scope of activities (such as scriptwriting, distribution or film promotion and all aspects of film production), introduces a higher maximum aid intensity level for cross-border productions, and limits the territorial production activity that can be required as an eligibility condition. In exchange, the new framework more explicitly acknowledges the limits of the Commission's regulatory autonomy regarding the application of the 'cultural test'. The Commission's detailed scrutiny of

---

[44]Commission Decision of 25 December 1998, N 486/97—the Netherlands - Support for film production [1999] OJ C 120/2; Commission Decision of 20 July 1999, NN 49/97 and N357/99—Ireland - Tax-based incentive scheme for investment in film production for the period 1999–2000 'Sect. 35/481' [1999] OJ C 375/4; Commission Decision of 21 April 1999, N4/98—Germany - Promotion of the film industry [1999] OJ C272/4; Commission Decision of 2 February 2000, N 748/99—Sweden—State aid N 748/99—Sweden—Scheme of aid to film production and film related activities (The Swedish Film Institute Agreement) [2000] OJ C 134/3.

[45]See e.g. Council resolution of 12 February 2001 national aid to the film and audiovisual industries [2001] OJ C73/3; Vivianne Reding, A New Approach to the Development of the Audiovisual Sector, Speech delivered at the Informal meeting of Audiovisual Ministers, Mons, 5 October 2001.

[46]I.e. the Commission verifies that the scheme does not contain clauses that would be contrary to provisions of the EC Treaty (now TFEU) in fields other than State aid, including the free movement provisions and the prohibition of discrimination on grounds of nationality.

[47]Communication from the Commission to the Council, the European Parliament, the Economic and Social Committee and the Committee of the Regions on certain legal aspects relating to cinematographic and other audiovisual works, COM/2001/0534 final [2002] OJ C43/6.

[48]For example, the limitation of the aid intensity to 50 percent of the film budget, one of the most contested provisions, was modified to allow for more flexibility. Exceptions for 'difficult and low budget films' could from now on, under the subsidiarity principle, be defined by each Member State according to national parameters.

[49]Communication from the Commission on State aid for films and other audiovisual works (2013/C 332/01) [2013] OJ C332/1.

verifiable cultural criteria, so as to ascertain that the aid could benefit from the cultural exception under Article 107(3)(d) TFEU,[50] had always been controversial.[51] To diffuse this particular conflict, the new Communication states that that the Commission will no longer scrutinize the detailed criteria used by the Member States.[52]

Consistent with the general trend towards a hardening of mature soft law, the new GBER codified the revised assessment criteria for State aid to films and other audiovisual works. Aid schemes with an annual budget below EUR 50 million that meet these criteria are now exempted from the notification requirement.[53]

7.3 State Aid to Sports Infrastructure

In the years 2011 to 2013, the Commission adopted no less than ten decisions on State aid measures for stadiums or other sports infrastructures. On the basis of this case experience, the Commission was able to codify the operational exemption criteria it had developed for aid to 'sport and multifunctional recreational infrastructures' in the 2014 GBER.[54]

Article 55 of the GBER sets out the specific compatibility conditions under which aid for sports and multifunctional recreational infrastructures,[55] which may take the form of investment aid or operating aid (only for sports infrastructure), can automatically be considered compatible with the internal market:

(1) The sports infrastructure is not to be used exclusively by a single professional sport user (i.e. it has to be offered to other professional or non-professional sports users for at least 20 % of the time capacity each year);
(2) Access to the infrastructure is granted on a transparent and non-discriminatory basis. Users that financed at least 30 percent of the investment costs may be granted preferential access. Pricing conditions for its use by professional sports clubs must be made publicly available;

---

[50]Aid that is aimed at promoting the development of the film industry, rather than promote cultural activities, can only be approved under Article 107(3)(c) TFEU.

[51]Pauwels et al. 2007; Schaefer et al. 2002.

[52]Communication from the Commission on State aid for films and other audiovisual works (2013/C 332/01) [2013] OJ C332/1, para 25.

[53]Commission Regulation (EU) No 651/2014 of 17 June 2014 declaring certain categories of aid compatible with the internal market in application of Articles 107 and 108 of the Treaty (GBER) OJ L 187/1, Articles 4 and 54.

[54]This category was added in the revised draft version of the GBER that the Commission presented in December 2013.

[55]The GBER does not provide a precise definition for 'multifunctional recreational infrastructure', but clarifies that it has a multifunctional character offering, 'in particular, cultural and recreational services with the exception of leisure parks and hotel facilities'. GBER, *Supra* n 53, Article 55(3).

(3) In case of a public-private partnership, the concessionaire is chosen on the basis of an open, transparent and non-discriminatory tender, having due regard to the applicable procurement rules;
(4) For investment aid, the aid amount does not exceed the difference between the eligible costs and the operating profit of the investment. For operating aid, the aid amount does not exceed the operating losses over the relevant period.

To benefit from an exemption, the aid measure must additionally comply with the common provisions of the GBER[56] and may not exceed the following thresholds: for investment aid max. EUR 15 million (with total costs not exceeding EUR 50 million) and for operating aid max. EUR 2 million per year.[57] Aid measures that do not fulfil all of the above criteria must still be notified to the Commission. This does not imply that the aid is deemed incompatible within the meaning of Article 107 TFEU. It merely means that the aid must be directly assessed under and declared compatible with the Treaty rules.

This section will discuss what triggered the sudden emergence of decisional practice since 2011 and how it accelerated the formalization process of sector-specific State aid rules. It shows that the Commission's enforcement practice must be understood in two distinct phases. In the first phase, general principles were articulated to consider the public financing of sports infrastructure outside the realm of State aid control (3.1). In the second phase, after the General Court brought infrastructure financing within the scope of the State aid rules, the Commission shifted those general principles, albeit in a more sophisticated form, to the compatibility level (3.2).

7.3.1 Phase 1: Football Stadiums as 'Public Service' Infrastructures

The public funding of infrastructure such as airports, railways, motorways, bridges, etc. has long been considered to escape the application of the State aid rules. It was understood that, if access and usage remained public (i.e. no advantages are conferred upon a specific undertaking or industry), the construction and operation of infrastructures would normally represent a general measure of economic policy and not an economic activity.[58] Accordingly, in its 2007 White Paper

[56]Ibid, Articles 5–9 (aid must be transparent, must have an incentive effect, must respect the rules on cumulation, and aid measures and awards must be published).

[57]Ibid., Article 4.1.

[58]See e.g. European Commission, Application of Articles 92 and 93 of the EC Treaty and Article 61 of the EEA Agreement to State aids in the aviation sector [1994] OJ C 350/5, para 12 ('The construction or enlargement of infrastructure projects (such as airports, motorways, bridges, etc.) represents a general measure of economic policy which cannot be controlled by the Commission under the Treaty rules on State aids'); European Commission, XXVth Report on Competition Policy (1995) p. 80 ('Governments have always used financial intervention as an essential tool

on Sport, the European Commission indicated that the public financing related to the construction of sports infrastructures can be considered not to constitute State aid, provided that certain conditions are fulfilled.[59] It had clarified this position for the first time in relation to the financing for the Niedersachsenstadion (now the HDI-Arena) in Hanover.

In 2000, when Germany was awarded the hosting of the 2006 FIFA World Cup, the Hanover stadium was selected as one of the hosting sites. Following the announcement that regional public authorities would fund part of its renovation, with total project costs amounting to around EUR 60 million,[60] the Commission received two complaints alleging unlawful State aid to the stadium's main tenant, the professional football club Hannover 96.[61] After a preliminary assessment of the project, the Commission concluded that the measures did not constitute State aid. In a letter to the German authorities, the Commission laid down some general principles. It stressed that a venue for public events (such as a football stadium), supporting different categories of activities, could be considered as embodying a typical State responsibility towards the general public (first principle). Furthermore, the Commission acknowledged that a stadium is a facility implying a large and risky investment, which the private market is unlikely to carry out in its entirety on its own (second principle). Based on these considerations, the Commission concluded that the funding of the stadium would not qualify as State aid so long as the infrastructure is not apt to selectively favour one (or more) specific undertaking(s) (third principle). If public authorities maintain ownership and management of the stadium, the selectivity requirement is not met when it is rented out to different users at market terms. If the management of the stadium is entrusted to a private operator, the concession must be awarded by means of an open, transparent and non-discriminatory tender and the nature of the stadium as a facility open to all operators must be preserved.[62] Since all the above conditions were met in the case at hand, the public investment in the stadium escaped the application of the State aid rules.

Footnote 58 (continued)

in their policy of infrastructure development. In principle, as long as access and usage remain public and general, such intervention will not constitute aid within the meaning of Article [107(1) TFEU] but will be normally regarded as being in the public interest … Such a public good provided by government benefits society in a collective manner and is not conferred upon any specific enterprise or industry (principle of non excludability). Consequently, public support for infrastructure will not normally constitute aid, but rather a general measure derived from the State's sovereignty in respect of economic policy, land planning and development').

[59]Commission Staff Working Document—The EU and Sport: Background and Context—Accompanying document to the White Paper on Sport, COM (2007) 391 final, Sect. 3.2.2.

[60]Siebold and Klingmüller 2004, p. 88.

[61]Gerlinger 2003, p. 9.

[62]The Commission reiterated these principles in administrative letters to the UK and Dutch authorities. The content of the letters are discussed in Santamato and Westerhof 2003, pp. 645–648; Koenig and Kühling 2003, pp. 289–298; Koenig and Haratasch 2004, pp. 393–398.

Based on the general principles set out in this precedent 'decision', public authorities could legitimately consider that the financing of sports infrastructure did not constitute State aid and that, accordingly, such measures did not need to be notified.

The principles were not unique to sports infrastructure. They were similarly applied to many other types of infrastructure funding.[63] The assumption that the construction and operation of sports infrastructure constitutes a general measure of public policy and not an economic activity, however, did showcase a generous approach. The Commission explicitly relied on the Amsterdam Declaration on Sport, which emphasizes that consideration should be given to the social significance of sport,[64] to assert that large major sports infrastructures satisfy general and basic needs of the general public. Even when considering that the infrastructure may also be used for concerts and other non-sports major events, this is quite a stretch. Surely, a football stadium does not perform a 'public service' function similar to open transport facilities (such as roads, railways, seaports and underground transport) or broadband infrastructures providing users universal connectivity in a given area. Moreover, the financing of sports infrastructures is clearly capable of conferring an advantage to certain operators (and users) that do carry out economic activities.

7.3.2 Phase 2: Commission Decisional Practice After Leipzig/Halle

The General Court's judgment in *Leipzig/Halle* (2011) marked a turning point in the Commission's approach to the public financing of (sports) infrastructure projects.[65] In the area of airport infrastructure, the Court had already invalidated the argument that the operation of such infrastructure for commercial purposes would not constitute an economic activity.[66] In *Leipzig/Halle*, the Court went one step further by clarifying that also the construction of that infrastructure must be

[63] Santamato and Westerhof 2003, pp. 646–648.

[64] Treaty of Amsterdam amending the Treaty on European Union, the Treaties establishing the European Communities and certain related acts - Declarations adopted by the Conference - Declaration on sport [1997] OJ C 340/136.

[65] Joined Cases T-443/08 and T-455/08, *Mitteldeutsche Flughafen and Flughafen Leipzig/Halle v Commission*, ECLI:EU:T:2011:117. The CJEU largely upheld the judgment in Case C-288/11, *Mitteldeutsche Flughafen AG and Flughafen Leipzig-Halle GmbH v European Commission*, ECLI:EU:C:2012:821.

[66] It was already clear from earlier case law that the management of airport infrastructure is an economic activity. See e.g. Case C-82/01 P, *Aéroports de Paris v Commission*, ECLI:EU:C:2002:617; Case T-196/04, *Ryanair v Commission*, ECLI:EU:T:2008:585.

characterised as an economic activity if the construction and operation are inseparably linked.[67] The fact that private investors would not have made the investment because it was deemed unprofitable is irrelevant in this respect.[68] In the case at hand, the Court upheld the Commission's finding that the public financing of the construction of a new runway at the Leipzig-Halle airport constituted State aid. Moreover, the Court rejected the claim that a considerable part of the public financing was for tasks falling within the exercise of public powers. Only compensatory payments relating to the performance of public duties (such as expenses relating security and police functions, fire-protection measures, and air-traffic control services) were considered to fall outside the scope of the State aid rules.[69]

According to the Commission, the judgment made clear that the economic character of the later use of an infrastructure determines whether the funding of its construction is subject to State aid control:

> after the *Leipzig/Halle* ruling, it cannot be denied anymore that the financing of *any type of infrastructure* (excluding infrastructure related to security, safety, etc.) that is later commercially exploited is State aid relevant. This also means *a contrario* that only the financing of infrastructure that is later *not commercially exploited* and built in the interest of the general public is in principle excluded from the application of the State aid rules. [70]

The judgment had vast implications for the public financing of *inter alia* sports infrastructures. Since most sports infrastructures are commercially exploited, it now became clear that the State aid rules apply to the way in which they are funded. As a result, Member States began to notify their support measures for sports infrastructures for approval by the Commission, triggering the development of decisional practice.

---

[67]In the case at hand, the Court upheld the Commission's reasoning that the publicly financed construction of a new runway at the Leipzig-Halle airport could not be dissociated from its subsequent operation for commercial purposes. The runway would not be made available free of charge in the public interest: its users would be charged for its use. Since the construction of the runway would permit the airport manager to increase its capacity and extend its business of operating the airport, it constitutes an economic advantage that must be classified as State aid. Joined Cases T-443/08 and T-455/08, *Mitteldeutsche Flughafen and Flughafen Leipzig/Halle v Commission*, ECLI:EU:T:2011:117, paras 94–100. The CJEU stressed, however, that the distinction between public remit and economic activities has to be made on a case-by-case basis. Case C-288/11, *Mitteldeutsche Flughafen AG and Flughafen Leipzig-Halle GmbH v European Commission*, ECLI:EU:C:2012:821, para 47.

[68]Joined Cases T-443/08 and T-455/08, *Mitteldeutsche Flughafen and Flughafen Leipzig/Halle v Commission*, ECLI:EU:T:2011:117, paras 114–115; Case C-288/11, *Mitteldeutsche Flughafen AG and Flughafen Leipzig-Halle GmbH v European Commission*, ECLI:EU:C:2012:821, paras 49–50.

[69]Joined Cases T-443/08 and T-455/08, *Mitteldeutsche Flughafen and Flughafen Leipzig/Halle v Commission*, ECLI:EU:T:2011:117, paras 225–226.

[70]European Commission, Note to DG REGIO on the Application of State aid Rules to infrastructure investment projects, COMP/03/2011. In the case at hand, only the contributions relating to security, safety, police, and customs measures and to activities regarding the control and supervision of airspace were considered to fall within the public remit and thus not to constitute economic activities.

The Commission adopted its first decision related to sports infrastructure funding in 2011.[71] It approved a Hungarian aid measure aimed at enabling professional sports organisations or clubs of the five most popular team sports (i.e. football, handball, basketball, ice hockey, and water polo) to modernize their sports infrastructures. The measure was part of a broader tax benefit scheme to incentivize undertakings to contribute to sports development.[72] The *Hungarian tax benefit scheme* decision was the first of a series of ten Commission decisions dealing with State aid to sports infrastructure in eight different Member States.[73] Most cases involved football stadiums, but there have also been decisions on aid for the construction and/or renovation of a swimming pool, an ice arena, a rugby stadium, a Gaelic games stadium, and multifunctional sport arenas. All of the aid measures were notified to the Commission, and, in the wake of the *Leipzig/Halle* judgment, the Commission was required to assess their compatibility with the internal market under Article 107(3)(c) TFEU.

The decisions reveal a consistent and favourable approach towards aid measures for sports infrastructure. For the most part, the Commission translated the general principles it had used during the first phase to find that there was no State aid in the meaning of Article 107(1) TFEU into operational criteria for exemption of the aid measures under Article 107(3)(c) TFEU.

Firstly, the Commission's acceptance that a sports infrastructure, supporting different categories of activities, could be considered as embodying a typical State responsibility towards the general public is now being used to find that the aid measure is aimed at a well-defined objective of common interest. For instance, in its decision concerning State aid for a stadium in the German town Erfurt, the Commission asserts that 'with regard to the achievement of a policy objective of common interest, the construction of venues for sport and other public events and supporting different types of activities which benefit the general public can be considered a State responsibility towards the general public'.[74] To further strengthen

---

[71]Commission Decision of 9 November 2011, SA.31722—Hungary—Supporting the Hungarian sport sector via tax benefit scheme [2011] OJ C364/1.

[72]In order to receive funding under the scheme, professional sports clubs have to design a strategy that includes initiatives for the public, such as the organisation of mass sports events, training of the young generation or reserving schedules for local citizens to use sports infrastructures.

[73]Commission Decision of 2 May 2013, SA.33618 Uppsala arena [2013] OJ L243/19; Commission Decision of 15 May 2013, SA.33728 Multiarena in Copenhagen [2014] OJ L152/32; Commission Decision of 20 March 2013, SA.35135 Multifunktionsarena der Stadt Erfurt [2013] OJ C140/1; Commission Decision of 20 March 2013, SA.35440 Multifunktionsarena der Stadt Jena [2013] OJ C140/1; Commission Decision of 18 December 2013, SA.35501 Financement de la construction et de la renovation des stades pour l'EURO 2016; Commission Decision of 2 October 2013, SA.36105 Fuβballstadion Chemnitz [2014] OJ C50/1; Commission Decision of 20 November 2013, SA.37109 Football stadiums in Flanders [2014] OJ C69/1; Commission Decision of 9 April 2014, SA.37342 Regional Stadia Development in Northern Ireland [2014] OJ C418/1; and Commission Decision of 13 December 2013, SA.37373 Contribution to the renovation of ice arena Thialf in Heerenveen [2014] OJ C50/1.

[74]Commission Decision of 20 March 2013, SA.35135 Multifunktionsarena der Stadt Erfurt [2013] OJ C140/1, para 14.

the argument that the aid measure in question is in line with the common interest, the decisions consistently make reference to Article 165 TFEU in addition to the Amsterdam Declaration on Sport.

Secondly, prior to *Leipzig/Halle*, the Commission acknowledged that the private market is unlikely to carry out the necessary investments for sports infrastructure on its own. In all of the decisions, the Commission continues to emphasize and acknowledge the problem of underinvestment in sports infrastructure, but now to conclude that the aid measure is necessary and well designed.[75]

For a measure to be declared compatible with the internal market, Member States must additionally demonstrate that there is an incentive effect (i.e. does the aid change the behaviour of undertakings?).[76] For example, in the *Football Stadiums in Flanders* case, the Belgian authorities argued that financial institutions would be more inclined to provide a loan for the renovation of football stadiums when the government finances (a small) part of the costs.[77] Similarly, in the *Hungarian tax benefit scheme* case, the Hungarian authorities showed that the investments concerned would not have been undertaken within the same timeframe without any State aid.[78] The other Commission decisions, however, simply state that without aid, there would be no sports infrastructure in the respective regions.[79]

Thirdly, the principle that the subsidized sports infrastructure is not to be used exclusively by a single professional sport user remains important. The Commission now applies that principle as a safeguard to ensure the proportionality of the aid measure and to limit its distortive effect. State aid by the Dutch authorities for the renovation of the ice skating arena Thialf, for instance, was found to be compatible under Article 107(3)(c) *inter alia* because 'the usage obligations with which the operating company will have to comply ensure that several types of users will be able to benefit from the ice skating facilities. The renovation, with public support, of the ice arena will therefore benefit professional and amateur

---

[75]See e.g. Commission Decision of 9 April 2014, SA.37342 Regional Stadia Development in Northern Ireland [2014] OJ C418/1, para 94. ('The aid is necessary and well targeted as it addresses the specific problem of underinvestment in sports infrastructure. The UK authorities have demonstrated that such infrastructure cannot be provided by market forces alone. The three stadia have not attracted sufficient private funding to deliver the reconstruction without significant public intervention'); Commission Decision of 9 November 2011, SA.31722—Hungary—Supporting the Hungarian sport sector via tax benefit scheme [2011] OJ C364/1, para 93 ('Taking into account the underinvestment in sport infrastructure facilities in Hungary in the last twenty years, the effects of the economic and financial crisis, the objectives of the measures cannot be achieved by any other means available for the government').

[76]See e.g. Case 730/79 *Philip Morris v Commission*, ECLI:EU:C:1980:209, para 17. The incentive effect criterion is also found in the 2014 GBER as a condition for its application. GBER, *Supra* n 53, Article 6.

[77]Commission Decision of 20 November, SA.37109 2013 Football stadiums in Flanders [2014] OJ C69/1, para 35.

[78]Commission Decision of 9 November 2011, SA.31722—Hungary—Supporting the Hungarian sport sector via tax benefit scheme, [2011] OJ C364/1, para 94.

[79]See for example Commission Decision of 9 April 2014, SA.37342 Regional Stadia Development in Northern Ireland [2014] OJ C418/1, para 96.

sports as well as the general public'.[80] The *Football stadiums in Flanders* case concerned State aid for sports infrastructure that will be used by one or more specific professional football clubs. The Belgian authorities, aware of the potential problem, introduced the condition that:

> the owner of the stadium (whether a local authority or a club) must commit to occasionally rent out the stadium to other clubs that wish to use it. The financial plan must show that conditions of access and use of the stadium for third parties are transparent and non-discriminatory and it must me proven that the lease of the stadium is comparable with a benchmark price established by the Flemish government.[81]

The Commission acknowledged that 'this pricing mechanism will serve to limit distortion of competition vis-à-vis privately owned and funded football infrastructure'.[82] Subsequently, it found that the aid does not affect trade and competition between Member States to an extent contrary to the common interest.

To conclude, although the *Leipzig/Halle* judgment subjected the public financing of sports infrastructure to State aid scrutiny, this did not result in a radical change in the Commission's policy. The general principles developed during the first phase clearly functioned as a blueprint for the operational exemption conditions used in the Commission's decisional practice since 2011. This also facilitated their rapid codification in the 2014 GBER (without the need for the standard intermediate stage of soft State aid rules).

7.4 State Aid to Professional Football Clubs

Regarding support measures granted by public authorities to individual professional sports clubs, the European Commission has not yet articulated sector-specific rules. In sharp contrast with State aid support for sports infrastructure, where the process of policy formalisation recently reached the stage of hard law, the Commission still has to adopt individual 'precedent' decisions on the compatibility of different types of State aid to professional sports clubs. It was only in 2013 that the Commission opened a series of in-depth investigations into various public support measures in favour of certain Spanish and Dutch professional football clubs (including tax privileges, the transfer and sale of land and property, State guarantees, bank loans, and debt waivers).[83]

---

[80] Commission Decision of 13 December 2013, SA.37373 Contribution to the renovation of ice arena Thialf in Heerenveen [2014] OJ C50/1, para 59.

[81] Commission Decision of 20 November 2013, SA.37109 Football stadiums in Flanders [2014] OJ C69/1, para 11.

[82] Ibid., para 41.

[83] Commission decision of 6 March 2013, SA.33584, The Netherlands - Alleged municipal aid to certain professional Dutch football clubs in 2008–2011 [2013] OJ C 116/19; Commission decision of 18 December 2013, SA.29769 Spain—State aid to certain Spanish professional football clubs [2014] OJ C69/115; Commission decision of 18 December 2013, SA.36387 Spain—Alleged aid in favour of three Valencia football clubs [2014] OJ C69/99; Commission decision of 18 December 2013 SA.33754, Spain—Real Madrid CF [2014] OJ C69/108.

This section will first discuss how a systematic lack of notifications by the Member States coupled with the Commission's position that it needed case practice to develop sector-specific State aid rules perpetuated a cycle of non-compliance (4.1). It will then explore the constraints on the Commission's independent agenda-setting abilities that triggered enforcement action in 2013 (4.2).

7.4.1 Before 2013: Implicit Tolerance of Non-compliance with the Notification Obligation

Prior to 2013, the Commission adopted only three formal decisions concerning support measures to professional sports clubs. Since it found that the support measures (subject to modifications) did not constitute State aid within the meaning of Article 107 TFEU, there was no need for a compatibility assessment in these cases.

In 2000, the French authorities notified a subsidy scheme under which local authorities would be able to grant subsidies to professional football, basketball, rugby, and volleyball clubs with State-approved youth training centres.[84] The aim of the scheme was to assist the clubs in providing education and training of young athletes. The Commission considered that these activities are part of the performance of public duties. The French authorities did have to ensure that there would be no cross-subsidization, namely by requiring separate accounts to be kept for training expenditures and for the club's economic activities.[85]

In 2003, the Commission opened an *ex officio* investigation into a new Italian law creating specific taxation and accounting rules for professional sports clubs including Serie A football clubs (the so-called Salva-Calcio law).[86] The law laid down urgent measures allowing sports clubs to offset capital losses (arising from the decreased value of the rights to exploit the performances of professional players, e.g. through injury) against future profits over ten years for tax purposes. The extension of the period over which losses could be deducted was considered to represent an economic advantage granted by forgoing tax revenues. At the Commission's request, the Italian authorities undertook to amend the law, ruling out the possibility of using the different accounting method for tax purposes. Although the amended law continued to grant sports clubs an advantage in terms of favourable accounting treatment,

[84]A previous version of the subsidy scheme was tacitly approved in 1995 because the Commission had raised no objections.

[85]Commission decision of 25 April 2001 on State aid N118/00—France, Subventions publiques aux clubs sportifs professionels.

[86]In parallel, the Commission opened an infringement procedure against Italy because the law also appeared to breach requirements laid down in the Fourth (78/660/EEC) and Seventh (83/349/EEC) Council Directives on companies' annual and consolidated accounts. Commission Press Release of 11 November 2003, IP/03/1529 Commission probes measures for professional sports clubs in Italy ('Salvio Calcio').

it no longer provided any tax advantage. The Commission, therefore, concluded that the measure no longer constituted State aid.[87]

In 2004, the Dutch authorities notified the Commission of the intention of the Dutch city of Almere to conclude service contracts with a local volleyball and basketball club. The city would compensate the clubs for services related to training, the promotion of physical activity in general and grassroots sports in particular, and citymarketing. According to the Commission, the contracts did not grant an advantage to the beneficiaries because they were being awarded under market conditions and drafted to prevent overcompensation.[88]

With the exception of the aforementioned Dutch and French measures, the Commission received no notifications of public subsidies to professional sports clubs in this period.[89]

In the field of amateur sports, Member State governments could legitimately assume that public aid to local clubs (mostly given by municipalities) does not constitute State aid. As acknowledged by the Commission, the criteria of Article 107(1) TFEU would generally not be fulfilled, for instance, because the beneficiaries are not considered undertakings or because the measure has limited effects on trade between Member States and/or does not create appreciable distortions of competition.[90] Furthermore, the amounts granted are typically limited and may fall under the *de minimis* threshold.[91]

In the field of professional sports, however, it is settled case law that clubs must be considered undertakings, subject to the application of EU competition law, to the extent they carry out economic activities (e.g. the transfer of players, the sale of tickets and media rights or the conclusion of sponsorship agreements).[92] Thus,

---

[87]Commission decision of 22 June 2005 on the measure implemented by Italy for professional sports clubs (Decreto Salva Calcio). In view of the amendments, the Commission also closed the infringement procedure against Italy. Commission Press Release of 13 October 2005, IP/05/1271 Commission closes case against Italy on accounting rules for professional sports clubs ('Salva-Calcio').

[88]Commission decision of 6 April 2005 on State aid N555/2004—Netherlands, Maatregelen ten behoeve van sportclubs: Basketbal Omniworld Almere en Volleybal Omniworld Almere.

[89]European Commission, Report from the 3rd meeting of the Expert Group on Sustainable Financing of Sport (XG FIN), January 2013. http://ec.europa.eu/sport/news/2013/20130111-eu-expert-group-fin_en.htm. Accessed 1 December 2015.

[90]See e.g. Commission Staff Working Document—The EU and Sport: Background and Context - Accompanying document to the White Paper on Sport, COM (2007) 391 final, Sect. 3.2.2; Commission Regulation (EU) N°651/2014 of 17 June 2014 declaring certain categories of aid compatible with the internal market in application of Articles 107 and 108 of the Treaty [2014] OJ L187/1, consideration 74. See also Council Regulation (EU) 2015/1588 of 13 July 2015 on the application of Articles 107 and 108 of the Treaty on the Functioning of the European Union to certain categories of horizontal State aid (codification) [2015] OJ L 248/1, consideration 14.

[91]Commission Regulation (EU) No 1407/2013 of 18 December 2013 on the application of Articles 107 and 108 of the Treaty on the Functioning of the European Union [2013] OJ L 352/1.

[92]See e.g. references in Commission Decision 2003/778/EC of 23 July 2003 (COMP/C.2-37.398—Joint selling of the commercial rights of the UEFA Champions League) [2003] OJ L 291/24, para 106; Case T-193/02, *Laurent Piau v Commission*, ECLI:EU:T:2005:22, paras 69–72.

there could be little doubt that selective aid from public resources to, for example, a professional football club, is likely to fall within the scope of Article 107(1) TFEU. It would be unconvincing (and legally irrelevant) for Member State governments to plead ignorance of the rules. A more credible explanation for the systematic lack of notifications would be that the State aid coordination body in the national or federal Ministry lacks (effective) supervisory authority over aid granted by regional and local public authorities.[93]

Although Article 108 TFEU formally requires Member States to notify all planned State aid measures (except for those measures exempted from notification), unnotified aid has always been the Achilles' heel of EU State aid control.[94] As noted earlier, when the reach of State aid control expanded to new forms of aid or new sectors, the Commission has typically extracted compliance from the Member States through precedents and the formulation of operational exemption criteria. Yet the Commission always maintained that it could only develop and clarify its policy in sport on the basis of individual cases.[95] To break this cycle of non-compliance, reliance on notifications was insufficient; precedent decisions were needed.

The detection of State aid that should have been notified is based either on complaints by third parties or on other sources that allow the Commission to launch investigations on its own initiative. Although some potential new cases are picked up through e.g. press reports, resulting in *ex officio* investigations, scarce resources and Commission discretion dictate that this is no standard practice.[96]

Outside of notifications, the Commission initiated two formal investigations into alleged unlawful State aid to professional sports clubs before 2013: one on the basis of an *ex officio* enquiry (i.e. into the Italian Salva-Calcio law) and one on the basis of complaints (i.e. regarding the sale of land to football club AZ in the

[93]The risk of non-notification is higher for aid granted by regional or local authorities; they only occasionally grant aid and therefore have limited knowledge of the State aid rules. The notification obligation is incumbent on Member State governments, not on decentralised granting authorities. When Member States are caught granting unnotified aid, they often argue that internal national procedures did not allow them to check the compatibility of the aid granted by regional or local authorities. Nicolaides 2002, pp. 260–261.

[94]Ibid.

[95]See e.g. European Parliament, Answer given by Mr Monti on behalf of the Commission to written Question E-1860/2003, 10 July 2003; European Parliament, Answer given by Mr Monti to written question E-2261/2003, 13 August 2003; Commission Staff Working Document - The EU and Sport: Background and Context - Accompanying document to the White Paper on Sport, COM (2007) 391 final, Sect. 3.2.2; European Commission, Report from the 3rd meeting of the Expert Group on Sustainable Financing of Sport (XG FIN), January 2013. http://ec.europa.eu/sport/news/2013/20130111-eu-expert-group-fin_en.htm. Accessed 1 December 2015; European Ombudsman, 'State Aid and European football clubs? Summary of recommendation by the European Ombudsman following a complaint against the EU Commission', 17 December 2013.

[96]The number of *ex officio* cases (e.g. 35 in 2009 and 18 in 2010) dwindles in comparison to the numbers of complaints (e.g. around 400 in 2009). European Court of Auditors, 'Do the Commission's procedures ensure effective management of State aid control?' (2011) Special Report No. 15, para 26.

Netherlands).[97] The latter investigation was terminated, however, after the parties had dissolved the sale agreement under scrutiny. Clearly, rigorous scrutiny of public funding to professional sports clubs was not an enforcement priority for the Commission.

7.4.2 The 2013 Formal Investigations

In view of the above, the European Commission's launch of in-depth investigations into eight distinct public support measures in favour of Dutch and Spanish football clubs in 2013 comes as a surprising about-turn. Why this sudden change?

Several authors have suggested that the investigations were prompted by complaints of citizens.[98] Indeed, in its decisions to initiate proceedings pursuant to Article 108(2) TFEU, the Commission indicates that it learnt about the measures, which were not notified, through press reports and complaints,[99] the vast majority of which were submitted by citizens. Given that State aid complaints are typically a product of private interest, the involvement of private citizens in this area is remarkable. The financial and economic crisis starting in 2008 undoubtedly has been a contributing factor. Particularly in countries like Spain, where citizens have personally perceived the social impact of the recession and austerity measures, public opinion towards State spending for professional sports clubs and mega sports events has shifted dramatically.[100]

Although the notable engagement of private citizens is relevant, a number of other contextual factors have additionally contributed to the sudden burst of enforcement activity. At the outset, the relevance of the Commission's 2012 information-gathering exercises relating to State aid to professional football clubs can be downplayed (4.2.1). Much more important factors appear to be the case law of the EU courts curtailing the Commission's discretion in handling complaints (4.2.2) and the pressure exerted by the European Ombudsman on the Commission to reflect on how the State aid rules should apply (4.2.3).

7.4.2.1 The 2012 Information-Gathering Exercise

In view of the accumulation of complaints alleging unlawful State aid between 2009 and 2012, the Commission wished to get an overview of the situation in all EU Member States.[101] First, it collected information concerning the financing of

---

[97]Commission Decision of 25 January 2006 on the State Aid implemented by the Netherlands for AZ and AZ Vastgoed BV [2006] OJ L 307/194.

[98]See e.g. Craven 2014, pp. 205–2017; Daley 2014, pp. 2–6.

[99]It remains unclear to what extent the various letters sent by citizens formally qualify as complaints. For the sake of convenience, however, we will refer to them as complaints.

[100]See e.g. Van Maren 2015, pp. 83–108.

[101]European Commission, 'State aid to professional football clubs', COMP/C4/WP/AH/ZZ/md–D*2012/98568, 1 October 2012.

European professional football through contacts with UEFA. Second, the Commission wrote a letter to all EU Member States asking them to provide an overview of the measures they have adopted in favour of professional football clubs, in particular tax breaks and reductions in social security contributions. In the letter, dated 1 October 2012, the Commission underlined that such measures may constitute State aid and reminded the Member States of their obligation to notify all aid measures. On the question why the focus had been on football only, the Commission later clarified that it was looking at potential disciplines where distortion was most likely to happen (i.e. football is the biggest market in terms of sponsorship and transfers).[102]

Responses to the Commission's letter, however, did not (yet) result in new State aid inquiries. There are at least two reasons for this. First, Member States might, as already indicated, misunderstand or misjudge the application of the State aid rules and/or be unaware of aid granted by regional and local public authorities. The Spanish authorities, for instance, assured the Commission it had no knowledge of any State aid measure in favour of professional football. Yet later the Commission became aware of possible State aid in the form of loan guarantees granted by the regional government of Valencia in favour of three football clubs in Valencia.[103] Second, when Member States did provide relevant information, e.g. on the Belgian fiscal regime regarding football, the Commission indicated that it had not prompted an investigation because it had received no complaint regarding the measure.[104]

The same is true for similar information-gathering exercises conducted in the past. Already in 1997, in the aftermath of the *Bosman* ruling, the Commission carried out a survey of aid granted to individual sports clubs. Notwithstanding the fact that most Member States had not indicated whether sports clubs benefited from fiscal aid, the Commission concluded from the responses that aid given to sports clubs is 'marginal and does not seem likely to affect trade between Member States'.[105] In 2003, the Commission sent a letter to several Member States to verify the existence of a preferential tax or social security regime for professional football clubs. All Member States answered the question in the negative.[106]

[102]European Commission, Report from the 3rd meeting of the Expert Group on Sustainable Financing of Sport (XG FIN), January 2013. http://ec.europa.eu/sport/news/2013/20130111-eu-expert-group-fin_en.htm. Accessed 1 December 2015.

[103]Commission decision of 18 December 2013, SA.36387, Spain—Alleged aid in favour of three Valencia football clubs [2014] OJ C69/99.

[104]European Parliament, Answer given by Mr Almunia on behalf of the Commission to written Question E-004261/13, 12 June 2013.

[105]European Commission, 'Preliminary guidelines on the application of the competition rules on sport', Internal Information Memo from Commissioner Karel van Miert to the Commission, 15 February 1999.

[106]European Commission, 'State aid to professional football clubs', COMP/C4/WP/AH/ZZ/md–D*2012/98568, 1 October 2012.

7.4.2.2 Case Law on the Handling of Complaints

Initially, the European Commission's increased reliance on complaints by third parties alleging unlawful State aid (from the second half of the 1980s) only had a minor impact on its independent agenda-setting abilities. The Commission was under no duty to investigate and adopt a position on a complaint. It thus exercised considerable latitude in choosing which complaints to pursue, opting for systematic enforcement action in some sectors and restraint in others.[107]

The Procedural Regulation No 659/1999 reflected the perceived role of complaints as mere information sources for the Commission. The procedural rights of complainants were limited to the minimum.[108] Article 10(1) of Procedural Regulation No 659/1999 imposed on the Commission the obligation to examine without delay any information in its possession 'from whatever source' regarding alleged unlawful aid.[109] Pursuant to Article 13(1), the examination shall result in any of the three types of formal decisions that the Commission may adopt in response to a notification: a decision that there is no State aid; a decision not to raise objections; or a decision to initiate the formal investigation procedure.[110] This seemed to rule out the possibility for the Commission to avoid the investigation of a complaint when it points to a possibly unlawful aid.[111] Article 20(2), however, offered an alternative course of action: '(w)here the Commission considers that on the basis of the information in its possession there are insufficient grounds for taking a view on the case, it shall inform the interested party thereof'. Accordingly, the Commission could refuse to investigate a complaint without the adoption of a formal decision. As a letter rejecting a complaint is considered to be an informal communication, not open to challenge,[112] complainants seeking to preserve their procedural rights could only bring an action for a failure to act under Article 265 TFEU.[113]

This explains why preliminary views of the Commission 'based on the information available' regarding alleged State aid to e.g. Real Madrid[114] or Valencia

---

[107]See e.g. Smith 2001.

[108]This restrictive approach reflected the case law preceding the adoption of the Procedural Regulation. Merola and Armati 2013, pp. 5–10.

[109]Council Regulation (EC) No 659/1999 of 22 March 1999 laying down detailed rules for the application of Article 93 of the EC Treaty [1999] OJ L 83/1.

[110]Ibid., Article 13(1).

[111]Pastor Merchante 2014, pp. 130–134.

[112]Case C-367/95, *Commission v Chambre syndicale nationale des entreprises de transport de fonds et valeurs (Sytraval) and Brink's France SARL*, ECLI:EU:C:1998:154, para 45.

[113]In addition to the considerable procedural costs, demanding procedural and substantive requirements (i.e. potential applicants must have standing and satisfy the applicable legal test) make the use of this remedy difficult.

[114]European Parliament, Answer given by Mr Monti on behalf of the Commission to written question P-2491/2002, 26 September 2002.

CF[115] never resulted in the adoption of formal decisions or why earlier complaints (such as in the case of alleged State aid to Greek football clubs[116]) could simply be dismissed by way of an administrative letter.

In a series of judgments starting from 2004, however, the EU courts have significantly enhanced the protection of complainants' rights in State aid procedure and clarified the Commission's duties when handling complaints. The CJEU judgment in *Athinaïki Techniki* (2008) is of particular importance. First, the Court recognized that State aid complainants, although they cannot rely on rights of defence, 'have the right to be associated with [the preliminary examination stage] in an adequate manner'.[117] Second, and subsequently, the Court stressed that when the information provided by the complainants is insufficient for the Commission to take a view on the case, the Commission must allow them to submit additional comments within a reasonable period.[118] Once those comments have been lodged, or the reasonable period has expired, 'Article 13(1) of Regulation No 659/1999 obliges the Commission to close the preliminary examination stage by adopting a decision pursuant to Article 4(2), (3) or (4) of that regulation'.[119] Thus, 'the Commission is not authorized to persist in its failure to act during the preliminary examination stage. Once that stage of the procedure has been completed the Commission is bound either to initiate a procedure against the subject of the complaint, or to adopt a definitive decision rejecting the complaint.'[120]

In other words, a complaint on allegedly unlawful aid inevitably brings the Commission to the preliminary examination stage, which must be closed with a formal decision addressed to the Member State. In *NDSHT* (2010), the CJEU further clarified that also when the Commission classifies a measure as existing aid, and thus refuses by implication to initiate the formal investigation procedure, it adopts a definitive position on the case that is open to challenge.[121]

---

[115]European Parliament, Answer given by Mrs Kroes on behalf of the Commission to written question P-5129/2006, 20 December 2006; European Commission, Commission decision of 18 December 2013, SA.36387, Spain—Alleged aid in favour of three Valencia football clubs, [2014] OJ C69/99, note 1.

[116]European Parliament, Answer by Mrs Kroes on behalf of the Commission to written question E-0315/2005, 16 March 2005.

[117]Case C-521/06 P, *Athinaïki Techniki AE v Commission*, ECLI:EU:C:2008:422, para 38. This brought the complainants' procedural rights closer to the field of antitrust where complainants are closely associated to the proceedings. See Council Regulation (EC) No 1/2003 of 16 December 2002 on the implementation of the rules on competition laid down in Articles 81 and 82 of the Treaty [2003] OJ L 1/1, Article 27(1).

[118]Case C-521/06 P, *Athinaïki Techniki AE v Commission*, ECLI:EU:C:2008:42239, para 39.

[119]Ibid., para 40. That is to say, a decision stating that aid does not exist, a decision not raise objections or a decision initiating the formal investigation procedure.

[120]Ibid.

[121]Case C-322/09, *NDSHT Nya Destination Stockholm Hotell & Teaterpaket AB v Commission*, ECLI:EU:C:2010:701, paras 50–54; Case T-182/10, *Associazione italiana delle società concessionarie per la costruzione e l'esercizio di autostrade e trafori stradali (Aiscat) v Commission*, ECLI:EU:T:2013:9, paras 30–32.

As a result of this jurisprudence, it became clear that in the State aid field, the Commission has little room for discretion in setting enforcement priorities. The requirements that a complaint must fulfil are very limited. Once the complainant gives information on a measure, which does not need to be detailed, and indicates that the measure is alleged to be unlawful aid, the Commission is under a duty to close the case with a decision on substance.[122]

As a way to safeguard administrative efficiency and its ability to focus its limited resources on the most distortive cases, the Commission introduced a series of filters when the Procedural Regulation was reformed in 2013.[123] Any submission that fails to pass these filters will not be registered as a complaint, but rather as mere market information that might be used at a later stage to conduct *ex officio* investigations.[124] There are essentially three filters: (1) the Commission's obligation to examine complaints is confined to those submitted by interested parties; (2) the interested party must duly complete a complaints form (as defined in the implementing provisions[125]); and (3) the interested party must provide the mandatory information requested in the form.[126] While persistent complainants could (easily) overcome the last two filters, the requirement to be an interested party[127] implies that natural or legal persons that have no legal standing before the EU courts shall no longer be treated as complainants.[128] Those without the requisite legitimate

---

[122]Case T-442/07, *Ryanair Ltd v Commission*, ECLI:EU:T:2011:547, para 46.

[123]Council Regulation (EU) No 734/2013 of 22 July 2013 amending Regulation (EC) No 659/1999 laying down detailed rules for the application of Article 93 of the EC Treaty [2013] OJ L204/14. Now replaced by Council Regulation (EU) 2015/1589 of 13 July 2015 laying down detailed rules for the application of Article 108 of the Treaty on the Functioning of the European Union [2015] OJ L 248/9.

[124]Pastor Merchante 2014, pp. 140–144. To this end, Article 10(1) of the original Procedural Regulation was amended. Article 12(1) of the current Procedural Regulation provides that 'the Commission *may* on its own initiative examine information regarding alleged unlawful aid from whatever source' (emphasis added) and that the Commission is only under an obligation to examine 'any *complaint* submitted by any interested party in accordance with Article 20(2)' (emphasis added). Council Regulation (EU) 2015/1589 of 13 July 2015 laying down detailed rules for the application of Article 108 of the Treaty on the Functioning of the European Union [2015] OJ L 248/9, Article 12(1).

[125]Commission Regulation (EU) No 372/2014 of 9 April 2014 amending Regulation (EC) No 794/2004 as regards the calculation of certain time limits, the handling of complaints, and the identification and protection of confidential information [2014] OJ L 109/14.

[126]Council Regulation (EU) 2015/1589 of 13 July 2015 laying down detailed rules for the application of Article 108 of the Treaty on the Functioning of the European Union [2015] OJ L 248/9, Article 24(2).

[127]Ibid, Article 1(h) defines 'interested party' as 'any Member State and any person, undertaking or association of undertakings whose interests might be affected by the granting of aid, in particular the beneficiary of the aid, competing undertakings and trade associations'.

[128]On the use of this higher standard for complainants to qualify as interested party, see European Commission, State Aid Manual of Procedures: Internal DG Competition working documents on procedures for the application of Articles 107 and 108 TFEU, July 2013, Sect. 7.4.

interest, such as individual taxpayers or non-governmental organizations,[129] may still submit information about alleged unlawful aid, but the Commission will merely register it as market information. Only complaints by interested parties will set in motion a preliminary investigation that will necessarily lead to a decision.[130]

Through the amended Procedural Regulation, the Commission was able to close a procedural gap that had arisen since the CJEU judgment in *Athinaïki Techniki*. It no longer has a duty, but instead a discretionary power, to investigate information received by persons other than interested parties. For example, in 2014 the Commission denied a number of individual supporters and minority shareholders of the Rangers Football Club, the status of complainants. They claimed that the Glasgow City Council had subsidized historic city rivals Celtic Football Club through a series of land transactions. The Commission rejected the 'complaint' through an administrative letter and decided not to investigate the matter on its own initiative.[131]

Between 2008 and 2013, however, the Commission was, pursuant to Article 10(1) of the original Procedural Regulation, bound to act on every complaint - regardless of the legitimate interest of the complainant. Subsequently, the citizen complaints alleging unlawful State aid to Dutch and Spanish football clubs that were lodged during this period automatically triggered the preliminary assessment stage, which must be closed either by a definitive decision rejecting the complaint or a decision opening the formal investigation procedure. Within this (and perhaps only because of this) peculiar legal context, the citizen complaints managed to seize the Commission's State aid policy agenda.

7.4.2.3 The European Ombudsman

In a much-publicized inquiry, the European Ombudsman opened up the Commission's reluctance to process a complaint alleging unlawful State aid to certain Spanish football clubs to public scrutiny. Even though there is no longer room for a selective policy of enforcement in State aid in terms of selecting complaints that pass the admissibility filters discussed above, the Commission is still entitled to give differing degrees of priority to the complaints brought before it.[132] There

[129]See e.g. Case T-188/95, *Waterleiding Maatschappij "Noord-West Brabant" NV v Commission*, ECLI:EU:T:1998:217, para 68 (rejecting the claim that individual taxpayers objecting to the manner in which tax revenue is spent on alleged unlawful aid qualify as interested party).

[130]Unless the Commission deems the case to be significant from a competition point of view and opens an investigation on its own initiative.

[131]G. Braiden, EC rules: Celtic FC didn't get 'state aid' in land deal with Glasgow City Council. The Herald, 13 November 2014. http://www.heraldscotland.com/news/13189309.EC_rules__Celtic_FC_didn_t_get__state_aid__in_land_deal_with_Glasgow_City_Council/. Accessed 1 December 2015.

[132]See e.g. Case T-475/04, *Bouygues SA and Bouygues Télécom SA v Commission*, ECLI:EU:T:2007:196, para 158.

are no legally binding deadlines for complaint handling.[133] Nonetheless, the Commission cannot prolong indefinitely its preliminary assessment into non-priority complaints about alleged unlawful aid, notwithstanding the complexity of the case or the politically sensitive nature of the subject matter.[134]

In November 2009, a representative of a number of investors in European football clubs had lodged a complaint about the preferential tax treatment of four major Spanish football and basketball clubs: Real Madrid CF, Athletic Club Bilbao, Club Atlético Osasuna (Pamplona) and FC Barcelona. More than 25 months later, and not having been informed about the progress of the case (which in fact had received priority status), the complainant turned to the Ombudsman. He argued that the Commission had failed to decide, in a timely way, whether or not to open the formal investigation procedure. Moreover, he suggested that the Commission's inaction might be linked to the fact that the Commissioner for Competition, Joaquín Almunia, supports one of the football clubs (Athletic Club Bilbao) and was a Minister in the Spanish government that decided on the tax advantages at the time. On 16 December 2013, the Ombudsman concluded its inquiry into these allegations and recommended the Commission to promptly make a decision on whether or not to start infringement proceedings.[135] It found no special circumstances that warranted the Commission's failure to decide on the case within one year. And although the Ombudsman did not establish whether there was a conflict of interest, it did stress that 'the continuing failure to decide on what to do in this case - more than four years now after the complaint was received - can only add to this perception .... Rather than allaying suspicions regarding a conflict of interests, and regarding inappropriate influences on the decision making process, the Commission's failures here have actually added to those suspicions'.[136]

Two days after receiving the Ombudsman's recommendation, the European Commission decided to open an in-depth investigation not only into the tax privileges granted to four Spanish football clubs, but also into State guarantees in favour of three Spanish football clubs in Valencia and land transfers by the Council of Madrid to Real Madrid.[137]

---

[133]There is only an indicative time frame of 12 months, within which the Commission should decide on whether infringement action is warranted. European Commission, State Aid Manual of Procedures: Internal DG Competition working documents on procedures for the application of Articles 107 and 108 TFEU, July 2013, Sect. 7.4.

[134]See e.g. Case T-17/96, *Télévision française 1 SA (TF1) v Commission*, ECLI:EU:T:1999:119; Case T-95/96, *Gestevision Telecinco SA v Commission*, ECLI:EU:T:1998:206.

[135]European Ombudsman, Draft recommendation of the European Ombudsman in the inquiry into complaint 2521/2011/JF against the European Commission, 16 December 2013.

[136]European Ombudsman, State Aid and European football clubs? Summary of recommendation by the European Ombudsman following a complaint against the EU Commission, 17 December 2013.

[137]Commission decision of 18 December 2013, SA.29769, Spain—State aid to certain Spanish professional football clubs, [2014] OJ C69/115; Commission decision of 18 December 2013, SA.36387, Spain—Alleged aid in favour of three Valencia football clubs [2014] OJ C69/99; Commission decision of 18 December 2013, SA.33754, Spain—Real Madrid CF [2014] OJ C69/108.

Commissioner Almunia made a number of critical observations regarding the Ombudsman's inquiry, in particular the 'insinuation' that his support for Athletic Club Bilbao could give the impression of a conflict of interests. He also firmly dispelled the assertion that the Commission's decision of 18 December 2013 was instigated by the Ombudsman's request.[138] Nevertheless, it is reasonable to conjecture that the maladministration investigation, rather than its final outcome, played a significant role in prompting the Commission to act on the complaint. The Ombudsman fully exploited the unusual features of the case (e.g. the identity of the beneficiaries of the alleged aid and the accusation of conflict of interests on part of the Commissioner), which increased the visibility of the inquiry, to attack the Commission's unjustified delay in reaching a decision on the complaint.[139]

7.5 Conclusions

When considering the general policy dynamics of EU State aid control, the 'late' emergence of State aid enforcement efforts in the (professional) sports sector—nearly twenty years after *Bosman*—is not as remarkable as it may appear.

The extension of the reach of State aid control to new sectors or new forms of aid has typically been the result of external constraints on DG Competition's independent agenda-setting abilities rather than notifications by Member States. These external factors include, for instance, complaints by third parties (e.g. the application of the State aid rules to films and other audiovisual works) or the Commission's wider political priorities (e.g. the application of the State aid rules to individual tax ruling practices of Member States).[140] In the case of sport, it was primarily the case law of the EU courts that pushed the Commission to enforcement action.

Regarding the public financing of sports infrastructure, public authorities did not need to notify such measures to the Commission because they were considered not to constitute State aid. As soon as the General Court invalidated this interpretation in its *Leipzig Halle* judgment, however, the Commission started to receive notifications, which triggered the development of decisional practice since 2011. An orthodox pattern of the articulation and formalisation of sector-specific rules enfolded.

Regarding the public financing of professional sports clubs, the Commission implicitly tolerated the Member States' non-compliance with the notification

[138]European Ombudsman, Letter from the Vice-President of the European Commission, Joaquin Almunia, to the European Ombudsman following the press release no. 23/2013, 20 December 2013.

[139]Martínez Navarro 2014, pp. 99–101.

[140]Commission Press Release of 17 December 2014, IP/14/2742 State aid: Commission extends information enquiry on tax rulings practice to all Member States.

obligation. The jurisprudence of the CJEU on the procedural rights of complainants eventually enabled citizen complaints to seize the Commission's State aid enforcement agenda between 2008 and 2013. The outcome of the pending formal investigations into alleged State aid to Dutch and Spanish football clubs is still to set in motion a process of policy formalisation.

Is this development long overdue? On the one hand, systematic non-enforcement of the State aid rules to a particular sector would be problematic. In the absence of an exemption from the Treaty, this could be criticized as a failure of the Commission to carry out its State aid control functions. In this context, the European Ombudsman rightly took up its role as guardian of the 'Guardian of the Treaties' in finding that the unjustified delay in the processing of a complaint alleging tax privileges to certain Spanish football clubs amounted to maladministration. On the other hand, there is a rationale for the Commission to selectively withhold vigorous (ex officio) State aid control in peripheral sectors in the face of dangerously contentious politics. Given that the Commission with its limited resources is burdened with the task of supervising many economically more significant and strategically more important sectors, it is quite comprehensible that EU control of State aid to professional sports clubs only now materialised due to exogenous factors.

References

Aydin U (2014) Issue framing in the European Commission: State aid policy and the single market. 12 Comp Eur Politics 2:141–159

Blauberger M (2009) Of 'Good' and 'Bad' subsidies: European State aid control through soft and hard law. West Eur Polit 32(4):719–737

Cini M (2001) The soft law approach: Commission rule-making in the EU's State aid regime. J Eur Public Policy 8(2):192–207

Craven R (2014) Football and State aid: too important to fail? Int Sports Law J 2014(3–4):205–217

Daley K (2014) Sport and State aid—reining in the populist gesture. Competition Policy Int Antirust Chronicle 1:2–6

Gerlinger M (2003) Stadiums for FIFA World Cup Germany 2006 and European law on State aid: a case of infrastructure measures? Int Sports Law J 2003(1):9–12

Koenig C, Haratasch A (2004) The logic of infrastructure funding under EC State aid control. 3 Eur State Aid Law Q 3:393–398

Koenig C, Kühling J (2003) Infrastrukturförderung im Ausschreibungsverfahren—EG-beihilfenrechtlicher Königsweg der Kompensation von gemeinwirtschaftlichen Pflichten. Deutsches Verwaltungsblatt 5:289–298

Martínez Navarro M (2014) The Ombudsman decision on the State-aid complaint concerning spanish football clubs: the Ombudsman as an alternative route for State-aid and anti-trust complainants? 6 J Eur Competition Law Pract 2:99–101

Merola M, Armati L (2013) Complainants' rights in State aid matters: lost in modernisation? Global Competition Law Centre Working Paper 01/13:5–10

Nicolaides P (2002) Control of State aid in the European Union compliance, sanctions and rational behaviour. 25 World Competition, Issue 3:249–262

Pastor Merchante F (2014) The role of competitors in the enforcement of State aid law. Unpublished Doctoral Dissertation, European University Institute, Florence

Pauwels C, De Vinck S, Van Rompuy B (2007) Lost in liberalisation? Can State aid in the film sector stand the proof of EU and WTO liberalisation efforts? In: Sarikakis K (ed) Media and cultural policy in the European Union. Rodopi, Amsterdam, pp 23–44

Piernas López JJ (2015) The concept of State aid under EU law: from internal market to competition and beyond. Oxford University Press, Oxford

Quigley C (2015) European State aid law and policy. Hart Publishing, Oxford

Rawlinson F (1993) The role of policy frameworks, codes and guidelines in the control of State aid. In: Harden I (ed) State aid: community law and policy. Cologne, Bundesanzeiger, pp 57–58

Santamato S, Westerhof JG (2003) Is funding of infrastructure State aid? 21 Europäische Zeitschrift für Wirtschaftsrecht 645–648

Schaefer K, Kreile J, Gerlach S (2002) Nationale Filmförderung: Einfluss und Grenzen des europäischen Rechts. 46 Zeitschrift für Urheber- und Medienrecht 3:182–194

Siebold M, Klingmüller A (2004) Sports facility financing and development trends in Europe and Germany 2003. 15 Marquette Sports Law Rev 2004:88

Smith MP (1998) Autonomy by the rules: the European Commission and the development of State aid policy. 36 J Common Market Stud 1:58–60

Smith MP (2001) How adaptable is the European Commission? The case of State aid regulation. J Public Policy 21(03):219–238

Stefan OA (2012) Hybridity before the court: a hard look at soft law in the EU competition and State aid case law. 37 Eur Law Rev 1:49–96

Van den Bogaert S (2010) Bosman: the genesis of European sports law. In: Maduro M, Azoulai L (eds) The past and future of EU law: the classics of EU law revisited on the 50th anniversary of the Rome Treaty. Hart Publishing, Oxford, pp 488–498

Van Maren O (2015) The Real Madrid case: a State aid case (un)like any other? 11 Competition Law Rev 1:83–108

Van Rompuy B (2015) The role of EU competition law in tackling abuse of regulatory power by sports associations. 22 Maastricht J Eur Comp Law 2:179–208

Weatherill S (2010) Bosman changed everything: the rise of EC sports law. In: Maduro M, Azoulai L (eds) The past and future of EU law: the classics of EU law revisited on the 50th anniversary of the Rome Treaty. Hart Publishing, Oxford, pp 480–487

Chapter 8
The European Social Dialogue: A New Mode of Governance for European Football?

Richard Parrish

Abstract In 2008 a social dialogue committee for European professional football was established and in 2012 it concluded its first agreement on minimum requirements in standard player contracts. The dynamics behind the establishment of the committee are numerous but the Europeanisation of industrial relations in football is strongly connected to the liberalisation of the European labour market for players following the European Court's judgment in Bosman. That social dialogue in European football can deliver more wide ranging agreements akin to those found in US sports remains a long term prospect, but in the shorter term the committee can be influential in recalibrating governance standards in European football and seeking solutions to specific problems within the sector.

Keywords Social dialogue · European football · Football transfer system · Football contracts · Sports governance · EU law

Contents

R. Parrish (✉)
Center for Sports Law Research, Edge Hill University, Ormskirk, UK
e-mail: parrishr@edgehill.ac.uk

A. Duval and B. Van Rompuy (eds.), *The Legacy of* Bosman,
ASSER International Sports Law Series, DOI 10.1007/978-94-6265-120-3_8

8.1 Introduction

The judgment of the European Court of Justice (CJEU) in *Bosman* had a liberalising effect on the European labour market in professional football.[1] Following the judgment, players were able to exercise enhanced rights of freedom of movement within the EU. They also anticipated that existing labour restraints, not specifically addressed by the Court in *Bosman*, would also be removed. Concerned at some of the perceived negative consequences of the ruling, the *Fédération Internationale de Football Association* (FIFA) and the Union of European Football Associations (UEFA), sometimes supported by the clubs, sought a re-regulation of this market. In particular, the FIFA Regulations on the Status and Transfer of Players (RSTP) introduced a series of measures that restrict a player's free circulation within the EU. The European Commission was a party to this agreement in 2001 but the settlement displeased the international football players union, FIFPro.[2] In an effort to facilitate a repair of industrial relations within the sector, shortly after the agreement the Commission began to advocate the use of the social dialogue provisions contained within the EU's Treaty. The Commission considered this a longer term method of finding solutions to labour related problems within the football sector, and a preferable alternative to litigation.

As will be demonstrated below, the Commission's ambitions have been only partly fulfilled. Since *Bosman* and the 2001 agreement, labour related disputes continue to be brought before the national courts, the European Commission and the CJEU. Litigation in sport is time consuming, expensive and the outcomes are uncertain. In that light, social dialogue has been promoted as a vehicle through which labour related disputes in football can be potentially resolved and avoided by way of dialogue between representatives of employers (clubs) and workers (players) – the so called social partners. A social dialogue committee in European professional football was established in 2008 and in 2012 it concluded its first agreement on minimum requirements in standard player contracts (MRSPC).

This chapter traces the origins of the football social dialogue committee, it assesses its first agreement, its implementation and it questions whether the committee can develop more far reaching agreements on contentious issues such as matters relating to the operation of the FIFA RSTP. It concludes by arguing that whilst binding agreements are an uncommon feature of social dialogue generally, the football committee can disturb traditional patterns of football governance and place pressure on sports bodies and the EU institutions to change existing sporting regulations.

---

[1]Case C-415/93 *Union Royale Belge des Sociétés de Football Association and others v. Bosman and others*, ECLI:EU:C:1995:463. For a discussion on its immediate effects, see Maguire and Stead 1998, pp. 59–73.

[2]FIFPro is the Fédération Internationale des Associations de Footballeurs Professionels, the international umbrella organisation for national player associations.

8.2 Labour Disputes in Sport: Application of EU Law[3]

The European labour market for professional players is fertile ground for labour related litigation. This is because labour practices in sport often diverge from the standards applied to 'normal' workers operating within the European single market. European Union law regulates economic activity and since 1974, the European Court has considered that EU law applies to sport whenever it is practiced as an economic activity.[4] From this perspective, professional athletes should benefit from the same labour protections as those enjoyed by other economically active workers. However, professional athletes have historically been considered a distinct category of worker and have been subject to rules, such as transfer systems, that place restrictions on their ability to take up employment with a new employer. It is this discrepancy between theory and practice that gives rise to the potential to litigate.

The prospect of successful litigation was, however, rendered somewhat uncertain by the Court's assertion in *Walrave* that the prohibition on nationality discrimination at issue in the case 'does not affect the composition of sport teams, in particular national teams, the formation of which is a matter of purely sporting interest and as such has nothing to do with economic activity'.[5] This gave rise to the expectation from sports bodies that their non-economic activity fell outside the scope of the Treaty, as did their rules which possessed an economic dimension but which were motivated by a purely sporting interest. The Court added that this was the position as long as the rule remained limited to its proper objectives.

Nearly twenty years later in *Bosman* the Court assessed the compatibility of international transfer rules and nationality quotas in European football with the requirements of EU law. In finding that both contested measures amounted to an unjustified restriction on a workers freedom of movement, the Court rejected submissions that 'a sport such as football is not an economic activity',[6] that 'only the major European leagues may be regarded as undertakings', that clubs in other leagues carry out only 'negligible' economic activity, that transfer rules 'does not concern the employment relationship between players and clubs'[7] and that 'nationality clauses are justified on non-economic grounds'.[8] The Court repeated its position first expressed in *Donà*[9] that EU law 'applies to the activities of pro-

[3]It is beyond the scope of this contribution to assess those cases heard before national courts and the dispute resolution mechanisms of sports bodies, such as the FIFA Dispute Resolution Chamber and the Court of Arbitration for Sport (CAS). For further reading, see Anderson 2010; James 2013; Lewis and Taylor 2014.

[4]Case 36/74 *Walrave and Koch v. Union Cycliste Internationale*, ECLI:EU:C:1974:140, para 4.

[5]Ibid., para 8.

[6]Case C-415/93 *Union Royale Belge des Sociétés de Football Association and others v. Bosman and others*, ECLI:EU:C:1995:463, para 72.

[7]Ibid., para 70.

[8]Ibid., para 122.

[9]Case 13/76 *Donà v Mantero* [1976] 2 CMLR 578, ECLI:EU:C:1976:115, para 12.

fessional or semi-professional footballers, where they are in gainful employment or provide a remunerated service'.[10] *Bosman* emphatically re-iterated that the relationship between a professional footballer and his club is an employment relationship to which the protections offered to workers under EU law apply.

At the turn of the millennium the CJEU handed down two further sports judgments. In *Deliège* the Court was willing to accept that even amateur sports men and women, in this case an amateur judoka, are capable of carrying out economic activity. It found that 'leading sports personalities could receive, in addition to grants and other assistance, higher levels of income because of their celebrity status, with the result that they provided services of an economic nature'.[11] However, the Court found that although the contested selection rules did inevitably have the effect of limiting the number of participants in a tournament,

> such a limitation is inherent in the conduct of an international high level sports event, which necessarily involves certain selection rules or criteria being adopted. Such rules may not therefore in themselves be regarded as constituting a restriction on the freedom to provide services.[12]

At the same time, in *Lehtonen*, the Court assessed the use of transfer windows in European basketball.[13] The Court established that whilst transfer windows amounted to a restriction on a workers freedom of movement, they could, subject to proportionality control, be compatible with EU law because late transfers could call into question the proper functioning of sporting competition.[14]

In *Meca-Medina* the Court considered a competition law challenge to doping sanctions imposed on two professional swimmers.[15] Although not a labour case, the Court established an important methodological framework apt for transposition into the free movement context. The Court first dismissed the relevance of the purely sporting rule defence by finding that 'it is apparent that the mere fact that a rule is purely sporting in nature does not have the effect of removing from the scope of the Treaty the person engaging in the activity governed by that rule or the body which has laid it down'.[16] It went on to establish the correct approach to take when assessing the compatibility of a contested measure with EU law which is to ask whether the consequential restrictive effects of the contested rule are inherent in the proportionate pursuit of the stated legitimate objectives.

---

[10] Case C-415/93 *Union Royale Belge des Sociétés de Football Association and others v. Bosman and others,* ECLI:EU:C:1995:463, para 73.

[11] Joined cases Cases C-51/96 and C-191/97 *Christelle Deliège v. Ligue Francophone de Judo et Disciplines Associées ASBL and others*, ECLI:EU:C:2000:199, para 13.

[12] Ibid., para 64.

[13] Case C-176/96 *Jyri Lehtonen and Castors Canada Dry Namur-Braine ASBL v. Fédération royale belge des sociétés de basket-ball ASBL (FRBSB)*, ECLI:EU:C:2000:201.

[14] Ibid., para 54.

[15] Case C-519/04 P *David Meca-Medina and Igor Majcen v. Commission*, ECLI:EU:C:2006:492.

[16] Ibid., para 27.

A further employment related dispute arose in *Bernard*.[17] Here, the European Court assessed the compatibility of the French Professional Football Charter with EU free movement law. In doing so, the Court declined to consider the inherency of the measure and instead returned to a classic objective justification assessment of the rule. The Charter required French youth players to sign their first professional contract with the club that trained them. The player in question, Oliver Bernard, refused the offer from Olympique Lyonnais and instead signed for English side Newcastle United. Olympique Lyonnais sought damages from the player and Newcastle United before the French Employment Tribunal. Following two appeals against initial awards, the case was referred to the European Court. The disputed French scheme was condemned by the Court as amounting to a system in which damages are paid to the training club at an amount unrelated to the training costs incurred by that club. This rendered less attractive the exercise of a workers free movement rights and so was considered incompatible with Article 45 of the Treaty on the Functioning of the European Union (TFEU). However, the Court upheld the principle that a system of training compensation in sport, as opposed to a damages system, which restricts the freedom of movement of players could be justified with reference to the objective of educating and training young players. In this connection, the Court stated that the compensation must be calculated on the basis of the actual training costs borne by the original club, although this could include the cost of training both future professional players and those who will never play professionally.[18]

The employment status of third country nationals has also given rise to complaints under EU law. In *Kolpak*, *Simutenkov* and *Kahveci*, the CJEU held that non-EU sportsmen and women covered by non-discrimination provisions contained within association agreements concluded between the EU and non-EU states cannot be discriminated against in terms of working conditions, remuneration or dismissal when they are legally employed in the territory of the Member State.[19]

8.3 The European Social Dialogue

The Commission has promoted social dialogue as a means through which the type of labour related litigation in professional football described above could be avoided. Social dialogue refers to discussions, consultations, negotiations and joint

[17]Case C-325/08 *Olympique Lyonnais v Olivier Bernard and Newcastle United FC*, ECLI:EU:C:2010:143.

[18]Ibid., para 45.

[19]C-438/00 *Deutscher Handballbund eV v Maros Kolpak*, ECLI:EU:C:2003:255; Case C-265/03, *Igor Simutenkov v Ministerio de Educación y Cultura and Real Federación Española de Fútbol*, ECLI:EU:C:2005:213; Case C-152/08 *Real Sociedad de Fútbol SAD and Nihat Kahveci v Consejo Superior de Deportes and Real Federación Española de Fútbol*, ECLI:EU:C:2008:450. An earlier case was removed from the court register, Case C-264/98 *Balog*, OJ C173/12 [2001].

actions involving organisations representing the two sides of industry, namely employers and workers (the social partners). Dialogue can take place at the cross-industry level, the scope of which covers all sectors of the EU's economy and labour market, or it can take place at the sectoral level covering one specific industry across the EU. Social dialogue forms part of the social model underpinning the EU's approach to labour relations and currently, the EU has supported the establishment of a number of cross-industry committees and over forty sectoral committees.[20] The consultative dimension of social dialogue can be traced to the foundation of the European Economic Community in 1957 and the negotiation element was added by the Amsterdam Treaty in 1997. The current legal base underpinning social dialogue is to be found in Articles 152–155 of the TFEU.

Article 152 TFEU establishes the duty of the EU to recognise and promote the role of the social partners at EU level and to facilitate dialogue between the social partners. Article 153 envisages the possibility of EU action to improve a number of employment conditions, including, amongst others: health and safety at work; working conditions; social security and social protection of workers; protection of workers where their contract of employment is terminated; the rights of third country workers and equality.

In relation to the above, the Council and Parliament can adopt Directives on minimum requirements for gradual implementation designed to encourage cooperation between Member States through initiatives aimed at improving knowledge, developing exchanges of information and best practices, promoting innovative approaches and evaluating experiences, excluding any harmonisation of the laws and regulations of the Member States. The coverage of issues within Article 153 has a relevance to sport. Since 1974, the European Court has recognised that sport is subject to European law whenever practiced as an economic activity[21] and that as a corollary, sports professionals are workers and professional clubs are undertakings.[22] In this connection, representatives of players and clubs can take their place at the heart of social dialogue as social partners.

Article 154 TFEU establishes that the task of the Commission is to promote the consultation of management and labour at EU level meaning that representatives of employers and employees have the right of consultation and opinion over new Commission proposals in the field of social policy. At this point, management and labour may inform the Commission of their wish to initiate the process provided for

---

[20]Monte 2013, p. 42.

[21]Case 36/74 *Walrave and Koch v. Union Cycliste Internationale,* ECLI:EU:C:1974:140, para 8.

[22]It is not in fact relevant for the purposes of the application of EU free movement law that the employer be defined as an undertaking. All that is required is the existence of, or intention to create, an employment relationship (see Case C-415/93 *Union Royale Belge des Sociétés de Football Association and others v. Bosman and others,* ECLI:EU:C:1995:463, para 74). Equally, EU rules on free movement apply not only to the actions of public authorities but also to rules of any other nature, such as rules of sports governing bodies, aimed at regulating gainful employment in a collective manner (see Case 36/74 *Walrave and Koch v. Union Cycliste Internationale,* ECLI:EU:C:1974:140 para 17).

in Article 153. The powers of the social partners are extended further by Article 155 which provides that the dialogue between management and labour at Union level may lead to contractual relations, including agreements. Such agreements can be implemented in two ways. The first is the voluntary route in which the so called autonomous agreement is implemented in accordance with customary national procedures. This agreement binds only the signatories and their affiliates. The second method is by way of a Council decision (a Directive). This type of agreement is binding on both sides of industry once the agreement is transposed into national law or national collective agreements. Therefore, the Treaty allows the social partners to intervene following a Commission initiative, and they also have the power of direct initiative themselves.

The power invested in the social partners of legislative intervention and initiative raises questions of democratic legitimacy insofar as this approach deviates from the classic EU legislative model which includes the participation of the democratically elected European Parliament and democratically legitimate Council.[23] To assuage these concerns, prior to the establishment of a social dialogue committee, the social partners must satisfy participation criteria established by the European Commission designed to ensure that the social partners genuinely represent those who they claim to represent. The criteria states that:

> (a) they shall relate to specific sectors or categories and be organised at European level; (b) they shall consist of organisations which are themselves an integral and recognized part of Member States' social partner structures and have the capacity to negotiate agreements, and which are representative of several Member States; and (c) they shall have adequate structures to ensure their effective participation in the work of the Committees.[24]

A formal agreement, whether implemented through the Directive or voluntary route, is only one possible outcome of social dialogue discussions. The social partners can also adopt *process-oriented texts* such as frameworks of action, guidelines, codes of conduct and policy orientations, and also *joint opinions and tools* which are intended to influence EU policies and share best practice.[25]

8.4 The Road to Social Dialogue in European Professional Football

The judgment in *Bosman* gave impetus to calls for employment related disputes within sport to be resolved by dialogue rather than recourse to law. The key development was the Commission's investigation into the operation of FIFA's international

[23] Smismans 2007. In a football specific context, this concern has been raised by Geeraert 2015, pp. 103–105.

[24] Commission Decision 98/500/EC of 20 May 1998, C(1998) 2334 - on the establishment of Sectoral Dialogue Committees promoting the dialogue between the social partners at European level [1998] OJ L 225/27 Article 1.

[25] Communication from the Commission of 12 August 2004, COM (2004) 557 final - Partnership for change in an enlarged Europe—Enhancing the contribution of European social dialogue.

transfer system and the subsequent protracted, and at times acrimonious, negotiations over its reform in 2000/01. The investigation stemmed from a number of complaints from private parties including a trade union and professional football clubs which, in 1998, led the Commission to issue FIFA with a statement of objections relating to alleged incompatibilities between the existing FIFA transfer regulations and aspects of EU law.[26] One such objection concerned the prohibition on players from transferring to another club following their unilateral termination of a contract, even if the player had complied with national law governing the penalties for breach of contract.[27]

With the threat of a negative decision looming, FIFA, UEFA and FIFPro joined negotiations with the Commission with a view to issue a new set of international transfer regulations. Despite protest from FIFPro, the principles underpinning the new regulations received Commission approval in March 2001[28] and FIFA subsequently gave effect to them following a decision adopted by them at its July 2001 Executive Committee meeting.[29] The content of the new international transfer regulations has received considerable comment elsewhere[30] and as the provisions essentially relate to the employment conditions of players, its content potentially falls within the scope of social dialogue discussions at European level.

The outcome of the transfer negotiations encouraged the Commission to place political support behind the idea of stakeholder dialogue as a means of avoiding and resolving disputes within the sports sector. For example, commenting in the European Parliament on the negotiations over the reform of the FIFA regulations governing international transfers, Viviane Reding, the Commissioner for Education and Culture remarked; 'discussions on transfers have clearly shown that dialogue at all levels is becoming a necessity and that all possible avenues for organising this should be explored, including collective agreements'.[31] The European Commissioner for Employment and Social Affairs added,

> I have strongly and repeatedly encouraged the clubs to start or pursue social dialogue with trade union representatives of the football players since the outcome of discussions in March 2001 between the European Commission and FIFA/UEFA on football transfers. The establishment of a structured European sector social dialogue in football could be an effective method to manage the impact of the different European policies in a pro-active way. These policies do not only affect the regulatory framework of football but also employment relations and the social situation in the sector.[32]

[26]Van den Bogaert 2005, p. 224.

[27]Parrish 2003, p. 141.

[28]Letter from Mario Monti to Joseph S. Blatter of 5 March 2001, D/000258; See also Commission Press Release of 5 June 2002, IP/02/824 Commission Closes Investigations into FIFA Regulations on International Football Transfers.

[29]FIFA Regulations for the Status and Transfer of Players 2001.

[30]See Parrish 2003, 2015; Van den Bogaert 2005.

[31]Speech by Mrs. Viviane Reding of 13 March 2001, 01/117.

[32]Letter of Commissioner Diamantopoulou of DG Employment and Social Affairs to Mr. Gerard Slager, chair of the European Federation of Professional Football Clubs (EFFC) of 4 February 2003.

The Commission then funded a number of research projects exploring the viability of social dialogue within the sports sector.[33] The Commission's position on social dialogue was formally set out in the 2007 White Paper on Sport.[34] In it, the Commission stated that governance issues in sport should fall within a territory of autonomy and that most challenges can be addressed through self-regulation which must however be 'respectful of good governance principles'.[35] In this connection, social dialogue in the sports sector was identified as being able to 'contribute to addressing common concerns of employers and athletes, including agreements on employment relations and working conditions in the sector in accordance with EC Treaty provisions'.[36] The Commission's support continued in the 2011 Communication on Sport in which the Commission committed itself to

> support social partners and sport organisations to create an EU-level social dialogue for the whole sport and leisure sector and to discuss new relevant items such as contractual stability, education and training, health and safety, employment and working conditions of minors, the role of agents or the fight against doping.[37]

The constitutional strength of this support was considerably enhanced following the entry into force of Article 165 TFEU which stated that 'The Union shall contribute to the promotion of European sporting issues, while taking account of the specific nature of sport, its structures based on voluntary activity and its social and educational function' and that 'Union action shall be aimed at: developing the European dimension in sport, by promoting fairness and openness in sporting competitions and *cooperation between bodies responsible for sports*, and by protecting the physical and moral integrity of sportsmen and sportswomen, especially the youngest sportsmen and sportswomen' [emphasis added].

A major impetus towards the establishment of a social dialogue committee for European professional football came with the *Oulmers* litigation. In this case, a dispute arose concerning how FIFA rules on the mandatory release of players interfered with the employment relationship between a club and its player.[38] These rules specified that for matches on dates listed in the coordinated international

---

[33]Commission Staff Working Document of 11 July 2007, COM (2007) 391 final - The EU and Sport: Background and Context - Accompanying document to the White Paper on Sport, footnote 149.

[34]Commission White Paper of 11 July 2007, COM (2007) 391 final - White Paper on Sport; See also Commission Staff Working Document of 11 July 2007, COM (2007) 391 final - The EU and Sport: Background and Context - Accompanying document to the White Paper on Sport.

[35]Ibid., Section 4.

[36]Ibid., Section 5.3.

[37]Communication from the Commission to the European Parliament, Council, Economic and Social Committee and Committee of the Regions, of 18 January 2011, COM (2011) 12 final - Developing the European Dimension in Sport, p. 13.

[38]Case C-243/06 *SA Sporting du Pays de Charleroi, G-14 Groupment des Clubs de Football Européens v Fédération Internationale de Football Association (FIFA)* ECLI:EU:C:2008:649. It has been removed from the Court register by order of the President of the Court of 25 November 2008.

match calendar and for all matches for which a duty to release players exists on the basis of a special decision of the FIFA Executive Committee, clubs are obliged to release their registered players for representative teams of the country for which the player is eligible to play on the basis of his nationality.[39] Clubs subject to this rule were not entitled to receive financial compensation and clubs refusing to comply with the mandatory release clause could be sanctioned by way of a points or game forfeiture.[40]

In *Oulmers*, the European Court was due to hear a challenge to this regime brought by Belgian football club Charleroi. The, as then, G14 grouping of leading clubs later joined the litigation.[41] The player concerned, Abdelmajid Oulmers, returned injured from international duty in 2004 following a compulsory call up for the national team and his team suffered financial and sporting losses as a result.

The referring Belgian court in *Oulmers* asked the European Court to consider the compatibility of the mandatory player release rules with EU competition and free movement laws. Shortly before the case was due to be heard it was removed from the Court register following an agreement concluded in January 2008 between FIFA, UEFA and the clubs. In it, the parties agreed that the case be withdrawn, the G14 be dissolved and replaced with the European Club Association (ECA), and that payment of financial contributions for player participation in European Championships and World Cups should be established.[42]

As part of the agreement, the ECA gained access to the Professional Football Strategy Council (PFSC), a UEFA consultative committee established a year before. In this committee, it was joined by representatives of the European Professional Football Leagues (EPFL)[43] and representatives of FIFPro (Division Europe). The PFSC is responsible for identifying solutions to improve collaboration between the various stakeholders of European football; dealing with problems pertaining to the social dialogue in European professional football matters; and dealing with questions related to the UEFA club competitions and their calendars.[44] As a consultative committee, the PFSC has no formal decision making function in UEFA, but it does report directly to UEFA's Executive Committee and according to the UEFA Statutes, it 'exercises a major influence on the decision-making of the Executive Committee'.[45]

---

[39]FIFA Regulations for the Status and Transfer of Players (2005) Annex I, Article 1.

[40]Ibid., Article 6.

[41]The G14 was established in 2000 to represent the economic interests of the elite football clubs in Europe.

[42]FIFA Media Release of 15 January 2008, Victory for football as a whole. http://www.fifa.com/about-fifa/news/y=2008/m=1/news=victory-for-football-whole-672438.html. Accessed 13 October 2015.

[43]The EPFL was founded in 1997, relaunched in 2005, and has as its membership 31 member leagues and associate members across Europe.

[44]UEFA Statutes 2014, Article 35.

[45]Ibid.

The *Oulmers* case is important, even though it was not decided by the Court. Whilst at one level, the litigation only concerned a challenge to one of FIFA's regulations, the underlying complaint of many professional football clubs concerned their perceived lack of influence in decision making committees of FIFA and UEFA. As the then G14 commented at the time of the Oulmers dispute:

> [P]rofessional clubs have no direct representation on the bodies that make the rules and, not surprisingly, these regulations favour federations over clubs. *The Charleroi/Oulmers* case is an example of how a lack of representation can lead to rules which favour one party over another. G14 believes that these rules, which are imposed on all clubs without their consent, are unfair, undemocratic and must change.[46]

Oulmers, therefore, represented a turning point for football governance in Europe. It demonstrated how litigation could drive governance reform and recalibrate power relations within it in favour of stakeholders. It added impetus to the formal organisation of club and player interests in European football and brought formal social dialogue a step closer.

8.5 The Social Dialogue Committee for European Professional Football

The social dialogue committee for professional football was established by the Commission in Paris in July 2008 following a joint request made by FIFPro and the EPFL in December 2007. Representing the workers in the committee is FIFPro (Division Europe). Two parties represent the clubs: the EPFL and the ECA. The representativeness of the social partners was confirmed by the Commission in March 2008, the ECA later being confirmed as complementing the representativeness of the EPFL.[47]

The work programme agreed at the launch event included the development of minimum conditions in players contracts throughout the EU and the possible conclusion of a collective EU level Framework Agreement based on Article 155 TFEU on these requirements.[48] Whilst this topic lies at the less contentious end of the potential topics that could have been discussed, it reflected concern that even basic minimum standards in player's contracts were not being respected, particularly in Eastern Europe.

---

[46]Fifa set for Charleroi court case. BBC Sport, 20 March 2006. http://news.bbc.co.uk/sport2/hi/football/europe/4825680.stm. Accessed 13 October 2015.

[47]Commission Press Release of 1 July 2008, IP/08/1064 - Footballers and employers launch new EU forum for social dialogue.

[48]European sectoral social dialogue committee in the professional football sector work program 2008–2009 (1 July 2008). http://ec.europa.eu/social/BlobServlet?mode=dsw&docId=9057&langId=en. Accessed 13 October 2015.

The social partners agreed to establish UEFA as an associate member and the Chair of the social dialogue committee and to establish a rule of procedure under which items are first submitted to UEFA's Professional Football Strategy Council. Once agreed there the item may then proceed to the formal social dialogue committee.[49]

The committee began work on discussions on MRSPC in the professional football sector in the European Union and the rest of the UEFA territory.[50] The agreement was concluded in 2012 and the parties agreed to transform the MRSPC into an autonomous agreement. The parties also agreed that the provisions of the EU Treaties, the Charter of Fundamental Rights of the European Union, and secondary EU law apply to professional football players' contracts without prejudice to more stringent and/or more specific provisions contained in the agreement. They also agreed that where appropriate, agreements on matters falling into the scope of Article 153 of the TFEU may be submitted to the Commission for adoption by Council decision in line with the procedure laid down in Article 155 TFEU.

The overall objective of the agreement is to ensure that certain minimum standards are provided for in player contracts. These include: contracts must be in writing; in the case of a minor the parent/guardian must also sign the contract; the club and the player must each receive a copy and a copy must be registered with the appropriate league /national association; the contract must state the relevant particulars of both parties including names, addresses and start and end date; the contract must define the equal rights of the player and the club to negotiate an extension and/or an earlier termination of the contract with early termination being founded in just cause; and the contract must state other persons involved in the negotiation or conclusion of the contract.

Article 5 of the agreement specifies that the contract regulates an employment contract for a professional player, and the national law of the country in which the club is located applies. Article 6 outlines the duties the club has to the player such as: the provisions on regular salary payments and the provision of other benefits; the protection and education of young players; the payment of relevant taxes under national law (which also applies to the player); paid annual leave entitlements which must amount to at least four weeks; protection of the player's human rights and non-discrimination; protection of the health and safety of the player including the provision of mandatory health insurance; and the keeping of confidential medical records.

---

[49]Article 4 of the Rules of procedure for the European sectoral social dialogue committee in the professional football sector provides for UEFA to become Chair of the committee and Article 2 of the aforementioned rules of procedure govern the relationship with the Professional Strategy Council. See http://circa.europa.eu/Public/irc/empl/sectoral_social_dialogue/library?l=/professional_football/2008/20080701_plenartagung/football_080702_1/_EN_1.0_&a=d. Accessed 13 October 2015.

[50]Currently the European Union has 28 Member States and UEFA 54 national associations.

Article 7 establishes the duties of the player which includes: an obligation to play to the best of his ability when selected; to train and maintain health and fitness; to obey club rules and accept reasonable club instructions; to attend club events, both sporting and commercial; to behave in a sporting manner; to abstain from other football activities or dangerous activities; to notify the club of injury, illness or accident and submit only to the clubs medical treatment; to comply with all relevant anti-discrimination rules; not to bring the club or football into disrepute; and not to gamble.

Image rights agreements are provided for in Articles 8 and 9 provides that the club and player must both agree to a loan move. Article 10 regulates disciplinary and grievance procedures. Article 11 establishes that the club and player comply with relevant anti-doping regulations. Dispute resolution is dealt with under Article 12. Here it is stated that subject to national law and national collective agreements, any dispute between the club and player on an issue relating to the contract is to be submitted to independent and impartial arbitration under the national association's statutes and regulations, or to the Court of Arbitration for Sport where no such national arbitration process exists. Article 12 states that labour disputes may be settled by the FIFA Dispute Resolution Chamber with an appeal to CAS. This procedure is regulated under the FIFA RSTP, although as the agreement makes clear, labour disputes are primarily a matter for national law and in some states arbitration on labour disputes is not permitted.

Article 13 states that the club and player must comply with relevant football regulations, such as those adopted by FIFA, UEFA and national associations. Article 14 provides that the club and the player must comply with national collective bargaining agreements. Article 15 regulates the final provisions of the contract including the applicable law, jurisdiction and language of the contract. Article 16 contractually commits both club and player to act against racism and other forms of discrimination.

The remaining Articles relate to the agreement itself. Article 17 provides that the social partners have the right to deviate from the agreement for the benefit of the players. This can be done by way of a national collective agreement or through an individual contract. Article 18 commits the parties to use their 'best endeavours' to ensure the implementation of the agreement at national level using the most appropriate legal instruments. Article 19 prevents signatories from amending the agreement without the consent of all parties. Article 20 establishes the length of the agreement at four years. Finally, Article 21 confirms the role of UEFA as an associate member of the committee and highlights the relationship between the committee and UEFA's Professional Strategy Council.

Given that the agreement extends not only to the 28 (at the time 27) Member States of the EU, but also to all 54 (at the time 53) members of UEFA, the manner of implementation is important. As explained above, implementation can be achieved through a Council Directive or through the voluntary route. Implementation by way of a Directive offers the strongest method of enforcement in EU28 as the agreement assumes the status of EU law. However, this would present problems in terms of the reach of the agreement as it would not be legally enforceable outside the EU28. By contrast, the voluntary route method would allow the agreement to be implemented more widely throughout the 54 member states of UEFA, but it requires implementation on a voluntary country-by country basis. The voluntary route also only binds the signatories and their affiliates and affects only them and only in accordance with the practices and procedures specific to them in their respective Member States.[51] Member States are not under an obligation to transpose the agreement into domestic law, although they can choose to if they so wish.

It was the choice of implementation that caused a substantial delay in the social partners signing the agreement. Whereas FIFPro wanted binding implementation, UEFA and the employers' representatives favoured the voluntary route. The employers did not want to expose their members to an additional legal burden and UEFA, it must be assumed, was reluctant for 'hard law' to regulate an area of traditionally sporting competence.

The solution that allowed all the parties to sign is located in Article 18 of the agreement and the accompanying Annex 8. Article 18 commits the parties to use their 'best endeavours' to ensure the implementation of the agreement at national level within EU and across the territory of UEFA, using the most appropriate legal instruments. Annex 8 explains that this means implementation in those countries where an existing collective agreement is in force. Where this is not the case, the social partners at the national level must evaluate the most appropriate and effective implementation method.[52]

This method of implementation acknowledges the variations in football industrial relations across the territory of UEFA and it naturally results in differing implementation outcomes. As the agreement concerns *minimum* requirements in player contracts, it is natural that in some national associations where a collective agreement is in force, standards equivalent to or higher than those specified in the agreement are already operational. In these 16 states, implementation of the agreement was not required. However, implementation is required in the remaining EU states and those non-EU states who are members of UEFA. In these states, Annex 8 envisages a number of potential implementation methods. First, the social partners are encouraged to establish stronger industrial relations at national level with the view to eventually implementing the agreement into a national collective agreement. Where this is not possible, alternative methods could be encouraged, such as implementation by agreement or through the relevant football authorities requiring compliance with the autonomous agreement through their internal regulations.

Implementation in those countries where a collective agreement is not in place is problematic and to monitor this and to discuss on a national level the best way

---

[51]Commission Communication to the Council and the European Parliament of 14 December 1993, COM (1993) 600 final - concerning the application of the Agreement on social policy.

[52]The Agreement Regarding the Minimum Requirements for Standard Player Contracts, Annex 8, para 1.5.

to implement the agreement, an implementation task force was established. In this regard, the quality of industrial relations within the football industry varies considerably throughout the UEFA territory. FIFPro has identified particular problems in Eastern Europe.[53] These include a problem with unpaid and overdue player salaries; poor state of club finances; a connected problem of match-fixing; abusive behaviour by clubs in relation to contracts such as pressure to sign a new contract, and contract termination without compensation or a reduction of salary. FIFPro also identify varying practice across Eastern Europe in terms of how a professional footballer is defined in labour status terms. In some countries, professional footballers are classified as self-employed workers and not employees, rendering problematic the representative nature of any employee association.[54] FIFPro has also highlighted the non-existence or relative immaturity of national dispute resolution chambers in some countries across Europe and this raises further problems in terms of the effective implementation of the agreement.[55]

8.6 Social Dialogue as a Forum for Reforming the Football Regulations

The first agreement of the social dialogue for professional football is modest in so far as it relates only to the basic requirements to be contained in a standard player contract. It is somewhat surprising that the social partners took four years to agree this. However, the delay was attributable, not to the content of the agreement, but rather to the form of implementation. It is, therefore, possible that the social dialogue committee can develop more far reaching discussions with a view to conclude agreements on a range of employment related issues in football. In particular, the social dialogue committee is an appropriate forum for discussions on the reform of the FIFA RSTP, or as a vehicle through which the social partners can regulate themselves matters contained within the FIFA regulations. This can be achieved by way of the social partners concluding and implementing a formal agreement according to one of the implementation methods discussed above.

Article 1 of the FIFA RSTP states that 'These regulations lay down global and binding rules concerning the status of players, their eligibility to participate in organised football, and their transfer between clubs belonging to different associations'. The scope for autonomous regulation by the social partners therefore

[53]FIFPro 2012, Black Book: Eastern Europe. The Problems Professional Footballers Encounter: Research, Hoofddorp: Netherlands.

[54]In this regard, the European Commission has launched a study on Mapping the Labour Status of Sports People under EU Law, DG Employment, Social Affairs and Inclusion 2015.

[55]FIFPro, Autonomous Agreement Moving Forward. FIFPro.org, 3 October 2014. http://www.fifpro.org/en/news/autonomous-agreement-moving-forward. Accessed 13 October 2015.

appears limited. However, the RSTP do specify that certain provisions must pay due respect to mandatory national law and collective agreements and any player or club has the right to seek redress before a civil court for employment-related disputes.[56] There is, therefore, scope for the social partners to regulate certain employment related matters outside the framework of the regulations. Given that the RSTP pay due respect to mandatory national law and collective agreements, the European nature of any such agreement does not compromise the 'global and binding' nature of the FIFA regime. Furthermore, despite the RSTP having global effect, the regulations already recognise that due to the requirements of EU law, certain special provisions relate only to the situation within the EU/EEA territory.[57] Even in the absence of a formal agreement, the social partners are uniquely well placed to be consulted and advise on the content of such provisions.

The right of players and clubs to seek redress on employment related matters before ordinary courts was inserted into the RSTP following the 2001 transfer system settlement. This provision enhances the prospects that some aspects of the RSTP will give rise to litigation under national and EU law.[58] In order to negate the threat litigation poses to legal certainty and the proper functioning of the football sector, the social partners could consider opening discussions on a reform agenda. Within the context of the RSTP, the social dialogue committee would be free to discuss a wide range of employment related matters currently regulated by FIFA.[59] These include: the status of players; the registration of players; the maintenance of contractual stability between professionals and clubs; the prohibition on third party ownership of players' economic rights; the protection of minors; the operation of the solidarity fund; and issues connected to dispute resolution. Of these, two aspects of the current RSTP are particularly apt for discussion within the social dialogue committee: contract stability and training compensation provisions.

8.6.1 Contract Stability

Title IV of the FIFA RSTP governs the 'Maintenance of Contractual Stability Between Professionals and Clubs'. Within this chapter, Article 17 establishes the

---

[56]The FIFA Regulations for the Status and Transfer of Players (2015), Article 22.

[57]For example, the provisions on the transfer of minors and training compensation for young players differs within the EU than that found outside. For minors, see FIFA Regulations for the Status and Transfer of Players (2015), Article 19(2) and for training compensation see Annex 4(6), Special Provisions for the EU/EEA.

[58]FIFPro Announces Challenge to Transfer System. FIFPro.org, 17 December 2013. http://www.fifpro.org/en/news/fifpro-announces-legal-challenge-to-transfer-system. Accessed 13 October 2015.

[59]T.M.C Asser Institute, Edge Hill University and Katholieke Universiteit Leuven (2008) Study into the identification of themes and issues which can be dealt with in a Social dialogue in the European professional football sector. Report for the European Commission.

consequences of a party unilaterally terminating a contract of employment without just cause. In the case of a player, unilateral termination without just cause can result in sporting sanctions being applied and compensation for the breach being payable.

The content of Article 17 was the product of the compromise negotiated between the Commission and FIFA and UEFA in 2001. In this regard, Article 17 makes provision for a 'protected' and 'unprotected' period in an employment contract.[60] The protected period was designed to satisfy the clubs' desire to see a period of contract stability enforced. Unilateral termination by the player within this period can result in sporting ban being imposed on the player and the requirement to pay compensation to the club. The provision of the unprotected period was designed to respond to the Commission's desire to see player's receive enhanced free movement opportunities within the latter part of their contract. Unilateral termination by the player outside the protected period will not result in sporting sanctions being imposed, but the player is liable for compensation. In the case of a dispute, the competent dispute resolution forums are the FIFA Dispute Resolution Chamber with an appeal to CAS.

The operation of Article 17, particularly the manner in which the CAS has awarded compensation sums payable by players who unilaterally terminate their contracts outside the protected period, has been subject to considerable criticism.[61] The potential for very high compensation sums to be attached to awards can give rise to concerns under national law[62] and EU law.[63] To mitigate these concerns, the social partners are best placed to regulate this aspect of the employment relationship outside the RSTP framework by, for example, agreeing the principles underpinning a clause that could be inserted into players' contracts governing the consequences of unilateral termination. Alternatively, the social partners could co-operate with FIFA and negotiate a special provision applicable to Europe that could be inserted into Article 17. Agreeing to amending Article 17, or regulating it through an autonomous agreement, will be a significant challenge, particularly for FIFPro who would have most to gain from reform. The social partners hold very divergent views on the operation of Article 17.[64]

8.6.2 Training Compensation

The 2001 transfer system agreement also contained provisions on training compensation.[65] This reflected the view that clubs involved in the training and devel-

---

[60]The protected period refers to a period of three seasons for players who entered into a contract prior to the 28th birthday of the professional and two seasons for those concluded over that age.

[61]Van Megen 2011; See also Parrish 2015.

[62]The Swiss Federal Supreme Court found that one such CAS award connected to enforcement of an Article 17 award to be in breach of Swiss public policy, Case 4A_558/2011, *Matuzalem*.

[63]This argument has been advanced in Parrish 2015.

[64]Compare Van Megen 2011 with Lambrecht 2011.

[65]Now provided for in the FIFA Regulations for the Status and Transfer of Players (2015), Article 20.

opment of young players should receive financial reward for that effort when either a player is registered for the first time as a professional or when a professional player is transferred between clubs of two national associations. A player's training and education takes place between the ages of 12 and 23 and training compensation is payable up to the age of 23 for training incurred up to the age of 21, unless it is evident that a player has already terminated his training period before the age of 21.

In the case of an international transfer, the obligation of the acquiring club to pay training compensation to those clubs involved in the player's training arises whether the transfer takes place during or at the end of the player's contract. Training compensation is calculated according to criteria established in the annexe accompanying the FIFA regulations. FIFA requires member associations to divide their clubs into a maximum of four categories. Category 1 clubs are deemed to have the highest quality training centres and category 4 the lowest. Training costs are then set for each category and are designed to correspond to the amount needed to train a player for one season multiplied by the number of players needed to be trained in order to produce that one player. This reflects the reality that not all trained players will play professionally yet the club has still incurred the costs of training them.

A number of potential legal issues arise from the application of the training compensation provisions. As the obligation of the acquiring club to pay training compensation arises whether the transfer takes place during or at the end of the player's contract, there is a risk that the regime could impede a player's freedom of movement guaranteed under EU law. In *Bosman*, the CJEU arrived at this conclusion in relation to out of contract transfer fees. In *Bernard*, the European Court upheld the principle that a system of training compensation in sport could be justified with reference to the objective of educating and training young players although this must be calculated on the basis of the actual training costs borne by the original club but could include the cost of training both future professional players and those who will never play professionally.

The principles underpinning FIFA's training compensation regime has therefore received high level judicial support. However, some issues remain concerning its practical operation. FIFA has admitted that it does not actually know the types of costs that national associations should take into account when establishing training compensation fees.[66] This is because many national associations failed to respond to a FIFA survey issued in preparation for implementation of the training compensation regime. This means that it cannot be established that the training compensation fees relate directly to the actual costs incurred, as required by the Court in *Bernard*. High training compensation fees could render less attractive the exercise of a player's free movement rights within the EU.

The social dialogue committee for European professional football is well placed to determine the types of cost that should be taken into account in the

[66] Ongaro 2010, pp. 78–80.

calculation of training compensation, although the committee is only able to determine these costs within the EU and UEFA territory. The committee is also able to discuss the operation of the special provisions contained within the training compensation regime that relate to transfers within the EU/EEA. Here, the regulations establish that if the player moves from a lower to a higher category club, the calculation shall be based on the average training costs of the two clubs and if the player moves from a higher to a lower category, the calculation shall be based on the training costs of the lower-category club. In addition, for intra EU/EEA matters, the final season of training may occur before the season of the player's 21st birthday if it is established that the player completed his training before that time. Finally, so that a club cannot claim training compensation for a player they have no interest in, training compensation cannot be demanded for a player who has not been offered a contract. In this situation, to claim training compensation, the club must present evidence justifying its claim.[67] This measure is in addition to the provision contained in the regulations, applicable globally, that no training compensation can be demanded for a player who has had his contract terminated without just cause. The special provisions applicable to Europe are designed to mitigate the threat of legal action brought under EU law, specifically EU free movement law. In this connection, in December 2014, the Bremen Court of Appeal, in the SV Wilhelmshaven case, found that FIFA Regulations on training compensation, as applied by the CAS, are incompatible with Article 45 TFEU on the free movement of workers.[68]

8.6.3 Other Potential Topics

Outside the RSTP framework, the social partners could also discuss the FIFA rules regulating the mandatory release of players and the fixing of the international match calendar. In addition, the FIFA regulations on working with intermediaries (the new name for agents) is a subject potentially capable of falling within the scope of social dialogue.[69] FIFA's agent regulations is fertile ground for litigation. A previous version of the FIFA regulations has been challenged before the European Court[70] and currently, the 2015 regulations are the subject to a legal challenge before the European Commission by the English Association of Football Agents. As intermediaries are not considered representative employers, their role in a social dialogue committee is problematic. However, the European Parliament's Mavrommatis report considered "that players' agents should have a

[67]FIFA Regulations for the Status and Transfer of Players (2015), Annex 4(6), Special Provisions for the EU/EEA.

[68]For discussion, see Duval 2015, pp. 248–249.

[69]FIFA Regulations on Working with Intermediaries (2015).

[70]Case T-193/02 *Laurent Piau v Commission of the European Communities* ECLI:EU:T:2005:22.

role within a strengthened social dialogue in sports, which, in combination with better regulation and a European licensing system for agents, would also prevent cases of improper action by agents".[71] The Commission's 2011 Communication on Sport also suggested that an EU-level social dialogue could discuss the role of agents.[72]

Below FIFA level a number of other football regulations could be subject to discussion within the social dialogue committee for professional football. For example, UEFA's rules on locally trained players, in so far as they relate to the employment relationship between clubs and players, are apt for discussion in the committee.[73] Equally, the participation of third country nationals within EU based competitions is a subject the social partners could discuss.[74]

8.7 Conclusions and Assessment

The European Court's judgment in *Bosman* had a liberalising effect on the European labour market for players. The football authorities, notably FIFA and UEFA, expressed concern that the judgment gave rise to a number of negative effects on the football sector including a diminution of competitive balance and a lack of incentives to educate and train young players. A process of labour market re-regulation took place, the fundamentals of which were enshrined in the 2001 agreement concluded between the European Commission and FIFA and UEFA. That agreement established the principles underpinning the 2001 edition of the FIFA RSTP. Elsewhere, re-regulation took a different form. For example, UEFA introduced regulations governing locally trained players.

Shortly after the 2001 agreement, the European Commission began to promote social dialogue as a venue through which disputes pertaining to labour issues in sport could be resolved. FIFPro enthusiastically supported this initiative as they objected to the terms of the 2001 transfer agreement and saw social dialogue as means of re-asserting their influence in international football governance. As social dialogue aims at improving workers' rights and conditions, FIFPro has most to gain from a European wide agreement. By 2008, a social dialogue for European professional football was established and in 2012 it concluded its first agreement on minimum requirements in standard player contracts.

---

[71]European Parliament Report of 14 April 2008, A6-0149/2008 - Motion for a Resolution on the White Paper on Sport, para 99.

[72]Communication from the Commission to the European Parliament, Council, Economic and Social Committee and Committee of the Regions, of 18 January 2011, COM (2011) 12 final - Developing the European Dimension in Sport.

[73]University of Liverpool and Edge Hill University (2013) Study on the Assessment of UEFA's Home-Grown Player Rule. Study for the European Commission EAC/07/2012.

[74]As recommended by KEA & CDES (2013), The Economic and Legal Aspects of Transfer of Players, Report for the European Commission, p. 8.

These developments indicate a strong connection between the European liberalisation of the football labour market that took place following *Bosman*, and the Europeanisation of industrial relations in European football. As a corollary, it cannot be discounted that, in time, industrial relations in European sport will follow a similar path to that found in the US where collective agreements are a more common feature of the industrial relations landscape in sport. For example, Halgreen observes that collective agreements in the US began as basic agreements on minimum conditions, as in the case of European football, but later developed into more substantial wide-ranging agreements following litigation.[75] FIFPro's challenge to the FIFA transfer system combined with their efforts at promoting social dialogue suggests that a similar pattern is observable in Europe.[76]

The potential for an Americanisation of sporting industrial relations is evident because social dialogue offers the social partners in the football sector the opportunity to regulate certain labour related issues outside the regulatory framework of the sports governing bodies. This far reaching power has the potential to effect major governance change in European football, and European sport more generally.[77] It does so by disturbing the traditional pyramid patterns of European sports governance in which the sports governing body assumes the primary regulatory function and stakeholders, such as clubs and athletes, subject themselves to this regulatory monopoly. Geeraert refers to this as a shift to a more networked style of governance in sport which is to the detriment of the hierarchic self-governance of sports.[78] In short, social dialogue both reflects, and promotes, the enhanced status and power of clubs and players in European football governance.

Such far reaching claims should, however, be tempered with caution. The social dialogue committee for professional football has, as yet, only concluded one agreement, on minimum requirements in standard player contracts. The relative lack of progress within the committee is not to be unexpected. Experience from other social dialogue committees suggests that employer groups prefer soft outcomes from discussion within the committee, such as joint statements and recommendations, rather than binding agreements.[79] Pochet calculates that fewer than 2 % of the texts adopted at sectoral level generally are agreements with binding effect.[80] The social partners, particularly employer associations, will only tend to

---

[75]Halgreen 2004, p. 210.

[76]T.M.C Asser Institute, Edge Hill University and Katholieke Universiteit Leuven (2008) Study into the identification of themes and issues which can be dealt with in a Social dialogue in the European professional football sector. Report for the European Commission.

[77]In June 2011, the European Association for Sports Employers (EASE) and the trade union for sports workers (UNI Europa Sport) signed a joint statement on the Informal European Sectoral Social Dialogue Committee for Sports and Active Leisure in which both social partners reaffirmed the importance of establishing a sectoral social dialogue committee for the whole sports sector. For discussion see Pierre and Buisine 2013.

[78]Geeraert 2015, p. 100.

[79]Keller 2005 cited in Léonard 2008, pp. 403–404.

[80]Pochet 2007.

engage at the hard end of social dialogue if other channels for delivering their goals are ineffective.[81] Social dialogue is also encouraged when the social partners can impose unacceptably high costs on one another and both see value in employing social dialogue as a venue for a negotiated settlement.[82]

Yet even in circumstances in which the European level social partners conclude agreements, they face the question of implementation. The principles of the first agreement were actually agreed in 2007 in a Memorandum of Understanding between FIFPro and UEFA.[83] The delay in concluding the agreement was attributable to the form the implementation took with the employer groups reluctant to adopt binding measures. Implementing agreements in the European football sector is rendered more problematic as the national industrial relations landscape in European football varies considerably in terms of its maturity. As European umbrella organisations, the social partners in football are creatures of their national affiliates. Concluding and implementing agreements at European level without a strong national mandate will be problematic. Not only do the strength of employer and employee associations vary considerably at national level, so do national cultures on football governance. Some national affiliates may see aspects of agreements concluded at European level as unwelcome and contrary to their national traditions. In other states, the absence of effective national affiliates frustrates implementation. It will take many years before it can be said that a mature, proper functioning and even model of national industrial relations operates throughout the European football sector.

Paradoxically however, it is the uneven nature of this national landscape that strengthens the argument that discussions are best located at the European level. Once the European football sector has a proper functioning model of national industrial relations, the incentives to engage at EU level diminish.[84] This raises the prospect that the football social dialogue committee could become a victim of its own success. By encouraging implementation at national level, and in doing so encouraging the establishment and proper functioning of representative employer and employee bodies, the committee is removing the incentives to engage at the supranational level. In time, governance change in world and European football may therefore be driven at the national level, not by litigation as is the current model, but through the conclusion of national collective agreements.

Using the social dialogue committee to drive through major governance change in European football is also likely to be frustrated by the current rules of procedure adopted by the social partners. These rules stipulate that the UEFA PFSC must first agree to items before they can be discussed in the social dialogue committee. This

[81]De Boer et al. 2005, pp. 55–56.

[82]Parrish 2011, pp. 228–229.

[83]Memorandum of Understanding between the Union des Associations Europeennes de Football (UEFA) and the Fédération Internationale des Associations de Footballeurs Professionnels "FIFPro division europe" (FIFpro) of 11 October 2007.

[84]De Boer et al. 2005, pp. 55–56.

gives UEFA, who are represented in the PFSC by four Vice Presidents from UEFA's Executive Committee, an effective veto over the emergence of new topics in the social dialogue committee. In this regard, UEFA is playing a multi-layered game.

First, they are, cosmetically at least, responding to the EU's agenda of integrating stakeholders into governance structures.[85] Second, they are mindful of the potential of social dialogue to undermine its own regulatory control. In this connection, UEFA is attempting to exercise some control over developments within the committee with a view to retaining their regulatory monopoly at the European level. This is supported through a complementary strategy of lobbying the EU institutions to secure more sympathetic treatment at EU level.[86] Third, UEFA sees value in the contribution social dialogue can make to better football governance throughout Europe, in particular better compliance with its own regulations at national level through the strengthening of national structures. Finally, UEFA must be compliant with the requirements of the FIFA Statutes. Article 20 of these statutes requires continental federations to 'to comply with and enforce compliance with the Statutes, regulations and decisions of FIFA'. UEFA would naturally want to exercise caution when being potentially party to an agreement at European level that contradicts the existing FIFA regulations.[87] Simultaneously, UEFA may see the value of social dialogue as means of effecting change at a global level, particular where FIFA regulations conflict with UEFA objectives.

Should UEFA exercise its veto, the business of the social dialogue committee could become frustrated. If this were to occur, the social partners retain the power to re-write the rules of procedure and remove the influence of the PFSC. It can also remove UEFA from the Chair of the social dialogue committee.

The transformative effect of social dialogue on European industrial relations, and more specifically European football governance, is therefore a longer term prospect. Nevertheless, in the short term evidence suggests that social partners use social dialogue as a lobbying strategy within the context of EU decision making.[88] In the context of professional football, social dialogue is a means through which the EU institutions can be lobbied on matters pertaining to labour related football governance.[89] It is also a vehicle for imparting pressure on FIFA and UEFA to adopt a more participatory style of governance and to effect regulatory change, such as in relation to the operation of the FIFA RSTP.

[85]Commission White Paper of 11 July 2007, COM (2007) 391 final - White Paper on Sport.

[86]Commission Decision of 14 October 2014, COM (2014) 7378 final adopting the Arrangement for Cooperation between the European Commission and the Union of European Football Associations (UEFA).

[87]Although, as stated elsewhere in this contribution, the FIFA regulations do recognise applicable national law and collective agreements.

[88]See Pochet 2007; De Boer et al. 2005; Dufresne et al. 2006, p. 274.

[89]Article 1 of the professional football committee's rules of procedure state that the committee's objectives are to "deliver opinions on labour matters to the Commission on initiatives with regard to social and employment policy and the development of European policy having consequences in the professional football sector".

The Commission is likely to be receptive to such lobbying. Not only is the Commission keen to encourage the greater engagement of the social partners within the European integration process 'as an alternative source of regulation and legitimacy',[90] it may also see the social partners as playing a role in the fulfilment of the sports policy objectives enunciated in Article 165 TFEU. For example, the promotion of 'fairness and openness in sporting competitions', the 'cooperation between bodies responsible for sports' and the protection of the 'physical and moral integrity of sportsmen and sportswomen, especially the youngest sportsmen and sportswomen' are objectives that are potentially deliverable by the social partners, where these objectives pertain to labour relations.[91]

References

Anderson J (2010) Modern sports law. Hart Publishing, Oxford

De Boer R, Benedictus H, Van der Meer M (2005) Broadening without intensification: the added value of the European social and sectoral dialogue. Eur J Indus Relat 11(1):51–70

Dufresne A, Degryse C, Pochet P (2006) The European sectoral social dialogue, actors, developments and challenges. Peter Lang Publishing, Brussels

Duval A (2015) The court of arbitration for sport and EU law: chronicle of an encounter. Maastricht J Eur Int Law 22(2):224–255

Geeraert A (2015) The European sectoral social dialogue committee in professional football: power relations, legitimacy and control. Soccer Soc 16(1):98–115

Halgreen L (2004) European sports law—a comparative analysis of the European and American models of sport. Forlaget Thomson Publishing, Copenhagen

James M (2013) Sports law. Palgrave Macmillan, Basingstoke

Keller B (2005) Europeanization at sectoral level. Empirical results and missing perspectives. Transfer 11(3):397–408

Lambrecht W (2011) Contractual stability from a club's point of view. Contractual stability in football. Eur Sports Law Policy Bull 1:95–114

Léonard E (2008) European sectoral social dialogue: an analytical framework. Eur J Indus Relat 14(4):401–419

Lewis A, Taylor J (2014) Sport: law and practice. Bloomsbury Professional, Hayward Heaths

Maguire J, Stead D (1998) Border crossing: Soccer, labour migration and the European union. Int Rev Sociol Sport 33(1):59–73

Monte G (2013) Towards an EU Social dialogue in sport. In: Siekmann R, Parrish, R, Smokvina V, Bodiroga-Vukobrat N, Sander G (eds) Social dialogue in professional sports: on some topics about European sports law. Shaker Verlag, pp 41–54

Ongaro O (2010) The system of training compensation according to the FIFA regulations on the status and transfer of players. The Bernard case: sports and training compensation. Eur Sports Law Policy Bull 1:69–92

Parrish R (2003) Sports law and policy in the European union. Manchester University Press, Manchester

Parrish R (2011) Social dialogue in European professional football. Eur Law J 17(2):213–229

Parrish R (2015) Article 17 of the FIFA regulations on the status and transfer of players: compatibility with EU Law. Maastricht J Eur Comp Law 22(2):256–283

[90]Dufresne et al. 2006, p. 20.

[91]Parrish 2011, p. 227.

Pochet P (2007) European social dialogue between hard and soft law. In: Tenth biennial international conference, European Union Studies Association (EUSA), Montreal
Pierre J, Buisine S (2013) Social dialogue in the sports sector. Eur Rev Labour Res 19(4):581–595
Smismans S (2007) The European social dialogue between constitutional and labour law. Eur Law Rev 32(3):341–364
Van den Bogaert S (2005) Practical regulation of the mobility of sportsmen in the EU post Bosman. Kluwer Law International, The Hague
Van Megen W (2011) Contractual stability from a player's perspective. contractual stability in football. Eur Sports Law Policy Bull 1:115–124

Chapter 9
Governing in the Shadow of Bosman: A Principal-Agent Perspective on Sports Governance and the EU

Arnout Geeraert

Abstract This contribution investigates the EU's (potential) role in sports governance by building upon insights from the Principal-Agent model. Highlighting the influence of Bosman, it explores the limitations and opportunities of the EU's power in relation to sports governing bodies (SGBs). Two EU bodies, the Court of Justice of the European Union and the European Commission, are conceptualised as principals and SGBs are conceptualised as agents. It shows that the EU is able to use the shadow of Bosman to influence the behaviour of SGBs because these bodies fear the costs of the ultimate EU sanction: a second Bosman case. However, drawing from the literature on the EU as a market power, this contribution demonstrates that several factors negatively influence the credible occurrence and magnitude of sanctions, limiting the EU's capacity to influence SGBs' behaviour. Moreover, it shows how SGBs are able to diminish the shadow of Bosman through a variety of strategies. The chapter concludes by offering concrete policy advice, indicating that there is certainly room for a more ambitious EU sports policy- devised and supported by the Member States - directed at SGBs.

Keywords Principal-agent · Market power europe · Sports policy · Internal cohesiveness · Regulatory capacity · Sports governing bodies

Contents

A. Geeraert (✉)
Leuven International and European Studies (LINES),
University of Leuven, Parkstraat 45, 3602, 3000 Louvain, Belgium
e-mail: arnout.geeraert@kuleuven.be

A. Duval and B. Van Rompuy (eds.), *The Legacy of* Bosman,
ASSER International Sports Law Series, DOI 10.1007/978-94-6265-120-3_9

9.1 Introduction

Friends and foes of football seemed to breathe a collective sigh of relief when *Fédération Internationale de Football Association* (FIFA) President Sepp Blatter resigned in 2015. Mr Blatter's announcement and the litany of corruption-related indictments in relation to FIFA suggest that the autonomy of sport may no longer be sacrosanct. One actor notably missing in the latest chapter of the FIFA soap opera is the European Union (EU), widely touted as the actor that has been the most capable of influencing sport governance at an international level. Indeed, 20 years on, the Court of Justice of the European Union (CJEU)'s ruling in *Bosman* has had a significant and continuing impact on sports governance. The ruling functioned as an agenda-setting event, boosting the demand of the Member States for a more coordinated EU approach to sport. It also showed unsatisfied sports stakeholders that the EU is an important venue for redress and made clear that sports governing bodies (SGBs) - private regulatory monopolies for a single sport that are mostly based outside the EU - have to abide by EU law. Doing so, *Bosman* propelled the EU to become a sports governance actor in its own right.[1] Twenty years later, however, both media and academics still lack a clear view on the EU's (potential) role in sports governance. There appears to be an abundance of academic literature on the ruling, yet few studies focus on its implications for the EU's power in relation to SGBs.[2]

Aiming to fill this void, this chapter explores and explains the EU's role in sports governance, building upon recent work by Geeraert and Drieskens and

---

[1]Geeraert and Drieskens 2015; Geeraert 2016; Geeraert and Drieskens, forthcoming.

[2]This contribution considers as SGBs the private associations that hold a monopoly on regulating sport competition at an international (i.e. global or continental) level. A crucial factor is that such organisations produce sports rules that have an effect within the EU's internal market. Thus, in principle, sport organisations that are not SGBs sensu stricto (because they do not govern a single sport), such as the International Olympic Committee or the World Anti-Doping Agency, also fall within the scope of this definition.

focusing on the EU's possibilities to govern SGBs.[3] In this respect, an important distinction must be made between *governance* and *governing*. According to Kooiman, governance is mainly concerned with describing 'the patterns that emerge from the governing activities of social, political and administrative actors', while governing can be defined as activities that make a 'purposeful effort to guide, steer, control, or manage (sectors or facets of) societies'.[4] Thus, in order to govern effectively, the EU should exercise power over SGBs. In the most rudimentary sense, such power implies that the EU is able to persuade SGBs to do something that they would not otherwise do.[5] Bringing the influence of *Bosman* to the forefront, this chapter aims to examine the roots of this power, as well as its limits and its opportunities, by building upon the Principal-Agent (PA) model.

The PA model relies (mostly) on assumptions derived from rational choice theory. In the rational choice paradigm, power emanates from the ability to exact costs. Actors behave rationally and make choices based on intelligent calculation, seeking to avoid accruing costs. The PA model has emerged as a useful tool to analyse power relations between two actors when one actor (the agent) acts on behalf of another (the principal). The model conceptualises imposed costs in terms of sanctions, which ultimately incentivise the agent to act in accordance with the principal's wishes, an action it would otherwise not execute given conflicting interests. Here, the CJEU and the Commission fulfil the role of principals and SGBs of agents. The central argument is that *Bosman* influenced the perceptions of agents about principals' capacity to sanction incompliance with both EU law and sports policy: because SGBs fear the costs of a second *Bosman* - meaning a ruling with far-going consequences for sports governance -, the EU is able to govern SGBs *in the shadow of Bosman*. However, several factors a priori negatively influence the credible occurrence and magnitude of sanctions, limiting the EU's capacity to influence SGBs' behaviour. Drawing from the literature on the EU as a market power, this contribution explores how the EU's market size, regulatory capacity and internal cohesiveness affect the magnitude and likelihood of sanctions and, consequently, the EU's capacity to govern SGBs.[6] Moreover, it demonstrates how SGBs are able to diminish the shadow of *Bosman* through a variety of strategies.

This contribution continues as follows. The next section introduces the PA model as a framework for analysing power relationships. Section 9.3 conceptualises the CJEU and the Commission as principals for SGBs, the agents, and explores how information asymmetries and conflicting interests necessitate invoking control instruments in order to push SGBs towards compliance. Section 9.4 explores the two routes that the EU uses to control SGBs: the EU law route and the EU sports policy route. It further demonstrates not only how *Bosman* casts a

[3] Geeraert and Drieskens 2015; Geeraert 2016; Geeraert and Drieskens, forthcoming.

[4] Kooiman 1993, p. 3.

[5] Dahl 1957, p. 202.

[6] Damro 2012.

shadow of hierarchy over SGBs, but also how several factors a priori affect the largeness of this shadow. Moving the focus from principals' *exerting* control to agents' *mitigating* control, Sect. 9.5 examines how SGBs diminish the shadow of *Bosman* by skilfully asserting themselves. The final Sect. 9.6 summarises the main findings and explores the way forward.

9.2 The Principal-Agent Framework

The PA model analyses different forms of *contractual* relationships between 'two (or more) parties when one, designated the agent, acts for, on behalf of, or as a representative for the other, designated the principal, in a particular domain of decision problems'.[7] Not a theory in itself, the PA model mostly relies on the theoretical assumptions of rational choice theory, which assumes that actors behave instrumentally so as to maximise the attainment of their (fixed) interests. In political science, rational choice theory finds resonance with the *new institutionalists*, a group that departs from the once-dominant theoretical approaches that considered institutions merely epiphenomenal; institutions are treated as 'political actors in their own right' instead.[8] This contribution aligns with the tradition of *rational choice institutionalists,* which holds that institutions are organisational forms that structure the behaviour of actors. These actors hold a fixed set of preferences and behave instrumentally.[9]

The basic assumption of PA analysis is that the relationship between the principal and the agent is inherently problematic because of conflicting interests and information asymmetries. It is assumed that the presence of interests different from those of the principal provides the agent with a *motive* to pursue its own interests at the expense of the principal. If principal and agent share the same interests, there is no reason for the agent to pursue conflicting interests. In the case of diverging interests, rational choice theory holds that the agent will behave instrumentally in order to maximise the attainment of its own interests. The presence of information asymmetries between the principal and the agent provides the latter with the *opportunity* to act against the principal's interests. If agent and principal have access to the same information, there is no room for the agent to minimise efforts or pursue private interests.

Agency slack - or independent action by the agent that is undesired by the principal - is likely where there are information asymmetries and conflicting interests.

---

[7] Ross 1973, p. 134.

[8] March and Olsen 1984, p. 738.

[9] Thus, this contribution assumes that SGBs are rational actors. Research demonstrates that this is the case for FIFA and UEFA, see Geeraert and Drieskens 2015; Geeraert 2016. Yet further research should explore if these assumptions hold true for other SGBs and, thus, succeed in correctly isolating the most important features of EU control, while also expanding our understanding of and leading to new insights into EU control of SGBs.

PA analysis suggests that principals can prevent and reduce the problem of agency slack by installing and deploying control mechanisms, which alter the incentives of the agent in such a way that acting in accordance with the principal's interests is more attractive.[10] After contracting from principal to agent takes place, the principal engages in three forms of control to limit slack, namely monitoring, steering and sanctioning. Several factors may complicate control, however.[11] Most importantly, the effectiveness of monitoring, steering and threats of sanctioning depend on credible and sufficiently large sanctions in the case of incompliance.[12] The agent can decrease the principal's incentive to control by skilfully asserting itself to 'manipulate' its principal's preferences.[13] If the agent brings the principal's preferences in line with its own, their interests will no longer be divergent and there will be no reason for the principal to control the agent.

The next section maps the Commission and the CJEU as principals for SGBs. It demonstrates how high degrees of information asymmetries and conflicting interests increase the likelihood of slack and necessitate the employment of control mechanisms in order to achieve compliance.

9.3 The Commission and the CJEU as Principals for SGBs

The EU has accumulated a body of law and related policies, commonly referred to as the *acquis*. Although the EU functions as an agent to its Member States to produce the *acquis*, it, too, functions as a principal in specific instances, delegating particular tasks to Member States and external bodies to aid compliance with *acquis* and other policies. In order to achieve compliance, the EU deploys a variety of control mechanisms.[14]

With regard to SGBs, there have been two EU institutions particularly involved: the Court of Justice of the European Union (CJEU) and the European Commission. In European governance, these institutions hold important enforcement and executive tasks. A dyadic PA setting thus emerges, wherein the CJEU and the Commission act as principals towards the SGBs, which act as agents. This section demonstrates how conflicting preferences and information asymmetries increase the likelihood of slack because SGBs have both the motives and the opportunity to act against the Commission and the CJEU's interests.

---

[10]McCubbins and Schwartz 1984; Kiewiet and McCubbins 1991; Pollack 1997; Geeraert and Drieskens 2015.

[11]See, e.g. McCubbins and Schwartz 1984; Pollack 1997; Huber and Shipan 2000; Nielson and Tierney 2003.

[12]Effectiveness means the extent to which targeted agents deliberately comply in response to these controls.

[13]Niemann and Huigens 2011, p. 432; See also Hawkins and Jacoby 2006, p. 212.

[14]Borzel 2010; Geeraert and Drieskens 2015.

9.3.1 Conflicting Preferences

In order for the PA model to have an explanatory use, there must be conflicting preferences between the principal and the agent; otherwise, there would be no reason for the agent to act against the principal's interests. According to McCubbins and Kiewiet, 'there is almost always some conflict between the interests of those who delegate authority (principals) and the agents to whom they delegate it'. Agents behave opportunistically, pursuing their own interests subject only to the constraints imposed by their relationship with the principal.[15] The *scope* for diverging interests will determine, however, the incentive for the agent to act against the principal's interests. Importantly, it is possible that the interests of the agent are altered by the deployment of control mechanisms or that the agent has manipulated those of the principal. Therefore, one must seek to uncover the principal and the agent's *initial* (core) interests.

Both the CJEU and the Commission - the principals in our setting- seek to achieve adequate compliance with EU law and policy. They seek 'a broader and deeper decision-making competence for the supranational institutions themselves and for the EU as a whole'.[16] The CJEU has systematically interpreted EU laws in ways that the Member States did not intend, developing legal doctrines and, thus, changing the EU legal system.[17] Furthermore, the Commission has often been portrayed as policy entrepreneur in the literature.[18] Pollack asserts that the Commission behaves as a 'competence maximizer', using its competences and discretion, amongst others, 'to create a single internal market free from internal trade barriers and distortions to competition'.[19] Turning to the case at hand, the Commission's immediate response to *Bosman* comes as a small surprise. Drawing on the support from the CJEU's ruling, it initially pressed for a far-reaching liberalization of the football players' market.

The core interests of the CJEU and the Commission conflict with those of their agents, SGBs, whose key interest in relation to public actors is to ensure as much decision-making autonomy as possible.[20] Pre-*Bosman* actions demonstrate that, unless compliance fits the governing body's private goals and objectives, SGBs will not comply with EU laws and policies in the absence of control mechanisms.

9.3.2 Information Asymmetries

In addition to conflicting preferences, most PA relationships entail some degree of information asymmetries. SGBs, however, are highly specialized organizations

---

[15]Kiewiet and McCubbins 1991, p. 5.

[16]Tallberg 2003, p. 28.

[17]Alter 1998.

[18]Laffan 1997.

[19]Pollack 2003, pp. 35–36, 321.

[20]Geeraert et al. 2014.

that are mostly based outside the EU. This implies that the principals have great difficulties observing the agents' actions and that they are confronted with hidden information. Moreover, SGBs are not known for adhering to a high degree of transparency. This provides them with many opportunities to act against their principals' wishes.

In conclusion, where the CJEU and the Commission do not deploy control mechanisms, SGBs feel little incentive to comply with EU laws and policies because they have both the motives and the opportunity to act against their principals' interests.

9.4 The EU's Options for Controlling SGBs

Geeraert and Drieskens demonstrate that the EU can and does use two routes to control the behaviour of SGBs: the EU law route and the EU sports policy route.[21] Each route incorporates three controlling instruments: monitoring, sanctioning and steering. In deploying them, the Commission and the CJEU can alter the incentives of SGBs, so that compliance with EU laws and policies is more attractive. This section briefly outlines the mechanisms the EU has at its disposal to control SGBs. It further demonstrates that *Bosman* was crucial in activating these mechanisms in both the EU law and the EU sports policy route as well as in defining their nature and effect.

9.4.1 The EU Law Route

SGBs act on behalf of a broad and diverse group of principals, including national federations, clubs, and athletes.[22] For instance, SGBs conduct a number of tasks on behalf of the latter, including the regulation of important parts of their employment. Athletes generally lack statutory options for sanctioning SGBs; yet this does not imply that they are powerless. *Bosman* demonstrated that stakeholders, including athletes, who are unhappy with sports rules, can turn to the CJEU to have their interests protected. Sports rules issued by SGBs often fall within the realm of the EU's internal market competence, most directly in relation to free movement and competition laws.[23] The CJEU and the Commission are interesting venues for redress for athletes and other principals, because they monitor and enforce compliance with EU law. The Commission steers and sanctions SGBs; the CJEU's powers are confined to sanctioning breaches of EU law.

---

[21] Geeraert and Drieskens 2015; Geeraert and Drieskens, forthcoming.

[22] Ibid., pp. 1450–1451.

[23] Parrish 2003.

9.4.1.1 Sanctioning

In PA terms, *Bosman* is an example of a classic form of sanctioning, namely 'overruling the agent'.[24] The CJEU, as enforcer of subjective rights, and the Commission, as public enforcer of competition law, can abolish a sports rule by taking judicial and quasi-judicial decisions, respectively. The short-term effect of *Bosman* was, thus, the abolishment of the system regulating the international transfer of football players - as defined by FIFA and the Union of European Football Associations (UEFA) - and a quota system restricting the number of foreign players in a team, both of which violated the free movement of workers. The CJEU overruled FIFA and UEFA because they demonstrated slack: their rules were incompliant with EU law. The ruling constitutes the first time that the CJEU sanctioned SGBs for breaching EU law, which implies a long-term effect as well. Indeed, even when sanctions are not imposed, merely acknowledging the possibility of a sanction 'provides a measure of latent control over the agent's actions'.[25] The CJEU can only rule on cases that stem from litigation. By demonstrating that stakeholders unhappy with sports rules can ultimately turn to the CJEU in order to secure their interests, *Bosman* shows that incompliance with EU law may lead to sanctions and this incentivizes SGBs to comply with EU law. Put simply, SGBs will avoid accruing costs and, consequently,—sanctioning.

9.4.1.2 Monitoring

By monitoring the agent's actions, the principal decreases information asymmetries concerning the agent's actions and interests, leaving fewer opportunities for the agent to act against the principals' wishes. *Bosman* resulted in a more rigorous monitoring of SGBs' compliance with EU law, because it empowered the Commission. Indeed, building on the ruling the Commission has more leeway to make use of its competences.[26] As guardian of the Treaties, it ensures that both the provisions of the Treaties and the institutions' decisions are implemented; as enforcer of competition law, the Commission is empowered to investigate whether SGBs' practices, qualifying as both undertakings and associations of undertakings, are anti-competitive. In PA terms, its capacities and actions are in line with *police patrol* monitoring, where the principal engages in continuous and detailed vigilance of the agent.

Yet *Bosman* also increased the occurrence of a second form of monitoring described in the PA literature as *fire alarm monitoring*, where the principal relies on third parties for information on slack.[27] Encouraged by the CJEU's ruling,

---

[24]McCubbins and Schwartz 1984; McCubbins et al. 1989; Pollack 1997.

[25]Calvert et al. 1989, p. 604.

[26]Tallberg 2003, p. 137. According to Parrish, '*the Commission used the ruling to justify greater scrutiny of sporting activity*', see Parrish 2003, p. 9.

[27]McCubbins and Schwartz 1984.

many unsatisfied sport stakeholders turned to the Commission. As a result, 'the Commission's sports-related competition law caseload swelled considerably'.[28]

9.4.1.3 Steering

Faced with an increased caseload after *Bosman*, the Commission is constrained by a lack of resources and political pressure. Accordingly, it turned to steering rather than sanctions in the form of prohibition decisions. Steering occurs 'when a principal does not actually use sanctions to induce compliant behaviour, but tries to change the actions of an agent in a pre-defined direction through bargaining or persuasion'.[29] Doing so, the principal tries to move 'the de facto behaviour of the agent in the direction of more perfect representation', thus limiting the leeway the agent enjoys after delegation has taken place.[30]

The implicit threat of sanctions in the case of incompliant behaviour casts a 'shadow of hierarchy' over the principal's steering efforts: a credible threat of sanctions creates an incentive for SGBs to change their behaviour.[31] Indeed, when SGBs' do not adjust their behaviour, the Commission retains the option of sanctioning. SGBs will avoid this cost and, therefore, be incentivised to comply.

9.4.2 The EU Sports Policy Route

Bosman increased the demand for a more coordinated approach to sport within the EU.[32] Moreover, the swelling caseload that surged after the ruling pointed at governance issues in SGBs: it was indicative of how many internal sport stakeholders were not satisfied with the way their interests are represented. This has resulted in (careful) EU efforts to improve the governance of SGBs. The Sport Unit emerged within the DG Education and Culture to coordinate the Commission's actions regarding sport and in 2009 the Lisbon Treaty granted the EU explicit competence for a direct sports policy. Article 165 of the Treaty on the Functioning of the European Union ('TFEU') grants the EU a formal role in the field of sport. As the EU was only given a supporting and coordinating sporting competence, EU policy-making in sport has remained limited to the use of non-hierarchical instruments—*steering* in PA terminology.

---

[28]Parrish 2003, p. 9.

[29]Geeraert and Drieskens 2015, p. 1454.

[30]Ibid., p. 1455.

[31]Scharpf 1994; Héritier and Rhodes 2011.

[32]Vermeersch 2009.

9.4.2.1 Sanctioning

In principle, the EU could overrule SGBs by issuing legislation. The geographical location of SGBs limits the EU's options, since most of them have established headquarters in Switzerland or in other non-EU countries. Nonetheless, the EU may issue legislation in certain areas, particularly related to the internal market, which would impact SGBs. The scope for these sanctions remains rather limited, nonetheless, because the EU's competences only cover a limited range of SGBs' activities and sanctions lack political support. *Bosman* did little to change this situation.

9.4.2.2 Monitoring

The EU institutions' more coordinated approach towards sport has resulted in coordinated attention for sporting issues following *Bosman*. The Commission is responsible for executing policies and closely follows the actions of SGBs in that regard.[33] In a manner similar to the EU law route, it can monitor in a direct manner (police patrol), discouraging agency slack via surveillance, or rely on third parties to alert it to agency transgressions (fire alarm).

9.4.2.3 Steering

As EU sports policy develops, the Commission increasingly engages in steering to influence SGBs' behaviour. A direct result of *Bosman*, the Commission's efforts in stimulating a social dialogue in sport in order to resolve labour conflicts is an example of steering. The Commission provides important financial resources, brings actors together, supports projects and studies, tries to reconcile differences between actors and exerts a light form of pressure on SGBs.[34] Remarkably, such steering efforts have been, in certain cases, successful in changing SGBs' behaviour despite the absence of imminent sanctions.

Both the (rational choice inspired) governance and PA literatures hold that the effectiveness of steering and monitoring (in terms of achieving deliberate compliance on the part of agents) largely depend on whether they operate under a shadow of hierarchy.[35] Put simply, the agent will adjust its behaviour because it fears the principal will impose costs in the form of hierarchical measures. Under the EU

[33]EU sports policy is devised in interplay between the Commission, the Council and the Parliament. As a result of the EU's limited sporting competence, the Council ultimately defines the EU's sports policy. Practice shows that both the Council and the Parliament set out priorities in resolutions and even request policy measures from the Commission.

[34]Geeraert 2014.

[35]Sharpf 1994; Pollack 1997; Héritier and Rhodes 2011.

law route, SGBs adjust their behaviour to comply with EU law because they fear (quasi-) judicial rulings by the CJEU and the Commission. By contrast, under the EU sports policy route, sanctions do not frame the Commission's steering and monitoring activities, since the Commission cannot replace its non-hierarchical instruments with hierarchy. Geeraert and Drieskens demonstrate that, nonetheless, FIFA and UEFA show a willingness to comply with the EU's steering because incompliance may reduce the Commission's goodwill in applying EU law to FIFA and UEFA. In addition, incompliance can potentially lead to legislation in (a limited number of) football-related areas.[36] In brief, incompliance with policy may thus indirectly lead to sanctions (and, thus, costs) under the EU law route.

Even though the EU does not have a strong sporting competence, steering in the EU sports policy route does operate under a shadow of hierarchy. *Bosman*, for a large part, imposed this 'shadow'. In fact, SGBs' compliance with steering under EU sports policy is a long-term consequence of *Bosman*. The next section demonstrates how SGBs in the post-*Bosman* era acknowledge the possibility of costly sanctions and conscious about potential sanctions, SGBs are more likely to comply with the EU's wishes.[37] Moreover, *Bosman* effectuated more rigorous monitoring of SGBs' compliance with EU law, which increased the likelihood of sanctions in the form of Commission decisions. This landmark case, thus, casts a shadow of hierarchy over SGBs, which in turn induces compliance.

9.5 The Shadow of *Bosman*

The previous section demonstrated how the EU's power is rooted in the ability to sanction SGBs. Costly sanctions provide SGBs with an important incentive to comply with the EU policies. However, in order to achieve significant compliance through monitoring, steering and (passive or active) threatening with sanctions, there must be (1) a credible threat of sanctions in the case of incompliance and (2) sanctions should be of a sufficiently large magnitude.[38]

SGB's perceptions of EU threats are, thus, a key factor in determining compliance. Before *Bosman*, SGBs did not give credence to the fact that the CJEU or the Commission would actually abolish a sports rule. As Parrish notes, sport and European law operated in separate realms in this period, as there was no hard enforcement of EU law on the sports sector[39]- there was no credible occurrence of sanctions. Although the CJEU's rulings in *Walrave*[40] and *Donà*[41] demonstrated

[36]Geeraert and Drieskens 2015, p. 1456.

[37]Calvert et al. 1989, p. 604.

[38]McCubbins et al. 1989; Scharpf 1994.

[39]Parrish 2003, p. 252.

[40]Case 36/74 *Walrave and Koch v. Union Cycliste Internationale*, ECLI:EU:C:1974:140.

[41]Case 13/76 *Gaetano Donà v Mario Mantero*, ECLI:EU:C:1976:115.

that sport is subject to EU law, no direct sanctions were imposed on SGBs. *Bosman* changed everything. Because it altered SGBs' perception of the EU's ability to sanction incompliance with EU law, increasing the probability that breaches of EU law will lead to costs.[42] In addition, it demonstrated the potentially high costs of a CJEU ruling: disruptive effects for sports governance and the subsequent decrease of decision-making autonomy due to the empowerment of the Commission and increased litigation, two elements that SGBs fear particularly.[43] Realising the far-reach of the enforcement of EU law, *Bosman* has encouraged SGBs to adopt a friendly demeanour towards the EU and to be open to its preferences and concerns in relation to both law and policy. The mixture of these factors constitutes the *Bosman* 'shadow,' which the EU employs to control SGBs.

Does this shadow function as a 'ring of power', to use Tolkien's Lord of the Rings trilogy as an analogy, bestowing upon the EU unlimited control over all SGBs? Certainly not. In fact, there are several indications that the *Bosman* shadow often does not loom large. First, despite the ruling, SGBs are not always fully aware of the EU's powers. Second, even when they are, several factors limit the credible occurrence and magnitude of sanctions and as such diminish the shadow of *Bosman*.

In order to assess the magnitude and likelihood of sanctions, this section draws from the market power literature because the sanction to overrule an SGB is, in essence, an externalisation of the EU's market principles.[44] The market power literature proffers that the size and relevance of the EU's market determine the extent of potential costs for incompliance and its regulatory capacity and cohesiveness determine the likelihood of inflicting sanctions. These factors a priori determine SGBs' perceptions of both potential costs of incompliance and the EU's ability to monitor and punish violations of EU law and policy. Higher or lower scores on each of these factors (which vary over time) thus influence the largeness of the shadow of *Bosman*.

9.5.1 Market Size and Relevance

According to Drezner, external actors adapt their standards to the EU's preferences because of the size and relevance of its market.[45] In other words, the higher the expected gains of market access, the greater the (potential) cost of non-adaptation

[42]Bach and Newman 2007, p. 832.

[43]IOC-FIFA Joint Declaration of 11 July 2007, EU white paper on sport: Much work remains to be done. Olympic.org. http://www.olympic.org/content/news/media-resources/manual-news/1999-2009/2007/07/11/ioc-fifa-joint-declaration---eu-white-paper-on-sport-much-work-remains-to-be-done. Accessed 7 July 2015; Infantino 2006.

[44]Damro 2012.

[45]Drezner 2005.

and sanctions. The EU internal market constitutes a very large and (often) very important part of the geographical area in which SGBs deploy their regulating activities. When a rule or a decision by these organisations is not in conformity with the EU provisions, they face the abolishment of this rule. Following this line of reasoning, when their actions are not in line with the common EU standards, they risk being overruled by legislation. This incentivizes SGBs to conform their market-related rules and decisions to the EU's standards. Tellingly, FIFA amended its transfer system in accordance with the CJEU's *Bosman* ruling, universally removing restrictive elements instead of only for the EU internal market. For European-level SGBs such as UEFA, the EU internal market covers an even greater part of the regulated area. These organisations face a higher likelihood that the rules they issue have an economic effect within the internal market.

Respectively, when the EU internal market does not constitute a significant area of economic activity for a particular SGB, that body faces significantly less costs for not complying with the EU's policy and incentives are considerably lower to change their behaviour. Indeed, the EU can only impose costly sanctions on SGBs when they produce sports rules which have an effect within the EU's internal market. In addition, the internal market must constitute a large and important part of the geographical area in which the SGB deploys its regulating activities. These conditions are only met by those SGBs that regulate a significantly commercialised sport.

9.5.2 Regulatory Capacity

Regulatory capacity pertains to the EU's ability to formulate, monitor, and enforce market-related rules and policies. It is shaped by three factors: *regulatory coherence*, *regulatory expertise* and *sanctioning authority*. Low regulatory capacity negatively influences the EU's 'ability to identify regulatory challenges, develop policy solutions, implement them, and provide competent monitoring'.[46] In PA terms, it decreases the likelihood that the EU will impose sanctions in response to slack.

Regarding sport, a distinction should be made between the EU's regulatory capacity under the EU law route and, respectively, the EU sports policy route. Whereas the EU's regulatory capacity in the former is generally high, this is not the case in the latter. Several reasons explain why the EU's regulatory capacity is not at a maximum level under either route. That the EU's regulatory functioning is less than maximal negatively influences the SGBs' anticipated application of sanctions.[47]

---

[46]Bach and Newman 2007, p. 831.

[47]Ibid., p. 832.

In the EU law route, *regulatory coherence* is high, since the authority to enforce EU law has been delegated to the CJEU and the Commission, which are two regulatory bodies with the authority to shape and enforce market rules. Both have a *sanctioning authority*: they can abolish a sports rule or decision if it breaches EU market principles. At the same time, the EU's level of *regulatory expertise* is not that high. Sport is still a relatively new legal issue and only limited CJEU case law is available. Most importantly, the Commission lacks the resources to deal with the increasing number of sports-related competition law complaints.

In the EU sports policy route, the EU's regulatory capacity is much lower. *Regulatory coherence* is low because sports policy is guided by the principle of subsidiarity. The EU holds only a supporting competence and does not have the capacity to harmonize Member State legislation and, thus, Member States have the ultimate authority over policy. Moreover, limited resources, including personnel, paralyze the EU's *regulatory expertise*. Sport is a relatively new EU policy endeavour, too, meaning that knowledge building is in its infancy and is ongoing. Finally, statutory authority to impose costs via *sanctioning* is also limited - if and when SGBs do not comply with sports policy or refuse to dialogue with the EU, the EU does not hold authority to impose fines or ban market entry.

Even though the Commission does not have statutory options for imposing sanctions on SGBs in the EU sports policy route, limiting the likelihood of sanctions, this chapter highlights that SGBs may still face sanctions when they do not comply with sports policy. SGBs fear that non-compliance with EU policy measures will decrease the Commission's goodwill in the application of EU law and the respect from the EU institutions for the autonomy of SGBs to regulate sport more generally. Non-compliance, thus, can potentially spark increased regulatory activities in sport-related areas.[48] The EU's low regulatory capacity in EU sports policy is counter-balanced by its higher degree of regulatory capacity in EU law, which corrects agency slack by increasing the likelihood of sanctions.

9.5.3 Internal Cohesiveness

The academic consensus is that the EU's power in the international realm cannot be understood without taking into account internal cohesiveness.[49] It reflects the degree to which Member States coagulate around a single message and manage 'to present that message with a single voice, without members of the group breaking away and undermining the collective message'.[50] While a 'single voice' does not automatically predicate the imposition of the EU's will externally, a lack of internal cohesiveness decreases the likelihood of sanctions.

[48] Geeraert and Drieskens 2015.

[49] Da Conceição-Heldt and Meunier 2014; Fioretos 2010; Quaglia 2014.

[50] Da Conceição-Heldt and Meunier 2014, p. 964.

Scholars agree that Member States demonstrate low cohesiveness regarding the appropriateness of EU interventions in sport.[51] In general, the Member States see national sovereignty as 'a positive value that is intimately bound up with the unity, identity, and raison d'être of the state'.[52] Certain Member States especially seek to retain national control over sports issues. Low cohesiveness influences negatively SGBs' anticipated application of sanctions[53]; it decreases the likelihood that SGBs' incompliance with legal or policy measures results in sanctions. For instance, research confirms that a lack of political will precludes the Commission's active use of its competition law competence in the field of sport.[54] The lack of a strong support from Member States explains why, in the aftermath of *Bosman*, the negotiations between the Commission and football SGBs on a new football transfer system lasted almost six years, and not all restrictive elements of that system were removed.[55]

9.6 Decreasing the Shadow of *Bosman*

The previous section demonstrates how certain institutional features a priori decrease the likelihood of sanctions. This section explores how SGBs have further eroded their credible occurrence. There is a growing consensus among PA scholars that the agent can decrease the principal's incentive to control by 'manipulating' the principal's preferences through skilful self-assertiveness.[56] If the agent alters the principal's preferences so they align with those of the agent, interests no longer diverge and there is no need for the principal to control the agent.

Indeed, SGBs are not powerless when faced with EU control. Purposeful and proactive actors, they deploy a number of strategies that allow them to alter the preferences of the Commission and football stakeholders in order to mitigate EU control.[57] Firstly, they lobby the Commission, the European Parliament, and Member States. Secondly, they manipulate the preferences of their stakeholders so that they do not seek recourse before the CJEU or the Commission. As a result, SGBs negatively influence the credible occurrence of sanctions.

---

[51]Parrish 2003.

[52]Tallberg 2003, p. 29.

[53]Bach and Newman 2007, p. 832.

[54]Niemann and Brand 2008, p. 98; *See also* Tallberg 2003, p. 137; Here, the Member States thus function as the Commission's principal, see Geeraert and Drieskens 2015 and Geeraert 2016.

[55]Irving 2002; Niemann and Brand 2008.

[56]Hawkins and Jacoby 2006; Delreux and Kerremans 2010; Niemann and Huigens 2011; Geeraert and Drieskens 2015.

[57]Geeraert and Drieskens 2015a.

9.6.1 Manipulating the Preferences of the Commission, the Parliament and the Member States

As a starting point, SGBs can manipulate the preferences of their principal - the Commission. The Commission is very open to lobbying, because it relies on the expert knowledge and legitimacy provided by non-governmental organizations.[58] SGBs certainly have a great deal of expertise regarding (regulatory) sport matters, but they can also help the Commission enhance its legitimacy in the sports policy realm, which strengthens its position in the inter-institutional decision-making process. SGBs give support to certain Commission initiatives that do not contradict their own preferences, such as the promotion of grass-roots sport or physical activity. SGBs have, subsequently, engaged with the Commission in order 'to promote awareness of sporting exceptionalism', manipulating the Commission's preferences in terms of both EU law and EU sports policy.[59] This has allowed them to obtain a more favourable application of EU (competition) law to sport as well as influencing the direction of EU sports policy.

Another point that deserves closer attention is that SGBs indirectly mitigate the Commission's control by manipulating the preferences of the Parliament, which is also very open to lobbying.[60] The Parliament's control over the Commission in sports policy matters has increased since the entry into force of the Lisbon Treaty. Although the Parliament initially called for increased EU control over SGBs, lobbying by sports actors resulted in strong support for the autonomy of sport and certain sports rules that may breach EU law.[61]

Finally, SGBs indirectly mitigate the Commission's control by manipulating the preferences of the Member States, which have ample control options over the Commission in the EU sports policy route and (albeit slightly fewer options) in the EU law route. Although it is generally acknowledged that lobbying Member States is much more difficult because of a more limited access for lobbyists, the sports sector holds a few advantages over other sectors with regard to influencing politics. Firstly, SGBs can prevent countries and their football clubs from participating in international competitions or withdraw their privilege of hosting important events. Acting contrary to SGBs' preferences may also harm a country's future chances to host a sporting event. Thus, Member States have been reluctant to include issues on the agenda that would enhance the EU's control, such as good governance in international sport organisations.[62] Secondly, the sports world maintains a close relationship with national politicians; national sport federations often have strong ties with their national governments and SGBs can capitalise on this.[63]

[58]Bouwen 2002, pp. 369–371.

[59]García and Weatherill 2012, p. 242; Geeraert and Drieskens 2015a.

[60]Coen and Richardson 2009.

[61]Geeraert and Drieskens 2015a, p. 1460.

[62]Ibid.

[63]Niemann and Brand 2008, p. 98; García and Weatherill 2012, p. 242.

Accordingly, SGBs have garnered support from the EU Heads of State and Government for the idea that they deserve special treatment under EU law and that the EU institutions should respect their decision-making autonomy.[64] Such direct lobbying moulded the Commission's rather generous treatment of sport cases.[65]

9.6.2 Influencing the Preferences of Stakeholders

The general consensus in the EU literature is that the CJEU is significantly more relieved from Member State and Parliament) control than the Commission.[66] This has two implications. First, as mentioned, the CJEU has interpreted EU laws in a way not intended by Member States and pursued a pro-integrationist agenda.[67] It has strengthened the EU through its rulings, enlarged the power of the Commission and the Parliament and increased the scope and effectiveness of EU law. Other chapters in this book emphasise that the CJEU continued to expand the applicability of EU law to sport rules. The further proliferation of jurisprudence in sport cases, including potentially a 'new' *Bosman*, would empower the Commission, since the latter has more leeway in relation to Member States when it draws on the support from a 'less constrained' CJEU.[68] The likelihood of sanctions would, therefore, increase inevitably. Second, SGBs stand little chance of indirectly manipulating the CJEU's preferences. Yet the CJEU's power 'is inherently limited by the reality that courts must wait for litigants to present [it] with cases'.[69] If SGBs influence the preferences of stakeholders who seek redress before the CJEU, they can prevent the proliferation of jurisprudence in sport cases.

Geeraert and Drieskens demonstrate that SGBs employ three strategies to this end: they have expanded the system of sports arbitration, settled cases outside the CJEU and institutionalised the consultation of stakeholders.[70] Firstly, SGBs have mitigated the proliferation of EU jurisprudence and regulatory practice by the Commission by expanding sports arbitration, a system that enables the sports world to settle disputes according to its own laws.[71] The Court of Arbitration for

[64]Conclusions of the Presidency of the European Council of 7–9 December 2000 (Nice), Annex IV – Declaration on the specific characteristics of sport and its social function in Europe, of which account should be taken in implementing common policies; Presidency Conclusions of the Brussels European Council of 11-12 December 2008, Annex V – European Council Declaration on sport Presidency Conclusions.

[65]Parrish 2003, p. 252; Weatherill 2003; Niemann and Brand 2008.

[66]Alter 1998; Pollack 2003; Tallberg 2003.

[67]Alter 1998.

[68]Tallberg 2003, p. 137.

[69]Alter 2012, p 84.

[70]Geeraert and Drieskens 2015a, pp. 1459–1461.

[71]Foster 2003; Duval 2015.

Sport ('CAS') provides sport stakeholders with a more cost-effective venue for control than the EU law route, since it is more flexible, less costly and allows for faster settlement. Such benefits entice stakeholders to seek redress before national arbitration courts and the CAS instead of the CJEU or the Commission.[72] Secondly, certain SGBs have settled cases outside the CJEU by offering stakeholders compensation rather than awaiting the Court's ruling. Finally, SGBs have frequently incorporated powerful sport stakeholders in their decision-making by involving them in consultative bodies.[73]

9.7 Conclusions

If it is assumed that SGBs act in a rational manner - seeking to maximise the attainment of their relatively fixed preferences, then it is clear that the Commission's and the CJEU's capacity to limit incompliance with EU laws and policies depends on the available control mechanisms and the credibility and magnitude of sanctions. *Bosman* plays a crucial role in this regard. This landmark ruling changed both the SGBs' perception of the EU's ability to sanction incompliance via EU law and demonstrated the potential costs of such sanctions. The fact that the EU has influenced the SGBs' behaviour both through the EU law route and the EU sports policy route is, therefore, for a large part, thanks to *Bosman*.

However, this chapter highlights that the shadow of *Bosman* does not extend infinitely. The EU's market size, regulatory capacity and cohesiveness a priori influence the magnitude and likelihood of sanctions. SGBs have employed successful strategies that limit their credible occurrence in case of incompliance. These caveats limit the power of the EU *vis-à-vis* SGBs; yet they do not render the EU powerless. Additionally, a change in one variable that determines the likelihood of sanctions may increase the power of the EU. More cohesiveness among Member States and more resources and expertise in relation to sports policy for instance may change the *status quo* significantly. A new *Bosman* ruling with far-reaching consequences for sports governance would empower the Commission, thereby increasing the shadow of hierarchy under which monitoring and steering encourage compliance with both law and policy. SGBs' strategies may have decreased the likelihood of a new *Bosman*, but the scope of sporting rules potentially infringing EU law remains large and the CJEU is much more detached from political pressure than the Commission.[74]

[72]Kiewiet and McCubbins 1991, p. 27.

[73]Irving 2002, p. 220; Holt 2006, p. 116; Geeraert et al. 2014.

[74]In *Meca-Medina* (Case C-519/04 P *David Meca-Medina and Igor Majcen v. Commission*, ECLI:EU:C:2006:492), the CJEU essentially held that the notion that a rule would have a purely sporting nature or aim does not suffice to automatically exempt it from the scope of the Treaty.

The Commission would be well advised to scrutinise sporting rules to keep the shadow of *Bosman* alive and consolidate its influence over SGBs. Most importantly, SGBs would have the incentive to comply with the Commission's steering when it acts via a strong mandate from Member States, because incompliance may change Member States' preferences. The Member States currently display a relatively stable preference for EU institutions to respect SGBs' decision-making autonomy, which dictates the Commission's generous treatment of sport cases under competition law. This current state of affairs may change should SGBs prove incompliant with Member States' wishes, increasing the likelihood of sanctions in the long run. These observations indicate that there is certainly room for a more ambitious sports policy, devised and supported by Member States, directed at SGBs. Twenty years after the seismic *Bosman* ruling, it is clear that the EU has only scratched the surface of its power in the governance of international sport.

References

Alter KJ (1998) Who are the "Masters of the Treaty"? European governments and the European court of justice. Int Org 52:121–147

Alter KJ (2012) Understanding the European court's political power. In: Zimmermann H, Dür A (eds) Key controversies in European integration. Palgrave, Basingstoke, pp 80–87

Bach D, Newman L (2007) The European regulatory state and global public policy: micro-institutions, macro-influence. J Eur Public Policy 14:827–846

Börzel T (2010) European governance: negotiation and competition in the shadow of hierarchy. J Common Market Stud 48:191–219

Bouwen P (2002) corporate lobbying in the European union: the logic of access. J Eur Public Policy 9:365–390

Calvert RL et al (1989) A theory of political control and agency discretion. Am J Polit Sci 33:588–611

Coen D, Richardson J (eds) (2009) Lobbying the European union. Oxford University Press, Oxford

Da Conceição-Heldt E, Meunier S (2014) Speaking with a single voice: internal cohesiveness and external effectiveness of the EU in global governance. J Eur Public Policy 21:961–979

Dahl R (1957) The concept of power. behavioural. Science 2:201–215

Damro C (2012) Market power Europe. J Eur Public Policy 19:682–699

Delreux T, Kerremans B (2010) How agents weaken their principals' incentives to control: the case of EU negotiations and EU member states in multilateral negotiations. J Eur Integr 32:357–374

Drezner DW (2005) Globalization, harmonization, and competition: the different pathways to policy convergence. J Eur Public Policy 12:841–859

Duval A (2015) The court of arbitration for sport and EU law: chronicle of an encounter. Maastricht J Eur Comp Law 22:224–255

Fioretos KO (2010) Capitalist diversity and the international regulation of Hedge funds. Rev Int Polit Econ 17:696 723

Foster K (2003) Is there a global sports law? Entertainment Law 2:1–18

García B, Weatherill S (2012) Engaging with the EU in order to minimize its impact: sport and the negotiation of the treaty of Lisbon. J Eur Public Policy 19:238–256

Geeraert A (2014) New EU governance modes in professional sport: enhancing throughput legitimacy. J Contemp Eur Res 10:302–321

Geeraert A (2016) The European Union in international sports governance. Palgrave Macmillan, London

Geeraert A, Drieskens E (2015) The EU controls FIFA and UEFA: a principal-agent perspective. J Eur Public Policy 22:1448–1466
Geeraert A, Drieskens E (forthcoming) Bipolar Power Europe: the EU as a force for good in international sports governance
Geeraert A, Mrkonjicb M, Chappeletb JJ (2014) A rationalist perspective on the autonomy of international sport governing bodies: towards a pragmatic autonomy in the steering of sports. Int J Sport Policy Politics. doi:10.1080/19406940.2014.925953
Hawkins D, Jacoby W (2006) How agents matter. In: Hawkins DG, Lake DA, Nielson DL, Tierney MJ (eds) Delegation and agency in international organizations. Cambridge University Press, Cambridge, pp 199–228
Héritier A, Rhodes M (eds) (2011) New modes of governance in Europe. Governing in the shadow of hierarchy, Palgrave, Basingstoke
Holt M (2006) UEFA, Governance and the control of club competition in European football. Football Governance Research Centre, Birkbeck University of London, London
Huber JD, Shipan CR (2000) The costs of control: legislators, agencies, and transaction costs. Legislative Stud Q 25:25–52
Infantino G (2006) Meca-Medina: a step backwards for the European sports model and the specificity of sport? Sports Law: Adm Pract 13:3–4
Irving J (2002) Red Card: the battle over European football's transfer system. Univ Miami Law Rev 56:667–726
Kiewiet DR, McCubbins MD (1991) The logic of delegation: congressional parties and the appropriations process. Chicago University Press, Chicago
Kooiman J (ed) (1993) Modern governance: new government-society interactions. Sage, London
Laffan B (1997) From policy entrepreneur to policy manager: the challenge facing the European commission. J Eur Public Policy 4:422–438
March JG, Olsen JP (1984) The new institutionalism: organizational factors in political life. Am Polit Sci Rev 78:734–749
McCubbins MD, Schwartz T (1984) Congressional oversight overlooked: police patrols versus fire alarms. Am J Polit Sci 28:165–179
McCubbins MD, Noll RG, Weingast BR (1989) Structure and process, politics and policy: administrative arrangements and the political control of agencies. Va Law Rev 75:431–483
Nielson DL, Tierney MJ (2003) Delegation to international organizations: agency theory and world bank environmental reform. Int Org 57:241–276
Niemann A, Brand A (2008) The impact of European integration on domestic sport: the case of German football. Sport Soc 11:90–106
Niemann A, Huigens J (2011) The European Union's role in the G8: a principal-agent perspective. J Eur Public Policy 18:420–442
Parrish R (2003) Sports law and policy in the European Union. Manchester University Press, Manchester
Pollack MA (1997) Delegation, agency, and agenda setting in the European community. Int Org 57:99–134
Pollack MA (2003) The engines of European integration. Delegation, agency and agenda setting in the EU. Oxford University Press, Oxford
Quaglia L (2014) The sources of European Union influence in international financial regulatory fora. J Eur Public Policy 21:327–345
Ross S (1973) The economic theory of agency: the principal's problem. Am Econ Rev 63:134–139
Scharpf F (1994) Games real actors could play: positive and negative coordination in embedded negotiations. J Theor Polit 6:27–53
Tallberg J (2003) European governance and supranational institutions. Making States Comply, Routledge, New York
Vermeersch A (2009) The future EU sports policy: hollow words on hallowed ground? Int Sports Law J 9:3–7
Weatherill S (2003) "Fair Play, Please!": recent developments in the application of EC law to sport. Common Market Law Rev 40:51–93

Chapter 10
The *Lex Sportiva* and EU Law: The Academic Lawyer's Path Before and After *Bosman*

Stephen Weatherill

Abstract The transformative effect of the Court's ruling in Bosman is widely recognised and has been the subject of much exploration. EU sports law is in important respects built on Bosman as a foundation stone. Bosman, in combination with the rapid pace of change in the broadcasting sector, has pushed sport and the law into an ever tighter embrace as a result of, in short, the rise of commercialisation. In this paper I look at Bosman's effect on academic law. Nowhere is the transformative effect more striking. Before Bosman there was … if not nothing, then remarkably little. Today EU sports law is well-established as an academic discipline. The Court's refusal in Bosman to grant sport a reliably defined zone of autonomy from the application of EU law lies at the root of this growth. Bosman changed (almost) everything.

Keywords EU law · Sport · Lex sportiva · Autonomy · Specificity

Contents

S. Weatherill (✉)
Law and Somerville College, University of Oxford, Oxford, UK
e-mail: stephen.weatherill@law.ox.ac.uk

A. Duval and B. Van Rompuy (eds.), *The Legacy of* Bosman,
ASSER International Sports Law Series, DOI 10.1007/978-94-6265-120-3_10

10.1 Introduction

A few years ago I was invited to contribute to the book which ultimately emerged as *The Past and Future of EU Law: the Classics of EU law revisited on the 50th anniversary of the Rome Treaty*, edited by Miguel Poiares Maduro and Loïc Azoulai and published in 2010 by Hart.[1] The idea behind the book was to choose the landmark cases of EU law—there were twelve—and, for each case, to collect four papers written by different authors tracing the impact of the decision and, most of all, to explain just *why* it rates as a landmark.

I was allocated *Bosman*. And I took as my title '*Bosman* changed everything: the Rise of EC Sports Law'. It was an exaggeration, of course, designed to grab attention. But it was not much of an exaggeration. *Bosman* might not have changed *everything*, but it was radically transformative on a number of levels. It marked the burial of any realistic aspiration of governing bodies in sport to find an *intellectual* basis to keep EU law at bay and it showed too that the days of finding *practical* ways to keep sport out of the courts were coming to an end. After *Bosman*, the Court of Justice of the European Union (CJEU) still had to perform some cleaning up of its legal reasoning, most of all achieved subsequently in *Meca-Medina*, and governing bodies still had to commit to some fights to protect their autonomy which they would learn from by losing. But *Bosman* set a new tone and, most of all, it set EU law and sport on the collision course which was ultimately mediated in the admission of sport to the formal scope of EU competence as a result of the entry into force of the Lisbon Treaty with effect from 2009. No one can make sense of Article 165 TFEU if they don't know their *Bosman*.

In this contribution I reflect on how *Bosman* changed the *academic* landscape. EU sports law is a thriving academic discipline and a vibrant community of scholars nowadays. There are books, there are conferences, there are specialist journals, there are research institutes, there are eager postgraduate students. It was not always so much fun. It used to be quite lonely. *Bosman* changed (almost) everything.

10.2 Before *Bosman*: The Case(S) for Sporting Autonomy

> 'If a player could do just as he liked at the end of the football season, the wealthier clubs would at once snap up the best players ….'
>
> 'All professional football leagues elsewhere in the world have the combined retention and transfer system or one that amounts to it, which shows that it has the unqualified approval of those best fitted to judge….'
>
> 'In considering the system as a whole, it should be borne in mind that the present system, based on a stable league, does secure benefits to players which a smaller organisation might not be able to secure'.

[1]Maduro and Azoulai 2010.

A brief inspection of these observations might suggest they were pressed on the Court in defence of the transfer system challenged in *Bosman*. But they were not. In fact they pre-date *Bosman* by almost thirty years. They are extracted from the judgment in *Eastham* v *Newcastle United Football Club Ltd. and Others*, a decision of Wilberforce J sitting in the Chancery Division of the English High Court in July 1963.[2]

The ruling in *Eastham* found unlawful a system which had in barely modified form existed since the nineteenth century. This had allowed a club not simply to demand a transfer fee but also to 'retain' the player if an acceptable fee were not offered by another club and, in certain circumstances, not to pay him at all. This was immensely imbalanced and could and did force players out of the game to seek employment elsewhere even where another football club wanted to offer employment: Eastham brought his case because Newcastle's intransigence had precisely this effect on him. The full story behind a system which had a strong taste of a nineteenth century master and servant relationship can be gleaned from Wilberforce J's judgment. It tells of a maximum wage, applicable at the time of the dispute although abandoned by the time the case was decided, which was fixed at £20 per week during the football season. It is commonplace nowadays to read of top footballers being paid £200,000 a week. Wilberforce J in the High Court found that 'retain' element to be an unreasonable restraint of trade and therefore contrary to the English common law. It went too far in privileging employer interests over those of the employee.

The court did not rule against a collectively agreed and enforced transfer system in some form. Wilberforce J took the view that the system 'provides a means by which the poorer clubs can on occasions, obtain money, enabling them to stay in existence and improve their facilities' and more generally 'it provides a means by which clubs can part with a good player in a manner which will enable them to secure a replacement'.[3] He did not declare explicitly how a revised system should be shaped: this would go beyond the judicial function in a restraint of trade case. But he clearly left room for football's governing bodies to devise a system that was less brutally restrictive and therefore lawful. A revised system focusing on payment of a fee in return for agreement to transfer a player's registration, while ameliorating the players' position to some extent by suppressing the ability of the first club simply to retain the registration and in practice force the footballer to give up his career, was shaped. So a revised system lived on after the *Eastham* decision in 1964.

This was the road that led eventually to *Bosman* in the CJEU in Luxembourg.[4]

It is the similarity between the arguments advanced and largely rejected in *Eastham* and those tried over thirty years later in *Bosman* which is illuminating. The law report on *Eastham* records the claims made by the club and the Football

[2]*Eastham* v *Newcastle United Football Club Ltd. and Others* [1964] 3 All ER 139.

[3]Ibid., p. 437.

[4]Case C-415/93 *Union Royale Belge des Sociétés de Football Association and others v. Bosman and others*, ECLI:EU:C:1995:463.

League in defence of the system, and they are those set out above. The claim in favour of a transfer system that 'If a player could do just as he liked at the end of the football season, the wealthier clubs would at once snap up the best players' is best summarised as an argument for the transfer system to serve as a means to achieve *balance* in sport. The point that 'All professional football leagues elsewhere in the world have the combined retention and transfer system or one that amounts to it, which shows that it has the unqualified approval of those best fitted to judge' is an argument rooted in expertise: sport knows best, courts should keep out. And finally the submission that 'In considering the system as a whole, it should be borne in mind that the present system, based on a stable league, does secure benefits to players which a smaller organisation might not be able to secure' is, even under a generous interpretation, no more than an obstinate refusal to imagine that the world could ever be different.

In short these combine to make one central claim – that sport should be allowed autonomy from legal regulation. That was the core of the case made in defence of the transfer system in *Bosman* too. In fact, much of what was argued in *Eastham* was recycled in *Bosman*. It was dismissed in both cases in a way that was not precisely in line, because restraint of trade under the English common law does not exactly match EU internal market law, but nevertheless the rejections had a common core – that however special football might be, it is not so special that it can claim to maintain a system as restrictive and burdensome as that at stake in the cases.

In *Eastham* Wilberforce J said:

> … it was said that this system, the combined system of registration, retention and transfer fees, or something like it, is operated in all professional leagues and has been so operated for a long time. This is claimed as evidence that those who know best consider it to be in the general interest of the game. I do not accept this line of argument. The system is an employers' system, set up in an industry where the employers have succeeded in establishing a united monolithic front all over the world, and where it is clear that for the purpose of negotiation the employers are vastly more strongly organised than the employees. No doubt the employers all over the world consider the system a good system, but this does not prevent the court from considering whether it goes further than is reasonably necessary to protect their legitimate interests.

This is very close to the heart of the *Bosman* ruling in Luxembourg thirty years later.

10.3 The Quiet Life of the Academic Sports Lawyer Before *Bosman*

The loud echo of *Eastham* that can be found thirty years later in *Bosman* reveals how stagnant sports law was. And the same was true of the lonely world of academic sports law.

Walrave and Koch was famously the first case concerning sport decided by the CJEU.[5] It generated some interest, but not much. It was followed two years later by *Donà v Mantero*.[6] But the floodgates stayed resolutely shut. No further litigation reached Luxembourg for twenty years, until *Bosman*. There was a strong sense that sport was able in practice to keep its disputes out of the courts. It does so fairly successfully nowadays thanks to the relatively dense network of arbitration which has the Court of Arbitration for Sport (CAS) at the pinnacle, but before CAS it was more a question of raw power that preserved the autonomy of sports bodies from litigation before the ordinary courts. Court proceedings are long; careers in sport are short. Litigants tread warily.

Academics tread warily too. Before *Bosman* there was not much attention paid to EU law and sport. It occupied an esoteric niche.

I wrote a paper entitled 'Discrimination on Grounds of Nationality in Sport'. It was published in 1989[7] so *Bosman* was not even on the horizon. Despite the title, the main preoccupation of the paper is not really sport. My main concern was with the treatment under EU law of labour practices that discriminated on grounds of nationality put into effect by private parties and, in particular, the overlap in coverage of such practices by free movement and competition law. The Treaty provisions on free movement affecting persons bind private parties, whereas those concerning goods do not, so, I thought, there was a special structural problem exposed by examination of such labour practices. It is, in fact, still even today a structural oddity in EU law.[8] The particular problem which I diagnosed as likely to generate practical problems was that the justifications available under free movement law are focused on public policy and so are much narrower than those available in competition law, which are attuned to the expectations of private parties. So a practice could be covered by both free movement and competition law and the question would arise whether the net of permitted justification should be the wider or the narrower.

Sport, especially football, was an excellent place to examine the problem, because there were plenty of such practices at national and EU level. In most, though not all, Member States restrictions were placed on 'non-national' players (those not qualified to play for the national team) and at the time there was a limit of four non-national players in the Union of European Football Associations (UEFA) club competitions. So I was able to use sport as an illustration, though a particularly vivid one.

My analysis was not too ill-directed. I argued that although *Walrave and Koch* had approved nationality discrimination at international level, nationality discrimination in club football was not compatible with EU law.[9] This was later confirmed

[5]Case 36/74 *Walrave and Koch* v *Union Cycliste Internationale*, ECLI:EU:C:1974:140.

[6]Case 13/76 *Gaetano Donà v. Mario Mantero*, ECLI:EU:C:1976:115.

[7]Weatherill 1989.

[8]See descriptively Weatherill 2013; normatively Schepel 2013, Prechal and De Vries 2009.

[9]Weatherill 1989, pp. 60–62.

in *Bosman*. I also argued that competition law could be used to attack practices that were not within the scope of free movement law, most of all those that appeared to be internal to a single Member State,[10] a point I made also in my subsequent case note on *Bosman*,[11] and which has been confirmed since, as competition law has become the more important basis for checking sporting practices against the demands of EU internal market law.

And in fact my main solution to the awkward overlap between free movement law applicable to private parties and competition law, which was to widen justification under free movement law to cover private interests and not just the public interests mapped at the time by Articles 48(3) and (4) EEC, is the one the Court adopted with little fuss in *Bosman*. It simply accommodated a general justification test, readily invoked by both public and private parties who were subject to the obligations drawn from the Treaty provisions on free movement.

It is an article that makes its points in laboured and clumsy fashion. It deserves a bit of credit for being at the time one of relatively few explorations of the field but generally it deserves to gather dust, and largely it has done so. The point of returning to it is to check the relatively bare terrain of EU sports law in which I was working. The density and high quality of writing on EU sports law is an established feature of the academic landscape today, but this certainly was not the case twenty-five years ago. *Bosman* was a watershed, but the ground on the far side of that divide was pretty dry.

In my 1989 article I cited just four academic articles dealing with the application of EU law to sport.

The first was an article published in 1986 under the authorship of Andrew Evans, entitled 'Freedom of Trade under the Common Law and European Community Law: the case of the Football bans'.[12] It addresses the ban on competing in European club competitions imposed on all English clubs in the wake of the deaths caused by rioting at the European Cup Final of 1985 in Brussels between Liverpool and Juventus. It was 1990 before English clubs were re-admitted. This was certainly an unfocused and disproportionate intervention in the freedom to provide services enjoyed under EU law by the English clubs whose record showed no pre-disposition to public disorder among their fans, such as Norwich City and Wimbledon who in the relevant period qualified to play in European club competitions but were not permitted to do so. It is not inconceivable that even in the case of clubs whose fans did have a poor record the ban could be considered unlawful: after all, repressive measures should be directed at lawbreakers not those with whom they choose to associate. The ban was, however, never challenged in court. The paper is imaginative and well-researched, though its main point of intellectual inquiry is not with EU law in itself but rather with the potential friction between common law and EU law notions of freedom to trade.

[10]Ibid., pp. 78–80.

[11]Weatherill 1996.

[12]Evans 1986.

The second paper I cited was by Giovanni Ubertazzi. This was 'Le domaine du droit communautaire. A propos de l'arrêt Walrave, Union cycliste internationale', published in 1976 in *Revue trimestrielle de droit européen.*[13] This is a case note on *Walrave*, though it is much more concerned with the matter of material competence than with the intricacies of sport. It shows how the ruling reveals the wide scope of EU law: 'tout ce qui rentre dans le domaine de l'économie appartient au domaine du droit communautaire'.[14] It notes too that (in the author's view) this has not always been fully appreciated in the academic literature. The paper also offers some comment on the nature of judicial reasoning and its place in the authority of EU law which, again, shows the author's ambition to be broader in his inquiry than simply the oddities of nationality discrimination in paced cycling.

The third paper was by Meinhard Hilf and it was entitled 'Die Freizűgigkeit des Berufsfussballspielers innerhalb der Europäischen Gemeinschaft'. It was published in 1984 in *Neue Juristische Wochenschrift.*[15] This piece argues that nationality discrimination in professional club football cannot survive challenge based on EU law. It carefully dismantles possible justifications for such practices, and the thoughtful analysis has much in common with that subsequently deployed so decisively to condemn discrimination in club football in *Bosman* itself. Hilf looks mainly at the DFB's rules but he is fully aware of the wider impact in other Member States.

The fourth paper I mentioned was by Heiko van Staveren. This appeared in *Sport and the law,* a 1989 publication of the Council of Europe.[16] As its Foreword notes: 'There is clearly a certain role for the State in regulating sports activities. On the other hand, given that sports organisations are protective of their independence, there is scope for conflict.'[17] One can only agree! In fact there is not much EU law in this publication. It mainly concerns national law and some comment on the possible role of the Council of Europe. Even the source I cited in my 1989 article, Heiko Van Staveren's paper 'The rules of the Sports Community and the Law of the State', only briefly touches on EU law. The interesting point it makes on which I relied was its comment that Walrave and Koch had not pursued the matter after the decision of the CJEU in 1974 'because, it is said, the UCI had threatened to remove their branch of sport from the World Championship'.[18] This is an intriguing little insight into the practical ability of sports bodies to resist unfavourable legal rulings. I confess I have never been able to pin down any first-hand source to support this claim. Van Staveren does not supply one and neither does his paper specify by whom 'it is said' that removal had been threatened. Hilf, in his above-mentioned 1984 article, makes the same observation in footnote 22,

[13]Ubertazzi 1976.

[14]Ibid., p. 642.

[15]Hilf 1984.

[16]Van Staveren 1989.

[17]Ibid., p. 5.

[18]Ibid., p. 6.

citing an article by Giltay Veth published in the 1978 Nederlands Juristenblad under the title 'Uitsluiting van buitenlandse voetballers: mogelijk binnen de EEG?'.[19] This is mainly about nationality rules in Dutch football, though it mentions also other sports and other jurisdictions too, and it looks at the key EU law cases on free movement. It reflects on what *Walrave and Koch* might mean for *club* football. Of present relevance it makes exactly the same observation as Van Staveren, namely that the UCI had threatened to remove the event from the calendar if Walrave and Koch continued to press their case, but the source given is simply 'van verscheidene kanten' - from several sides. None is named.

So I cited just *four* academic papers touching EU law and sport! There were admittedly other sources that I did not cite, such as Veth's above-mentioned insightful paper in *Nederlands Juristenblad* and also Laura Forlati Picchio's 'Discriminazioni nel Settore Sportivo e Comunità Europee', published in 1976 in the Rivista di Diritto Internazionale, an examination of *Walrave and Koch* and *Donà v Mantero*.[20] But there was not much more, though I should mention, and did cite, the Report on the freedom of movement of professional footballers drawn up and published in 1989 on behalf of the Parliament's Committee on Legal Affairs and Citizens' Rights, with Mr Janssen Van Raay serving as Rapporteur.[21] This vigorously attacked the transfer system, decrying it as a latter-day version of the slave trade, and condemning nationality discrimination which it argued was a violation of EU law. This generated a flurry of political activity and newspaper heat. Andy Williamson, spokesman for the English Football League, was quoted as observing that 'This is another example of bureaucrats considering an issue they don't understand … The fee paid for a player is actually compensation to the club for their investment in developing his skills'.[22] The claim that superior expertise justifies sporting autonomy is perfectly captured by this comment. And the car crash the football authorities would meet in *Bosman* was inevitable with such complacent drivers at the wheel. Gordon Taylor, chief executive of the Professional Footballers' Association, reportedly said 'many Football League clubs would go to the wall if they no longer received fees from players once their contracts expire'.[23] So even those paid to represent the interest of players were prepared to line up dutifully in support of the *status quo*. Of course no such thing happened once *Bosman* brought about exactly the horror foreseen by Mr Taylor.

After I wrote my article for the 1989 *Yearbook on European Law* but before *Bosman* loomed large, there were one or two more sources which emerged in the childhood years of EU sports law. A book edited by Michael Will, *Sportrecht in*

[19]Veth 1978.

[20]Forlati Picchio 1976.

[21]Resolution of the European Parliament of 11 April 1989, A2-415/188 on the Freedom of Movement of Professional Football Players in the Community, OJ C120.

[22]Europeans in league to save transfer deals. The Independent, 13 April 1989, p. 40.

[23]Transfer system under fire. The Times, 12 April 1989, p. 47.

Europa, published in 1993, contained ten essays, all in German.[24] A short ten-page introduction by Manfred Zuleeg under the title 'Der Sport im europãischen Gemeinschaftsrecht' begins by stressing that sport has an economic dimension which brings it within the scope of EU law, and then deals mainly with basic free movement law. Then national reports on France, England, Italy, Portugal, Spain, Greece and Poland follow, with two concluding chapters on on the access of foreign players to professional football in the EU (Peter Karpenstein), and a final essay on free movement of players within the EU (Gerhard Renz). Both are very good, and are still interesting for tracing the shaping of the Commission's attitude to the prevalence of nationality restrictions in club football in the light of EU law, which involved a degree of negotiation with UEFA—and which to the Commission's embarrassment was subsequently exploded by *Bosman*. It was, the editor conceded unnecessarily in his Vorwort, 'ein bescheidenes Debűt'—a modest debut.

A paper entitled' European Law and Football' by Andrew Evans, published as Colloquium paper 120/90 of the EUI at Florence, was a product of a colloquium on *Le football et l'Europe*, held in Florence on 3-5 May 1990.[25] It is a good, though relatively short, survey of free movement and competition law, picking out points, such as nationality rules, where friction may be anticipated.

Edward Grayson's *Sport and the Law*, an eccentrically entertaining expedition across the intersection of sport and the law energised by a romantic commitment to protect sport from 'the insidious and pernicious influence of the so-called permissive society', was published in its first edition by Butterworths in 1988.[26] The book is rated by some as a formative influence in the discipline of sports law in England. There is little EU law in it. *Walrave and Koch* appears on just two of the book's 376 pages. It is spelled incorrectly ('Walgrave') in the table of cases, which is doubtless not the author's fault, though the garbled attempt to suggest EU law might help professional cricketers subject to disciplinary action for playing in the apartheid (but not permissive) society of South Africa presumably is.[27]

In the period before *Bosman* invigorated EU law scholarship pertaining to sport there was certainly plenty of literature on sports and the law available from North America, but the antitrust exemptions there applicable and matters such as the single entity theory had little ready application to EU law or to European sport more generally. One could—one still can—enjoy the contrast between the deeply interventionist patterns of North American sport designed to promote competitive balance and the powerful place of labour unions found there and the much more free market typical European model: quite the reverse of wider assumptions about how American and European societies are structured. But exactly these deep gulfs limited the viability of comparative legal analysis.

[24]Will 1993.

[25]Evans 1990.

[26]Grayson 1988. The quote is in the Preface, page ix. Not the least of the book's delights is the cover, the design of which is awful beyond parody.

[27]Ibid., p. 212.

The relative scarcity of academic attention to EU law and sport was in part driven by the visible practical power of sport in keeping disputes out of the ordinary courts. There was also a sense that in any event there was not much of intellectual worth at stake. I speak to some extent from personal experience. No one ever suggested to me that scholarly pursuit of the interaction between EU law and sport was a smart career move. A few suggested the opposite.

Advocate General Warner's Opinion in *Walrave and Koch* captures the mood that there is nothing of intellectual depth at stake in understanding EU law's intersection with sport:

> Suppose that an officious bystander, at the time of the signing of the EEC Treaty, or, for that matter, at the time of the signing of the Treaty of Accession, had asked those round the table whether they intended that Articles 48 and 59 should preclude a requirement that, in a particular sport, a national team should consist only of nationals of the country it represented. Common sense dictates that the signatories, with their pens poised, would all have answered impatiently 'Of course not'—and perhaps have added that, in their view, the point was so obvious that it did not need to be stated.

'Common sense' is a subjective and unstable basis for interpretation of legal texts, but the Court in truth did little better in *Walrave and Koch* in finding a firmer footing for explaining the circumstances in which a sporting practice may escape condemnation under EU law when it appears to conflict with its demands of non-discrimination and free movement. It stated that EU law's prohibition of nationality-based discrimination 'does not affect the composition of sport teams, in particular national teams, the formation of which is a question of purely sporting interest and as such has nothing to do with economic activity'.[28] Its controlling device was contained in the next paragraph: the 'restriction on the scope of the provisions in question must however remain limited to its proper objective'.[29] But the claim that the rule involves 'a question of purely sporting interest and as such has nothing to do with economic activity' is evident nonsense. Not only is international football big business, even in 1974, but moreover players enhance their profile and popularity, and therefore their commercial potential, as a result of selection for international teams, and especially for the bigger and more successful countries. It would be economically rational for a top footballer to prefer to play for Germany rather than Scotland, just as a top-flight banker would, all things being equal, be likely to earn more money in Frankfurt than in Edinburgh. There are good reasons to permit nationality discrimination in international football despite the control exercised by EU law but those reasons lie in the very nature and distinctive representative character of the activity, which is not to be found in banking, not in a denial of their economic consequence.

The Court's ruling in *Walrave and Koch* was important in the general sweep of EU law for it emphasised the Treaty's broad material scope, triggered by economic activity.[30] But, as far as the particular instance of sport was concerned, it

---

[28]Case 36/74 *Walrave and Koch* v *Union Cycliste Internationale,* ECLI:EU:C:1974:140, para 8.

[29]Ibid., para 9.

[30]Stressed by Ubertazzi 1976.

was off the right track in its hapless quest to find rules that involve 'purely sporting interest', with no association to economic activity. Even in *Bosman* the Court cited the unhelpful formula that EU law does not 'prevent the adoption of rules or practices excluding foreign players from certain matches for reasons which are not of an economic nature, which relate to the particular nature and context of such matches and are thus of sporting interest only',[31] although, repeating the controlling proviso that that restriction on the scope of the provisions in question must remain limited to its proper objective, it refused to find that national discrimination in *club* football could benefit from this ill-shaped concession. *Bosman* didn't change *everything*: it didn't kill off the idea of the 'purely sporting' rule as worthy quarry. It is only more recently that the Court has stopped trying to place emphasis on the notion of the 'purely sporting rule' on which it relied in *Walrave and Koch* and has preferred instead to adopt the more realistic view that most sporting practices are both sporting and economic and that what really counts is a case by case inspection of whether the specific nature of sport directs that room be allowed for its peculiarities. This is the model of conditional autonomy found in the landmark ruling in *Meca-Medina*[32] in which the Court borrowed from general EU competition law and insisted that the compatibility of rules with EU competition law cannot be assessed in the abstract. In applying Article 101(1) TFEU, account must be taken of the overall context in which the arrangements are struck and, more specifically, of their objectives. The test, which the Court extracted from the landmark ruling in *Wouters*,[33] asks whether the consequential effects restrictive of competition are inherent in the pursuit of those objectives and are proportionate to them.[34] This is to open up the legal assessment of sporting practices that restrict competition to include assessment of their objectives and it leaves room to treat sporting practices as compatible with EU law without having to resort to the mystical and frankly deceitful suggestion that they are 'purely sporting' in nature. Anti-doping rules and their associated sanctions, approved by the Court in *Meca-Medina* despite their effect on competition and athletes' freedom of action, offer a perfect example: they are both economic and sporting in effect, and are assessed – favourably by the Court - with an awareness of both dimensions. The approach is functionally similar to that used in *Bosman* but in fact it is analytically superior. And it leads to a case-by-case inspection of sporting practices in the light of EU law, which may admittedly lead to a degree of (unavoidable) unpredictability but, crucially, is an examination conducted with receptivity to the particular features of sport that may justify practices that would not be tolerated elsewhere.

[31]Case C-415/93 *Union Royale Belge des Sociétés de Football Association and others v. Bosman and others*, ECLI:EU:C:1995:463, para 127.

[32]Case C-519/04 *P Meca-Medina and Majcen v Commission*, ECLI:EU:C:2006:492.

[33]Case C-309/99 *J. C. J. Wouters, J. W. Savelbergh and Price Waterhouse Belastingadviseurs BV v Algemene Raad van de Nederlandse Orde van Advocaten, intervener: Raad van de Balies van de Europese Gemeenschap*, ECLI:EU:C:2002:98.

[34]Ibid., para 42.

This approach is in effect, albeit not explicitly, codified today by the embrace of 'the specific nature of sport' located in Article 165 TFEU. In *Olympique Lyonnais v Olivier Bernard* the Court cited its familiar acceptance, first found in *Bosman*, that the considerable social importance of sporting activities and in particular football in the European Union leads to the finding that the objective of encouraging the recruitment and training of young players must be accepted as legitimate.[35] This, it added, meant that assessment of the transfer system, as a restriction on free movement, shall embrace 'the specific characteristics of sport in general, and football in particular, and of their social and educational function'.[36] It added that 'The relevance of those factors is also corroborated by their being mentioned in the second subparagraph of Article 165(1) TFEU'.[37] *Bernard* avoids treating the Lisbon Treaty as transformative. Instead Article 165, applied in the interpretation of the free movement rules, becomes simple confirmation of pre-existing judicial practice in Luxembourg. The ruling is significant for confirming that although Article 165 is not explicitly tied to the Treaty provisions governing the internal market, it will nevertheless be used by the Court in this cross-cutting fashion. But this too is simply to confirm what the Court has always been willing to do. It did it in *Bosman*.

10.4 *Bosman* Changed Everything! (Well, Almost)

EU law and sport mattered a great deal more after *Bosman*. The intellectual interest was stronger as a result of the Court's careful engagement with free movement law and also by its evasion of competition law, because it was perfectly clear that such evasion could be short term only.[38] Academics certainly do not and should not need juicy high-profile case law to work themselves into an intellectual frenzy. In fact focus on the latest case can be a very good way to make one's work of ephemeral value and a very bad way to develop a career as a scholar. But a fast-moving landscape can provoke extra stimulation. *Bosman* suddenly changed the pace of EU sports law – from backwater to fast flowing current. Academic interest was carried along. In fact academic interest helped to speed the flow.

The practical importance of *Bosman* rested in part on the Court's careful rejection of a whole series of claims advanced by UEFA which were in different ways all directed at one main aim – the preservation of sporting autonomy. This is why the ruling was so savage in exposing sport to the control exercised by EU law. A

[35]Case C-325/08 *Olympique Lyonnais SASP v. Olivier Bernard and Newcastle United FC*, ECLI:EU:C:2010:143, para 39; Case C-415/93 *Union Royale Belge des Sociétés de Football Association and others v. Bosman and others,* ECLI:EU:C:1995:463, para 106.

[36]Case C-325/08 *Olympique Lyonnais SASP v. Olivier Bernard and Newcastle United FC*, ECLI:EU:C:2010:143, para 40.

[37]Ibid., para 40.

[38]This was a strong message of Weatherill 1996.

lot of optimistic assumptions held by sporting bodies about their autonomy from EU law were exploded.

There were eight claims to absolute or unconditional autonomy advanced by the football authorities, each of which was methodically rejected by the Court:

1. It was argued that only the major European football clubs may be regarded as undertakings within the meaning of EU law. But this did not matter. EU law applies to economic activity and this embraces the activities of professional or semi-professional footballers.
2. It was argued that the matter did 'does not concern the employment relationships between players and clubs but the business relationships between clubs and the consequences of freedom to affiliate to a sporting federation', and that so the Treaty rules on the free movement of workers did not apply.[39] This is utterly baffling. The Court treated it as such.
3. UEFA sternly advised the Court that any decision concerning the situation of professional players 'might call in question the organization of football as a whole'.[40] The Court sternly advised UEFA that possible consequences for the organization of football as a whole could not 'diminish the objective character of the law and compromise its application'.[41] The only concession made by the Court in this direction was to place a temporal limitation on the application of its ruling to the transfer system (but not to the effects of nationality discrimination in club football).
4. The German Government submitted that sport has points of similarity with culture. The Court did not disagree, but would not allow this to disable completely the application of internal market law.
5. The German Government referred to the freedom of association and autonomy enjoyed by sporting federations under national law. The Court did not disagree, but would not allow this to disable completely the application of internal market law.
6. The German Government, citing the principle of subsidiarity, argued that intervention by public authorities, including those of the EU, must be confined to what is strictly necessary. The case concerns football, but had cricket been involved we would certainly note that by this stage the Court was playing with a straight bat. Its response to this submission was not to disagree, but it would not allow this to disable completely the application of internal market law.
7. It was pressed on the Court that Article 48 EC, today Article 45 TFEU, did not apply to private parties such as the governing bodies of a sport, but the Court, citing its ruling in *Walrave and Koch* and adopting the reasoning used there, declared that the action of public authorities is subject to control under

[39]Case C-415/93 *Union Royale Belge des Sociétés de Football Association and others v. Bosman and others,* ECLI:EU:C:1995:463, para 70.

[40]Ibid., para 71.

[41]Ibid., para 77.

EU law governing the free movement of workers but so too are 'rules of any other nature aimed at regulating gainful employment in a collective manner'.[42] Were it otherwise, inequality in application of EU law would arise in consequence on the different patterns of private and public actors across the several Member States. At this point the Court addressed the concern that had animated my 1989 article, mentioned above.[43] UEFA's objection that such an interpretation unfairly burdens private parties who, unlike Member States, may not rely on limitations justified on grounds of public policy, public security or public health was dismissed on the basis that individuals *may* rely on such justifications.[44] This lays the foundation for justification as the place to argue about sport's specificity.

8. Finally, it was argued that the dispute concerned a situation purely internal to a single Member State, Belgium. It concerned a Belgian player detrimentally affected by the conduct of a Belgian club and a Belgian association.[45] This was true, but Bosman's case was not 'purely internal'. His prospective new employer was a club in France. So the Court treated the transfer system as a direct impediment to a worker's access to the regulated market, the labour market in France, and it did not serve to exclude EU law that he would have been subject to the same hindrance even had he been trying to move to another club in Belgium.

At this point, with the score standing at 8-0 in favour of the jurisdiction of EU law to exercise review of the sporting practices that were the subject of the litigation, the game would seem to be over. But it was not. This was half-time. EU law applied. But in the second half of the game the next question needed to be answered: EU law applied, but did it permit or did it prohibit the practices in question?

The Court would not yield to sporting autonomy in any absolute sense, but it did write into EU law an explicit recognition of the special features of sport. This was the famous para 106 of *Bosman*, which declares that:

> In view of the considerable social importance of sporting activities and in particular football in the Community, the aims of maintaining a balance between clubs by preserving a certain degree of equality and uncertainty as to results and of encouraging the recruitment and training of young players must be accepted as legitimate.[46]

This statement is foundationally important in the development of EU sports law. Article 165, which entered into force in 2009, embraces 'the specific nature of sport': here, in the 1995 ruling in *Bosman*, are its roots. Any autonomy granted to sport by EU law is *conditional* on meeting the expectations located in the tests of justification

---

[42]Ibid., para 82.

[43]Weatherill 1989.

[44]Case C-415/93 *Union Royale Belge des Sociétés de Football Association and others v. Bosman and others*, ECLI:EU:C:1995:463, paras 85–86.

[45]Ibid., para 88.

[46]Ibid., para 106.

recognised by EU internal market law. And it is in the shaping of the environment of justification that sport needs to aspire to embed its claims to be 'special'.

As has been skilfully summarised:

> La spécificité sportive intervient juridiquement au niveau de l'application et non de l'applicabilité du droit de l'UE [47] et ne saurait par conséquent être définie a priori, mais seulement *in concreto* en fonction des normes de la *lex sportiva* soumises au contrôle du droit de l'UE.[48]

The structural point is that the Court, having spent much time in *Bosman* explaining why it was refusing to accept the claims of sports bodies to absolute autonomy from the application of EU law, turned to address the possibility for justifying practices that fall within the scope of EU law, and immediately embraced a recognition that sport has distinct characteristics. Sport is special – in at least the two respects identified in para 106 of *Bosman*.

> … la fonction de la spécificité sportive n'est donc pas de définir des territoires, mais de garantir l'ouverture du droit de l'UE à son autre juridique : la *lex sportiva*.[49]

EU law aspires also to be sports law, just as, in Wouters, it aspires to be a law of professional standards,[50] as in Cassis de Dijon it aspires to be a law of consumer protection,[51] as in Bluhme it aspires to be a law of biodiversity conservation[52] and as in Omega Spielhallen it aspires to be a law of human dignity.[53] Free movement and competition law are porous to non-market values. The story is admittedly far from perfect: in Viking Line the Court claimed in much less happy circumstances to make EU law a law of labour rights.[54] The field of application claimed by EU law plainly places a huge weight on the capacity of Court (and sometimes the legislature) to perform the necessary balancing of interests but at least the Court tries to do so. It does not present internal market law as a simple deregulatory bloodbath.

The transfer system challenged in *Bosman* could not survive this test but an amended version was put in place which, though not subject to any direct challenge before a court (yet), is less restrictive and so more likely to survive. This

---

[47]Martucci 2011, p. 381.

[48]Duval 2015, p. 202.

[49]Ibid., p. 224.

[50]Case C-309/99 J. C. J. Wouters, J. W. Savelbergh and Price Waterhouse Belastingadviseurs BV v Algemene Raad van de Nederlandse Orde van Advocaten, intervener: Raad van de Balies van de Europese Gemeenschap, ECLI:EU:C:2002:98.

[51]Case 120/78 *Rewe-Zentrale AG v Bundesmonopolverwaltung für Branntwein*, ECLI:EU:C:1979:42.

[52]Case C-67/97 *Ditlev Bluhme*, ECLI:EU:C:1998:584.

[53]Case C-36/02 *Omega Spielhallen v Oberbürgermeisterin der Bundesstadt Bonn*, ECLI:EU:C:2004:614.

[54]Case C-438/05 *International Transport Workers' Federation v Viking Line ABP*, ECLI:EU:C:2007:772; Case C-341/05 *Laval un Partneri Ltd v Svenska Byggnadsarbetareförbundet, Svenska Byggnadsarbetareförbundets avdelning 1, Byggettan and Svenska Elektrikerförbundet*, ECLI:EU:C:2007:809. For criticism, see Azoulai 2008.

conformed to *Eastham*: a green light for *a* transfer system, a red light for *this* transfer system. Meanwhile, nationality discrimination in club football, previously granted an amber light by the Commission, was given a clear red light by the Court in *Bosman*.

10.5 Beyond *Bosman*

Bosman did not change *everything*. It prompted and promoted further litigation and sport has certainly become a far more intensively juridicalised arena in the twenty years since *Bosman*. *Bosman* gave litigants the vocabulary needed to exploit EU law as a basis to lever open entrenched practices and perhaps it gave them the courage to suppose they could succeed. But the main reason for the more aggressive engagement of law with sport has been the increasing commercial dimension to sport, driven most of all by technological and regulatory change in the broadcasting sector. More money, more litigation: plus smart advocates, a bold court (and Commission), and perhaps some pointers from academics, though they would have to wait until *Meca-Medina* for the Court to move more firmly away from the deceptive concept of the 'purely sporting' rule than it had been willing to do in *Bosman*.

Article 165 stands for a (doubtless grudging) acceptance by sporting bodies that they are better off inside the EU system where they are equipped with language—the specific nature of sport—that may help to soften its impact on their autonomy than they are in standing outside shouting 'keep away'. The story in this vein of the negotiation of what is now Article 165 has been told elsewhere: it shows how at crucial moments in the negotiations through the first decade of the new millennium sports bodies were able to press their case with some success but never to the point where they were able to secure a complete exemption from the rules of the EU game.[55] In fact the trend whereby some sports bodies were inclined to adopt a co-operative relationship with the Commission in particular, for purely pragmatic reasons, was noticed by Borja Garcia operating beyond the particular context of Treaty negotiations. UEFA, in particular, was notable for adapting its strategy towards a more co-operative model.[56] This was induced by *Bosman*.

The current debates over Financial Fair Play (FFP) are a clear current example of this strategy. Those designing FFP have been quick to secure a dialogue with the Commission and they have been able to extract some modestly encouraging comments from the Commission about its view of the compatibility of FFP with EU law. So, for example, in 2010 M. Barnier, answering a question posed by an MEP, stated that the 'The Commission considers that the rationale of UEFA's plan

---

[55]García and Weatherill 2012.

[56]García 2007.

seems to be in accordance with one of the objectives of the EU's action in the field of sport, namely with the promotion of fairness in sporting competitions' and he cited Article 165 TFEU. He added that 'The Commission also notes that any measure taken in this framework has to respect the EU's Internal Market and competition rules'.[57] The Commission certainly has no current intention to challenge FFP despite its anti-competitive taint as a horizontal restraint on spending that is, moreover, likely to foreclose entry into the market to supply top-level football by new clubs. This is not decisive and could yet be upset by private litigation. However, *Bosman* is the root of this co-operative approach which seeks to embrace the Commission as a partner in the shaping of the *lex sportiva*, because *Bosman* so comprehensively exposed the failure of attempts made by UEFA to find a jurisdictional basis to keep EU law out of the development of the *lex sportiva*.

Bosman started it all. But it certainly has not finished it.

References

Azoulai L (2008) The court of justice and the social market economy: the emergence of an ideal and the conditions for its realisation. Common Market Law Rev 45:1335–1355

Duval A (2015) La Lex Sportiva Face au Droit de l'Union Européenne: Guerre et Paix dans l'Espace Juridique Transnational. Doctoral Dissertation, European University Institute, Florence

Evans A (1986) Freedom of trade under the common law and European Community law: the case of the football bans. Law Q Rev 86:510–548

Evans A (1990) European Law and football. colloquium paper 120/90, European University Institute, Florence

Forlati Picchio L (1976) Discriminazioni nel settore sportivo e Comunità europee. Rivista di diritto internazionale:745–760

García B (2007) UEFA and the European Union: from confrontation to co-operation. J Contemp Eur Res 3:202–221

García B, Weatherill S (2012) Engaging with the EU in order to minimize its impact: sport and the negotiation of the treaty of Lisbon. J Eur Public Policy 19:238–256

Grayson E (1988) Sport and the law. Butterworths, London

Hilf M (1984) Die Freizügigkeit des Berufsfussballspielers innerhalb der Europäischen Gemeinschaft. Neue Juristische Wochenschrift 10:517–523

Maduro M, Azoulai L (2010) the past and future of EU Law: the classics of eu law revisited on the 50th anniversary of the Rome treaty. Hart Publishing, Oxford

Martucci F (2011) Coupe du Monde et droit de l'Union européenne. In: Maisonneuve M (ed) Droit et Coupe du Monde. Economica, Paris, pp 357–391

Prechal S, De Vries S (2009) Seamless web of judicial protection in the internal market? Eur Law Rev 34:5–25

Schepel H (2013) Freedom of contract in free movement law: balancing rights and principles in European Public and private law. Eur Rev Private Law 21:1211–1229

Ubertazzi G (1976) Le domaine du droit communautaire. A propos de l'arrêt Walrave, Union cycliste international. Revue Trimestrielle de Droit Européen, pp 635–647

[57]Parliamentary Question E-4628/10 (2011), Answer given by Mr Barnier on behalf of the Commission, OJ C 170 E. http://www.europarl.europa.eu/sides/getAllAnswers.do?reference=E-2010-4628&language=MT. Accessed 1 December 2015.

Van Staveren H (1989) The rules of the sports community and the law of the state, published by the council of Europe, 18th colloquy on European law, Sport and the law. Strasbourg, pp 64–69

Veth G (1978) Uitsluiting van buitenlandse voetballers: mogelijk binnen de EEG? Nederlands Juristenblad 53:504–513

Weatherill S (1989) Discrimination on grounds of nationality in sport. Yearb Eur Law 9:55–92

Weatherill S (1996) Annotation of the European court's ruling in *Bosman*. Common Market Law Rev 33:991–1033

Weatherill S (2013) The elusive character of private autonomy in EU law. In: Leczykiewicz D, Weatherill S (eds) The involvement of EU law in private Law relationships. Hart Publishing/ Institute of European and Comparative Law, Oxford, pp 9–28

Will M (ed) (1993) Sportrecht in Europa. Műller Juristischer Verlag, Heidelberg, C.F

MIX
Papier aus verantwortungsvollen Quellen
Paper from responsible sources
FSC® C105338

If you have any concerns about our products,
you can contact us on
ProductSafety@springernature.com

In case Publisher is established outside the EU,
the EU authorized representative is:
Springer Nature Customer Service Center GmbH
Europaplatz 3, 69115 Heidelberg, Germany

Printed by Libri Plureos GmbH
in Hamburg, Germany